The states of Egypt, India, Mexico, and Turkey have all developed extensive public enterprise sectors and have sought to regulate most economic activities outside the state sector. Their experiences have been typical of scores of developing countries that have followed similar paths of industrialization. This study examines the origins of these state sectors, the dynamics of their growth and crises, and the efforts to reform or liquidate them.

It is argued that public ownership creates its own culture and pathology, which are similar across otherwise different systems. The logic of principal–agent relations under public ownership is so powerful that it obscures culture and peculiar institutional histories. Whereas public sectors accumulate powerful associated interests over time, against most predictions these prove relatively powerless to block the reform process.

EXPOSED TO INNUMERABLE DELUSIONS

POLITICAL ECONOMY OF INSTITUTIONS AND DECISIONS

Editors
James E. Alt, Harvard University
Douglass C. North, Washington University in St. Louis

Other books in the series
James E. Alt and Kenneth Shepsle, eds., *Perspectives on Positive Political Economy*
Yoram Barzel, *Economic Analysis of Property Rights*
Robert Bates, *Beyond the Miracle of the Market: The Political Economy of Agrarian Development in Kenya*
Gary W. Cox, *The Efficient Secret: The Cabinet and the Development of Political Parties in Victorian England*
Leif Lewin, *Ideology and Strategy: A Century of Swedish Politics* (English Edition)
Gary Libecap, *Contracting for Property Rights*
Matthew D. McCubbins and Terry Sullivan, eds., *Congress: Structure and Policy*
Douglass C. North, *Institutions, Institutional Change, and Economic Performance*
Elinor Ostrom, *Governing the Commons: The Evolution of Institutions for Collective Action*
Charles Stewart III, *Budget Reform Politics: The Design of the Appropriations Process in the House of Representatives, 1865–1921*
Gary J. Miller, *Managerial Dilemmas: The Political Economy of Hierarchy*
Jean-Laurent Rosenthal, *The Fruits of Revolution: Property Rights, Litigation, and French Agriculture*
Jean Ensminger, *Making a Market: The Institutional Transformation of an African Society*
Jack Knight, *Institutions and Social Conflict*

EXPOSED TO INNUMERABLE DELUSIONS

Public enterprise and state power in Egypt, India, Mexico, and Turkey

JOHN WATERBURY
Princeton University

CAMBRIDGE
UNIVERSITY PRESS

Published by the Press Syndicate of the University of Cambridge
The Pitt Building, Trumpington Street, Cambridge CB2 1RP
40 West 20th Street, New York, NY 10011-4211, USA
10 Stamford Road, Oakleigh, Melbourne 3166, Australia

© Cambridge University Press 1993

First published 1993

Printed in the United States of America

Library of Congress Cataloging-in-Publication Data
Waterbury, John.
Exposed to innumerable delusions : public enterprise and state
power in Egypt, India, Mexico, and Turkey / John Waterbury.
p.   cm. – (Political economy of institutions and
decisions)
Includes bibliographical references and index.
ISBN 0-521-43497-1. – ISBN 0-521-43549-8 (pbk.)
1. Government business enterprises – Developing countries – Case
studies.   2. Government ownership – Developing countries – Case
studies.   I. Title.   II. Series.
HD4420.8.W38   1993
338.9'009172'4 – dc20   92–45784
                                                              CIP

A catalog record for this book is available from the British Library.

ISBN 0-521-43497-1 hardback
ISBN 0-521-43549-8 paperback

To Charles Issawi,
ustadh al-jiil

The sovereign is completely discharged from a duty, in the attempting to perform which he must always be exposed to innumerable delusions, and for the proper performance of which no human wisdom or knowledge could ever be sufficient; the duty of superintending the industry of private people, and of directing it towards the employments most suitable to the interest of the society.

Adam Smith, *The Wealth of Nations* (1937:651)

Contents

Tables, figures, and illustrations

Tables, figures, illustrations

ix

Tables, figures, illustrations

Series editors' preface

The Cambridge series on the Political Economy of Institutions and Decisions is built around attempts to answer two central questions: How do institutions evolve in response to individual incentives, strategies, and choices, and how do institutions affect the performance of political and economic systems? The scope of the series is comparative and historical rather than international or specifically American, and the focus is positive rather than normative.

In this pioneering book John Waterbury examines the origins, growth, scope, and reform of state sectors in industrializing countries. Comparing Egypt, India, Mexico, and Turkey, all of which developed extensive public enterprise sectors, he explains a logic of principal–agent relations under public ownership that transcends national cultural and institutional histories. He describes how public officials became rent seekers, state-owned enterprises became a net drain on public finances, and their productivity sank and costs rose. Waterbury argues forcefully that coalitions of interests dependent on public enterprise are able to create formidable obstacles to reform. However, these same coalitions turn out to be weak, fragmented, and incapable of resisting the fundamental restructuring through privatization with which governments in some of these countries have attempted to remove public enterprise from the reach of politics. Backed by a mass of rich empirical evidence, Waterbury's application of insights from agency and collective action theories provides a perspective on state-owned enterprise that will inform, engage, and encourage further responses from a broad range of social scientists interested in the political economy of the public sector.

Preface

In 1971 I began seriously to study Egypt's public sector enterprises, and part of my findings were eventually published in 1983. About a year later I took the first steps in elaborating a comparative analysis of public enterprise and identified the four countries that are the focal point of this book. The actual field research was carried out in 1985 and 1986 in Egypt and India, with three return trips to Egypt in subsequent years, and one to India in 1990. Research in Turkey and Mexico was carried out in the course of four separate visits each between 1987 and 1992.

As I lay out in greater detail in the Introduction, the targets at which I had taken aim refused to stand still, and some of the questions with which I set out seemed of considerably less importance as the research proceeded. In the early 1980s, state-owned enterprises were coming out of a long period of expansion. By the time my research was completed, they appeared to have entered an era of secular decline. In 1988, in Mexico City, I interviewed the managing director of a large state-owned company. The gentleman was standing behind a large desk with about five telephones, all of which were ringing. As he talked on each in turn, secretaries scurried in and out with letters for him to approve and sign. Finally, in the midst of this bustle, he turned to me with a puzzled look and asked me, "I'm sorry – who are you and what is it that you want to see me about?" I explained briefly that I was carrying out research for a comparative study of public enterprise. He looked at me and said "Ah, so you must be an archaeologist."

The long gestation of this study means that the debts I have accumulated are commensurately large. From the beginning the Woodrow Wilson School of Public and International Affairs, and above all its Center of International Studies, generously supported my research, including funding for trips to Mexico, Turkey, and India. In the fall of 1985 I was a Fellow of the American Research Center in Egypt, whose support afforded me five months of field research. During the first six months of 1986, I was the beneficiary of an Indo-American Fellowship, and the New Delhi office of that program provided me invaluable logistical support during the Indian leg of my research. I was also affiliated with the Center for the Study of Developing Societies in old Delhi, whose outstanding team of researchers gave me welcome intellectual companionship. For a considerable portion of my stay, I lived at the India International Centre. Anyone familiar with the IIC will know the quality of its library, its members, its facilities, and its kitchen. In both Ankara and Istanbul I resided at the respective American Research Institutes in Turkey, and I want to thank the two directors, Drs. Toni Cross and Antony Greenwood, for their help and goodwill during my sojourns.

In 1989–90 I was the recipient of a John S. Guggenheim Fellowship as well as a fellowship from the Institute for Advanced Study at Princeton. The latter fellowship was funded through a grant to the IAS from the John D. and Catherine T. MacArthur Foundation. During that year I began to write up my findings in a setting – and with colleagues – that left absolutely nothing to be desired.

Literally hundreds of people helped me in my research with no expectation of recompense or even acknowledgment. I am deeply grateful to all those who shared their time and expertise with me, but in the confines of this preface I can thank by name only those who went far beyond any normal call to duty or collegiality.

Part of my debt is owed my colleagues at Princeton, especially those involved in a project on public sector reform and privatization that yielded the publication edited by Ezra Suleiman and myself, and published in 1990 (see Bibliography). Coauthoring an article with Henry Bienen on privatization contributed greatly to focusing my own ideas, while Atul Kohli and Ben Schneider, through their writing and their kibitzing, have been of incalculable help to me. My work over the years with Alan Richards of the University of California, Santa Cruz, has, in a general way, been formative.

Further afield, and probably unbeknownst to them, Yair Aharoni, Leroy Jones, and John Nellis have been important sources of inspiration, as any one familiar with the study of public enterprise would recognize. In the course of circulating this manuscript for publication several anonymous and nonanonymous readers provided much needed critical comment. Among those known to me I wish to acknowledge Miguel Centeno, Stanley Kochanek, Atul Kohli, Sylvia Maxfield, Şevket Pamuk, John Sheahan, and Raymond Vernon.

I have lived and worked in Egypt since 1970; my debts to Egyptians are on a scale with that country's to the rest of the world. Nonetheless, with respect to this study I owe particular thanks to Tahar al-Bishr, Heba Handoussa, Ahmad Seif al-Din Khurshid, Khalid Fouad Sharif, and Taha Zaki, and to the fine team of social scientists at the *al-Ahram* Center for Strategic and International Studies, whose members critiqued some of my ideas in a seminar in late 1985. Over the years Hilmy Abderrahman and Tahsin Bashir have been unfailing guides to Egypt's economy and politics.

The USAID library, a treasure trove of project documents and sectoral analyses, was vitally important to my research. My thanks go to Sylvia Mitchell, who organized the collection, and to Lou Ann McNeil, who carried on the good work. The U.S. Embassy Post library is no longer the well-kept secret it once was. Nadia Rizq, who put it together and has managed it for years, is a special friend and colleague. I was fortunate that Ryan Crocker, George Laudato, and Frank Wisner were where they were during portions of my Egyptian research. Finally, my student and friend Dr. Abdesslam Maghraoui undertook a fine analysis of a set of annual reports of the Graduates Association of the National Institute for Administrative Development, the results of which are presented in Chapter 6.

Phil and Veena Oldenburg not only taught me about India but nursed me through a rather nasty liver infection during my stay in New Delhi. They also introduced me to Hari Pillai, who gave me a view of state-owned enterprises that was truly unique. At the Center for the Study of Developing Societies, Bashirrudin Ahmed was a constant source of informed guidance on India's political system. In and around the state enterprise system itself. G. Bandopadhyay, Hiten Bhaya, R. P. Billimoria, R. C. Dutt, Waris Kidwai, V. Krishnamurthy, Lavraj Kumar, Sharad Marathe, Laxmi Narain, R. C. Nath, Sam Patil, K. L. Puri, P. C. Sen, and Prakash Tandon shared their extraordinary experiences and insights with me. My Princeton colleague John P. Lewis has taught me more about Indian development than he probably ever suspected. A former student, Joydeep Mukherji, acted as a research assistant in India over a six-month period, and he carried out several interviews and document searches that proved essential to my analyses of public firms. I appreciate also the help Nandita Parshad extended to me during my visit to India in 1990, as well as that of Supriya RoyChowdhury, whose fine doctoral dissertation did not come too late to be incorporated into this study.

Carlos Bazdresh not only educated me with respect to Mexico's political economy but opened many doors for me. My student and friend Denise Dresser and her mother, Geni Dresser, were equally instrumental in advancing my research. Denise also acted as a research assistant during my investigations and unearthed a wealth of documents and articles. Her own work on PRONASOL figures prominently in my analysis of coalitions in Chapter 7. Felix Velez at ITAM was unstinting in his help and companionship. His colleague at ITAM, Juan Ricardo Perez, the Mexican academic who has probably followed privatization most closely, was also generous with his time and knowledge. Special thanks are owed Maria del Carmen Pardo, Juan Leipen, Marco Provencio, Benito Rey Roman, Reiner Steiken, Jorge Tamayo, Luís Teller, Marco Vorcj, and also Emilio Ocampo, the right man but for a time very much in the wrong place.

My thanks to Yeşim Arat and Şevket Pamuk for their friendship, help, and shared knowledge of Turkey. My acknowledgment to them here is grossly inadequate. Likewise Hasan Ersel and Mustafa Aysan were both generous hosts and mentors during my stays in Turkey. Müge Göcek and her parents helped me immeasurably at the beginning of my research in Turkey. Special thanks are also owed Korkut Boratav for his friendship and insights. Many other Turkish academics and experts gave generously of their time; primary among them are Ayşe Buğra, Cem Çakmak, Mehmet Çoşan, Yücel Ertekin, Timur Kuran, Hocam Ahmet Kuyaş, Ziya Öniş, Ergun Özbudun, and Galip Yalman. Hakan Yilmaz, over several months, collected newspaper articles on Turkish public enterprise and helped me painfully decipher them.

For all the above the customary absolution is offered and no doubt will be accepted.

The final and in many ways most important acknowledgment is to Paulomi Shah, who helped produce this manuscript with superb professionalism and with a level of concern that frequently exceeded my own.

Two further preliminary remarks are in order. I have made heavy use of World Bank reports in this study. Many of them have been "grey cover" reports with restricted circulation and not for citation. As these are documents drawn up in collaboration with the Bank's client states, only those states have the right to release the contents of the reports. The reality is, however, that those reports do receive wide circulation, routinely winding up in academic or think-tank offices, or on the desks of interested journalists. I simply want to state here that no World Bank official violated any trust so far as my research was concerned, and my access to grey cover reports came through third parties.

Second, I have an abhorrence for acronyms, yet it is the fate of anyone studying public enterprise to be immersed in them. They go with the turf, and there is no happy way to avoid them. They are displayed in all their finery in the list that follows. I tried resolutely not to invent any of my own, but I failed in one major respect. It would have been tedious and space-consuming to spell out Egypt, India, Mexico, and Turkey each of the countless times I had to mention that quartet. So I invented the acronym EIMT. My apologies.

List of acronyms, abbreviations, and foreign terms

AHMSA	Altos Hornos de México, Sociedad Anonima, S.A.
AICC	All India Congress Committee
ANAP	Motherland Party (Ana Vatan Partisi)
ASSOCHAM	Associated Chambers of Commerce and Industry of India
ASU	Arab Socialist Union
BHEL	Bharat Heavy Electrical Corporation (India)
BPE	Bureau of Public Enterprises (India)
CANACINTRA	Cámara Nacional de la Industria de la Transformación
CAOA	Central Agency for Organization and Administration (Egypt)
CAPMAS	Central Agency for Public Mobilization and Statistics (Egypt)
CCE	Consejo Coordinador Empresarial
CCM	Confederación Campesina Mexicana
CEO	chief executive officer
CFE	Comisión Federal de Electricidad
CGOCM	Confederación General de Obreros y Campesinos de México
CGT	Confederación General del Trabajo
CIF	cost, insurance, and freight
Çitosan	Turkish Cement Ltd.
CMD	chairman and managing director
CMIE	Centre for Monitoring the Indian Economy (Bombay)
CNC	Confederación Nacional de Campesinos
CNOP	Confederación Nacional de Organizaciones Populares
CNT	Central Nacional de Trabajadores

CONASUPO	Compañía Nacional de Subsistencias Populares
CONCAMIN	Confederación de Cámaras Nacionales de Comercio e Industria
CONCANACO	Confederación de Cámaras Nacionales de Comercio
CONCARRIL	Constructora Nacional de Carros de Ferrocarril
COPARMEX	Confederación Patronal de la República Mexicana
CROC	Confederación Revolucionaria de Obreros y Campesinos
CROM	Confederación Regional de Obreros Mexicanos
Crore (one)	10 million
CTLD	convertible Turkish lira deposits
CTM	Confederación de Trabajadores de México
CUP	Committee of Union and Progress (the so-called Young Turks)
DESIYAB	State Industrial Development Bank, Turkey
DFI	direct foreign investment
DINA	Diesel Nacional (México)
DISK	Federation of Revolutionary Workers' Unions (Turkey)
DYP	True Path Party (Doğru Yol Partisi)
£E	Egyptian pound
EEC	European Economic Community
EIMT	Egypt, India, Mexico, Turkey
ELG	export-led growth
Erdemir	Ereğli Steel Corporation (Turkey)
ESOP	employee stock ownership program
ETUF	Egyptian Trade Unions Federation
FCI	Food Corporation of India
FERA	Foreign Exchange Regulation Act (India)
FERTIMEX	Fertilizantes Mexicanos
FICCI	Federation of Indian Chambers of Commerce and Industry
FICORCA	Fideicomiso para la Cobertura de Riesgos Cambiarios
FSTSE	Federación de Sindicatos al Servicio del Estado
FSTU	Federación de Sindicatos de Trabajadores Universitarios
FTDF	Federación de Trabajadores del Distrito Federal
GATT	General Agreement on Tariffs and Trade
GDP	gross domestic product
GFCF	gross fixed capital formation
GNP	gross national product
GOFI	General Organzation for Industry (Egypt)

HEC	Heavy Engineering Corporation (India)
HMT	Hindustan Machine Tools
HSL	Hindustan Steel Ltd.
IAS	Indian Administrative Service
ICOR	incremental capital output ratio
IFC	International Finance Corporation
IIM	Indian Institute of Management
IMF	International Monetary Fund
IMSS	Instituto Mexicano de Seguridad Social
INAP	Instituto Nacional de Administración Pública
INFONAVIT	Instituto Nacional de Fomento de Vivienda para Trabajadores (Institute for the Development of Workers' Housing)
INP	Institute of National Planning (Egypt)
INTUC	Indian National Trade Union Congress
IRI	Institute per la Ricostruzione Industriale (Italy)
ISCO	Indian Iron and Steel Company
ISI	import-substituting industrialization
ITAM	Instituto Tecnológico Autónomo Mexicano
JPC	Joint Plant Committee (India)
Lakh (one)	100,000
LDC	lesser developed country
Lok Sabha	National Parliament of India
MHPPF	Mass Housing and Public Participation Fund (Turkey)
MRTP	Monopoly and Restrictive Trade Practices Act (India)
NAFINSA	Nacional Financiera, S.A.
NBI	National Bank for Investment (Egypt)
NDP	National Democratic Party (Egypt)
NTC	National Textile Corporation (India)
NTPC	National Thermal Power Corporation (India)
OECD	Organization for Economic Cooperation and Development
ONGC	Oil and Natural Gas Commission (India)
OYAK	Armed Forces Mutual Support Fund (Turkey)
PAN	Partido de Acción Nacional
PECE	Pacto de Estabilidad y de Crecimiento Económico (replaces PSE)
PEMEX	Petróleos Mexicanos
PERL	Public Enterprise Reform Loan (World Bank)
PESB	Public Enterprise Selection Board (India)
PNR	Partido Nacional Revolucionario

PRC	People's Republic of China
PRD	Partido de la Revolución Democrática
PRI	Partido Revolucionario Institucional
PRM	Partido de la Revolución Mexicana
PRONASOL	Programa Nacional de Solidaridad
PSBR	public sector borrowing requirement
PSE	Pacto de Solidaridad Económica (12/87)
RPP	Republican People's Party (Turkey)
SAIL	Steel Authority of India Ltd.
SCOPE	Standing Committee on Public Enterprises (India)
SEE	state economic enterprise (Turkey)
SEKA	Turkish Cellulose and Paper Corporation
SICARTSA	Siderúrgica Lázaro Cárdenas, Las Truchas, Sociedad Anonima
SIDERMEX	Siderúrgica Mexicana (Steel Sector Holding Company)
SNPTRM	Sindicato Nacional Revolucionario de Trabajadores Petroleros de la República Mexicana
SNTE	Sindicato Nacional de Trabajadores de Enseñanza
SOE	state-owned enterprise
SOMEX	Sociedad Mexicana de Crédito Industrial
TCDD	Turkish Railways
TEK	Turkish Electricity Corporation
TELMEX	Teléfonos de México
TFP	total factor productivity
THY	Turkish Airlines
TISCO	Tata Iron and Steel Company (India)
TISK	Turkish Confederation of Employers' Unions
TL	Turkish lira
TMO	Soils Products Office (Turkey)
TPAO	Turkish Petroleum Corporation
TRENCO	Transport and Engineering Company (Egypt)
Türk-Iş	Confederation of Turkish Labor Unions
TÜSIAD	Turkish Industrialists' and Businessmen's Association
USAID	United States Agency for International Development
USAŞ	Air Services Ltd. (Turkey)
WB/IBRD	World Bank/International Bank for Reconstruction and Development
WDR	World Development Report
YDK	High Control Board (Turkey)

The glowing industrial future. Originally printed in *Industry*, 11/28/16, vol. 3, no. 8, and reprinted as the cover of Zafer Toprak, *Türkiye'de "Milli Iktisat" (1908–1918)* (Ankara: Yurt Yayincilik A.Ş., 1982).

1

Introduction: Property and change

The illusions to which the sovereign is exposed are, in current economic and political language, unintended or unanticipated consequences. The illusion is that sovereign political authorities, in trying to make markets work according to a centrally crafted design, will inevitably trigger actions by all economic agents that weaken, if not run directly counter to, the grand scheme. This, in short, is the history of contemporary economic experiments combining import-substituting industrialization (ISI) and state-owned enterprise (SOE). Both the strategy and the chosen instrument to implement them are the subject of this book.

While both the strategy and the instrument appear to have foundered on sovereign illusions, my argument is not that the whole experiment was perverse in its effects, that is, some costly blunder. Rather it is that the experiment did not achieve the goals it set for itself, for example, self-sustaining heavy industrialization, integrated domestic economies, and a significant level of insulation from international markets. These were the illusions. But the experiment did achieve a great deal in building the skills, infrastructure, and industrial habits that *may* allow several countries successfully to pursue radically different policies. These were and are the unanticipated consequences.

There is no necessary connection between ISI and state-owned enterprise, but in scores of developing countries the direct link is an empirical fact. The possibility of relying on private interests to carry forward the industrialization drive has in those countries been dismissed as unrealistic and the involvement of foreign capital in strategic sectors as threatening to national sovereignty. In the four countries examined in subsequent chapters, SOEs were seen as indispensable to accomplishing the productive and distributional goals of national policy. The macroproblems of ISI interacted with the institutional problems peculiar to SOEs in such a manner that both strategy and instrument were eventually called into question.

1

Exposed to innumerable delusions

What I seek to explain in this study is the logic by which ISI, founded on extensive state ownership of productive assets, was launched in Egypt, India, Mexico, and Turkey (henceforth EIMT), the nature and causes of the crises that eventually led to its reform or abandonment, and the capacity of coalitional interests that had been created or reenforced by ISI itself to resist change in their entitlements. I offer no monocausal framework to answer these questions. Rather I reassemble from detailed case studies the evidence to contribute to five ongoing debates. I now present my arguments in schematic form with some indication of the chapters in which they are more fully developed.

1. The legal designation of property counts. In contrast to some neo-classical arguments, as well as to those of some apologists for public ownership, extensive public ownership of industrial, financial, and service sector assets seems to have necessary, economically suboptimal consequences. I make this case primarily through an examination of the institutional context of principal–agent relations (Chapter 4) and the use of public enterprises for political purposes (Chapters 5 and 7).

If public assets are managed like private assets in competitive factor markets with hard budget constraints and the possibility of exit, then there is no economic advantage to retaining the assets under public ownership. On the other hand, the distributional role of the state-owned enterprise (SOE) sector, and the public sector in its broadest sense (Chapters 7–9) dwarfs its economic role, and, over time undermines the economic efficiency of the SOEs. Theoretically, the distributional role could be separated from the economic, but in practice it seldom is, and were the distributional component to be suppressed, then the question of the logic of retaining assets under public ownership would again arise.

Culture, class structure, and historical specificity are of relatively little use in explaining the performance of public property regimes and the crises to which they are subject. By contrast, public ownership nurtures its own culture (and pathology), which is similar across otherwise different systems. The logic of principal–agent relations is so powerful that it swamps culture and peculiar institutional histories. I develop these points further below and in Chapters 4–6.

2. Public sectors cannot be reformed although individual enterprises can. A specific enterprise can be made economically viable without destroying the distributional logic of the sector as a whole. To render the whole sector viable would entail the destruction of that logic and pose once again the question of the retention of any assets under public ownership. The decision to keep enterprises under public ownership will be a political, not an economic, one. I do not wish to prejudge the normative issue of whether or not monopolies should be kept under direct public ownership.

2

3. The argument is that the structures of the economy and society have retarded change but have not determined its course. In this respect the argument is voluntaristic. Heads of state, supported by insulated change teams, have overcome structural "retardants," both with respect to the launching of ISI (Chapter 2) and to the promotion of marketization (Chapter 5). Over time the structural differences among the four countries have become sufficiently great (compare the 25% of Mexico's population employed in agriculture to India's 70%) that it would be hard to argue that either the crises faced by the public sector or the remedies applied to deal with them have been structurally determined.

Nonetheless, I argue that in the absence of determined leadership, insulated change teams, and *economic success*, which ISI for a time supplied, structural features may paralyze the impetus toward change. Moreover, in Mexico and Turkey, where change has proceeded furthest, it is still too early to say if the structural features of their economies, and the institutional interests associated with ISI, have been overcome definitively. As for Egypt and India, change is at its very inception and hence quite reversible. In neither country is there yet determined leadership or an *insulated* change team.

4. We can approach the contrasting dynamics of the initiation and carrying forward of systemic change by incumbent leaders as opposed to those more or less distant from existing distributional arrangements who come to power by coup or election. Understandings inspired by the literature on rent seeking and distributional coalitions generally do not specify how incumbent leaders will shred the entitlements of the coalitions that put them in power. My explanation, neither startlingly original nor stiletto sharp, is that deep economic crisis will alter the nature of interests resisting reform and allow for strategic breaks. The test case is Mexico under Salinas de Gortari, a president produced by a decades-old system that he has profoundly altered.

5. Vested interests have so far been relatively ineffective in defending their entitlements and in thwarting change (Chapters 6–9). My reasoning is that they view reform as a collective bad and survival of change as a kind of lottery. They hope that others will bear the costs of reform while they survive by negotiating new deals with the leadership, just as they or their predecessors negotiated their entitlements in the first place. Moreover, in many instances entitlements were originally bestowed and not won. Hence, the emerging interests did not develop the organizational sinews and history of struggle and cooperation that would have afforded them a coherent defense of their interests.

There is an admitted ambiguity in the way in which I treat vested interests: They are sometimes portrayed as powerful, a perception shared by political leadership, World Bank experts, and itinerant academics; and

3

as weak, because of their recently observed inability to defend their interests. But this perceived weakness may be highly contextual. I would hypothesize that were the reform efforts in Poland, Czechoslovakia, or Russia to be reversed, a new national statism, managed by old interests, might well emerge, sending encouraging signals to these interests' beleaguered counterparts in other countries.

1. THE CASE FOR THE CASES

The four countries under consideration are all large, highly diversified developing economies that followed ISI strategies in which state enterprise played the leading role. As Table 1.1 shows, they vary greatly along important socioeconomic variables. India's population is ten times the size of Mexico's, the next largest,[1] while its per capita income is only a sixth of Mexico's, a quarter of Turkey's, and half of Egypt's. India remains by far the most agrarian of the four countries and Mexico by far the least. But these figures may obscure more than they reveal. All four are still poor developing countries with large pockets of absolute poverty, especially in the rural areas. The structural disparities among them hint at differing political strategies, governmental expenditure patterns, and social welfare programs, but in terms of their industrialization strategies and the role of public enterprise, the disparities have relatively little explanatory value.

The state enterprise sectors of all four are relatively old. The state-owned enterprise sector dates in Turkey from the late 1920s and the 1930s, in Mexico from the 1930s, in India from the late 1940s and 1950s, and in Egypt from about 1954 on. Thus, relative to most lesser developed countries (LDCs), we find in these four the maximum possibility for the formation of coherent managerial elites in the public sector (see Chapter 6), for the development of dependent, privileged labor organizations (see Chapter 9), and for enterprise longevity and tradition. We may hypothesize that in these countries the defense of the public sector is likely to be the strongest, the resistance to reform the most pronounced, and the range of vested interests affected by reform and privatization broader than elsewhere in the developing world. Hence, if we find major change in the structure of the public sector, we should be able to say with some confidence what forces stood in its way and what elements allowed it to go forward.

The state in each of the countries has been interventionist along a broad front. While a certain degree of improvisation was always present, at specific moments in the early period of building the state sector, they each elaborated ideological justifications for public property. They cited the quest for industrial catching-up, economic sovereignty, and social

4

Property and change

Table 1.1. *Population, agricultural population, GNP, and per capita GNP in EIMT, 1987*

	Population millions	% Population in ag. sector	GNP $ millions	Per capita GNP $
Egypt	50.1	52	34,068	680
India	798.0	68	239,400	300
Mexico	82.0	30	150,060	1830
Turkey	52.6	55	63,646	1210

Source: WDR (1988) and census data for each country.

equity as the raisons d'être of public enterprise, relegating the private sector thereby to a decidedly subordinate role (see Chapter 2).

Flowing from the initial ideological and programmatic commitment, there have been attempts at multiyear planning, far-reaching regulation of all economic activity, administered pricing and efforts to guide market forces, quantitative trade restrictions, and substantial if not total control of banking and other financial institutions by the public sector. They all still maintain plan organizations, draw up four- or five-year plans, and see the state as coordinator of all major economic activity (see Chapters 3 and 4).

Each of the four has a private sector of varying strength. The states in question, however, attributed to them two common characteristics. First, existing private sectors were for some time depicted as weak, given to speculation and profiteering, and prone to sell out the national good through alliances with foreign capital. Much of the rationale for heavy state intervention in the economy was to protect the poor from private greed and to undertake what short-sighted, unskilled, and undercapitalized private actors could not. Second, each radical ideology held out the prospect that some day a truly nationalist, enlightened, farsighted entrepreneurial bourgeoisie might emerge, one, however, that would always play a supporting role in strategies laid down by the state (see Chapters 2 and 8).

The policy makers and leaders of all four countries have, in the last decade or so, expressed disappointment with the way in which ISI has proceeded and in the performance of SOEs. Chronic loss-making SOEs contributed importantly to burgeoning domestic deficits, and their inability to generate significant exports, coupled with heavy import-reliance, exacerbated balance of payments problems. Organized labor and sheltered private sectors developed recognized claims to public resources (wage packages and soft credit), which in several episodes fueled

5

inflation, leading to overvalued currencies. In order not to compromise distributional arrangements, deficit financing and external borrowing increasingly became the norm. Something approaching crisis, especially in external accounts, was manifest by the middle 1970s, to some extent driven if not caused by the external oil shocks. The initial response was an attempt to streamline and "rationalize" the statist experiments, to replace redistributive state socialism with cost-effective state capitalism.

The four countries differ in the course of adjustment after the first attempt to deal with the mid-1970s crisis. Mexico and Egypt, increasingly fat with oil and external rents (workers' remittances, tourism), abandoned the stabilization-cum-structural adjustment programs with which they briefly flirted in 1976 and 1977. Mexico was driven back to the reform agenda in the early 1980s by the exigencies of servicing its enormous external debt. The Egyptian regime faced cost-of-living riots when, in January 1977, the government tried to reduce consumer subsidies. It abandoned the reform agenda at that time and, until 1991, avoided far-reaching adjustment by its ability to attract strategic rents. India did not enter into crisis until 1990–91. Supplemented by the discipline of the emergency period, 1974–77, it managed, through careful fiscal and trade policy, to protect its fundamental ISI and statist strategy. Finally, Turkey dealt with its severe domestic and external accounts crisis of 1978–79 through a military take-over and the authoritarian implementation of a structural adjustment program and a shift to export-led growth.

Schematically, then, within the time frame of this study, we have two cases of systems maintenance – India and Egypt – in which SOE reform has been designed to prolong the viability of existing arrangements including the ISI strategy itself, and two cases of systems transformation – Mexico and Turkey – in which privatization and a greater opening to international markets are supposed to alter profoundly the coalitional base of the ISI era. With the exception of Turkey, the process of change, whether structural or marginal, has been carried forward by incumbent elites.

In their specifics, these systems vary a great deal, especially in the extent of state intervention in the economy, in the place of foreign investment (Chapter 3), in the relative strengths of their private sectors (Chapter 8). Where they tend to be similar is in the internal dynamics of the public property regimes and in what I have called the pathology of public sector performance. The analysis seeks to hold some variables more or less constant (within generous parameters; see Chapter 3) – ideology, goals, public–private balances, size of economy and level of development – while letting others – especially history, culture, class configurations, the structures of political competition, and relations to dominant economic powers – vary.

6

Property and change

In the next section, I examine, in order to minimize their importance, some of the frequently invoked independent variables that are alleged to explain how the state deals with its citizens and its assets. If a major part of the problems of ISI and public ownership stem from ineffective monitoring of the performance of state agencies and firms, then these putative explanations are of considerable importance, especially if wrong.

2. CULTURE AND CLASS

2.1. Culture

It would be hard to imagine four countries more culturally and historically diverse than EIMT. Their geography, their ethnic, religious, and lingual composition, their precapitalist modes of production, and their history vis-à-vis industrial Europe and North America are widely if not wildly different. I cannot explore these differences in any detail and must hope that the reader has some general knowledge of them. Some important factors, however, are that Turkey never experienced colonial rule, and Mexico's colonial experience is nearly a century and a half in its past. Egypt's and India's political sovereignty is much more recently acquired, so that if colonial subjugation is purported to influence the way independent states and economies function, then there should be clear differences between Turkey and Mexico on the one hand, and Egypt and India on the other.[2]

Many reputable observers of EIMT and other countries have been quick to invoke cultural factors in explaining basic aspects of economic and political life. In addition, in my interviews with officials and managers in EIMT, several interlocutors cautioned me with the words "To understand this, you must also understand our historical and cultural legacy...." The next words might invoke India's caste system, or *caciquismo* in Mexico, or Egypt's *fahlawi* (verbal servility and ingratiation), or Turkey's warrior code of valor and obedience. Then would follow a series of characteristics that were remarkably similar across all four countries. I do not want to overstate the similarities or to minimize the very real and observable differences among the four, but what my interlocutors frequently saw as cultural flaws with sui generis origins could be reduced to common attitudes and behavioral patterns in systems where power has been concentrated and is used arbitrarily, and where poverty and relative powerlessness are the norm for most inhabitants.

Each society has its code words. In Egypt, the pharaonic past coupled with renderings of hydraulic society and docile *fallahin* are used to explain the feigned deference of the average Egyptian and the overweening powers of the state. The two together inhibit change or the accurate assessment

7

of failed policies. But then, we can shift to Turkey with its tribal past, and its warrior traditions. Despite them Turkish scholars often invoke the Father State (*devlet baba*) to explain why authority is seldom challenged (see Heper, 1985).

Perhaps it all has something to do with Islam as the older orientalist school would have suggested. But the same sorts of characterizations emerge in caste-ridden Hindu India and Catholic Mexico. Octavio Paz has made much of the impact of the mestizo on Mexico's political culture, and, echoing him, Hansen (1974:142) writes of the "mestizo's pathological fascination with and craving for power . . . To the present day this characteristic of mestizo psychology pervades Mexican public life." Miguel Basáñez (1990) likewise stresses the importance of Mexican political culture, which promotes false deference, double codes of behavior, toleration of corruption, and a disdain for work.

Taken together, these critiques are really concerned with flaws that they see as the absence of responsible leadership, and hence of empowered citizens, a rational approach to problem solving, a spirit of public service, and a nonthreatening environment in which people can speak their minds. The flaws may well be there, and they have obvious relevance for the issues of public sector performance and accountability, but I doubt that they are culturally determined.[3]

Some cultural elements do seem to influence process and outcomes in ways that distinguish the four countries. For example, the proposition that India's top leadership and the elite of the administrative services have been dominated by Brahmins who disdain the merchant castes may well have shaped India's experiment in statist socialism. And I am willing to concede that there is a "Bengali factor" when it comes to labor–management relations in that state. Such examples, however, are rare.

Culture also makes a difference in terms of a theme that arises frequently throughout this book: transaction costs. To the extent that culture provides understandings of obligations and rights among various actors in a given cultural system, it also provides self-enforcing norms for all sorts of transactions, including those in markets. It should be noted that ideologies serve similar purposes (North, 1989). Shared cultural norms and ideological values thus reduce the costs involved in carrying out exchanges and in enforcing implicit and explicit contracts.[4]

The, so far, unique economic successes of South Korea, Taiwan, and, of course, Japan have evoked a great deal of speculation as to their cultural origins. What we come out with is a delicate chemistry involving Confucian norms, nationalism, the distribution of wealth at the beginning of the growth period, and the relations of citizens to their governments. The chemistry is not the same for each of the three. Gustav Ranis (1989:1446–47) has posited that the key lies in "organic nationalism" by which citizens' obligations are well defined and generally accepted while the organs of government remain relatively insulated from societal pressures. Peter Evans (1989), and also Alice Amsden (1991), described this phenomenon as "embedded autonomy," and Chalmers Johnson (1982), as one in which politicians reign and technocrats rule.

No one has advanced a standard formula for this chemistry (although Wade, 1990, comes close), but what it suggests is that culture cannot be dissociated from institutions that themselves may be acultural or extra-cultural in origin. In trying to explain the differing economic performance of societies in the last two centuries, Lloyd Reynolds (1985:976; cf. North, 1990) concluded that the "single most important explanatory variable is political organization and the administrative competence of government."

Culture modifies but does not determine, and it is frequently over-whelmed by other forces. Public institutions, like modes of production, yield patterns of behavior and norms that catch up all who work within them. For the questions that I seek to address, institutional cultures are more powerful than the cultural characteristics of the society at large. The Virgin of Guadalupe provides no answers to my riddles.

The director general of a large Mexican SOE recounted to me what a typical board meeting is like. The board members are largely government functionaries with varying although generally limited understanding of the firm. They are the representatives of the owner(s), but they have no stake in the performance or profitability of the firm. They follow a kind of bureaucratic imperative to prove they can exercise control and to demonstrate their power. Management (the agents) thus sees the repre-sentatives of the owners (the principal) as interfering, irresponsible, and destructive. Criticism voiced in board meetings by the government rep-resentatives can never be taken at face value but is assumed to indicate a political decision taken somewhere else for reasons not directly related to the firm. Unless such a decision is at stake, no criticism is voiced. Nonetheless, after a polite meeting, the government representatives will scatter and frequently engage in low-scale acts of sabotage of management – once again to demonstrate their power. This sort of depiction was given to the author in all four countries, and it is not too much to suggest that we are in fact looking at a clash of institutional cultures. Resort to the mestizo personality or Brahmin arrogance does little to illuminate what drives the actors.

It could be hypothesized that the differing bureaucratic traditions and ethos of EIMT would explain some part of the differing economic per-formance of their public sectors. It turns out however that this factor says more about how principal–agent interaction is structured than about the overall performance of the governments and their assets. This issue is treated in greater detail in Chapter 6, but we may note here that if professionalism, predictable career paths, and functional specialization are expected to enhance administrative and managerial efficiency, then Egypt should boast the most efficiently managed public sector of the four. Need I add that it does not? If long historical tradition and the slow accretion of bureaucratic skills are likewise deemed crucial, then Turkey's administrative corps, descended from the Ottoman bureaucracy, should outperform the others. There is no unambiguous evidence to that effect either. If the existence of a powerful bureaucratic elite with real esprit de corps affects performance, then surely the Indian Administrative Service (IAS) should set India apart but does so only partially. Finally, if unpredictable and frequently broken careers among the upper echelons of the administration are expected to yield poor bureaucratic performance, then Mexico should be the most affected. The effect is not immediately visible. The very real differences that exist among the four in terms of administrative history, coherence, and professionalism are neutralized by the similar property regimes within which they operate.

2.2. Class

If the four states were or are the instruments of a dominant bourgeois class operating within an essentially capitalist mode of production, then we might have the key to all questions concerning the logic of the public sector (building or reenforcing capitalism) and of its crises. We cannot make that leap, however, because the strengths of the indigenous bourgeoisies in EIMT are so different that they could not have produced state sectors with far less difference among them (see Chapters 2 and 8). Moreover, the relations between the public and private sectors have varied significantly across EIMT. For most of the period under scrutiny for each of the cases, the state has enjoyed considerable autonomy from any constellation of class actors. This does not mean that societal forces have not *constrained* the state, for they have. But that is a far cry from the instrumentalist vision of class *control*. The broad similarities in the evolution of the four public sectors cannot be satisfactorily explained by resort to class analysis.[5]

There are two types of class actors that frequently recur in the analysis of the state in developing countries. One is the petite bourgeoisie and the other is the state bourgeoisie.[6] With respect to the first, the basic proposition is that the postcolonial state lacks both a mature bourgeoisie and a significant proletariat. The state comes to be dominated by a stratum of white-collar professionals and petty capitalists who are typically nationalist, populist, and hostile to foreign capital. They use the state and state enterprise to promote themselves as a class and to foster

10

an environment in which they can translate state power into individual, private economic power. Michal Kalecki, in an influential article (1976), characterized these as "intermediate regimes," and his propositions were adopted by numerous South Asian scholars (Raj, 7/7/73; Jha, 1980; Sobhan and Ahmad, 1980; Nayar, 1989).

Inherent in this view is that there is no fundamental antagonism between the state and private sectors and that once the state has provided conditions suitable for the development of indigenous capital, it will gradually disengage from direct intervention in the economy. Because something like this process can be observed empirically, the argument would seem to have some power. I argue, however, that the process of disengagement is sustained not by evolving class interests but rather by failed state intervention.

Two facets of the argument appear particularly suspect. One is the notion that the petite bourgeoisie needs public enterprise to further its interests, and the second, directly related, is that the state is more far-sighted than the private actors in whose name it rules. On the first count, it seems implausible that this economically weak petty bourgeois class could snatch political power from extant indigenous bourgeoisies, colonial forces, and multinational corporations and yet be seen as incapable of managing its own private economic interests. The proposition that it must create assets within the public domain in order to further its own development is unconvincing. One could counter that the main obstacle to its development as a private sector entrepreneurial class was and is capital, and that to satisfy its needs it might, once having captured political power, create public banks and investment institutions to provide preferential credit to petty bourgeois entrepreneurs. There would be no need, indeed no logic, in placing much manufacturing, trade, and service activity under state ownership, yet that is exactly what happened in all four countries.[7]

We have, in fact, an example of a self-promoting (petty?) bourgeois regime in Salazar's Portugal, where even banking, along with mining, manufacturing, electricity, telecommunications, and the airline were in private hands. Yet for Eric Baklanoff (1986) there is no doubt that the Portuguese private sector until the 1960s was subordinate to the guidance of the state. If, in fact, the petite bourgeoisie were a dominant class in the making, then we should expect replication of the Portuguese "model."

The proponents of the petty bourgeois, would-be dominant class thesis, would argue that it is not enough that the class use state assets to build its future, but more, it must have the state act as the farsighted helmsperson of economic policy, resolving contradictions between labor and capital and charting economic strategy. In this light, protectionist ISI can be seen as a quintessentially petty bourgeois project.

For many analysts, there need be no direct connection between a petite bourgeoisie and the clairvoyant state. The latter idea, however, flies in the face of a body of literature (to be discussed in section 4 of this chapter) positing the structural shortsightedness of public bodies and the generally counterproductive effects of political interference in the process of private calculus. Be that as it may, I cannot see why the same class that is depicted as too inexperienced to build a real private sector can develop the expertise to plot a rational growth strategy to nurture its interests.[8]

Sometimes joined to the analysis of intermediate regimes is the notion of a state bourgeoisie. For Mahmoud Hussein (1971), for instance, the state bourgeoisie is drawn from the petite bourgeoisie, and exploits its control over state assets to convert public into private wealth. Thus rent seeking and corruption become part of a class strategy for the privatization of public wealth. This putative class, however, lies more in the eye of the beholder than in itself. Pending a fuller discussion in Chapter 7, we may say that it is possible to identify such a class by enumerating formal positions in the state apparatus and particularly in the management of the SOEs. But it is difficult to discern any actions of these functionaries that would indicate a strategy of reproduction and of defense of class interests. To the extent class action is observable, mainly in the form of foot dragging and sabotage when its interests are under assault (see Chapter 5), it is undertaken more by top-level civil servants than by public enterprise managers who are nominally in control of the means of production. Otherwise what characterizes the state bourgeoisie, like so many other class actors in the twentieth century, is mobility: the fact that neither its material nor its intellectual wealth is tied to a particular constellation of productive means. In fact, the top-level state managers do not try to reproduce themselves as a class. If any reproduction is going on, it is among the lower echelons of the state apparatus – the "peasants" of state systems – and there it is not by design.

An alternative view of state elites is as follows: Those groups that seized control of the state apparatus and its economic appendages were not the vanguard of the petite bourgeoisie, nor were they the instrument of a quasi-dominant entrepreneurial class. Very often they were *of* the petite bourgeoisie (although in India initially they were not), but, I argue, that is merely because there was no other stratum from which sufficient numbers of educated personnel could be drawn to people the new state apparatuses. The topmost among them believed in the efficacy of state action and had an abiding suspicion of their own private sectors and a conviction of their inherent weakness. They were no less suspicious of foreign private investment. They received considerable encouragement for their state projects from mainstream development economists and from Western governments and businesses.[9]

As we shall see in greater detail in Chapter 2, the explicit commitment to prolonged, if not indefinite, state intervention was stronger in India and Egypt than in Turkey and Mexico. In the latter two there was always a vague promise that the state would eventually cede its place to a fortified national private sector. But once considerable assets were concentrated in the state sector, a dynamic was begun, sustained by interested managers and politicians, to protect and expand the resources at the disposal of the state. In India and Egypt, where the ideological commitment to state ownership was more powerful, so too was the dynamic.

Thus, as long as economic performance was adequate, there were no class or other structural elements that would have forced the state into retreat. As John Freeman has written with respect to the mixed, corporatist systems of Western Europe, these "were not half-way stops between capitalism and socialism" (Freeman, 1989:46–47; see also Pollock, 1982, and Nayar, 1989:214) but, rather, were taken as self-perpetuating. To that extent there was and is a concern for reproduction but not a strategy. When the ISI projects experienced severe fiscal constraints and fell into stagflation, the need for change was recognized and to a more limited extent actually begun. For some this was proof that the petite bourgeoisie had fulfilled its historic role, but if that were at all the case, one would not expect it to make its move in economies undergoing severe crisis in which much private enterprise survives only by the grace of public sector banks.

3. PROPERTY REGIMES

I shall make a qualified argument that the legal disposition of property counts in the sense that public and private ownership are rooted in different expectations, and they necessarily generate different criteria for measuring performance. Derivatively both owners and managers under the two legal forms respond to qualitatively different incentives.

Property regimes are institutions that allow economic actors, who are in no other way linked than through the market, to develop interdependencies with some confidence that the rules governing their interaction will be observed. It is normally the state that enforces the rules, but if the costs of monitoring and enforcing contractual arrangements are not to be prohibitive (i.e., excessive transaction costs), then the regimes must be embedded in norms that allow for a considerable degree of self-enforcement (North, 1989:1320).

There are many analysts who argue that property regimes, especially in advanced industrial societies, do not really matter in any of the ways just listed. The two principal reasons for minimizing the significance of legal ownership are, first, the similar distance separating shareholders in private regimes and taxpayers in public regimes from the assets they nominally own (Sappington and Stiglitz, 3/87). In both instances there is little effective owner control. Management, with little or no ownership stake in the firm, can and does operate it in inefficient and self-serving ways. Put in rational choice language, monitoring can be seen as a collective good the benefits of which cannot be denied any of the nominal owners of the asset, but toward which no individual owner will have any incentive to contribute. Each will instead try to free-ride in the hope that someone else will carry out the monitoring. If everyone behaved "rationally," no monitoring would take place.[10] The second observation is that large bureaucratic structures, be they giant private corporations or large public enterprises, will generate similar incentives for current spending, blurred responsibilities, and duplication of tasks. When one reads that in 1982 Exxon slashed 80,000 employees of a total of 182,000, including 1,000 of 1,360 bureaucrats in its New York headquarters, without sacrificing production, one must question the distinction between public and private (see *New York Times*, 4/2/89:sec. 3). There is, however, a difference: Had Exxon been an SOE, it might not have made the personnel cuts.

Under certain circumstances economic theory suggests that there may be little difference in how publicly and privately owned assets perform.[11] The crucial condition is that they be subjected to competition in capital, final goods, and management markets (Picot and Kaulmann, 1989; Stiglitz et al., 1989:31; Comisso, 1990:593). Shapiro and Willig (1990) assert that under "optimally" designed regulatory and tax regimes there should be no difference in performance between public and private enterprise. Indeed, it is claimed that governments (principals) enjoy advantages of information regarding their SOEs that would be denied them were they to replace ownership with regulation of private activity. In this respect some public assets may be more efficiently run than private ones. In short, Stiglitz as well as Shapiro and Willig dismiss on theoretic grounds any operational distinction between publicly and privately held assets, and instead stress differences in available information and regulatory arrangements.[12]

As these and other authors readily concede, a competitive environment is frequently lacking, especially in LDCs. However, what they do not sufficiently acknowledge is that the governmental owners of public assets frequently do not have adequate information about the management of these assets. As Solís (1976:139) notes, for bureaucrats and managers, information is a strategic resource and its sharing is seen as a dissipation of power. It will be released only for strategic advantage. In addition, the empirical record shows that managers of public assets doctor their books, hoard goods, evade taxes, hide profits, and collude with other enterprises to defraud the government. Informational and regulatory advantages between principals and agents in the public domain appear to be mainly theoretical.

It is striking that the leaders of many LDCs, and certainly the founding fathers of the public enterprise sectors of EIMT, believed that the legal designation of property matters greatly. They believed this both in terms of efficiency and of equity. SOEs were to be harnessed to a rational multiyear plan for growth and to become the principal instruments in its execution. Being direct appendages of the state, the SOEs would require much less monitoring than private firms. Transaction costs would be less. Moreover, because they would not be measured by profitability alone, the SOE could be put to specific social purposes of provision of low-cost products, employment generation, and the development of backward regions.

All of this hinged on one crucial assumption, or illusion, as it turned out. The plan, the market, and equity targets had to be managed by selfless public officials who would resist the temptation to exploit the power that state administration of markets and assets provided them. It did not seem ill-advised to set up state monopolies because they would be run for the public interest. Monopolies in private hands, it was believed, would inevitably produce exploitation. Administered markets would serve social purposes while unregulated markets would serve private greed. Any distortions or gross inefficiencies that might emerge in regulated markets and in SOEs would be handled by bureaucratic controls (auditing, inspection, policing) and by enlightened senior management. The three main illusions that were inherent in the faith in public property were

1. that bureaucratic controls would work as designed;
2. that devoted management could be sustained over time;
3. that planners could devise rational strategies that would lead to self-financing growth in publicly owned assets.

It is also significant that when, more recently, voices are raised advocating privatization of public assets, their rationale is based on the real distinction between legal dispositions. In EIMT and most LDCs the supply of competent management is limited and much of it may be concentrated in the public sector. Thus, the advocates of privatization are suggesting not that the private sector will provide new managerial talent but, rather, that the same managers will run their firms more efficiently under private ownership. Indeed, public sector managers themselves are the most likely to espouse this view.

Those who defend SOEs generally cite the one or two efficiently run public firms in their economies and conclude that there is nothing inherently inefficient about this form of ownership. That, as Stiglitz (1989) and others argue on theoretic grounds, may well be true (although I shall contest it on political grounds), but it misses the main point. The consequences of inefficiency, poor management, and business failure are much different for private than for public enterprise. When private enterprises fail, they (sometimes) go out of business. The annual rate of declared bankruptcies in the United States is eloquent testimony to this. By contrast I would be hard put to cite any liquidation of a major SOE in EIMT before that of Fundidora de Monterrey in Mexico in 1985. Exit of SOEs, it is well known, is not a threat their managers have to face. In Egypt, Law 97 of 1983, which until 1991 defined the juridical status of SOEs, stated that they cannot be declared bankrupt (although private firms accumulating losses equivalent to 50% of their capital can).[13] It should be noted that private firms are not always allowed to exit when they fail, and in all four countries the state has often taken over, by refinancing, failing private firms. In India the absorption of "sick" industries into the public domain has become almost ritualistic. One Indian pundit has remarked that "when a private firm goes sick, we nationalize it. When a public firm goes sick, we try to privatize it."

Public assets need not be managed in economically inefficient ways, nor need all state intervention in markets be distorting.[14] The fact that public assets most often are managed inefficiently and that many interventions do yield unintended and unwanted consequences cannot be swept aside on theoretic grounds. The vicious triangle of no-exit, noncompetitiveness, and the soft budget constraint, made famous by János Kornai, has become the hallmark of SOEs in most countries. It is often those who advocated or sired them and believed in their capabilities who have become their most trenchant critics. Kornai figures prominently here. In India, I was told by a person who had been the chief executive officer (CEO) of one of the largest state holding companies and then a member of the Planning Commission, that public ownership "contains a genetic flaw." His disillusionment was shared by many others.

4. THE STATE AS ENFORCER OF PROPERTY REGIMES

The discussion of property regimes has hinted at a fundamental cleavage in the conceptualization of the state. In the post–World War II era there was an optimism shared by newly independent LDCs and by development economists that public authorities would be capable of marshaling scarce resources and designing and implementing policies that could put their economies on the path toward sustained growth. The shared view of the state was that it consisted of a disinterested set of instrumentalities that, constrained only by their competence and revenues, would faithfully

	Instrumental (I)	Autonomous (A)
Benevolent (B)	**IB** Liberals see the state as fulfilling the programs of democratically elected interests. Marxists see the state as furthering the interests of the dominant class.	**AB** Weberians and some Neo-Marxists see the state for more or less long periods of time carrying forward a developmental project relatively unfettered by forces in society.
Malevolent (M)	**IM** For Marxists the state exploits society for the benefit of the dominant class.	**AM** Neoliberal, neo-conservative (New Political Economy) analysts see the state and its agents as acting fundamentally in their own interests at the expense of society.

Figure 1.1. A matrix of state logic

pursue projects aimed at the general welfare. This seemed to be the lesson of the Western state as it dealt with the 1930s depression and reconstruction after the war.

As decades of experience and observation accumulated, another understanding gained currency. In contrast to the benevolent characteristics already depicted, an image, arising out of public choice theory (and now sometimes referred to as the new political economy), saw the state as a collection of self-interested actors concerned mainly with extracting resources from society and elaborating the "myths" by which to legitimize this extraction. This is a decidedly malevolent understanding of the state, one that in its extreme forms has given rise to labels such as "predatory" (Levi and North, 1982; Lal, 1988) or "mafia" states (Tilly, 1985).

Cutting across the benevolent–malevolent divide are understandings that see the state as predominantly the instrument of societal forces or as predominantly autonomous from them. Marxist and liberal analyses stress the instrumental nature of the state while Weberians, neo-Marxists and neoliberals in specific situations stress its autonomy. These are admittedly gross characterizations, which I have tried to summarize in Figure 1.1. Even at this level of abstraction, they are important because they posit a logic to state action that has direct implications for the degree to which states intervene in markets, who benefits from such intervention, and what variables change the nature and scope of state intervention.

The matrix is of necessity static. The nature of the state is not, and it changes over time. Indeed, Douglass North (1989:1323), whose understanding would often place him in the *AM* quadrant, sees the evolution of states from mafia-like to more rational-legal (benevolent) forms as "a major part of the history of freedom." Each quadrant, at any moment

17

in time, and even for different parts of the state, may capture the essence of its nature. I make no claim that any single understanding is, more often than not, the correct one. That said, for the time period covered in this study, EIMT are best understood as falling in quadrants *AB* and *AM*. It is for that reason that in the next paragraphs I discuss only those two quadrants.

Jones and Mason (1982:24) present a view that, I think, summarizes the understanding of *AB* succinctly:

[The state is a] rational decision-making entity exclusively concerned with maximizing economic welfare through a choice among a wide variety of centralized and decentralized institutions . . . Benefits can be had from government intervention where market failures lead a profit maximizing private producer to behavior incompatible with social welfare maximization . . . Public enterprise is . . . one among many tools available for achieving the government's goals, and the choice of this tool is a function of the costs and benefits associated with its use as compared to those of other institutional forms.

The authors admit there is a mythical quality to this abstract state. However, many observers took it as approximating reality,[15] including, predictably, many heads of state. The assumption of inherent state benevolence (and autonomy) is implicit in remarks made by Nehru in 1954 (as cited in Nayar, 1989:223; cf. A. H. Hansen, 1959; John Lewis, 1962:202–20; Tello, 8/88:27). The state, he said, had to preempt basic industries from the private sector

because not only they might prove to be very profitable but because it gives them economic power. I think it is highly objectionable that economic power should be in the hands of a small group of persons, however able or good they might be. Such a thing must be prevented.

In short, quadrant *AB* would include much of the literature on modernization, state capitalism and state socialism.[16]

The protagonists grouped in quadrant *AM* argue that the concentration of power in extensive state bureaucracies, undergirded by overwhelming coercive force, will sooner or later yield perverse effects and the abuse of the public welfare. The state will tend over time to exploit its monopoly position to extract resources from the disorganized many to reward the organized few with whom its leaders are allied. These could be subordinate classes (Bardhan, 1984), distributive coalitions in the Olsonian sense (Olson, 1982), or privileged groups formed within and dependent upon the state itself (Keyder, 1987, and Chapter 6).

Levi and North (1982:318–19) define the state as "any organization with an absolute advantage in violence extending over a geographic area whose boundaries are determined by its power to tax constituents." All reference to Weberian legitimacy is omitted, and the authors state that

18

the ruler designs property rights intended to maximize the power and wealth of those individuals or coalitions already powerful.

The benevolent and powerful state is thus oxymoronic. That it could be more farsighted than private actors pursuing their own interests is improbable. States, in this view, will improve welfare only if their powers are strictly checked or widely dispersed. Mahatma Gandhi sought precisely that through his quest for an independent India based on empowered villages. The rise of Nehru in the Congress Party, with Gandhi's blessing, signaled his retreat in the face of the inevitable. But he never shared Nehru's faith in the welfare-producing effects of state action.[17]

States and state intervention have been frequently characterized as predatory. The image itself is explicit. States tend to devour the populations and resources from which they live. The farsighted predator will look to the reproduction of his resource base (evoking more the image of bovine recycling than of gazelle hunting; see Lal, 1988:294; Evans, 1989, 1992). The predatory image is ancient, and hence, one might suspect, well founded: "He [George III] has erected a Multitude of new Offices, and sent hither Swarms of Officers to harass our People, and eat out their substance" (from the Declaration of Independence, 1776). Subsumed under the label "predatory" are two elements. There is, on the one hand, the monopolistic extraction of resources in exchange for the enforcement of property rights and the provision of some law and order (both being public goods), and, on the other, rent-seeking behavior on the part of public officials and those in civil society bidding for state favors.[18] The state grows at the expense of society which, over the long term, is surely unsustainable.

Microeconomists have supplied the analytic framework for rent-seeking behavior and for the broader concept of directly unproductive profit-seeking (DUP).[19] The basic proposition is that governments, through discretionary regulation of economic activity, create opportunities for profit that entail no change in the productive forces of the economy. Resources will be expended by economic actors to bid on privileges provided by public policy (licenses, tariffs, import permits, etc.). If the bidding is fully competitive, the gains from privilege will be totally offset by the expenses of bidding with no net gain to the economy.[20] Highly interventionist states will create a vast range of rent-seeking incentives. The best entrepreneurial talent will be diverted from directly productive pursuits as will the resources they control. Once the rent seekers have established "title" to their rents, they will resist any efforts to dismantle the regulations that yield them.[21]

Finally, quadrant *AM* includes a body of analysis that fastens on the expected behavior of public officials. State agencies pursue their own interests even at the expense of other public entities. Planners become

19

brokers among sectoral lobbies. In the absence of any effective monitoring by taxpayers, the managers of public resources press constantly for their expansion. They prefer current to future expenditures because they tend to move among agencies. They prefer front-loaded, capital-intensive projects to labor-intensive programs with slowly disbursing recurrent budgets (Niskanen, 1975:639; Kornai, 9/10/81:966–69).[22]

Because of ineffective monitoring, costly collusions among bureaucrats, public and private interests, and politicians form and lead to the pillaging of the public sector. Some public officials whom I interviewed were among their severest critics. A senior Indian official compared the public sector to a carcass being picked over by vultures – labor, politicians, managers, bureaucrats. They all have a vested interest in poor management, he said, in losses and in complicated accounting. They can pilfer a losing company more easily than a sound one. Company bankruptcy is of no concern. The state will cover the losses. All they care about are immediate revenues and their foreign bank accounts. Leopoldo Solís, writing in 1976 (pp. 136–38) as an inside man in the Echeverría administration, mused: "Perhaps no other group can be as detrimental to reform as the bureaucracy itself ... The influence of the bureaucracy is especially strong on the spending side ... Regardless of their functions, bureaucrats pursue their own interests ... a bureaucracy owes its first loyalty to itself."[23]

In the periods under study, EIMT established mixed property regimes in which the state was proprietor of a vast range of strategic and productive assets (the so-called commanding heights). There were no class actors of sufficient strength to control the states which for the most part enjoyed considerable autonomy.[24] At various points the states and their functionaries turned to projects of national development with some devotion and selflessness. Over time, however, as the leadership began to realize the magnitude and complexity of what they had undertaken, policy drift and rent seeking came to predominate. In terms of Figure 1.1, EIMT had begun to move from *AB* to *AM*. But these four states were never predatory in the sense of feeding off an increasingly impoverished populace. They did extract high levels of resources from society, particularly from the agricultural sector, but their predation, if such it was or is, was of the deferred variety: through deficit financing and external borrowing the appetite of the state was sated at the expense of future generations.

5. STASIS AND CHANGE

The contents of the four quadrants in Figure 1.1 imply the existence of systems of power and resource allocation with different consequences for the process of change. Quadrant *IB* suggests a process of constantly adjusting interests allowing for the establishment of new equilibria. *IM* would predict that a dominant class will maintain its grip indefinitely or until such time as a dialectical response leads to its overthrow. *AB* suggests a process by which the autonomous state wins the development battle leading to an increasingly differentiated society with large pockets of economic wealth outside state control. The state gradually loses its autonomy. Quadrant *AM* predicts coalitions of revenue-maximizing state and private interests that defend the status quo until economic collapse or violent overthrow ensue.

In none of them is the crucial question of the possibility for endogenous transformation of systems sufficiently explored (Grindle, 1989; Haggard and Kaufman, 1992), and within the terms of this study it is the case of Mexico that demands an answer to that question.

5.1. Stasis

Over the decades in which EIMT implemented ISI, the resultant system of resource allocation helped create a broad-based and costly coalition of organized interests. This coalition came to rest on a set of entitlements, sometimes referred to, as in Egypt, as the social pact, and that pact became the cornerstone of regime stability (see Chapter 7). With their emphasis on revenue maximization, distributional coalitions, and rent seeking, choice theoretic approaches provide powerful tools for understanding this sort of stability and stasis. They would predict regime-generated change of an incremental, system-sustaining variety, tending toward new equilibria within existing arrangements. This, I shall argue, was indeed the reform agenda of Anwar Sadat and Husni Mubarak of Egypt, Rajiv Gandhi of India, and Miguel de la Madrid of Mexico. Initially I had expected that this book would focus on the role of the public sector in promoting or thwarting this adjustment process. However, Mexico and Turkey in the 1980s began experiments intended to be system transforming, and in the case of Mexico such experiments were begun by the incumbent political regime. How that came about demands close attention.

When we look at the array of interests that have benefited from state-led ISI, it appears a formidable alliance until we think of the collapse of similar alliances in the Soviet Union and Eastern Europe (Przeworski, 1991:6). Political leadership in EIMT came to treasure the broad discretionary powers afforded it by the instruments of production and social engineering within the public sector. Leaders enjoyed the discretionary use of public resources to redirect flows to targeted groups, to keep opponents off balance, and to disrupt any autonomous accumulation of wealth in society. Even leaders who come to office with a mandate to diminish the economic weight of the state may find it very hard to part

21

with its attendant powers. This was the story of the Turkish government in the 1950s. It was committed to privatization, but at the end of its incumbency the public sector had actually grown through the founding of what were called "election factories" (Ahmad, 1977:128). Thus, leaders for strategic purposes, and politicians, whether *apparatchiki* of single-party regimes or elected officials, for purposes of patronage developed strong interests in the maintenance of the public sector, and, indeed, in its expansion.

Many governmental agencies in EIMT were created expressly to monitor and supervise public enterprise. Their officialdom, and, of course, the managers of the SOEs themselves, shared an interest in maximizing resource flows to the public enterprise sector. Civil servants, who controlled contracting and who acted as gate keepers and toll takers in complex regulatory regimes, drew personal reward from their power. When all these elements were combined they produced a kind of inertial expansionary force that overwhelmed the logic and purposes for which individual public agencies had been founded (for a case study of Nacional Financiera in Mexico, see Bennett and Sharpe, 1/80).

Outside the state, but to varying degrees dependent upon it, were organized interests that benefited directly from the state domain: the large-scale private sector, organized labor, and the "intelligentsia." The private sector, as we shall see, was in part the creation of the public sector, but even when it enjoyed some autonomy antecedent to ISI (e.g., in India and Mexico) it came to thrive on state business: public credit, production subsidies, tariff protection, supply and purchasing contracts, tax incentives, and the like. The resources used in bidding for rents may have been more than offset by the fact that the state absorbed risk for private actors and tolerated high rates of profit.

Typically the nonagricultural work force was split by the state into a disorganized majority scattered through myriad small-scale enterprises, and an organized minority of more skilled workers concentrated in the state sector itself. Corporatist collaboration among the state, the large-scale private sector (if it existed), and the peak labor unions produced a certain degree of labor discipline in exchange for relatively high wages and benefits and virtually guaranteed employment. Alongside organized blue-collar unions were the civil servants, sometimes organized, sometimes not, but representing the bulk of white-collar employees in the economy (see Chapter 9).[25]

The "intelligentsia" generally refers to virtually anyone in these countries with a high school degree or better. Its status in society is dependent on its educational qualifications, and those of its members who are actually educationists, intellectuals, and pundits have generally been profoundly statist and articulately hostile to the private sector. Moreover, higher education has tended to become a kind of closed circle in which universities, as public entities, produce state employees. The intelligentsia is thus internal to the state, and although its members are frequently critical of it, the criticism generally deals with how the state might better intervene. Because the intelligentsia can give voice to its apprehensions, it has become the most conspicuous defender of the status quo.

Finally, among the beneficiaries of state-led ISI are the military establishments. Many SOEs are, in fact, in the military-strategic sector; military establishments may be at the cutting edge of new technologies in, say, computers, lasers, satellite imagery, and so on; their claims on the national budget are large and unquestioned (see Chapter 3); they have carved out large niches in the civilian economy; they often enjoy duty-free imports of their "necessities" and overvalued rates for foreign exchange. The military, one might assume, would fear being swept up in a more general drive to roll back the state. In Mexico, however, we have a state in which the military, since the 1940s, has been marginalized, in both political and economic terms. It is not clear if this has facilitated the efforts of Carlos Salinas de Gortari to undertake economic reform.

In most respects this array of vested interests and entitlements conforms to the spirit of Mancur Olson's analysis of distributional coalitions. He sees organized interests as rent seekers, acquiring over time rights to quasi-monopoly status in some occupational or product market. He posits that stable societies with fixed boundaries will accumulate more and more such "collusions," that they will tend to reduce economic efficiency and technological innovation, and that, unless the losses to the economy as a whole are several-fold greater than the specific rewards to special interests, the latter will always have an incentive to perpetuate the collusion (Olson, 1982:43). Olson's theses have been subjected to telling criticism on both empirical and conceptual grounds, but they do isolate, it seems to me, important dynamics for stasis that are at work in EIMT.[26]

5.2. Change

His theses are less helpful in specifying the conditions under which change can come about. It can be hypothesized that this may happen in three nonmutually exclusive ways. Established beneficiaries can be displaced by new interests, through coup, revolution, or the ballot box, and once in command of the state apparatus use public revenues in radically different ways. External powers with various points of leverage over a particular polity can impose a new strategy. The regnant strategy may reveal itself to be so flawed that the beneficiaries no longer benefit or that they fear being swept away by the growing numbers of nonbeneficiaries.

These three factors are mediated by institutions in the public sphere. As used here, public institutions[27] are neither the simple tools of class interests nor are they rational calculators. Rather, they have historical memories, conform to rules of what is appropriate rather than rational, and engage in strategies of satisficing rather than maximizing. However, if we are dealing with transformative change in the public sector, then we are confronted with an anomaly with which institutional theory is ill equipped to deal. The agents of change are likely to be its first victims (Solís, 1976; Kornai, 1989), and it seems neither rational nor appropriate that they would be willing accomplices to their own demise.

I emphasize in this study the importance of domestic factors in explaining the determinant sources of change, but it must be stressed that that is very much a *ceteris paribus* proposition. The international context is important (Cameron, 1978, 1988; Haggard, 1990), and in periods of crisis may be determinant. The most difficult analytic issue is to determine the source of the crisis. For example, it was the crisis brought about by the deterioration in the terms of trade for primary product exporters in the 1930s that *partially* led to the first elaborations of the ISI strategy. Today, the intelligentsias of many developing countries see the changes adumbrated in the form and scale of state economic intervention as being wrung from unwilling and beleaguered policy makers by a powerful alliance of international creditors and academic ideologues. However, as shown in subsequent chapters, those pressures have reenforced a growing recognition on the part of indigenous policy makers that new approaches were needed.

The interaction between external and domestic stimuli in bringing about policy change thwarts attempts to disentangle lines of causality. Domestic policies that produce large public deficits render small economies vulnerable to external pressures. Cheap commercial credit from international banks in the late 1970s led to crippling debt burdens in the 1980s. But some countries, like South Korea, managed their deficits and debt obligations much more effectively than others, like Argentina, and those differences, I believe, ultimately must be attributed to domestic factors.[28]

In seeking explanations for transformative change we may turn to the initiation and spread of ISI as a growth model. It sheds light on the current efforts in Mexico and Turkey, and to a much lesser extent in Egypt and India, to streamline the state's economic interventions, to deregulate markets, and to compete internationally.

ISI was intended to, and in fact did, represent fundamental change in the economies of the periphery and semi-periphery in the interwar years. It was sometimes, although not always, initiated by new political incumbents – that was the case for three of the four countries under examination here.[29] It was not designed by Western donors or commercial banks, although it eventually received ample support from them, as well as fr' m multinational corporations (Maxfield and Nolt, 1990). Like the neo-classical frameworks now being urged upon the developing world, ISI bore the intellectual imprimatur of a host of development economists. It was in this sense not imposed from outside but, rather, was the result of the diffusion of ideas and models of diverse origins (Friedrich List, Keynes, ECLA, the Soviet Union, etc.) whose time had clearly come.

It was not the logical outcome of some unfolding of class forces, although it was, of course, a partial response to the challenge of predominant agricultural sectors with low productivity and low per capita incomes. This notwithstanding, the constituency for ISI was no more *structured* than are the groups that today advocate reform of its legacy in the public sector. It was a response to the crisis embodied in the collapse of world trade and primary commodity markets in the 1930s, although the response could be pragmatic and piecemeal, as in Mexico (Kaufman, 1990), or comprehensive and strategic, as in Turkey. It was also importantly a response to a perceived crisis in national self-assertion in the face of dominant industrial powers. The designers, aware of the structural impediments, talked frequently of skipping stages and leaping directly into the industrial age.

The leaders were narrowly based and, to varying degrees, had to create their own constituencies. The relative lack of structured opposition to ISI that favored its inception, in turn made its sustainability problematic until such time as the new beneficiaries in labor, the military, the state sector itself, and the salariate could develop organizational underpinnings.

It is important to note that this constituency-building process was generally "inclusionist," in Guillermo O'Donnell's (1973) sense of the term, whereas the same process under way today in Mexico and Turkey is distinctly "exclusionist."[30] That is, the current adjustments will rest on a much more narrow political base. ISI had a populist appeal that structural adjustment will never enjoy.

Finally, and perhaps most importantly, ISI produced growth over fairly long periods of time. This growth ranged from Mexican or South Korean highs to what Raj Krishna dubbed the Hindu rate of growth, but growth it was. The simplistic but powerful corollary is that sustainability is ultimately anchored in performance.

We can extract at least three explanatory variables from the change wrought by the introduction and application of ISI. First, the international context, characterized by the twofold crisis outlined above, provided an impetus for change. Second, regnant strategies and policies for economic growth were seen by domestic elites to be deficient. Third, the initiation of new strategies, as in all four countries under scrutiny here, came as the result of sharp discontinuities with previous political arrangements (see Chapter 2).

5.3. Reform and change in property regimes

The framework in which contemporary strategic change takes place is that of structural adjustment. Structural adjustment is usually triggered by what is seen as a short-term, conjunctural crisis but consists in long-term policies to liberalize markets, allow prices to reflect real scarcities in the economy, weed out unviable enterprises, and reduce government spending and the public deficit while using public investment to support private production. Adjustment may also entail improving the domestic terms of trade for agriculture and an effort to promote exports. The SOE sector is implicated in every facet of the adjustment process: It is a subsidy taker and a subsidy provider, it runs large deficits, it may determine the terms of trade with the agricultural sector, and, outside of the petroleum sector, it seldom exports.

As conjunctural crises unfold – as in the early 1970s after the first oil shock or in the 1980s as arrears on debt servicing accumulated – the initial response will be to try to reform existing arrangements to make them more efficient. The protectionist and regulatory apparatus of ISI may be partially dismantled and measures undertaken to improve SOE efficiency. Each member of EIMT entered this phase of structural tinkering in the mid- or late 1970s, and Egypt and India are only now, possibly, about to leave it. In these two countries, the initial reform efforts may not defuse the crisis nor improve macroeconomic efficiency. If realization of that fact is coupled with another conjunctural crisis, such as the mounting external debt and plummeting oil revenues of Mexico in the early 1980s, then a phase of *transformative* change may follow. Two decades of tinkering may be followed by wholesale dismantling of policies, and SOE reform may be replaced by privatization and liquidation.

Moreover, a marked change in coalitional strategy may also ensue. In the first reform phase the object of leadership is to bring about change without seriously disrupting existing coalition partners (those already sketched out). In the second phase, leadership will try to remake the coalition, reaching out to all segments of the private and informal sector, consumers as opposed to employees, and market-oriented farmers. None of these have much benefited from the decades of ISI and may be willing to support transformative change (for the Turkish case, see Waterbury, 1992). The second phase may begin, if it begins at all, under radically different circumstances. In Turkey it came after the military had dis-

26

mantled the old coalition, whereas in Mexico it has begun with the old coalition still in place.

The sequential shift, if it is to proceed, will be managed by what I will call a change team. It will consist in technocrats with few or no links to the political arena although their prominence in the realm of macrostrategy may lead to such links. But in their capacity as the brain trust of the political leadership they will be politically isolated and dependent on the patronage of the head of state. Conversely, for the team to move, an agenda will require the visible and consistent support of the head of state. Such teams were frequently crucial in carrying forward the ISI project in its initial stages.[31] The crucial factor is the public backing of the team by the head of state.

It is also important that there be considerable consistency in views and the setting of priorities among the team's members, although it is in the nature of political leadership to want a variety of views at its disposal and to balance contending camps. For that reason, and because turnover in change teams tends to be high, it is hard for them to maintain momentum. In Mexico, Finance Minister Pedro Aspe has clearly been the driving force of the change team, but he has rivals in other ministries, the Bánco de Mexico, and in the presidency itself. In Turkey, Özal's team of young, foreign-trained technocrats (two-passport Turks, as the local press sometimes describes them) saw a number of members fall from grace or move off into the private sector, a trend sharply accelerated by an electoral defeat in the fall of 1991.

Change teams are to varying degrees shielded from the groups whose interests will be gored in the reform process. They will be dealing with facets of a crisis that is felt throughout society, but by the very severity of which the populace has been numbed or rendered indifferent to the policy process itself. Defenders of old policies can no longer mount a coherent or coordinated defense. It will be clear, then, that policy initiatives originate within the state apparatus itself and only infrequently can be seen as the result of domestic lobbying (for earlier examples, see Hirschman, 1965:309).

In examining the initiation of ISI as well as the initiation of neoclassical reforms, it is possible to isolate an important dynamic that inheres in the delegation process. Political leaders may have a few general preferences and targets that they seek to realize. They select among available experts a team sharing those preferences and technically competent to pursue them. The head of state, we may hypothesize, is a pragmatic problem-solver, wedded to some extent to the status quo. The team he or she selects, however, may develop an ideological and programmatic approach to the problems it has been charged to solve. In Egypt in the early 1960s, Nasser, whom I see as a trial-and-error statist, put the organization of

27

the economy and of the political system in the hands of subordinates who wanted to build socialism. More recently in Mexico, an equally pragmatic de la Madrid, and a marginally less so Salinas, have set loose technocratic teams in pursuit of an internally consistent neoclassical blueprint. Pragmatic problem-solving has given way to programmatic transformation. If the top leadership becomes alarmed at the zeal with which the transformation is being pursued, it may disperse the team, thereby jeopardizing even pragmatic change. If it stands by the team, we may witness a process of cascading reform (for the British case, see Keegan, 12/31/89). Reform sequencing is examined in much greater detail in Chapter 5.

6. CONCLUSION

When trying to grasp the significance of large state sectors for the macroeconomy and political systems of EIMT, and to understand their performance and their pathologies, we find that broadly similar property regimes and formal institutions explain far more than variables of culture and class, which vary considerably among the four.

Sustainable transformative change in such systems depends on sharp breaks and discontinuities. Revolutions and wars are the most spectacular of these, but coups and elections can also provide them. I argue that economic crisis can in itself constitute a break of such magnitude that self-interested, incumbent elites may try to change the foundations upon which their power has long rested.[32] The crises may have been brought on by economic strategies so flawed that over time they caused structural distortions, but if one looks at the record of ISI in India and Mexico, such a conclusion is by no means obvious (see Chapter 3). On the other hand, I do not accept that the kinds of change we are witnessing in EIMT can be explained in class-structural terms, that is, as the unfolding of a dialectic.

Political power rests on explicit or implicit coalitions. They are likely to be heterogeneous, including class actors, functionally defined groups, ethnic or religious interests, and interests from the state itself (see Chapter 7). Change inevitably affects coalitional interests, and in the case of change in ISI, the array of entitled beneficiaries is formidable. Yet, as we shall see, resistance to change has been surprisingly weak. Rational actor models provide clues as to why this is so.

Incumbent coalitions may regard structural reform as a collective bad; no one can be excluded from its costs (or benefits). Those who benefit will want to do so without contributing to the costs of change. Those who may suffer, rather than directly oppose change, which might entail high costs of its own, will seek to protect their own privileges while

28

hoping that all others will bear the costs. They will try to free-ride rather than throw themselves in the path of the bus.

There is a sequence in resistance to change that corresponds necessarily to the change sequence itself. In the phase of system-maintaining reform, the beneficiaries deny there is anything fundamentally wrong. They denounce as malicious or corrupt any critics who suggest otherwise. They present a fairly united front so long as they maintain control of the reform process. In this phase an objectively defined crisis may go on for some time before bold measures are adopted to deal with it (Egypt's position from 1976 to 1991).

Then comes the phase of avowal. The crisis persists and deepens, and change can no longer be denounced as betrayal. The issue then becomes who will bear the burden of it, and in approaching it the coalition fragments into microstrategies of *sauve qui peut*. The fragmentation gives determined leadership the chance to push through transformative change packages, while the disorganized free riders look on, sometimes but perhaps not always until it is too late. In the LDCs and in Eastern Europe, this process of transformative change is too recent to exclude the possibility of a crisis in the change process itself – such as that witnessed in Brazil and Argentina in the early 1980s – that may allow the old coalition to regroup and recentralize. In that spirit, my story of change in EIMT will be carried forward only as far as the data permit. But if transformative change in the older patterns of allocation under ISI is arrested or reversed, we should avoid attributing the phenomenon to rearguard actions by "conservatives" or sabotage by blocking coalitions. As likely an explanation, as was the case with ISI, will be the inconsistencies and incoherence of the reform and restructuring policies themselves.

The chapters of this book are organized according to the following logic: Chapter 2 deals with the process by which ISI and the development of large public sectors in EIMT was carried forward. It also provides the historical context necessary to understand the remaining chapters. Chapter 3 explores, first, the changing macroeconomic characteristics of the four countries, and, second, the relative characteristics of their SOE sectors. The performance of publicly owned assets and the efforts to reform or privatize them are examined in Chapters 4 and 5, which also analyze the "culture" of principal–agent relations in public property regimes.

The crucial issue of the state managers, the most significant "agents" in the state economic sector, is raised in assets under their control. As the managers would seem to have a kind of proprietary interest in the assets they manage, we shall want to determine how they respond to efforts to reform or sell them. The managers are undisputably key members of the dominant ISI coalitions. Chapter 7 examines as a whole these coalitions and the strategies for holding them together, then singles out for detailed analysis the private sector (Chapter 8) and organized labor (Chapter 9). Thus, Chapters 6 through 9 should explain the interests of those constituencies most attached to existing patterns of the use of public resources and in a position to thwart attempts to change them. Why they may prove ineffectual in their blocking role is a theme developed in these chapters.

2

The will to transform

This chapter sketches the process by which state-led industrialization was launched in EIMT. It will provide about as much straightforward history as is to be found in this book. Its goals, however, are more ambitious. We shall look at the great initiators of change in EIMT and some of their successors. The initiators, it is argued, were not representatives of an economic class, nor were the economic structures of their societies conducive to the heavy industrialization they set out to achieve. To the contrary, the initiators wanted to break through these, largely agrarian, structures and to drag what they rightly believed were reluctant societies toward an industrial future. To a considerable extent they succeeded.

Furthermore, because the initiators were not rooted in any existing set of social or economic interests, they were "statists"; the state was their chosen instrument of change, and in their vision it was to be self-perpetuating. It would deal with class interests either by creating them or subordinating them, but in no event were these interests to challenge the primacy of the state. The state, as regulator of social and economic activity, would be handed down from generation to increasingly professionalized generation of civil servants and technocrats.

We need to grasp, however, the medium-term goals of the initiators, or what they hoped to accomplish in their lifetimes. Such goals were driven by concerns for national strength and sovereignty, self-sustaining industrial growth, mass literacy, the end of rural poverty and servitude, and equitable prosperity for a grateful citizenry. With the exception of Kemal Atatürk, all of the initiators lived to see their goals partially foiled as well as the onset of the first attempts to modify their experiments. The will to transform *radically* in EIMT was exerted for a relatively short time and diminished in the face of both domestic and international pressures. But the modifications, I stress, did not come from new or old class actors but rather from strategic flaws within ISI and from the impossible tasks assigned to public enterprise (see Chapter 4).

31

The will to transform. Diego Rivera, 1934, The progress of man toward the future. Palacio de Bellas Artes, Mexico City. Reproduction authorized by the Instituto Nacional de Bellas Artes y Literatura.

The voluntarism of the initiators must be carefully put in context. The initiators in EIMT may have been of unusual ability and determination relative to leaders in other developing countries. Crises need not call forth high-quality leadership, but in these four cases they did. Because I often resort to choice-theoretic explanations of human activity, it is logical to ask what motivated these men; what was in it for them to take on so much with so little organized support or expert help? I will adduce five factors without attributing weights to them. First is ideological conviction, which the initiators had in abundance. Second is strategic behavior; transformation meant necessarily destroying the power bases of, and preempting resources from, existing adversaries, whether domestic (for example, agrarian elites) or foreign (for example, metropolitan corporate interests). Third is inadvertence; policy directions were turned over to change teams that took them further than the initiators may have intended. Fourth is lack of alternatives; the international context may have been perceived to have dictated certain initiatives. Finally, there is hubris; the initiators simply underestimated the magnitude of what they had undertaken or, at any rate, thought they were more than up to the task.

My case for voluntarism is problematic in a second sense. The stories of EIMT during the two great episodes of initiation and then structural reform have been repeated throughout the developing world. How can such similar processes of change result from "Leninist" leaders fixated on their own country's circumstances? Both the adoption of ISI and the more recent celebration of the market, the private sector, and exports were and are so widespread that voluntaristic explanations must surely lead us astray. To reiterate an argument made in Chapter 1, the crucial question is the adoption of ISI. Once adopted, its own internal dynamics played out in similar ways so that the response to crises stemming from ISI took on a certain sameness, although the timing was different across countries.

ISI, to repeat, did not flow from internal structural necessity except in the sense that it was seen as the weapon with which determined elites could *overcome* the structural givens of "backwardness." The subsequent gradual and halting reabsorption of many LDCs into the international (capitalist) order would lend credence to earlier forecasts from the *dependencia* school and from Marxists that the elites that launched ISI were bound to fail because the capitalist world order would sabotage their projects, they would be betrayed by their own private sectors who would ally with foreign financial interests, or they would betray themselves by reverting to their petty bourgeois origins and by using the state to promote the interests of that class.[1] Although there is little dispute about the spread of market orthodoxy and the questioning of state intervention in the developing world, neither, I argue, is the result of the forces identified

33

by dependency or Marxist analysis. Rather, the gradual abandonment of state-led ISI resulted from the strategy's internal flaws. It had become, within its own terms, inviable. Neither international creditors nor domestic bourgeoisies needed to explain that to beleaguered public policy makers. Moreover, as I hope to demonstrate, the initiators really did seek a new order; they were not merely clothing class or personalistic designs in radical rhetoric.

Voluntarism implies choice. What choices did the initiators really have? For all intents and purposes the range was very limited. They could have forgone industrialization and accepted their comparative advantage niche in world primary product markets. They could have sought industrialization in close cooperation with what became multinational corporations. They could have forgone protection for domestic industries, whether or not foreign-owned, and engaged in enclave industrialization for upscale domestic markets and for export. With the examples of German, Japanese, and the Soviet industrialization before them, coupled after World War II with the powerful intellectual messages emanating from the Economic Commission for Latin America (ECLA) school as well as from Western Keynesianism, it is hardly surprising that these choices were rejected in favor of ISI. Without any far-reaching consultation among them, the leaders of many LDCs before and after World War II moved confidently in the same direction.

The experiences of EIMT show the range of forms that ISI could take in terms of political arrangements, the extent of public ownership, the relations between public and private capital, and so forth. It is in the shape given to ISI and public ownership that the initiators left their marks, and there was absolutely nothing foregone about the directions in which they moved. At crucial junctures voluntaristic choices were made, and a kind of internal "path dependency" set in motion. These junctures and resultant paths are the subject of the rest of this chapter.

As we approach them, we need to pay attention to the rhetoric of the leaders, for it is in their declarations and revered documents[2] of the transformation that goals and expectations are set forth. It is also here that we see the long struggle for legitimacy that is essential to acquiring voluntary compliance to the regime's goals. Some analysts have doubted not only the structural possibility of radical transformation but the very intent or will of the leaders to try to effect it. We shall see that the leaders of the statist experiments in EIMT shared a formidable will to transform.[3]

It is easy to see rhetoric and radicalism used for strategic purposes. That leads some to believe that the rhetoric is a device, invoked *only* for purposes of maneuver and advantage. Thus Cárdenas's radicalism was clearly a weapon in his struggle with Plutarco Elías Calles, but it was also sincerely held. Indira Gandhi brandished a radical stick in her 1969

34

confrontation with the "Syndicate" in Congress. Nasser outmaneuvered Naguib in 1954 by rallying statist officers to his cause, and his 1961 socialist decrees and nationalizations were partially designed to preempt resources from a potentially hostile private sector. All of these leaders shared Atatürk's concern that the state occupy the commanding heights not only in the economy but in education, culture, and politics as well. All that this amounts to is that the founding fathers were politicians as well as idealists.

The experiments were all begun in the wake of fairly shattering crises, that is, in the context of sharp discontinuities with the immediate past. It is important to note, however, that the experiments all showed some continuity with earlier intellectual, and sometimes official, formulations in the same spirit. They did not emerge out of a vacuum. For example, in the interwar years debates were under way in the Congress Party about India's socialist future, the proper industrial policy, and the respective role of the public and private sectors, once independence was won. Mexico's experiment of the 1930s has some roots in the Porfiriato of the final quarter of the nineteenth century. Kemalist Turkey pursued policies that could be traced back at least to the Young Turks at the turn of the century. Nasserist Egypt's break with the immediate past was the cleanest, although some Egyptian historians like to portray Nasser as having resurrected a statist project first launched by the Ottoman governor Muhammed 'Ali at the beginning of the nineteenth century.

The discontinuities are more striking. Nasser and his officer colleagues came to power through military coup in 1952, following the disastrous campaign against the new state of Israel in 1948. The statist economic project was launched in the aftermath of the Suez War of 1956. The independent Indian state was born in the midst of the carnage and population exchange associated with the hiving off of Pakistan, both West and East. Mexico's experiment followed a decade of civil war in which some 600,000 (out of a population of ca. 15 million) Mexicans died or emigrated (Hernández Laos, 1985:26). The Turkish Republic was founded in the midst of a war of liberation against foreign occupiers, and accompanied by the exchange of nearly 2 million people between Turkey and Greece. Crises created opportunities; which ones were seized needs to be explained. The country cases are presented in the chronological order in which the statist experiments were begun.

1. TURKEY

Kemalist Turkey represents the oldest experiment among the LDCs to transform society from top to bottom. In ideology, it was the least radical of our four countries, that is, the least leftist, but what it achieved in real terms has probably been more far-reaching than in the other three. Moreover, the founding of a secular, Turkish republic in the wreckage of the Ottoman Empire was probably the least likely outcome that one might have predicted during World War I. More likely would have been the occupation and annexation of parts of Anatolia itself by foreign powers, above all the Greeks. There might have been a puppet regime in Istanbul, controlled by the victorious European powers and built around the Sultanate. What Mustafa Kemal, later known as Atatürk (father of the Turks), achieved by the strength of his own will and political cunning was no less remarkable than Lenin's propelling the Bolsheviks to power a few years earlier.[4]

Atatürk's transformation of Turkey was as much cultural as it was economic. The story of his assault on official Islam, the abolition of the Caliphate, the introduction of the Latin alphabet, the creation of a national educational system, the reform of Turkish as a language, the introduction of civil commercial and criminal law codes, and the inculcation of a strong sense of national pride, is well known and need not be retold here.[5] I shall concentrate on economic transformation.[6]

In the early twentieth century Ottoman social thinkers, as well as the members of the Committee for Union and Progress (CUP; known familiarly as the Young Turks), turned their attention to the means by which the Ottoman Empire could be made modern. Intellectuals like Ziya Gökalp, a follower of Emile Durkheim, and Yusuf Akcura, bemoaned the nonorganic nature of Ottoman society, especially the fact that Turko-Muslims constituted the administrative and military corps of the society, whereas Greeks, Armenians, and Jews dominated crafts, trade, and commerce. In particular what was vitally needed if Ottoman society was to become whole, organic, and dynamic was a Turko-Muslim commercial and industrial bourgeoisie. Although the CUP dissolved during World War I, Atatürk and his Kemalist supporters carried forward the project first adumbrated at the beginning of the century.[7]

In a similar vein, economic analysts looked to Germany for inspiration, especially to Friedrich List (Toprak, 1982:29–34), and also to Japan (Ahmad, 1980:333). There is no doubt that Atatürk came to see his mission of nation building as similar to that of Bismarck. Consequently, like many Turks, he was taken by List's arguments for the (temporary) protection of infant industries, because no truly sovereign nation could be without a heavy industrial base. It was then a logical conclusion that in the absence of a Turko-Muslim bourgeoisie, the state would itself have to establish the infant industries, all the while creating the class that would eventually own them. That conclusion was not reached, however, until the early 1930s.

In 1915, in the regions of Istanbul and western Anatolia, there were only 264 industrial establishments concentrated in spinning, weaving, and food processing. Of these, 172 were owned by non-Turkish minorities (Aysan, 1982:47; Toprak, 1982:192). With the support of the CUP around 80 new joint stock companies were founded during the war, owned for the most part by Turkish Muslims. Class building through state support was under way.

Turkey and Atatürk enjoyed the rare advantage among developing countries of having established the new republican regime and introduced the first sweeping institutional changes on the heels of an extraordinary string of military successes against would-be foreign occupiers, especially the Greeks. The Turkish Republic was born in pride and some confidence. It also inherited the battle-tested remnants of the Ottoman armies and the legions of the Ottoman bureaucracy, perhaps as many as one hundred thousand civil servants. At the same time, the wars and the subsequent peace lead to the death or expulsion of some 2.5 million Greeks and Armenians. Nearly all the prewar bourgeoisie was gone (Mardin, 1980:37; Keyder, 1987:69). The new republic had to absorb some four hundred thousand Turks gathered in from the former Balkan provinces of the Empire.

The Republic of Turkey was not internationally accepted within its de facto borders until the Lausanne Conference of 1923. Part of the price of acceptance was the imposition of low tariff walls for Turkish industry until 1929. The period 1923–29 thus witnessed a state-inspired attempt to construct a new bourgeoisie within the context of a free-trade regime.

This was a brief liberal economic interlude. It was launched with the Izmir Economic Conference, inaugurated by Atatürk and partially designed to send reassuring messages to the European conferees at Lausanne (Finefrock, 7/81; Boratav, 1982:14). The state in this period was to play handmaiden to the nascent private sector, and the conference laid down the principle, henceforth honored in the breach, that "the task of the state begins where the activity of the private sector ends" (Hershlag, 1968:40).

The conference also drew up the Principles of Economic Contract, which emphasized the mutual responsibilities of labor and capital in building economic sovereignty. This contract embodied what the Turks called solidarism, or what is now more commonly referred to as corporatism, and it became a lasting feature of the Turkish political economy. In that spirit, in 1925, all leftist organizations were banned, unions placed under strict control, and the right to strike denied.

The state maintained direct control of a number of monopolies in tobacco, alcohol, salt, matches, sugar, and petroleum. In addition, the first modern SOEs were founded in tobacco processing, wool milling, cotton weaving, silk spinning, and sugar beet refining. These initiatives were in accord with the Izmir Conference, and the main emphasis was placed on promoting private industry. Atatürk founded in 1924 and took an equity position in the hybrid Business (İş) Bank that was designed to help new private industries find their way. In 1927 the Law for the Encouragement of Industry was issued, and by 1932 nearly 1,500 enterprises were benefiting from it. Yet, as Boratav (1981:171) notes, doubts as to the intentions of private capital had begun to spread among policy makers shortly after the law was promulgated.

In 1929 Turkey regained control of tariff policy and became free to protect. Even before the onset of the world depression, Turkey had begun to experience external account difficulties. By 1930 there had begun an era of protectionism, which was not to end until 1983 (and even then only partially). In that year Prime Minister Ismet İnönü used the term "etatism" for the first time, reflecting the basic concerns of Atatürk and his associates. These were national strength through industrialization, the avoidance of foreign debt, and a favorable trade balance. Etatism was subject to many interpretations, but Peter Sugar has rendered its essence (1964:170): "*Etatism* was and is a curious mixture of private and state enterprise invented by people who understood the importance of economic growth but only as a factor in national power." In 1931 etatism was adopted as one of the official principles of the Republican People's Party (RPP), and in 1938 it was incorporated into the republic's constitution.[8]

Atatürk balanced two groups within his following, one that we can call liberal statists, the other more radical. Both were skeptical that private enterprise could deal with the economic crisis of the 1930s, let alone build the nation's economic sovereignty. Atatürk himself said (as cited by Aysan, 1982:89):

Private interests, most of the time [are] in opposition to the general interest... Individuals and companies are weak compared to state organizations. Free competition has social dangers, such as leaving the weak and the strong in a face-to-face confrontation.

His views were consistent over time and conformed to what he called "moderate statism" (*mutadil devletçilik*). In 1931, he stated (as cited in Hershlag, 1968:69):

[W]e desire to have the Government take an active interest, especially in the economic field, and to operate as far as possible in matters that lend themselves to the safeguarding of vital and general interests, or, in short, that the Government ensure the welfare of the nation and the prosperity of the State.

In 1935, at the Izmir Fair, his tone had scarcely changed (as cited in Aysan, 1982:48):

The will to transform

Born of Turkish needs, this [etatism] is a system peculiar to Turkey. Private enterprises and businesses of individuals are well rooted, but taking into consideration all the needs and the myriad tasks to be done, the national economy is taken in hand by the State.

Under this benevolent umbrella more ambitious and more radical lieutenants sallied forth. For a brief time policy momentum shifted to P. M. Inönü, Recep Peker, the secretary general of what had become Turkey's single party, the RPP, and to Mustafa Şeref Bey, who became minister of economy in the spring of 1930.

Inönü in October 1933 set the tone of the statist experiment in the pages of *Kadro* (from the French word *cadre*), a Marxist journal run by intellectuals supporting industrialization and public ownership. He dismissed as naive anyone who thought the economic crisis and the long-term goal of industrialization could be dealt with without the state taking the lead (Aydemir, 1968; Göymen, 1976:99). For his part, Peker sought to allay fears that the experiment would promote class warfare and emphasized that etatism would in fact produce social solidarity. That said, he was an advocate of forced-pace change (as cited in Karpat, 1959:72): "to tear away from a social structure the backward, the bad, the unjust and harmful, and replace them with the progressive, the good, the just and the useful elements."

It was Şeref who popularized the term "etatism," and by it he meant the obligation of the state to intervene broadly in economic life to overcome the shortsightedness of private actors – in short, he saw the state as autonomous, benevolent, and concerned with the long haul (Kuruç, 1987:97).

The long haul meant industrialization based on local markets and local raw materials. Industrialization, in turn, required financing and special banking facilities. In 1932 the State Industrial Office was created to guide industrial policy for both public and private sectors, and the Turkish Industrial Development Bank was established to target industrial finance. Şeref, however, did not couple these goals with any pronounced concerns for social equity. His only manifest gesture in this direction came in modifications to the 1925 labor law that sought to protect child and female labor.

Seref's main accomplishments lay in state regulation and market interventions, through the creation of the Central Bank, the establishment of import controls and the placing of sugar, coffee, and tea imports solely in the hands of the state, and the authorization of the Agricultural Bank to buy and sell in rural grain markets in order to stabilize prices. Other than put coastal shipping under state monopoly, the Şeref interlude did not witness much expansion in SOEs. Nonetheless, he antagonized the still weak private sector, and in September 1932 was replaced in the

Ministry of Economy by a "liberal," Celal Bayar, the director of the Business (İş) Bank.

State intervention did not lessen, however, and, indeed, there was a pronounced expansion in SOEs. Bayar might be best seen as a state capitalist with a relatively benign attitude toward a regulated private sector. In 1936 he was to say to the Grand National Assembly (as cited in Göymen, 1976:104):

I cannot even pronounce "liberalism," this word is so foreign to me... we want to establish the principles of government-controlled economy and we are heading towards these new principles.

And this he did. His main instrument, created in June 1933, was Sümerbank, which in fact was more a public holding company than a bank. To some extent it displaced the State Industrial Office and the Industrial Development Bank. It was to become the hub of industrial planning and finance, seeking cofinancing of large industrial ventures with the private sector. The battle cry was to break with the "colonial economy" and move into heavy industry. Bayar proclaimed his faith (Kuruç, 1987:113): "The claim of progress by a civilization without steel or coal is empty words." In 1936, the general director of Sümerbank, Nurullah Esat Sümer, declared (Kuruç, 1987:114) that

the establishment of basic industry in state hands in Turkey, which to Turkey is like air, water, and sun, will never be neglected... In Turkey, the state, to be exact, has taken in hand the creation of an organic, planned economy.

Sümerbank was intimately linked to the First Five Year Plan, begun in 1934. This plan truly launched the SOE sector with some twenty large-scale industrial projects built around the "three whites" (textiles, sugar, and flour) and the "three blacks" (coal, iron, and petroleum: Wålstedt, 1980:66).[9] Turkey negotiated credits from the Soviet Union worth $8 million to help finance the plan (negotiated by Şeref Bey), to be repaid in Turkish exports.[10] The industrialization drive was intensified in the mid-1930s. In July 1935 the Etibank was founded to establish the state's control over mining and ore processing. In 1936 work was begun on the Second Five Year Plan, which projected one hundred new industrial ventures in metals, glass, ceramics, spinning and weaving, cement, and petrochemicals. The centerpiece was to be the Karabük iron and steel complex (with British funding) and the development of the Zonguldak, Black Sea region as an industrial growth pole. Projects in sugar, yarn, and cement were slated for the "backward" regions of eastern Anatolia as well. Atatürk had a hand in drafting both five-year plans, and the second, in its preamble, depicted its logic as thwarting the goal of the industrialized nations to keep economies such as Turkey's in an agrarian mode (Aysan: 1982:89).

Table 2.1. *The share of Sümerbank in the volume of industrial output, 1939*

Industry	Sümerbank share (%)
Cotton textiles	35
Wool	60
Artificial silk	100
Leather	62
Shoes	90
Paper and cardboard	100
Cement	55
Coke	70
Iron	70
Superphosphates	100
Steel	80
Lubricating oils	80

Source: Hershlag (1968), 96. Used by permission.

The second plan was adopted by the Grand National Assembly in 1938 on the eve of Atatürk's death. It had to be scrapped in 1939 with the outbreak of World War II. Nonetheless Turkey achieved high rates of growth during the 1930s. The productivity of capital was high as public investment averaged only about 5% of national income with private investment at a somewhat lower rate.

By the outbreak of the war, the SOE sector was well established. It was now organized by Law 3460 of 1938 that sought to rationalize the sector through uniform personnel and accounting practices and reduced firm autonomy, putting each under the tutelage of a specialized ministry and under the financial supervision of the Ministry of Finance and the High Control Board (Wålstedt, 1980:77). According to some observers the law destroyed Atatürk's moderate statist vision that emphasized firm autonomy, flexibility and the possibility of acquisition by private investors. Sümerbank, which had acted as the central planning, and, along with Etibank and the Maritime Bank, as the central funding agency for the plans, came to dominate the public sector (as shown in Table 2.1) although its domain was now impinged upon by tutelary ministries and auditing agencies.

Under conditions of war and disrupted international trade, the Turkish bourgeoisie developed rapidly through investment, speculation and profiteering. At the end of the war it was in a position to push for the liberal etatism, personified by Celal Bayar, and, indeed, he came to champion private capital in industry and commercial agriculture. He was to help found and lead the Demokrat Party that challenged the RPP in 1946, losing in what were regarded as rigged elections, and then winning in 1950. The confrontation is accurately depicted as one between a newly assertive alliance of private interests, created by etatism, and the old military-bureaucratic alliance that had founded the republic.[11] The shift was pushed forward by Turkey's need to win favor with the United States and to benefit from the Marshall Plan. External pressure and domestic power shifts combined to produce a major but short-lived change.[12]

The triumphant party's program of May 1950 stated (cited in Aysan, 1982:51): "The basis of our economic and financial views, it can be said, is to shrink as much as possible the state sector and to broaden as much as possible the private enterprise sector and to provide it security."

The Ministry of Economy and Commerce was put under the charge of Muhlis Ete, who began to prepare a firm-by-firm (many of them belonging to Sümerbank) plan for privatization. The overall economic situation was good, coinciding with excellent harvests and a boom in international commodity prices caused by the Korean War. The new government, under Prime Minister Adnan Menderes, with U.S. assistance under Point Four, pushed agricultural mechanization and the development of highways and rural roads.

By 1952, however, Menderes backed away from privatization, saying the goal was not to transfer ownership to the private sector but to encourage new private investment (Aysan, 1982:52). The collapse of commodity prices after the Korean War preceded a new round of elections in 1954, and the Demokrat government discovered the attractions of the SOE sector as dispenser of jobs and patronage in hard times (Ahmad, 1977:128). The Demokrat Party survived the 1954 elections and probably rigged those of 1957. The state's finances deteriorated rapidly, forcing Turkey to enter into a stabilization agreement with the International Monetary Fund (IMF) at the end of the decade.

In the 1950s the private sector came to benefit fully from the protective measures enacted in the 1930s with the main purpose of sheltering the SOEs. At the same time, the Demokrat Party fostered the growth of the SOE sector. In 1950 government investment accounted for 28% and SOE investment for 15% of total investment. In 1958, the corresponding figures were 40% and 24% (Okyar, 1976; Hale, 1981:91). No significant act of privatization was undertaken by the Demokrat government.

The deteriorating economy and the widespread corruption of the Menderes regime led to a military coup in 1960. For a brief time the military-bureaucratic interests that had undergirded the Turkish experiment in the 1930s were back in control. A third variant of etatism was born. The junta immediately created the State Planning Organization, which, in 1962, drew up a five-year plan for industrial deepening. This was partly in preparation for Turkey's formal application for membership in the EEC (European Economic Community, or Common Market). Under the draft plan the SOE sector was to be reorganized to stress profitability, but according to Ahmad (1977:275), the Turkish private sector, which had an interest in the relative inefficiency of the SOEs, was able to scuttle the reorganization. Be that as it may, the SOEs in the coming decades and up to the present time were to be concentrated in the production of intermediate and capital goods and the management of power and infrastructure in support of protected private enterprise (Pamuk, 1981:28).

A year after the coup, a group of professors drew up a new constitution that was liberal, democratic, and explicitly concerned with the state's obligations to promote social equity. It formalized rights of association and expression, and greatly relaxed the controls on labor organization and the right to strike (see Chapter 9). If the 1950s saw the takeoff of the Turkish bourgeoisie, the 1960s saw a corresponding takeoff of organized labor. The 1960s and 1970s in fact represented a kind of "Keynesian entente" in which all the major parties, including the remnants of the Demokrat Party, rebaptized as the Justice Party, accepted the need for a large state sector. Given an average rate of gross national product (GNP) growth of 7% per annum between 1962 to 1977, politicians could enjoy the patronage advantages of the SOE sector at no immediate cost to the economy. During this period of Turkish "populism," the real wages of the work force grew in tandem with the economy and the expansion of the public sector (Boratav, 1989:11–17).

In 1965 civilian government was restored when the Justice Party won an absolute majority in the Grand National Assembly. Although there was another military intervention in 1971, the period 1965–80 was characterized by regularly held parliamentary elections giving rise in most instances to coalition governments with costly agendas. Each military intervention was followed by a sorting out of "radical" and "conservative" interventors, in both instances in favor of the latter. Whatever economic projects the divided officer corps may have wished to pursue were soon swamped by the electoral contests played out between the Justice Party and a refurbished Republican People's Party. After 1966 the RPP was led by the civilian intellectual Bülent Ecevit, who converted it into a social democratic party, at least in philosophy. Each party held power in coalition with either the National Salvation Party, representing Islamic interests seeking to reverse Turkey's secularism, or the National Action Party, representing a neofascist brand of Turkish nationalism.[13] The coalitions were unable to agree on effective measures to deal with

43

the growing violence brought about by clashes of leftist and fascist elements on the campuses and in the shantytowns.

During the period 1973–79 different coalitional combinations presided over a sharp increase in public outlays and deficit financing. As in all the countries of EIMT, the 1970s were a period of marked public sector expansion. In Turkey the soaring costs of imported oil were partially offset by increased remittances from Turkish workers in West Germany and elsewhere. By the end of the decade external accounts spun out of control while domestic inflation took off. Turkey fell into arrears on servicing its rapidly mounting external debt. The private sector for the first time publicly denounced the governments' economic mismanagement. It was a kind of coming-of-age.

Once again the Turkish military stepped in to restore order and to pursue vigorously a program of structural adjustment begun under the last Justice Party coalition. This intervention, as it turned out, broke a basic line of continuity, based on ISI, protection, and a large SOE sector, that had prevailed since 1929. The intelligentsia and left-wing organized labor were badly battered in the wake of some 26,000 arrests. The left-wing Federation of Revolutionary Workers' Unions (DISK) was dissolved, as were the main political parties of the 1970s. Martial law was proclaimed and basic rights suspended. In 1982 the new constitution drafted under the watchful eyes of the generals dropped all mention of etatism. It prepared the way for elections in 1983 and the restoration of civilian rule under a new party, the Motherland Party (ANAP), led by Turgut Özal.

The generals, having clamped civil society under tight controls, in 1980 placed economic policy in the hands of a small team led by Özal himself. He had served in the last Justice Party government, led by Süleyman Demirel, and had engineered the first steps toward structural adjustment. Between 1980 and 1982, he began to put together the policies that would move Turkey toward export-led growth accompanied by substantial deregulation of the domestic economy and some dismantling of the protective tariff regime. When he returned as prime minister in 1983, having defeated the handpicked candidate of the military, he began to fashion a new coalition of interests out of the wreckage of the 1970s, one that could sustain his economic policies politically. The single-minded purpose with which this was begun eroded as the years went by, but the economic edifice put in place by Atatürk has been profoundly altered.

2. MEXICO

Just as Turkey's outward-looking war for liberation shaped the goals of the new republic, so too did Mexico's inward-looking revolution, the violent phase of which spanned the period from 1910 to 1921. The biggest stake in the revolution was the redistribution of land, and that question dominated the postviolence phase at least up until 1940. The defining document of the revolution was the 1917 constitution, which laid down the legitimizing values of what came to be known as Mexico's "Revolutionary Family."[14] In its Article 27, the right to private property was made contingent on its use for socially beneficial purposes, and the state was charged with the duty to supervise the use of property and to regulate all economic activity. This delegation of power gave rise to the principle of the "rectorate of the state" (*rectoría del estado*). The constitution also reserved to the state strategic sectors of the economy including basic infrastructure, energy, and mines (see Womack, 1969:315; Cuadernos de Renovación Nacional, 1988:37; Roldán, 1988:17). Finally, the constitution enshrined, in reaction to the long grip on power of Porfirio Díaz, the principle of non-reelection at all levels of the political system. From this was born Mexico's peculiar and extraordinarily important institution of the nonrenewable six-year presidency (*sexenio*), which continues to shape the pace and nature of policy making and implementation.[15]

In marked contrast to Turkey, the 1917 constitution, and, indeed, many of the subsequent initiatives in state-led social and economic transformation, came in partial response to the needs and demands of social groups, economic interests, and nascent classes. The revolution had brought to the fore a congeries of peasant groups, militant labor, and an intelligentsia liberated from the strictures of the Porfiriato. Alongside them were powerful landowners, an important industrial bourgeoisie mainly in the city of Monterrey, and large enclaves of foreign investment. None of these alone or in combination were able to determine the course of the revolution and in fact were regularly trumped by fractious generals and warlords produced in its course. Where the Turkish republic had to create new class actors, the Mexican had to nurture what already existed.

The task of consolidating the revolution fell to generals Alvaro Obregón and Plutarco Elías Calles. The latter in many ways exhibited preferences close to those of Atatürk. He continued the radical educational reforms begun under his predecessor and designed by the remarkable figure José Vasconcelos. Calles sought to subjugate the Catholic hierarchy and the church and to marginalize the role of the armed forces in political life. He had to absorb the rural jacqueries and urban syndical anarchists cast up in the turmoil of the revolution.

Calles was hostile to foreign capital, a fact that in the United States earned him an ill-deserved reputation as a fellow traveler. He was anything but that. He did place the foreign-owned power sector under state regulation, and he began the building of what became the Mexican public sector. During his incumbency the Bank of Mexico was launched as the

45

state's central bank, and parastatal organizations were created to supervise irrigation and road building. Like Atatürk, he wanted to use the state's rectorate to strengthen the indigenous bourgeoisie, and, again like Atatürk, he was a fiscal conservative.

He began the corporatization of Mexican politics by creating the Partido Nacional Revolucionario (PNR) and the subordinate peak labor organization, the Confederación Regional de Obreros Mexicanos (CROM). He also began the process of domesticating leaders of corporate organizations by giving them seats in parliament, in local office, and in the state sector itself. Finally, he slowed the pace of the agrarian reform prescribed by the 1917 constitution.

Had Calles been able, as he intended, to control his successors to the presidency, Mexico might have come to look very much like Turkey in the 1930s; that is, a state-capitalist regime with only modest commitments to social welfare. However, in 1934 the PNR elected General Lázaro Cárdenas to the presidency with Calles's acquiescence. Partly because Cárdenas was determined to wrest power from Calles and partly because he was sincerely committed to the promotion of social equity, the experiment entered a radical phase.[16]

The *sexenio* of Cárdenas is particularly interesting in that he was the product of the very system he set out to change. In this respect the task he faced was similar to that of Salinas de Gortari fifty-four years later. It is the case, however, that the system built by Calles was by no means as institutionalized as that inherited by Salinas, and the combination of postrevolutionary political flux and the world depression meant that Cárdenas did not have to break entrenched entitlements or thwart long-held expectations, except, perhaps, in the all-important military.

It was clear to Calles early in the *sexenio* that Cárdenas was not to be manipulated. In March 1935, Calles tried to recapture the PNR and the system by challenging Cárdenas and his labor allies. Within four days the challenge had collapsed, Cárdenas cleansed the system of Callistas, and Calles himself went into exile. The extraordinary power of the presidency that has been the hallmark of the Mexican system ever since was convincingly demonstrated (Cornelius, 1973:440).

Cárdenas sought to build an alliance of peasants and workers linked and subordinate to the government. Toward that end he greatly accelerated the agrarian reform. He concentrated his efforts on the restoration of communal farms (known as *ejidos*). Between 1934 and 1940, *ejidal* land rose from 13% to 47% of all cultivated acreage, and some 45 million hectares were distributed to more than 800,000 peasant families. He established a state bank whose sole function was to lend to the *ejidal* sector (see Hansen, 1974:91; and Sanderson, 1984:57). Toward the end of the *sexenio* he created the Confederación Campesina Mexicana (CCM) to incorporate the clientelized *ejidal* peasantry.

With respect to labor, in 1936 he founded the Confederación de Trabajadores de México (CTM), under the leadership of Lombardo Toledano, and through it he was able to capture organized labor from the CROM (Marván, 1977). He accepted and even encouraged a high level of strike activity, and state arbitration boards systematically found in favor of labor. Wages were determined by the same boards according to their estimate of what firms could afford to pay. Like the communally managed and owned *ejidos* Cárdenas hoped that much industrial enterprise would fall under worker management. In 1936 he encouraged private entrepreneurs who could not take the pressure of labor demands to turn over their enterprises to the workers (Wilkie, 1967:73; Cornelius, 1973:421; Hansen, 1974:92; Collier, 1982:69).

In 1937, Cárdenas began to arm the workers and envisaged similar measures for the *campesinos*. These measures were designed to counterbalance the armed forces that might have been tempted to intervene. He brought into his cabinet General Saturnino Cedillo, a conservative Catholic, as secretary of agriculture. This momentarily defanged growing opposition from both the church and the military. However, after the nationalization of the foreign oil companies in 1938 described later in this section, Cedillo himself led an abortive rebellion during which he castigated Cárdenas for his atheism and Bolshevism.

Most observers concede that Cárdenas accepted the inevitability of class struggle (see Wilkie, 1971:72; Cornelius, 1973:420; Brun, 1980:88), but despite this he sought to channel it into the straitjacket of corporatist representation. In 1938 he overhauled the PNR, creating out of it the Partido de la Revolución Mexicana (PRM). Within a few years this became the Partido Revolucionario Institucional, or PRI. The CTM and the CCM became the sole organizations representing peasants and workers with which the state dealt officially. The white-collar work force and intelligentsia were represented through the Confederación Nacional de Organizaciones Populares (CNOP). For a brief time the military was represented at the national level of the PRM, but that was ended in 1940 when elected military representatives were reaffiliated in CNOP. Finally, a new entrepreneurial bourgeoisie closely allied to the state through credit and contracts, and to some extent made up of former state functionaries, military officers, and labor leaders, was grouped together under the Confederación de Cámaras Nacionales de Comercio (CONCANACO).

Cárdenas did not focus his energies on state-led industrialization and the building of the SOE sector. That task lay to his immediate successors. He wanted the reorganized agrarian sector to increase production in order to supply urban consumers and industries, and, after the end of his *sexenio,* the agrarian sector did perform that role (Sanderson, 1984:57). His attitude toward private industrial capital was ambivalent as he protected it against foreign competition and foreign investors but exposed it to labor militancy. In July 1935, his director of statistics used words that could have come directly from Mustafa Şeref (as cited in Womack, 1969:326):

We are convinced that the evils of capitalism are not to be found in the application of machinery to the productive process, but rather are due to a merely legal question: who is the owner of the machinery.

In private hands, industry exploits; in public hands, it promotes the general welfare.

There was nothing in the Cárdenas period to rival Turkey's First Five Year Plan and the founding of major public industrial undertakings. On the other hand, Cárdenas nationalized the U.S.-owned oil companies in 1938, thus effectively bringing the oil sector within the state domain where it has, with constitutional recognition, remained ever since. He also took over some foreign-owned railroads. The process of labor agitation did lead to the transfer to worker cooperatives of enterprises in textiles, fishing, bus and truck transport, lumber, printing, foundries, bakeries, and so forth. With time these became part of the SOE sector. Cárdenas's goal, according to Cornelius (1973:421), was the gradual "socialization" of the means of production.

In April 1934, Nacional Financiera, S.A. (NAFINSA) was founded to help develop a capital market in Mexico, coordinate investment banking, and promote Mexican private industry. Because of the agrarian focus of Cárdenas's *sexenio,* NAFINSA did not really develop its role as industrial promoter and holding company until after 1940 (Blair, 1964; Bennett and Sharpe, 1980; Ramirez, 1986:63). Nonetheless, its founding represented an important step in the state's assertion of control over development financing.

It is hard to see Cárdenas as the witting or unwitting agent of some form of capitalist transformation of Mexico, except with the benefit of hindsight (Brun, 1980:37; Hamilton, 1982; Leal, 1986:33). He certainly fooled his adversaries, who obviously took his radicalism very seriously. By the end of his *sexenio,* elements of the armed forces, the church, the private sector, which founded the Partido de Acción Nacional (PAN), and the United States were arrayed against Cárdenas's experiment. The period, in Cornelius's words (1973:392), "is without parallel in Mexican experience and perhaps in all of Latin American experience with the exception of the early years of the Cuban Revolution."

Calles and Cárdenas became archetypical figures of the Mexican revolution, and various of their successors shaped their *sexenios* in the spirit of one or the other. It was Cárdenas's minister of defense, Avila Camacho, who succeeded him and reinvoked the state capitalist themes first introduced by Calles. But it was during the *sexenio,* 1946–52, of Miguel Alemán that Mexico's economic miracle developed momentum. For more than three decades thereafter the economy grew at average rates of 6% per annum, and, despite the country's high rate of population growth, gross domestic product (GDP) per capita grew at rates well over 3% per annum until 1982.

This was the beginning of a long period of successful ISI during which foreign exchange needs were met by foreign investment and external borrowing. Alemán set the state on the course of supporting the Mexican private sector. Rates of gross fixed capital formation (GFCF) doubled between 1940 and 1954 and remained at levels of 20% of GDP thereafter. At the same time the share of the public sector in GFCF declined from 62% in 1939 to 33% in 1962 (Clark Reynolds, 1970:tables 7.8, 7.9). This is evidence of a successful handmaiden role, and it was articulated by Alemán himself (as cited in Vernon, 1964:88):[17]

The private sector ought to have all the freedom and be supported by the State in its development, particularly when this is done positively for the benefit of the collectivity. Ownership of real estate ought to be primarily in the hands of nationals, following the principles established in our charter; but foreign capital that comes to share the destiny of Mexico will be free to enjoy its legitimate profits.

The general pattern of development was dubbed "stabilizing growth," and it was accompanied by expansion of the public sector itself. Bennett and Sharpe (1980) have shown how NAFINSA, after World War II, was gradually transformed into an industrial development bank whose goal was to promote the deepening of the industrial sector as it moved beyond the easy phase of ISI. With time it began to take over failing private enterprises and maintained majority ownership in a number of enterprises it had helped launch. The view developed within NAFINSA that the private sector was deficient and that the tecnicos within NAFINSA could supervise these investments better than private entrepreneurs. NAFINSA began to compete with the private sector for finance capital for its rapidly expanding holdings. NAFINSA's evolution lends credence to those analyses of public institutions that stress their inherent tendency to capture new resources and expand operations transforming their original goals in the process.

The rectorate of the state, both conceptually and in practice, was never abandoned, and during specific *sexenios* the state was set on a radical course. This was particularly true of the *sexenios* of Adolfo López Mateos

(1958–64) and Luis Echeverría (1970–76). López Mateos gained the presidency coincident with the advent of Fidel Castro in Cuba. There followed a period of what might be called preemptive radicalization throughout Latin America, and Mexico was no exception. López Mateos nationalized all foreign power companies, with a book value of $400 million (Wionzcek, 1964:42; Schüking, 1982:21). In what Rey Romay termed an assertion of national sovereignty (1987:63), the president assembled in the public sector the strategic chain of petrochemicals, fuels, and energy in the form of SOEs (Fertilizantes Mexicanos, or FERTIMEX; Petróleos Mexicanos, or PEMEX, and Comisión Federal de Electricidad, or CFE). It was a period of marked tension between the state and the private sector resulting in some capital flight and the blocking of a tax reform program in 1964 (Solís, 1976:60–61).

The pendulum swung to the right during the *sexenio* of Díaz Ordaz (1964–70) and then sharply leftward under that of Echeverría, 1970–76. Mexico had been traumatized in 1968 by the student demonstrations that led to the Tlatilolco massacres and that seemed to signal a more deeply rooted demand for redistributive policies. Echeverría attempted to meet that demand without alienating the private sector. The slogan of "stabilizing" development was replaced by that of "shared" (*compartido*) development. The result, however, was an incoherent set of policies that pushed up foreign borrowing and the public deficit while avoiding resort to devaluation to encourage exports.[18] As had López Mateos, Echeverría intensified the agrarian reform so that by 1976 the cumulative total of land distributed since the 1920s reached 79 million hectares with 2.5 million beneficiary families (Sanderson, 1984:83).

The SOE sector grew rapidly throughout the 1970s, especially through the helter-skelter absorption into the public domain of failing private enterprises. Horacio Flores de la Peña was put in charge of the Ministry of Public Property. He was a self-proclaimed leftist, hostile to the private sector and to the conservative policy makers in Hacienda and the Bank of Mexico. As the former director of the School of Economics at the Universidad Nacional Autónomá de México (UNAM) he was Echeverría's bridge to the intelligentsia (Solís, 1976:67). Echeverría himself forcefully restated the philosophy of the *rectoría del estado* (as cited in Roldán, 1988:46):

The mixed system established by the constitution presupposes that public investment possesses sufficient power to direct growth. Free enterprise can be fruitful only if the government possesses sufficient resources to coordinate the accomplishment of the major national objectives.

Mexico entered into a fiscal and external payments crisis at the end of Echeverría's *sexenio,* and stabilization measures, including the first devaluation of the peso since 1954, were briefly introduced only to be abandoned by President López Portillo as Mexico began to reap the benefits of the second surge in international petroleum prices. For a few years it was possible to pay off all segments of the Revolutionary Family and to finance private sector expansion. Much new investment was covered by a spurt of foreign commercial borrowing. Public sector expansion in Mexico, under a populist umbrella, closely paralleled that of Turkey in the same period, despite the fact that the first had oil and the second did not.

Three years after Turkey, in 1982, Mexico entered into a severe crisis signaled by its inability to service its debt. The crisis was accompanied by further devaluation of the peso and the nationalization of the major banks in an effort to stem capital flight.[19] The nationalization destroyed the little confidence that López Portillo had been able to build with the private sector. He left to his successor, Miguel de la Madrid, the huge external debt, high inflation, and a private sector no longer willing to invest.

De la Madrid came out of the Ministry of Budget and Planning as a kind of financial tecnico rather than as a PRI politician. He was a statist of the right, in some ways of Calles's spiritual lineage. He wanted to make the state more efficient, not to dismantle it. Because the state had so little money, public expenditure necessarily had to be drastically cut. De la Madrid made modest overtures to the private sector by reducing the public share in bank equity to 66%, by bringing private sector managers into the banks, and by "overcompensating" the former owners. "To nationalize," he said, "is not to statize. Nationalized banking must be the people's and not that of a new minority of managers" (Rodríguez, 1987:251).

De la Madrid introduced important amendments and additions to the constitution. The commitment to strategic sectors reserved to the state was kept,[20] and, in Article 28, bank nationalization was made a constitutional principle. The 1982 amended constitution affirmed that state ownership of certain assets was in itself not sufficient to assure the *rectoría* and must be paralleled by control over decision making and administration. At the same time the 1982 constitution did away with the two-sector, public–private hierarchy and replaced it with three sectors on an equal footing – the public, the private and the social (Rodríguez, 1987:249; Cuadernos de Renovación Nacional, 1988:35).

The worsening of the economic situation in the mid-1980s outpaced de la Madrid's efforts to repair the old economic and political system. Debt servicing was using up nearly all state finances, the private sector held its money outside the country, inflation increased as the public deficit grew, and there were no new lines of commercial credit. It was in this context that de la Madrid took several emergency initiatives setting the state on a course that came to entail a fundamental restructuring of its constituencies and its role in the economy. Privatization of SOEs was begun, Mexico joined the General Agreement on Tariffs and Trade (GATT) and slashed its external tariffs, and public expenditures were further cut. In December 1987 he drew up with labor and the private sector a pact of economic solidarity (the Pacto de Solidaridad Económica, or PSE) to introduce wage and price controls and, a year later, a crawling peg for the peso (Kaufman, Bazdresch, and Heredia, 1992). It was up to his successor, however, to intensify the process of restructuring. Salinas de Gortari, himself the architect of the austerity measures under de la Madrid, increased the pace of privatization leading finally to the reprivatization of the banks beginning in late 1990.

Doubtless Salinas's bold moves were partially driven by the pressing need for new sources of investment while the state continued to devote most of its resources to debt servicing. The move toward a free-trade agreement with the United States was also driven by that concern. Nonetheless, what had begun under de la Madrid as pragmatic and step-by-step measures to rescue the old system became under Salinas and his finance minister Pedro Aspe a programmatically driven neoclassical transformation of the economy.

3. INDIA

Of all the radical transformers under consideration, Jawaharlal Nehru was the most ideologically sophisticated and easily the most ambitious in what he set out to do. His goal was the socialization of the means of production, without violence and within the institutional and legal framework of democracy. It is hard to imagine India's political and economic evolution after 1947 without attributing much of it to the single-minded purpose of Nehru. Despite the awful precedent of partition, the country held together through a series of strategic compromises over language and ethnicity. Despite wars with Pakistan and China, the country did not fall under military dictatorship. Despite an ideological commitment to public enterprise, punitive policies of nationalization were, until 1969, avoided. Somehow, as one of the poorest countries in the world, India managed to maintain democratic procedures and the rule of law to a degree unparalleled among the developing countries.

The gap between what Nehru wanted to do and what he could do has produced the clearest contrast between the will to transform and its results. The fact that he fell well short of his goals has led some, mainly on the left, to question the sincerity of his pronouncements. For my part, I have little doubt that Nehru sought a socialist economy for India, but he believed, perhaps naively, that this could be achieved gradually with private capital cooperating in its own quiet demise. At the Congress Party conference at Lucknow in 1936, Nehru, having visited the Soviet Union, told the party (as cited in Rao, 1982:131):

I see no way of ending the poverty, unemployment, the degradation and subjection of our people except through socialism...That means the ending of private property, except in a restricted sense, and the replacement of the present profit system by a higher ideal of cooperative services.

The Congress Party was a broad nationalist front that included wealthy capitalists and doctrinaire socialists at opposite ends of its spectrum. Despite Mahatma Gandhi's deep misgivings regarding the young Nehru's faith in socialism, the state, and industrialization, he ceded the party to him in the postwar years. "As far as I am concerned," he once said, "the evils inhere in industrialization and no dose of socialism can make them disappear" (cited in Bernard, 1985:25). Thus, Nehru's rise to prominence was not a foregone conclusion. Gandhi chose not to block him, and, in any case, Gandhi's assassination in January 1948 removed a pivotal figure from the Indian political scene. In addition, in 1939, Subhas Chandra Bose led the radical Bengali Forward Block out of Congress, thereby removing a radical populist threat to Nehru. In 1950 the consummate politician and party financier Sardar Patel, closely linked to the party's business interests, died. Nehru was then in a position to try to fashion the party and the nation's development course in accordance with his own preferences (see Frankel, 1978:25–26).

India moved into ISI not because of the depression, as in Turkey, nor in an ad hoc way as under Cárdenas in Mexico. India's move was carefully planned in the postwar years and premised on the coherent actions of a benevolent state pushing the economy on to a heavy industrial footing. The origins of the industrial plans lay, in fact, in the 1945 White Paper prepared by the Labour government in Britain (Tandon, in Nigam, ed., 1984:95; Marathe, 1986:18). The same Labour government, be it noted, made no such plans for the industrialization of Egypt. The main lines laid down at that time were the promotion of strategic public enterprise, regulation and licensing of private enterprise, and the take-over by the government of private enterprises when such would serve the public interest.

In 1947 at the Jaipur meeting of the All India Congress Committee (AICC), Nehru and his radical allies pushed through resolutions that led to the founding of the Planning Commission and to a "soak the rich" budget (Frankel, 1978:25–26; Nayar, 1988:211). Soon thereafter the socialist and Gandhian wings of the party, unhappy for different reasons with the way in which the party was being led, left it, leaving Nehru isolated against the more conservative elements. The first Industrial Policy Resolution, issued in 1948, tried to restore business confidence. It emphasized the need for increased production, eschewed all mention of socialism, and declared a ten-year moratorium on nationalizations. The First Five Year Plan, 1951–56, was basically one of postpartition rehabilitation with little emphasis on public enterprise.

After the death of Sardar Patel in 1950, Nehru, who was already prime minister, was elected to the presidency of the Congress Party. At the same time the Planning Commission, which was to become the intellectual and policy heart of Nehru's efforts to build socialism, was founded. He lured the socialists, led by Jayaprakash Narayan, back to the Congress. By the last years of the First Five Year Plan, Nehru was in a position to drive the party and the economy onto a much more radical course. In late 1954, Nehru declared that "the means of production should be socially owned and controlled for the benefit of society as a whole." The Lok Sabha (parliament) immediately took up his words and resolved that the objective of the Indian state was to establish a "socialistic pattern of society" (Nayar, 1988:223).

There followed a decade of profound internal transformation and external setbacks. After the zamindari abolition,[21] agrarian reform ground to a halt in the face of local elites who were vital to the Congress Party in mobilizing the rural vote. Unlike Cárdenas, therefore, Nehru could not pursue rural socialism (despite his initial fascination with China's communes), and instead sought his socialist goals in the commanding heights of the industrial sector.

In 1956 two key documents were drawn up: the second Industrial Policy Resolution and the Second Five Year Plan. The first was inspired by T. T. Krishnamachari, the minister of industry and a close friend of Nehru's. This Brahmin businessman from Madras was known as the "red capitalist" (Tandon, 1980:372), and in many respects he was the father of the Indian SOE sector. The Industrial Policy Resolution segmented the industrial sector into three "schedules." Schedule A, the so-called commanding heights, was reserved to SOEs. Schedule B was open to both public and private capital (eventually fertilizers were put in Schedule B). Schedule C was reserved predominantly for private capital. The resolution also tightened government controls on the licensing of new capacity and on market shares.

The Second Five Year Plan was largely the work of P. C. Mahalanobis, a leftist mathematician-statistician who was put in charge of the Planning Commission. This plan was to be the blueprint for heavy industrialization within the public sector and the beginning of India's socialist transformation. Bernard summarized the shift thus (1985:160):

The will to transform

The preparation of the Second Plan (1956–1960) was the stage for an intellectual revolution: it witnessed the passage from a Keynesian to a Marxist model. The efforts of Professor Mahalanobis were in fact inspired by the schemes of Karl Marx regarding the reproduction of capital and a model based on them developed by the Soviet economist, Feldman, in the 1920s.

Nehru himself, in a speech to the Lok Sabha in 1956, acknowledged the importance of the private sector but predicted that "gradually and ultimately it will fade away" (Nayar, 1988:233–34; see also Bhagwati, 1985:61, and Chand, 1965:11–12).[22] The change team Nehru and Mahalanobis led was out ahead of their party and their society. The very fact that Nehru saw no need to resort to nationalization indicated that he saw little threat from the industrial bourgeoisie, despite the fact that by 1959 it had formed its own party, the Swatantra.[23] The Indian bourgeoisie, like the founders of the PAN in Mexico in 1939, did not see Nehru as their witting or unwitting ally. In sum, as Frankel put it (1978:114): "From 1955 to 1964, Nehru's pivotal position permitted a handful of men to determine national economic and social policy and methods of development."

The Third Five Year Plan (1961–65) was designed to consolidate the preeminence of the public sector and to set the society on an irreversible course of socialist transformation. Nehru is said to have personally drafted the plan's first chapter. His frame of mind is well represented in a speech to the Lok Sabha at the inception of the plan in 1960 (as cited in Banerjee, 1984:57):

A number of textile mills in Ahmedabad or Bombay or Kanpur is not industrialization; it is merely playing with it. I do not object to textile mills; we need them; but our idea of industrialization will be limited, cribbed, cabined and confined by thinking of those ordinary textile mills and calling it industrialization. Industrialization produces machines, it produces steel, it produces power . . .

Factors inherent in the plan itself coupled with some "exogenous shocks" prevented many of its objectives from being reached. India's defeat by the People's Republic of China in their border war of 1962 shook the regime's confidence in much the same way as the 1967 June War shook Egypt. At the same time, that conflict and the subsequent clashes in 1965 with Pakistan heightened India's concern with the commanding heights, especially in the defense industry sector (Bhagwati and Chakravarty, 1969; Nayar, 1972; Toye, 1981; Bernard, 1985:214–21).

Other shocks took the form of monsoon failures toward the end of the plan, and, of paramount importance, the death of Nehru in 1964. The result was lagging momentum in the heavy industrialization push. A foreign-exchange crisis developed as India faced mounting food imports alongside industry-related imports. The country became increasingly dependent on foreign aid. Moreover, employment targets were not being met as the plan unfolded. With Nehru gone, there was a trimming back of objectives and investment levels. Lal Bahadur Shastri, who succeeded Nehru to the prime ministry, presided over a plan holiday and an assessment of the shortcomings of India's version of the great leap forward.

Indira Gandhi, who became prime minister after Shastri's death in 1965, did not immediately reverse the more cautious policies he had introduced. Indeed, in 1966 she was obliged to devalue the rupee under pressure from the IMF. Her fortunes and those of the Congress Party reached their nadir in the wake of the electoral setback of 1967. From this crisis Indira Gandhi drew the conclusion that she must assault the so-called syndicate within Congress, that is, conservative, probusiness elements that had gained power within the party after Nehru's death. To isolate the syndicate, and to reverse Congress's electoral fortunes, she launched a campaign aimed at constructing a broad-based coalition. Her slogan became *garibi hatao,* or remove poverty, while her opponents, led by her own minister of finance, Morarji Desai, countered with their own slogan, "remove Indira."

The major instrument in the assault on poverty and the isolation of her opponents was the 1969 nationalization of fourteen major banks that controlled 85% of all deposits. Once in the public domain, the banks were to orient their loan programs toward the rural poor and the "backward sectors" in a more general sense. The move was enormously popular, and Gandhi's adversaries could not confront her over it. Small businesses applauded the nationalization, while major business associations, such as the Federation of Indian Chambers of Commerce and Industry (FICCI) lavished faint praise upon it. Big business evidently hoped that Indira Gandhi would mismanage the nationalizations, thereby discrediting both the move and herself in the process.

Parallel with these moves Indira captured Congress itself. Soon after the electoral defeats of 1967, she formed an alliance with the Communist Party of India and with Marxist-oriented elements in her own party known as the Congress Forum for Socialist Action. They became part of her ideological change team. The party split in November 1969, with the syndicate and its allies moving out to establish their own rump Congress Party. Her handpicked Congress president, Shankar Dayal Sharma, castigated the syndicate and denounced the "influence of big money and monopolists on the affairs of state" (Frankel, 1978:467–79; Hurtig, 1986; Nayar, 1989:296). She also brought into her government, as minister of steel and mines, S. Mohan Kumaramangalam, a staunch advocate of socialist transformation and state-led heavy industrialization.

What was in the making, beginning in 1969, was probably the most spectacular reassertion of radical transformation witnessed in any of the members of EIMT. The reprises of the Turkish military after 1960 or the policies of López Mateos and Echeverría pale in comparison. Indira Gandhi and her leftist supporters adopted nationalization as a primary means of building the state sector and taming private interests. They abandoned Nehru's strategy of allowing the state sector to displace gradually private interests. The constitution was amended in 1971 so as to make private property rights contingent on their conformity with the public good (as was the case in the 1917 Mexican constitution).

In 1969 not only were the major banks nationalized but all private medium- and large-scale enterprise was placed under a highly restrictive regime laid down in the Monopolies and Restrictive Trade Practices Act, which placed more detailed restrictions on capacity expansions, market shares, and new investments. It was premised on the assumption that near punitive regulations were the only way to control private greed. It has often been pointed out that the large private groups were able to buy their way out of the regulations, and that they in fact prospered in the 1970s. That result, however, is much more a function of bureaucratic rent seeking than of the unrevealed preferences of the regime. One of the state managers from that period, Sharad Marathe, later wrote (1986:18–19; see also Krueger, 6/74, and Bhagwati, 1985:37):

It would appear that by the early 1970s the whole apparatus of control and regulation of industry had acquired a momentum of its own. It was seen that the scope for conferring or denying favors meant considerable accretion of power and patronage to the political system . . . [resulting in] the emergence of the combined and powerful vested interests of politicians, bureaucrats and businessmen.

In 1971, Congress won a crushing victory at the polls, and Gandhi's power was virtually unchallenged. She immediately began to back away from her leftist allies, eventually dissolving the Congress Forum in 1973 (the same year in which Kumaramangalam died in a plane crash). Nonetheless, the expansion of the state sector was accelerated. In 1971, 106 insurance companies were taken over by the state and then nationalized in 1972. The coal sector was nationalized in 1972, as was the Indian Iron and Steel Company (ISCO), one of two private sector integrated steel mills. That same year 46 textile mills were taken over and added to 57 that had been seized in 1968. All 103 were nationalized in 1974 and held within the National Textile Corporation (NTC). The state then moved to control all basic grain trade, despite the alleged alliance of the Congress with the rural bullock capitalists. In the midst of all this India signed a treaty of friendship with the Soviet Union.

Once again exogenous shocks forced the government to slow the pace of change. Successive years of poor monsoons lowered agricultural production and obliged the state to abandon plans to bring rice trade under central control. The sudden increase in the price of imported petroleum after 1973 fell heavily on energy-intensive industries in both the public and private sectors. By 1974 the government had introduced a series of stabilization measures to dampen inflation and encourage exports (Ahluwalia, 1986). Spending cuts and wage controls were introduced, and in a sharp break with the populist policies in place since 1969, Gandhi crushed a major strike among railroad workers in 1974. Simultaneously she fought losing battles in the courts against charges of electoral improprieties. Adverse judgments led her to proclaim a state of emergency in September 1975. During the following two years she disciplined organized labor and, although gross investment declined, presided over a marked improvement in economic performance. Indira Gandhi introduced political controls of a corporatist variety, and both the Rudolphs (1987:241) and Nayar (1989:335) saw the signs of incipient bureaucratic-authoritarianism. Thus, in the space of five years Indira Gandhi had virtually toppled the two pillars of her father's experiment: She directly assaulted the private sector through nationalizations and she briefly put parliamentary democracy in limbo.[24]

The emergency, which ended in electoral defeat for Congress and the constitution of the Janata Party government between 1977 and 1980, gave rise to an era of state capitalism that has prevailed up to the present time. The Janata government differed from Congress mainly in its emphasis on rural development and servicing constituents among the rural middle class. It shared Indira Gandhi's suspicions of the private sector and made George Fernandez, a prominent labor leader, minister of industry. He threatened to break up the big private holdings, such as the Birlas, and talked of nationalizing India's most successful steel firm, Tata Iron and Steel Company (TISCO). The Janata interlude was short-lived and Indira Gandhi returned to power in 1980.

The government's approach, especially as embodied in the Sixth Five Year Plan, was markedly different from that of the years of *garibi hatao*. Gandhi's chief advisor was L. K. Jha, who had first gained prominence during the brief incumbency of Lal Bahadur Shastri. He was bent on tightening public expenditures, achieving greater efficiency in public investment and in the operations of the SOEs, and in stimulating the private sector through deregulation and liberation of the capital market. The sixth plan concentrated on the power, coal, and transport sectors to support both public and private enterprise. Much greater stress was placed on SOE performance, which Indira Gandhi herself qualified as "a sad thing" (Nayar, 1989:351).

After her assassination in 1984, Indira Gandhi's son, Rajiv, acceded

SOCIALISM: The state that India will reach when both rich and poor are totally eliminated to give rise to an altogether new breed of "socialist creature."

Looking back on the great transformation in India. Source: *As Indians Do*, text by Ajit Gopal, illustrations by Jar (Bangkok: Media Transasia Ltd., 1987):79. Used by permission.

to the prime ministry in a wave of national commiseration and sympathy. Rajiv was young, clean, and seemingly bent on fundamental change. He kept on L. K. Jha as a major advisor and brought in "whiz kids" like Montek Ahluwalia to design a program of deregulation and liberalization to open a system that had been in place at least since 1955. Those interests that were likely to be gored in the process, concentrated in the Congress Party itself, denounced Gandhi for disavowing his mother's legacy and India's socialism. These protests were disingenuous as Indira Gandhi had begun the reforms herself, but they were effective in stalling the reform program for a time (Kohli, 1990).

Rajiv Gandhi was soon swept up in the hurly-burly of state and ethnic politics, the crony capitalism that linked powerful public and private actors, and the complex electoral games that Congress has always had to play. He played his hand badly on nearly all counts (see Kohli, 1990) and was driven from power through electoral defeat in late 1989. During the 1980s, however, the economy continued to grow briskly, especially in the industrial sector, which had been the subject of long academic debates on India's industrial malaise (see Chapter 3). Cautious deregulation of private enterprise, efforts to stimulate exports and to lower tariff barriers, and the ability of private firms to raise capital on the booming Bombay exchange undergirded the growth surge. But the state sector remained huge, and in the last half of the 1980s public finances and expenditures began to run out of control. The domestic and external debt mounted rapidly (a reflection of the growing government deficit), and inflation started to creep upward. The first signs of a crisis on a scale of what we have seen in Mexico and Turkey in the late 1970s and early 1980s became visible. The Congress defeat of 1989, and the subsequent formation of coalition governments, weakened fiscal discipline, leading in 1991 to the announcement of a tough reform program in the orthodox mold.

4. EGYPT

In comparison to the other three countries, Egypt's radical transformation began with the least certain trumpets but ultimately, in structural terms, went furthest. Extensive agrarian reform begun in 1952, followed by massive nationalizations in 1961, produced an economy in which the state controlled or owned *all* significant means of production. The basic contours of Egypt's economy by the mid-1960s were more like those of Yugoslavia or Hungary than those of Turkey, Mexico, or India.

Between 1952, when General Naguib and Colonel Gamal 'Abd al-Nasser and other officers seized power, and 1956 when the Suez Canal Company was nationalized, Egypt's military regime groped its way toward some form of state capitalism and an accommodation with foreign investment.[25] Its major effort at redistribution consisted in the agrarian reform of 1952 which, in essence, destroyed the land base of the royal family and some two thousand large landowners who had dominated Egypt's political and economic life. In successive phases of the reform a cumulative total of about 14% of Egypt's cultivated surface was redistributed to about 10% of its farm families (Waterbury, 1983:266–67). The twin goals of the reform were, first, to allow the new regime to consolidate its political power at the expense of the old aristocracy, and, second, to build up the stratum of middle and small-scale capitalist farm-

60

ers as a source of higher productivity and of political support in the countryside.

In terms of industrialization, the thrust of the regime was similar to that of India during the First Five Year Plan or of Mexico under Alemán: to use state resources to develop infrastructure, power, and large-scale industries to provide producer goods for private enterprise. Such projects as the electrification of the old Aswan Dam, the Kima Fertilizer plant, the Helwan Iron and Steel complex, and the High Dam at Aswan were studied or launched in the period leading up to 1956. Indeed, Robert Tignor (1987) has argued that had it not been for the Suez War of 1956, it is likely that the Naguib–Nasser regime would have reached an accommodation with foreign capital such that the state would have limited itself to a handmaiden role for privately financed growth. Instead of the socialist economy that developed in the 1960s, we might have seen a public–private balance more akin to that of Ayub Khan's Pakistan or of Chung Hee Park's Korea. I am skeptical that Tignor is right, but it is true that the "revolutionary" regime of 1952 came with no revolutionary blueprint for the future.

A major reason for my skepticism is that Nasser, who by 1954 had ousted Naguib from power, consistently showed suspicion and hostility toward Egypt's private sector and, above all, toward foreign capital. Any accommodation he was able to strike would have been tactical and not strategic. His suspicions lacked the ideological sophistication of Nehru's, and in some ways they probably reflected a crude political calculus that unless the (his) state controlled most wealth in society, it would inevitably be exposed to the machinations of those who did. In its inception after 1956, Nasser's socialism was essentially preemptive.

The trigger of the transformation of Egypt (leaving aside the agrarian reform) was exogenous and consisted in four steps. First, in mid-1955, Egypt negotiated with Czechoslovakia the first large-scale purchase of Soviet weaponry by any Arab state. Second, as a result of the purchase, the World Bank, the United States, and Great Britain withdrew their offers to finance the construction of the High Dam at Aswan. Egypt, in the third move, then nationalized the Compagnie Universelle du Canal de Suez in order to capture all its revenues and use them to finance the construction of the dam. Finally, in collusion with Israel, France and Great Britain launched a military campaign against Egypt to seize the canal and to provoke the overthrow of Nasser. The latter effort failed, mainly because of U.S. opposition to the aggression.

For our purposes the important fact is that the Egyptian public sector, heretofore confined to the projects already mentioned and to some military industries, received an enormous fillip in the wake of the war when Egypt took over French and British assets in the country. Within a year the regime's basic slogan of "unity, discipline, and work" gave way to "democratic, cooperative socialism." There was no talk of selling the seized assets to the private sector, and in fact they were grouped in Egypt's first public holding company, the Economic Organization. A ministry of industry was created, and put under ʿAziz Sidqi, a Harvard-trained civilian planner, who drew up a three-year industrialization plan and won Soviet funding for it. The ministry was to promote and finance the SOE sector and to license the founding and expansion of all private industrial establishments. Policy momentum shifted to military and civilian technocrats enamored of state intervention and to a certain number of ideologues who began to write of Egypt's socialist path.[26]

In 1960, Egypt drafted its first five-year development plan into which the original three-year industrial plan was folded. A ministry of planning was created and entrusted to a member of the military Revolutionary Command Council. The plan's objective was to double national income in ten years.[27] The private sector was not consulted in the drafting of the plan but was called upon to undertake a major share of the financing. This it failed to do, so the regime alleged, and in July 1961 the famous Socialist Decrees were issued, which by 1964 brought the entire large-scale private sector under public ownership. No other country in EIMT undertook anything remotely as sweeping as Egypt's nationalizations and confiscations. By the time the measures were implemented, the following sectors were under state ownership:

1. all banking and insurance
2. all foreign trade
3. all "strategic" industries and all medium and heavy industries; all large textile, food-processing, and sugar-refining plants
4. all air and most maritime transport
5. all public utilities and mass transit
6. a limited proportion of urban retail trade
7. major department stores, hotels, cinemas, and theaters
8. all newspapers as well as importation and distribution of newsprint
9. all reclaimed land and all surface irrigation infrastructure
10. all agricultural credit and supply of fertilizer, seed, and pesticides
11. all major construction companies
12. all infrastructural assets such as the High Dam, Suez Canal, power stations, ports, airports, railroads, etc. (Waterbury, 1983:76)

In 1962, the National Charter was drawn up, which defined Egypt's socialism and reserved major sectors of the economy exclusively for the public sector. The charter explicitly declared Egypt's course to be that of socialist transformation, and Nasser moved leftward in a far more programmatic way than heretofore. So dramatic were his rhetoric and the nationalization and sequestration measures carried out between 1961 and 1964, that some Soviet analysts, principally Georgi Mirskii, saw Egypt to be on the noncapitalist path to socialism, in contrast to India, whose regime had failed to decapitate the bourgeoisie (Carrère d'Encausse, 1975:159–67). In May 1964, after Nasser had released the Egyptian Marxists from detention at the time of the inauguration of the High Dam, Nikita Khrushchev declared Egypt to be "building socialism" and made Nasser a Hero of the Soviet Union.

By 1965, Nasser had constituted a change team that consisted of a few officers of radical persuasion, such as ʿAli Sabry, who was prime minister until mid-1965 and then was made secretary general of the single legal political organization, the Arab Socialist Union (ASU); technocrats, such as ʿAziz Sidqi; and ideologues from among the released Marxists who were inducted into the ASU. The ASU was dubbed "the alliance of working forces," and parallel to its corporatist structures, Nasser, mimicking the Yugoslav model, fostered a vanguard organization to drive forward the revolution.

Nasser's pronouncements in these years reveal a good deal more than pragmatic populism and statism. As early as 1961, when Syrian private interests, alarmed at the Socialist Decrees, conspired with the Syrian military to break up the union with Egypt, Nasser voiced his profound suspicion of the Egyptian bourgeoisie. He said to his fellow officer ʿAbd al-Latif al-Baghdady that Lenin had made the mistake of accommodation with the bourgeoisie. Nasser, by contrast, warned (as cited in Ansari, 1986:88): "We have no other alternative but to liquidate them by arresting all of them and putting them in Wadi al-Jadid [the concentration camps]."

Nasser consistently denied any legitimacy to class struggle while recognizing the factors that give rise to it. The public economic sector and the ASU were to work together to "melt class differences" by providing work, welfare, and representation for all the functional parts of society. Although he never embraced Marxism–Leninism, he did see himself as part of a global socialist transformation (as cited in Waterbury, 1983:324):

Socialism in general means the eradication of man's exploitation by man. But the socialist application varies from one country to another. There are people who like to call it Arab socialism on the basis that this is a socialism with a particular trademark. It is my opinion that it is an Arab application of socialism and not an Arab socialism. I believe that there is only one type of socialism and that there are basic socialist principles.

By 1965, Egypt had begun to experience the same structural flaws in its state-led industrialization program, as had India at the same time. In this instance there were no external shocks, save Egypt's involvement in the Yemeni civil war after 1962, contributing to the crisis. Rather the large, ISI-oriented industrial sector developed a voracious appetite for imports while contributing almost nothing to exports. Nor was it yet capable of generating much of a surplus that the state could tax. The result was that the domestic deficit began to mount and the balance of payments to deteriorate. Egypt was obliged to increase its foreign borrowing, but even then it faced a major financing shortfall for a second five-year plan. In fact the plan was never launched. It was, instead, replaced by a one-year investment program and then entirely abandoned in the debris from the military defeat of June 1967.

By late 1965, when the USSR, now led by Leonid Brezhnev, proved reluctant to advance new lines of credit to Egypt, Nasser began to address issues of SOE efficiency. At the end of 1966 he assembled all the senior managers of the SOEs, and, calling them the sons of the revolution, he exhorted them to improve operations: "less philosophy and more production!" (Hussein, 1971:227). He went on to say that the state capitalism Egypt had adopted was the first stage in the transition to socialism and, at some unspecified point, would be superseded by worker self-management and the withering away of the state itself (Mu'nis, 1984:244).

The high tide of Egyptian radicalism came in 1965–66. Nasser had to retreat from the heady expansion of the state sector of the early 1960s as sources of external funding dried up. In 1966 his signals were very mixed. On the one hand, he talked of nationalizing even small-scale activities including private trucking and wholesale trade in food commodities. On the other, he tried to stimulate the private sector and provide incentives for it to export, primarily to the Eastern Bloc. He talked about establishing free enterprise zones in the Canal zone cities in order to attract foreign capital.

The June War of 1967 fatally crippled Nasser and thrust Egypt into economic decline for at least five years. But in the period 1957–66, Nasser led an experiment that had no observable underpinnings in the class structure of Egypt. He moved far ahead of his own comrades-in-arms, many of whom retired from politics in the 1960s in quiet protest of Nasser's growing "Bolshevism." It takes a fertile imagination to see Nasser as the agent of the interests of the Egyptian bourgeoisie and as a necessary catalyst to Egypt's capitalist development (for the contrary view, see Hussein, 1971, and Riad, 1964).

Anwar Sadat was elected president of Egypt after Nasser's death in September 1970. After the October War with Israel of 1973, he adumbrated an open-door policy that came to be known as *al-infitah*. Sadat was immediately branded by the Egyptian left as bent on the destruction of Nasserism and of the state sector (Mursi, 1974). It is my view that Sadat was more nearly analogous to Alemán succeeding Cárdenas (at the remove of one *sexenio*) or to Indira Gandhi succeeding herself after the Janata interlude. Sadat certainly did abandon socialist sloganeering: first, because he had never been comfortable with it, and second, because he wanted to attract Arab and foreign investment to Egypt. Here it is interesting to note that Egypt faced a fiscal crisis of substantial proportions before any of the others in EIMT. The state was no longer able to finance its own investment and had to turn to outside sources.

The main thrust of *infitah* was to liberalize the banking sector, allowing foreign commercial banks to operate in foreign currencies in what had been a public sector banking monopoly. Foreign exchange regulations and the import regime itself were relaxed. An Arab and Foreign Investment code was drawn up (Law 43) to attract new capital flows. Efforts were made to stimulate the capital market, moribund since 1961. The hope was that through joint ventures with foreign capital, the SOEs would gain access to advanced technology and management techniques, and, with enhanced efficiency, begin to compete for external markets as well as to produce better products at lower cost for the domestic market. *Infitah* also entailed a shift away from trade dependency on the Eastern Bloc and toward markets in which Egypt could earn hard currency. What *infitah* was not was an attempt to dismantle the state sector or to reduce the state's intervention in the economy. In fact, the SOE sector grew prodigiously during the 1970s and the state gave up none of its regulatory powers.

Egypt very nearly had to adopt programs of stabilization and structural adjustment in 1976. The subsidies on some consumer items were lifted in January 1977, provoking widespread rioting in Cairo and elsewhere and resulting in about one hundred deaths. Sadat rescinded all austerity measures and toured the oil-rich states of the Arabian peninsula soliciting aid. Henceforth Egypt grew habituated to external strategic rents. When rents from Arab countries were suspended after Egypt signed the Camp David Accords in 1979, the United States stepped in with a billion or more dollars in aid in all the succeeding years. Several other Western governments opened lines of credit to Egypt as well. Coinciding with this flow of strategic rents were augmented flows from petroleum sales, worker remittances, Suez Canal tolls, and tourism. In aggregate these sources generated well over $10 billion per annum by the early 1980s.

Flush with foreign exchange, Egypt postponed its stabilization and structural adjustment programs indefinitely and used its new resources to finance an import and consumer binge. The basic structure of industrial production, with all its flaws, was left basically untouched (World Bank, 1/83; Handoussa, Nishimizu, and Page, 1986). Even when petroleum prices plummeted in the mid-1980s, with an accompanying downturn in worker remittances, Egypt was able to avoid structural reforms by trading its cooperative role in the "peace process" for concessional aid and credit flows. By 1990, Egypt's external debt stood at about $50 billion, or well over 100% of GDP. Were it not that much of the debt was government-to-government, rather than commercial, Egypt would have found itself in a crisis more severe than Turkey's of 1979–80 or Mexico's of 1982.

In 1981, Anwar Sadat was assassinated by Muslim extremists and was succeeded by his vice-president, Husni Mubarak, who had been a pilot and commander of the Egyptian air force in 1973. Mubarak was and is far less flamboyant than Sadat, but he continued his predecessor's policies. Since the late 1950s, the statist experiment had engendered a number of large, semiorganized interests in the state bureaucracy, the trade and labor unions, the intelligentsia and professional groups, and in the armed forces on which the regime depended. Any structural adjustment program with teeth would have cut deeply into the entitlements these groups had built up over time. Mubarak undertook piecemeal reforms, adjusting exchange and interest rates, lowering consumer subsidies, and slowing the pace of public hiring. But these reforms never dealt with the root causes of the economy's malfunctioning: the huge government deficit, the poor export performance, the distorted price signals that led to major resource misallocation, and the creeping inflation that administered prices only partially masked.

Mubarak is an interesting counterpoint to Salinas de Gortari. Both are reformers from within the system that produced them, but Mubarak has never confronted the blocking coalitions that have thwarted far-reaching reform. Mancur Olson could take comfort in the Egyptian case, for there distributional interests have, in the pursuit of maximizing their own utilities, led to suboptimal and unsustainable results for the economy as a whole. In Turkey, General Evren smashed the older entitlements after 1980, and, with strong financial support from the World Bank and the Organization for Economic Cooperation and Development (OECD), launched the reform process.

Egypt's participation in Operation Desert Storm in 1991 afforded Mubarak two opportunities. First, the United States and a group of Egypt's official creditors, known as the Paris Club, agreed to forgive about half of Egypt's external debt, contingent on the government's *implementation* of deep reforms and sharp reductions of the deficit. Second, the domestic popularity that Mubarak had earned led him to seize the moment and commit the country to the reform package.

The will to transform

5. CONCLUSION

I have argued that in EIMT the process of state-led industrialization was begun and sustained by determined leaders, assisted by small change teams, who operated independently from and in advance of the economic and class structures of their societies. This was less the case for Mexico under Cárdenas and much more the case for Turkey under Atatürk and Egypt under Nasser. In most instances they in fact had to use their state apparatuses to strengthen or create new class actors, particularly in the private industrial sector and in commercial agriculture.

The experiments they launched produced far-reaching social and economic change as well as a broad, albeit inefficient, industrial base. None of these leaders had real respect for their indigenous private sectors, nor did any see foreign capital as anything better than a necessary evil. Because, after thirty years or so of their statist projects, their respective private sectors emerged strengthened (except in Egypt), some observers concluded that such was the logic of the project. This is an untestable hypothesis, but arguing against it is abundant evidence that the private sectors themselves saw the project as hostile and threatening (see Chapter 8). Deals were cut and fortunes made as state agencies interacted with private interests, but that result has about as much to do with the logic of the projects as does, say, the police colluding with the Mafia.

Each experiment yielded a relatively brief radical phase, no more than a decade in length in the cases of India and Egypt, and only a few years in Turkey. On the other hand, Turkey, Mexico, and India demonstrate that radicalism and retrenchment tend to move in cycles, or to alternate: The authors of Turkey's 1960 coup sought to rekindle and intensify the Kemalist etatism of the 1930s; López Mateos and Echeverría invoked the credo of Cardenismo; and in 1969, Indira Gandhi revived the spirit of the Second Five Year Plan and embellished it with *garibi hatao*.[28] I have tried to represent the swings in policy in Figure 2.1.

The radical optimism of the initiators was not inherited by their successors. The flaws in their designs had already become manifest, but the entitlements created in the early years had also become entrenched. Returning to Figure 1.1 in Chapter 1, the state sector had begun to move perceptibly from Autonomous–Benevolent to Autonomous–Malevolent, and although many recognized that fact, no one with the power to do so had any incentive to take painful remedial measures. The crisis had to intensify, and by the beginning of the 1980s in Mexico and Turkey, and by the beginning of the 1990s in India and Egypt, it had.

Over time, the varied nature of state intervention became clear. There was an alternance in EIMT of statists of the left and the right with the supreme leaders, like Atatürk and Nasser, raising or lowering the prom-

67

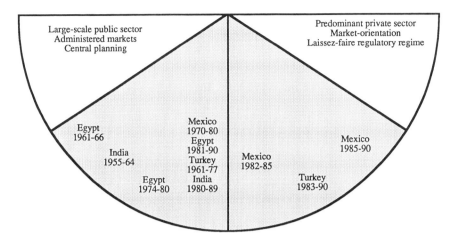

Figure 2.1. Pendular swings in state economic intervention in EIMT, 1960–90

inence of both sets of technocrats. The leftists stressed income redistribution, job creation, industry at any cost, and containment of the private sector; the rightists emphasized fiscal restraint, productivity and profits, and the need to stimulate private initiative. Neither in any way questioned the appropriateness of the state to orchestrate all aspects of the development process. Over time the rightists gained ascendancy and were to begin the process of neoclassical transformation.

3

Bald comparisons

The task of this chapter is twofold. First, using simple statistical measures, it tries to get a comparative hold on the most salient characteristics, above all those contributing to the crises, of the ISI experiments in EIMT. The timing and relative magnitudes of the macropathologies of ISI will be laid out. For the reader already familiar with the recent economic performance of the four countries, this is not essential reading. The second part of this chapter singles out the SOE sectors and compares their sizes, functional characteristics, and contribution to the macropathologies of ISI. The material in the second part is not commonly available in a comparative context, and it is important for the in-depth analysis of the SOE sectors in Chapter 4.

1. STRATEGIES AND POLICIES OF INDUSTRIALIZATION

1.1. The military-industrial complex

A hallmark of ISI has generally been the specific attention to the founding of a military-industrial complex, part and parcel of building a credible military establishment. ISI, national defense, and defensible independence became intertwined. For Atatürk, Nehru, and Nasser the interlinkage was obvious and compelling. Public expenditure in the name of national security and sovereignty removed the defense sector from cost accounting and civilian scrutiny. The anomaly here is Mexico, whose experiment with ISI was launched by a general, Lázaro Cárdenas (see Figure 3.1). He began a process of whittling away at the claims on public resources of the Mexican military that was continued by his successors to the point that, in 1987, outlays on defense represented only 1.4% of total public expenditures. The corresponding figures for the others in 1987 were:

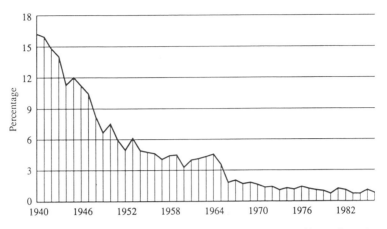

Figure 3.1. Defense outlays in Mexico as a proportion of total public outlays. Source: Basáñez (1990), 135. Used by permission.

Egypt   19.5%
India   21.5% (of central government outlays)
Turkey   11.4%

It could be that Mexico's exceptional neglect of its military establishment contributed to the high and steady economic growth rates of the 1950s and 1960s, but it did not save the country from crises in the 1970s and 1980s as severe as any experienced in the developing world.

1.2. Savings and investment

What Michael Lipton has called urban bias (Lipton, 1977) appears to be inherent to the initial attempts to finance ISI and is potentially crippling. Developing countries have had to turn to their own predominant agricultural sectors as the principal source of savings to finance industrialization. These sectors are tapped less by direct taxes than by various administered prices that systematically turn the terms of trade against agriculture. The trick is, of course, to keep the agricultural sector producing while stripping it of part of its savings. Few developing countries, Taiwan being a notable exception, have been able to bring this off. What typically happens is that rural living standards stagnate, new industries face inadequate domestic (especially rural) demand and are too inefficient to enter into exports, and losses are covered by deficit financing and foreign borrowing.

Turkey's statist experiment in the 1930s was a harbinger of this dilemma, and its severity may have provoked the defeat of the single-party

government in 1950. Despite substantial rural support for the new Demokrat Party incumbents, the 1950s did not witness a reversal of urban
bias. However, by the late 1960s and 1970s the terms of trade shifted
decisively in favor of agriculture, only to be reversed under the export-
led growth strategy of the 1980s (Boratav and Yalman, 10/89).[1]

Similarly in India, upon whose experience Lipton built his original
thesis, the heavy-industrialization push of the late 1950s led to various
devices to promote a net flow of resources from agriculture to industry
and the urban areas. But, as in Turkey, electoral pressures and the specific
role of the growing ranks of middle-size commercial farmers appear to
have reduced, if not eliminated, those flows in the 1970s and 1980s.[2]

Mexico presents a more ambiguous case. It was in 1945 that Mexico
formally launched its ISI strategy (Solís, 1971:22). It was also at this time
that the country's agricultural sector became highly dualistic with an
extensive, underfinanced *ejido* (communal) sector that held the bulk of
the rural population and a modernized commercial sector in the north,
benefiting from state-financed, large-scale irrigation projects. The *ejidal*
sector has been something of a vote bank for Mexico's PRI, and substantial compensatory flows have gone in its direction. The fact remains,
however, that Mexico is characterized by widespread poverty and low
productivity. Its large population has not been able to constitute a significant market for the industrial sector. Rather, it has exported labor to
the cities and to the United States. Mexico's structural transformation,
which has produced a situation in which more than two-thirds of the
population lives in cities and towns, has been the result not of labor
shortages in the cities and rising productivity in the countryside (the key
elements of successful structural transformation) but, rather, of productivity failures and poverty.[3]

Since the mid-1950s the Egyptian state has engineered a consistent net
flow of resources from agriculture to the nonagricultural sectors, and the
principal mechanism has been through administered prices (Cuddihy,
1980; Dethier, 1989). There have been substantial return flows in the
form of surface irrigation systems, subsidized fertilizers, fuels, and electric
power. Egyptian agriculture is not dualistic, and although productivity
has not grown satisfactorily, it has grown. Nonetheless, this sector has
been unable to form an adequate market for the top-heavy public industrial enterprise system, which in turn is so heavily protected that it
has never approached the levels of productive efficiency necessary for
entry into export markets.[4]

In three of the four countries domestic savings have been impressive,
whereas Egypt's savings effort has been uneven and somewhat unsatisfactory. In 1978–79, India achieved a gross domestic savings rate of 24%
of GDP, of which about 17% was in the household sector (Lal,

71

1988:257), and levels of more than 20% have been maintained throughout the 1980s. This is a remarkable performance for a low-income economy without oil. Mexico's domestic savings rate has been equally remarkable, reaching 21% of GDP in 1978, falling to 17% in 1982, but rising once again, to 25% in 1986 (Brothers, 12/88:table 2). We find similar rates for Turkey, where domestic savings rose from 15% of GNP in 1964, to 20% in 1979, and 25% in 1988. Private savings in the latter were 18% of GNP (TÜSIAD, 1989:10).

In Egypt, by contrast, gross domestic savings rose to about 18% of GNP at the end of the First Five Year Plan in 1965 then fell steadily for a decade to about 9% in 1974 (Waterbury, 1983:38; Central Bank of Egypt, 1987b:table 3). It is important to remember that Egypt fought two major wars in this period: in 1967 and again in 1973. The first in particular had severe repercussions on Egypt's productive capacity. In the late 1970s, buoyed by new oil revenues, the national savings rate recovered to attain levels in excess of 20% of GNP, but once petroleum prices tumbled after 1982, national savings sank with them to 11% of GNP in 1986–87 (Central Bank of Egypt, 1987b:table 3).

What I stress here is that all four countries were able to generate high levels of savings to underwrite their development strategies. The real issue was the efficiency with which savings and investment were used. As we shall see, especially with regard to India, unacceptably high incremental capital output ratios (ICORs) vitiated the national savings efforts in all four. In addition, investment levels, reaching in some instances 30% of GNP, were in excess of available domestic savings. By the end of the decade, what troubled Indian economists most was the combination of a high rate of savings and investment and low rates of industrial growth. The pattern became manifest after independence, and to characterize it the late Raj Krishna coined the phrase "the Hindu rate of growth," which is to say, GNP growth in the area of 3% per annum, very slightly ahead of the population growth rate of about 2.5% per annum.

In the 1960s and 1970s the incremental capital output ratio increased dramatically, especially in the public sector. ICORs of 4 in the 1950s grew on average to 10 in the succeeding decades, and in specific sectors, such as power generation, to well over 20 (Acharya, 1985; World Bank, 3/90). For industry as a whole, growth rates accelerated between 1957 and 1966 to 7.1% per annum on average and then fell off to 5.4% between 1967 and 1981 (Ahluwalia, 1985:13 measuring growth rates in net value-added). All observers were disturbed that India was generating high rates of domestic savings and then wasting them through inefficient investment.

The search for the causes of this performance stimulated an interesting

Bald comparisons

debate in the late 1970s and early 1980s.[5] Pranab Bardhan's (1984) analysis saw the problem as lying in a triumvirate of class actors – commercial farmers, the industrial bourgeoisie, and the state sector itself – the satisfaction of whose conflicting demands on the public exchequer required vast and inefficient capital outlays. Others saw the problem as lying in insufficient domestic demand owing especially to what was seen as a chronically depressed agricultural sector (i.e., variants on the effects that Lipton, 1977, attributed to urban bias).

Against the structuralists were those who saw the issue as one of remediable public policy. Beginning with the "plan holiday" of 1966 to 1969, investment, particularly in the railroads, declined. Moreover, what investment was taking place was in areas such as power generation, where initial outlays were large and the rate of return initially very low. Finally there were those who stressed overregulation as the culprit. As early as 1973, Jagdish Bhagwati vividly described the situation (Bhagwati, 1985:37; see Marathe, 1986:262, for similar conclusions), noting that

the maze of meaningless controls that India continues to work with, so that the Invisible Hand is nowhere to be seen [sic], represents a regression, *reductio ad absurdum* that does its intelligence little credit and the economy much harm.

Almost as soon as the various contributions to this debate appeared in print, new evidence on industrial performance became available. Between 1983 and 1989, Indian industry grew at an average annual rate of 8.2%. Industrial ICORs dropped into the range of 4 to 5 (although they continued to be substantially higher in the public than in the private sector: World Bank, 1990:appendix, p. 5). The economy as a whole grew at a rate of 5.8% per annum, despite a couple of failed monsoons. For a time, at least, the Hindu rate of growth had been shattered.

There is not much consensus about what is taking place, but the only changes introduced since 1980 in fact consist in considerable deregulation, eased industrial licensing procedures, and liberalized imports (World Bank, 1990:40–51). Investment levels did not increase, and in fact fell in the late 1980s, but the efficiency with which capital and labor are used did increase (World Bank, 3/90:14).

Whether or not India can sustain these higher rates of growth is moot. They have been accompanied by a marked deterioration in fiscal discipline. The domestic debt has risen from 35% of GDP in 1980 to 56% in 1989 (Bhattacharya and Guha, 4/14/90:781), inflation is creeping up, and the external debt, although modest, is growing. India's economy is entering the kinds of crises that had afflicted the other three countries. Undoubtedly the defeat of the Congress Party in the polls in 1989, followed by the formation of two coalition governments, contributed to

73

fiscal indiscipline, and it was the seemingly weak, Congress-led coalition of Prime Minister Rao that committed India to a major reform program.

1.3. The deficit and deficit financing

To fill the investment resource gap all four countries have resorted to deficit financing with the attendant problems of rising inflation and possible crowding out from domestic credit markets of private borrowers. We shall look more closely at the specific role of SOEs in generating deficits in the second part of this chapter. For the moment, I simply present the overall size and trends in public deficits.

Compared to average levels of deficits to GNP of 5.8% for middle-income developing countries, and 5.1% for industrial economies (WDR, 1988:46; figures for 1985), the countries under examination here, except for Egypt, fall fairly close to the average. Egypt's total budget deficit (presumably including interest payments) has been consistently very high, averaging 22% of GDP over the period 1976 to 1982, a period corresponding to the highest levels of petroleum revenues (Ahmed, 1984:12). As those revenues fell and some efforts at financial adjustment were undertaken, the deficit was imperceptibly reduced to about 21% of GDP between 1983 and 1986, then surged forward once again to levels of more than 25% of GDP (World Bank, 3/87:12; AI, 4/30/90:32). By this measure alone, one can grasp the depth of Egypt's structural crisis. Expenditure and revenue patterns have become relatively fixed over time, and until its letter of intent to the IMF in 1991, Egypt's political leadership has been reluctant to make other than marginal changes in them (see Chapter 7).

India's balances are far more tolerable, but they too represent some ingrained patterns of expenditures and revenues. India's ISI experiment has been characterized by financial prudence in both domestic and foreign borrowing. Even so, trends in the last ten years have been alarming. From the early 1970s to 1980, the government deficit was, on average, less than 6% of GDP. That level rose steadily throughout the 1980s (see Figure 3.2), climbing to more than 10% in 1991. This rise has occurred even though GDP itself has grown rapidly, and it has paralleled a series of liberalizing reforms and deregulation in the Indian economy. The reforms, however, have been accompanied by a major expansion in public outlays, in sharp contrast with the experience of Mexico in the 1980s.

In many ways, Mexico's post–World War II experience with ISI was the most remarkable of the four, yielding high and steady rates of growth over nearly three decades. Its public financial deficits were commensurately low, averaging, for instance, 2.5% of GDP for the period 1965–70 (Rivera Ríos, 1987:table III). With the Echeverría *sexenio* and the

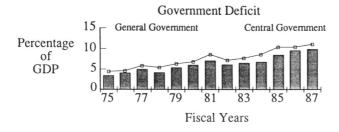

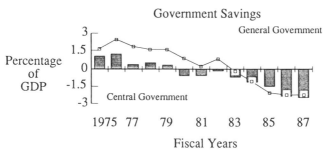

Figure 3.2. The evolution of India's government deficit and savings, 1975–87. Source: World Bank (1989), 60. Used by permission.

beginnings of the oil boom, deficit spending accelerated sharply to 8.8% of GDP for the period 1974–76. Short-lived efforts at stabilization after 1976 reduced the level to 7% between 1977 and 1979, but then, under López Portillo and the impact of the second surge in international oil prices, caution was thrown to the winds, and the deficit jumped to 14% of GDP by 1982. Although fluctuating, that level was maintained through 1988, after which preliminary figures indicate a reduction to about 5% of GDP (*Plan Nacional de Desarrollo*, 1989:142) and to 1.9% in 1990 (*Latin America Monitor*, 3/91:869). It is very important to note that by 1987, the primary deficit, net of interest payments, was actually converted into a surplus of 5.7% of GDP.

As we shall see in other respects, Turkey's vaunted experiment in export-led growth and structural adjustment has not led to appreciably greater fiscal discipline than that which prevailed in the much maligned and "profligate" 1970s. In that decade Turkey's overall deficit fluctuated between lows of 5% and highs of 10% of GDP. The rate in the 1980s, however, has averaged nearly 6% of GDP, and there are indications of declining discipline toward the end of the period. The budget deficit for 1990 was estimated at about 10% of GNP (Öniş and Özmucur, 1988a:75; World Bank, 3/15/88, Vol. II:table D.12; ICOC, 1990:57; TÜSIAD, 1/90:41). An era of inclusionary social democracy in the earlier decade has been replaced by a nominally pro-private sector and narrowly based coalition in the 1980s. But, like the transition from the statist, single-party regime to the two-party liberalizing system after 1950, re-markably little in the structure and depth of state economic intervention was changed.

Table 3.1 summarizes the relative sizes of the public deficits for all four countries. It is important to note that the same measures are *not* being used in each country (see note beneath the table), but the general orders of magnitude and the trends are accurate.

1.4. Foreign borrowing, external rents, and foreign investment

Directly related to the running of deficits in order to fill the resource gap was the growing resort to foreign borrowing. For once Egypt is not the egregious actor under this rubric. In fact, Turkey's payments crisis of 1977–80 should be considered the first among the current round of LDC debt crises. Mexico's has been more spectacular but came later. Egypt has had the luck of regular access to multilateral and government-to-government lending (a facet of the strategic rents issue already mentioned), thereby avoiding, for a while, reliance on commercial bank lending.[6] By the late 1980s, however, Egypt was falling seriously in arrears on all its external obligations. Table 3.2 shows the absolute size and per capita shares of the disbursed external debts of the four countries. In absolute terms, but above all in per capita terms, India's debt is quite modest, testimony once again to the prudent financial management that has characterized the country since independence. Like its deficit figures, the small size of India's debt suggests that unmanageable levels of foreign obligations need not be an intrinsic part of ISI.

Despite the fact that one exported oil and the other imported it, Mexico and Turkey found themselves in severe difficulties for roughly the same reasons. They both followed expansionary, high-growth programs throughout the 1970s with large public outlays for investment and welfare. In Mexico, borrowing was designed to finance the development of infrastructure and the public deficit at the same time that it filled the foreign-exchange gap and allowed the government to maintain an over-valued exchange rate. This policy could not be sustained, as the current account deficit quadrupled between 1970 and 1975. In 1975 efforts to "rationalize" tariffs were undertaken with the maximum rate set at 75%. Then, in 1976, the outgoing Luis Echeverría was forced to introduce the first devaluation of the peso in twenty-two years (Villareal and Villareal, 1980; Villareal, 1988a:317; Zedillo, 1986). As already noted, further

Table 3.1. *Comparative sizes of the public deficits in EIMT, 1974–89 (percentage of GDP)*

Year	Egypt	India	Mexico	Turkey
1974	21.0	5.5	8.8	5.2
1975	29.0	5.5	8.8	4.0
1976	21.0	5.5	8.8	6.7
1977	17.0	5.5	8.8	9.6
1978	23.0	5.5	6.8	6.5
1979	27.0	5.5	6.8	8.7
1980	18.0	6.1	6.8	6.5
1981	23.0	6.1	14.0	4.8
1982	21.0	7.0	14.0	5.0
1983	20.2	7.0	9.1	6.0
1984	20.2	7.0	9.1	7.7
1985	21.2	7.0	9.1	5.0
1986	23.0	8.9	13.8	5.0
1987	20.0	8.9	13.8	6.8
1988	17.0	8.1	..	5.5
1989	..	8.2	5.5[a]	6.0[a]
1990	..	..	1.9[a]	10.0[a]

Note: Egyptian figures refer to gross public deficit presumably including interest payments and SOE deficits; Indian figures are labeled "overall deficit" and probably include the same items. Mexico's are labeled "financial deficit" and probably include interest payments but perhaps not SOE deficits. Turkey's figures equal the sum of the budget deficits and the SOE deficits.

[a] Estimated.

Sources: Egypt: World Bank (10/5/83), 135; USAID Cairo, 1989 Statistical Compilation. India: World Bank (1989), 60, 63. Mexico: *Plan Nacional de Desarrollo, 1989–1994* (1989), 142; Rivera Riós (1987), Table III; Urzúa (1990), 22; Turkey: unpublished compilation of World Bank Statistics (1989); World Bank (3/15/88), vol. II, Table D.12; Osman Ulagay, 3/16/90; Öniş and Özmucur (1988b), 24.

adjustment was avoided as the second oil shock generated an enlarged flow of earnings for the Mexican economy.

Turkey's debt trebled in less than a decade, rising from $3.3 billion in 1973 to $15.3 billion in 1980. By the end of the decade petroleum came

Exposed to innumerable delusions

Table 3.2. *Total and per capita nonmilitary external debt in EIMT, 1988 (in $U.S.)*

	Year	Total (billions)	% GDP	Per capita
Egypt	1989	45	119[a]	882
India	1989	50	20	62
Mexico	1988	104	55	1238
Turkey	1988	38	52	710

[a]1986.

Sources: WDR (1989) and *International Financial Statistics* (1989).

to represent in value about half of all Turkey's imports. Simultaneously, because of recession in Europe, worker remittances fell off sharply. The foreign exchange shortfall forced Turkey into arrears on some $2.3 billion in special convertible Turkish lira (TL) accounts. The second surge in oil prices in 1978–79 pushed Turkey to the brink of default (Celâsun and Rodrik, 11/87). It was left to Bülent Ecevit, the left-of-center prime minister from the Republican Peoples' Party, to try to deal with the mess. He pushed through a 23% devaluation of the Turkish lira in 1978, but his efforts to cope with the deficit were neutralized by large, inflationary wage settlements in the public sector.

Turkey's debt more than doubled in the ensuing eight years. The new borrowing in the 1980s came largely through official channels (governments, the World Bank, and the IMF), so that in 1985 only 31% of Turkey's debt was owed commercial banks. The corresponding figure for Mexico was 91%. In that same year Turkey's debt was equivalent to 54% of GNP while Mexico's was only slightly higher at 55%.

Mexico and Turkey dealt with their crises in radically different manners, although there was little choice involved. Three factors marked Turkey off from Mexico. First, at the inception of the debt crisis there was a substantial transfusion of new external financing that was sustained well into the 1980s.[7] That, in turn, permitted Turkey to maintain a fairly high real rate of growth in GDP and a fairly high level of imports. The third factor was the military intervention of September 1980, which led to severe repression of organized labor and the imposition of martial law for three years. These factors combined to yield a dramatic shift in economic strategy away from ISI and toward a remarkably successful export drive. Exports increased from $2.5 billion in 1980 to more than $12 billion in 1989. High levels of imports provided the inputs necessary for

78

industrial exports. Idle capacity in the industrial sector that had built up after 1977 permitted fairly rapid shifts from domestic to external markets, and the lead industries could count on enforced labor discipline in the process.

These conditions gave rise to an experiment that the donor community touted as a model of adjustment, particularly regarding export performance (inter alia, Balassa, 1983; Öniş, 1989). There is disagreement, however, on how to weight the key elements. The World Bank (3/15/88) has emphasized the role of the real devaluation of the Turkish lira on a continuing basis after 1980. Celâsun and Rodrik (11/87), on the other hand, minimize that role and stress instead the massive infusion of capital, the relatively small size of the external debt at the beginning of the crisis, the relative absence of wage indexing in the Turkish economy, the low dependence on primary exports, and the maintenance of high levels of imports. To these we should add the rupture represented by the military coup itself. Once civilian rule was restored in 1983, the old political coalitions and their organizational embodiments that had dominated the 1970s had either been banned or broken up. It was relatively easy for new political actors to introduce substantially different expenditure patterns that allowed the "miracle" to continue.

By contrast, Mexico did not benefit from any international bailout after 1981 and, indeed, contemplated a partial default on its external obligations. Because most of its borrowing was from commercial sources, it found itself cut off from new infusions of capital. Its only recourse, as petroleum revenues plummeted, was to restrict imports, introduce severe demand-management measures, and allow the economy to drop to negative levels of growth. Adjustment policies were worked out in the context of stabilization agreements with the IMF in 1983 and 1986, and in the latter year the IMF set the precedent of calculating the budget deficit net of interest payments. With the economy in severe recession, Mexico was able to effect an impressive turnaround in its trade performance, racking up large trade surpluses between 1982 and 1986. Like the expansionary policies of the 1970s, the contractionary policies of the 1980s could not be sustained indefinitely.

By 1985, de la Madrid had concluded that a major overhaul of the "populist" policies of the 1970s was required. Mexican industry, both public and private, had to be made more competitive, and his government tied the economy to the mast by bringing Mexico within the GATT framework. An assault on the primary deficit was launched through curtailed public expenditures and large layoffs of public personnel. The first steps toward whittling down the claims of labor and other organized interests on public funds was begun. But the political risks were enormous. Inasmuch as little new capital was coming into Mexico, the trade surplus had to be used to service the debt. The government had no resources for new investment and job creation. The economy and the general wage level continued to decline. In 1988 the government and the PRI paid the price in the presidential elections, barely winning a majority in what many regarded as rigged elections.

What is astonishing is that de la Madrid's designated successor, Carlos Salinas de Gortari, pushed ahead with the reforms with even greater vigor. Succeeding. chapters examine the specific instances of Salinas's program involving privatization and confrontation with organized labor. The important point to note here is that, unlike Turkey, there was no sharp rupture in regime continuity, no housecleaning by military coup, no prior dismantling of the vested interests that had sustained the PRI for decades. It may well be that the very depth of Mexico's crisis constituted the element of discontinuity that allowed Salinas to move ahead.

Neither Egypt nor India has been faced with debt crises to rival those of Mexico and Turkey. Like Mexico, Egypt was driven to adoption of a stabilization plan in 1976–77, but with the availability of large new external rents after 1978, the plan was abandoned. Only after the collapse of oil prices in the early 1980s, which also adversely affected worker remittances, Suez Canal traffic, and foreign investment, was Egypt obliged to consider far-reaching adjustment measures. Moreover, its foreign debt, although mainly owed public creditors, was presenting major servicing problems. Egypt tried, not very successfully, to reduce public spending, especially by eliminating subsidies, to raise interest rates, and to approximate the market exchange rate for the Egyptian pound (£E). In this instance, until 1991 the inertia of the incumbents had won out against the pressures for structural change. This may be bad for the Egyptian economy but comforting for political scientists.

India weathered the oil shocks of the 1970s in good order. It managed to maintain high (although declining) levels of investment and marked expansion in the SOE sector itself while avoiding balance of payments crises and snowballing external debt.

In Mexico, but above all in Egypt, external rents came to fund a substantial portion of the resource gap. For both, petroleum rents in the boom years of the late 1970s and early 1980s were used to support high levels of investment and consumption. Both tapped into remitted earnings of nationals working abroad. In Egypt in the 1980s remittances became the single most important source of foreign exchange in the economy. Both collected substantial rents from international tourism. Only Egypt could collect rents from the Suez Canal, and only Egypt benefited from the enormous strategic rents paid by the United States in return for the Camp David Accords of 1979 and for Egypt's continuing role in promoting an overall Arab understanding with Israel. U.S. economic assis-

Bald comparisons

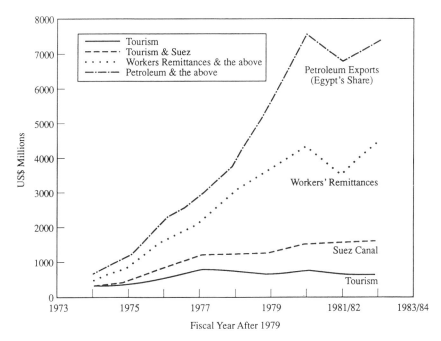

Figure 3.3. Egypt: Development of exogenous resources. Source: Ahmed et al. (1985), Table 1.1, 3. Used by permission.

tance to Egypt totaled $13.2 billion between 1975 and 1990, with an additional $3.2 billion through the Commodity Import Program. Military assistance, begun in 1980, reached $12.6 billion by 1990. The total flow of U.S. assistance thus cumulated to $27.4 billion over fifteen years.

In the early 1980s gross receipts from petroleum sales, Suez Canal tolls, tourism, and remittances (known in Egypt as the Gang of Four) was in the area of $12 billion per annum, or about half of GDP (see Figure 3.3). This foreign exchange cushion was not used to promote structural adjustment but rather to fuel consumption. Domestic savings shrank proportionately. Mexico, which began efforts at structural adjustment in 1976, similarly abandoned them as petroleum rents flowed into the economy after 1977.

For long periods the four countries under consideration regarded foreign investment with considerable suspicion, and in Egypt and India it was for a time discouraged. Only in Mexico has direct foreign investment (DFI) played a substantial role in the economy, indeed a dominant one in the automotive industry. But it would be hard to argue that even in Mexico such investments were large enough and sufficiently well placed to force the pace and direction of public resource outlays. For example,

81

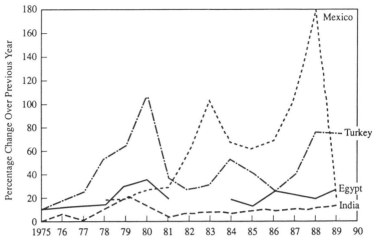

Figure 3.4. Inflation rates in EIMT, 1975–89

over the period 1972–83, net flows averaged about $500 million per year, with sharp increases to more than $1 billion in 1980 and 1981, followed by an equally sharp decline to $374 million in 1983 (Zedillo, 1986:table 2). After 1984, DFI began to pick up markedly, rising to $3.2 billion in 1987 or 2.2% of GDP. This should be measured against total fixed investment in 1987, which was 19% of GDP. The cumulative total for 1984–87 was $5.6 billion (much of it returning flight capital and debt–equity swaps).

The trend for DFI in the remaining three countries is also up. In India the amounts remain extraordinarily small, $62 million in 1984–85, rising to $253 or about 1% of GDP, in 1987–88 (World Bank figures; see also Lal, 1988:257). In Turkey, the cumulative total of *approved* foreign investments for the period 1980–88 was $2.9 billion. This sum was thirteen times greater than the entire flow of the preceding twenty-eight years (TÜSIAD, 1989:97). Finally, in Egypt the cumulative total of DFI over the period 1974–88 was $3 billion, excluding investment in the petroleum sector, and more than half this total was subscribed by Egyptians. In sum, it can be concluded that none of these economies has been captured by multinational corporations, and that they would all welcome far more DFI than they have enjoyed heretofore.

1.5. Inflation

In Figure 3.4, we see the familiar pairing of the countries in terms of inflation, especially in the 1980s. India, reflecting its relatively careful

82

Bald comparisons

Table 3.3. *Relative weights of foreign trade in the four economies, 1987 (U.S. $millions)*

	Exports	Imports	Total trade	GNP	Exports/ GNP %	Total trade/ GNP %
Egypt	4,040	8,453	12,493	34,068	11	37.0
India	12,548	18,985	31,533	239,400	5	13.2
Mexico	20,887	12,731	33,618	150,060	14	22.4
Turkey	10,190	14,163	24,353	63,646	16	38.0

Note: For Mexico and Egypt exports do not reflect the pre-1986 high export prices for petroleum. Egypt's import figures reflect its high agricultural dependency, Mexico's the depth of recession.

Source: WDR (1989), 164, 190–91.

financial management, registered the lowest inflation rates of the four, and the sudden bursts in some years testify either to monsoon failures or to the two oil shocks of the 1970s. Egypt should have displayed much higher rates of inflation given its enormous public deficit. But external rents, an overvalued currency, and huge subsidy programs allowed the government to contain inflationary pressures. Unlike India, Egypt's tolerable rates of inflation have been achieved by shifting the costs of deficits and external borrowing to future generations.

Turkey and Mexico predictably entered periods of very high inflation in the late 1970s and early 1980s. In both instances the rates were driven by deficit financing, rapid increases in debt servicing, and currency devaluation. It has already been mentioned how the two countries chose to deal with inflation: Turkey trying to keep it within manageable bounds while maintaining high rates of GNP growth; Mexico, through severe demand management and curtailed public expenditures. Mexico's burst of triple-digit inflation in 1987–88 led to the negotiation of the Pact of Economic Solidarity (PSE), which led to the imposition of wage and price controls. Inflation fell off sharply in 1989, and real growth returned to the economy. Turkey, however, continues inertially at rates of 60% to 70% per year.

1.6. Trade and protection

ISI did not mean withdrawal from world trade. All four countries are heavily involved in external markets. Table 3.3 shows the weight of foreign trade in GNP for the four countries in 1987. India, unsurprisingly,

83

مسئول المنسوجات

— وعدم تصــــديرنا دلوقت دليل جودة اقمشتنا .. لأن
اللى صــــدرناه من عشرين سنة لسـه مادابش .. !!

Egypt's export performance. The Director of Textiles (with cigar): "Our lack of exports today is an indication of the quality of our cloth... What we exported twenty years ago still hasn't worn out... !!" Source: *Ruz al-Yussef*, 11/18/85:25.

is the most self-contained economy, which reflects its continued commitment to the ISI formula. Its huge domestic market allows it this privilege. Nonetheless, in the 1980s India became much more concerned about its export performance. During the Seventh Five Year Plan period, the rupee was allowed to devalue by 40%. In overall terms, India's exports grew modestly in the latter half of the 1980s, but manufactured exports picked up markedly after 1985.

Egypt has remained faithful to the same ISI formula, but its involvement in world trade is proportionately much larger. This is because of the country's very large import bill, especially for food, and its petroleum exports. Although Egyptian policy makers have emphasized the imperative need to promote Egyptian industrial exports, there have been scant changes in the country's decades-old pattern. As a USAID report put it (1990:32): "If exports of petroleum, cotton and textiles are excluded, Egypt would be left with no meaningful commodity export."

Turkey, and to a lesser extent, Mexico, have commanded the attention of the international donor and business communities for their energetic shift to an export-led growth strategy in the 1980s. Their success demonstrates that economies structured by long periods of ISI are nonetheless capable of adapting to the rigors of international competition. South

Bald comparisons

Korea is perhaps the most striking example of this, but so too are Brazil and some other Latin American countries (Pazos, 1987; on Turkey, Eralp, 1990:223, and Kirim, 1990).

Turkey took its first steps toward the transition with the devaluation of the TL in 1970. While maintaining its basic ISI structures (as Mexico did after the devaluation of 1976), the country gave a boost to its exports. The results were not spectacular. Primary exports grew unevenly throughout the decade. Manufactured exports increased their share of total exports from 19% to 29%. The share of total exports to GNP rose from 3.5% to 5.8% (Öniş, 1989:19, and Öniş and Reidel, 1990:59). A second devaluation in 1979 anticipated the comprehensive shift to export-led growth after 1980. A range of export incentives, customs and tax rebates, preferential credit arrangements, the establishment of private trading houses (on the Korean and Japanese model), and the resort to continuous real devaluation of the TL undergirded the spectacular rise in manufactured exports (and some services such as in the construction sector) that ensued. By 1989 exports had quintupled in value, and manufactured goods exports accounted for 80% of the total. More than 60% of total exports went to OECD countries. Turkey had clearly made a competitive breakthrough.

Mexico, of course, entered the 1980s as a major exporter, but that was because of its petroleum. It also was a heavily protected economy. With petroleum prices falling in the early 1980s, the Mexican government decided in July 1985 to bring the country within the GATT framework, a move that had been theretofore blocked by opposition on the part of private industry and organized labor. Tariffs were slashed across the board, and various incentives to encourage exports were put in place. Devaluations of the peso occurred in 1982, in 1985, and in 1988, after which the peso was allowed to devalue continuously through a managed float. The devaluations have stimulated an impressive growth in exports, which rose to $27 billion in 1990 (owing partially to the recovery of oil prices). Manufactured exports grew to nearly $14 billion, or about half the total.

It is unlikely that outside the minerals sector the SOEs will play much of a role in exports. For the most part SOEs will help prop up, but not lead, the export drive. The shift to determined export promotion will entail a commensurate shift in the promotion of the private sector. The kind of symbiosis between large private conglomerates and mercantilist, facilitating states that has already been seen in Japan and Korea may spread.

For decades all four EIMT countries resorted to high tariff walls and quantitative trade restrictions to protect their new industries. Even as policy makers identified the need to open their economies to world trade,

Exposed to innumerable delusions

Table 3.4. *Mean tariffs on manufactured goods in EIMT, 1984–85*

	Intermediate goods	Capital goods	Consumer goods
Egypt	← (50%: range 0–300%) →		
India	123.0	114.5	128.5
Mexico	23.5	23.5	32.2
Turkey	29.4	34.9	55.3

Source: For Egypt, World Bank (6/89), 47–49. For the last three entries, World Bank (1989), 14.

the walls were kept fairly high. Table 3.4 shows average levels of pro-tection by type of goods for the mid-1980s. What it does not show are subsidies to industry that increase the effective rate of protection, or goods whose importation is totally banned. In Egypt, for example, there were, in 1989, 275 categories of goods whose importation was totally or partially restricted, and the list had grown from 210 in 1986. After 1986, Egypt lowered tariffs within a range of 0% to 110%, with an average level of 31% (World Bank, 6/13/89). India likewise has main-tained very high levels of protection, which have actually been increasing in the 1980s.

Only Mexico has made a direct assault on its structures of protection (see World Bank, 1986).[8] The number of items subject to import licensing was reduced by 75%, and the average tariffs were lowered to about one-fifth of their 1985 levels. Throughout the 1980s, Turkey made good but inconsistent progress in tariff reduction. For some sectors, especially con-sumer durables and automobiles, levels remain high. Although Turkey has sharply reduced the categories of goods subject to licensing, it has added various taxes and surcharges on imports, some of which provide earmarked flows for extrabudgetary funds (see Chapter 7), that have actually increased the total import tax (including tariffs) to about 25% of their cost, insurance, and freight (CIF) value in 1987 (World Bank, 4/13/88:23).

1.7. Conclusion

ISI did lead to significant industrialization in EIMT, as Table 3.5 shows. The share of industry in Mexico's economy is on a par with the most advanced industrial nations, although somewhat behind South Korea, another late industrializer. But not only has the share of industry in GDP probably reached its limit in these four countries, we may in fact expect

86

Table 3.5. *Relative shares of industry in GDP in EIMT*

	Egypt		India		Mexico		Turkey	
	1973	1986/87	1974/75	1985/86	1965	1987	1973	1988
Industry	16	14	22	27	27	35	21	26
(Manufacturing)	..	..	(16)	(17)	(20)	(25)	..	..

Sources: Figures all drawn from various World Bank reports. In addition, for Turkey, Celâsun (1983) and TÜSIAD (1989). The Egyptian figures do not include the petroleum sector. In general these figures, taken from country-specific reports, are well below the World Bank's own estimates in recent issues of the *WDR*. I cannot account for the discrepancies.

some relative regression as protection is reduced, investment more care-fully and parsimoniously undertaken, and as some of the behemoths of an earlier era are liquidated. One must distinguish between the petroleum and power sectors, where growth is likely to be strong, and manufac-turing, where the going will be much rougher, especially when export promotion is involved.

ISI has played itself out, although India will be able to tinker with the model for many years to come. It has by no means been a disaster. It did, after all, promote significant industrialization in unlikely milieux. It built skills among blue- and white-collar work forces that can be turned to other purposes and strategies. It has proved flexible enough to allow a shift toward export-led growth in two of the four countries. Finally, if export-led growth leads to the buffeting of highly leveraged private sec-tors by international trade and business cycles, it is not at all out of the question that some variant of ISI may once again exert its appeal.

2. THE SIZE AND CHARACTER OF THE SOE SECTOR

Our task here is to describe, as simply and succinctly as possible, the comparative contours of the public enterprise sectors in the four countries under examination. In terms of the range and type of activities under-taken, there are basic similarities among them. However, the economic spaces they each occupy differ significantly. Here, we shall try to measure those differences and similarities, while assigning the explanation for their occurrence to Chapters 1 and 4.

2.1. The Four in a larger universe

Developing countries after World War II leapt aboard a train that had gathered speed in the more advanced industrial nations of the West and in the Soviet Union since the turn of the century. With the advent of the Depression and World War II, government expenditures as a proportion of GNP surged from levels between 10% and 15% to 25% to 35%, from which they have never declined (Kohl, 1983:210). According to OECD figures, by 1981 the public sectors of industrialized nations on average expended 41% of GDP, up from 29% in 1961. The last decade has witnessed a halt in that steady growth, but no diminution of the weight of public expenditures.[9]

There is in fact a clear positive correlation between levels of national per capita income and the size of public expenditures (World Bank, *WDR*, 1988:46), such that low-income developing countries (i.e., between $125 and $500 in 1985 dollars) average about 28% of GNP in public ex-

Table 3.6. *General government and state-owned enterprise expenditures as a proportion of GDP in EIMT*

	Year	General govt. expenditures/ % GDP	SOE expenditures/ % GDP	Total public expenditures/ % GDP
Egypt	1988/89	44.0	17.3[a]	61.3
India	1985	9.0	15.5	24.5
Mexico	1988	27.0	12.0	39.0
Turkey	1988/89	21.0	28.0	49.0

[a]1987.

Sources: Egypt: *Middle East Economic Digest* (7/14/89), 5 and unpublished World Bank and USAID estimates. India: World Bank (10/88), Report 7294-IN:2. Indian figures do not include outlays at the state level. Mexico: René Villareal (1988b), 147 and World Bank figures. Turkey: unpublished World Bank figures.

penditures, while middle income ($501–$2,000) average about 33%, and upper income ($8,001–$20,000) average a little more than 40%.

The problem in LDCs, then, is not bigness per se but, rather, the nature of public expenditures. The largest items in the expenditures of the industrialized nations come in the area of social services (health, education, and social security), although for some, such as the United States, defense claims a big piece of public outlays (Stiglitz et al., 1989:19). Outlays on public enterprise as a proportion of GDP are relatively low, ranging in 1982 between 6% and 11% for a select group including Sweden, France, the United Kingdom, and the United States. For a group of Latin American nations in the same year, the weighted average was 19%, with Peru, Mexico, and Venezuela averaging 34% (Schneider, 1991:table 2.1).

Table 3.6 shows that these generalizations do not hold up very well in our four cases. Levels of income do not predict public sector size, with India confirming the proposition and Mexico refuting it. What we do see is that public enterprise occupies a major place in overall governmental expenditures. Egypt's and Mexico's figures reflect the declining weight of the state petroleum sectors after 1985. In fact, in all four countries since the mid-1980s the share of the public sector in the economy has declined marginally from the peaks attained in the late 1970s or early 1980s. Mexico's public sector expenditures, for instance, reached 49% of GDP in 1982 or 42% excluding PEMEX (Zedillo, 1986:975). This table accurately indicates general orders of magnitude with Egypt's public sector being two and a half times as large as India's, and a third again as big as Turkey's.

89

Table 3.7. *Public sector and public enterprise deficits in EIMT*

	Year	Public sector deficit % GDP	Primary deficit % GDP	Public enterprise deficit % GDP
Egypt	1986/87	26.3	..	9.0
India	1988/89	10.4	6.3	3.2
Mexico	1987	14.0	6.0	2.0
Turkey	1990	6.1	..	2.7

Sources: Egypt: World Bank (3/87), 12 and USAID (1989?), Tables 1.0 and 1.1. India: World Bank (1989), 60, 63, 75; World Bank (10/88), 18; Ministry of Finance, *Economic Survey 1989/90* as cited in Sarma (1990); World Bank (3/90), 22; BPE (1990), 6. Mexico: Zedillo (1986), 975; Cuadernos de Renovación Nacional (1988), 110, 115–16; *Plan Nacional de Desarrollo, 1989–1994* (1989), 142; De la Madrid (1986), 45. Turkey: Statistical compendium compiled from World Bank figures, unpublished, World Bank (4/88), 83; Ulagay (1990) citing figures from Treasury and Foreign Trade Secretariat.

Public enterprise in developing countries has borne much of the opprobrium for the poor economic performance that has characterized all but the "little tigers" of Asia since the early 1970s. The opprobrium is not misplaced. To the extent that SOEs have been a drain on public resources, rather than generating surpluses for the exchequer (nearly always the case except for the petroleum sector), it is the SOEs that account for the bulk of public sector deficits in developing countries.[10] The overall deficits of public enterprise sectors are a particularly large component of government deficits in LDCs. For industrial countries overall SOE deficits averaged 2.1% of GDP over the period 1974–77, while for developing countries the average was 4.6% (Short, 1984:145–58).[11]

As can be seen in Table 3.7, EIMT ran much larger deficits than the average for all developing nations as well as for their national income groups. Egypt, as in all other respects, is the outlier, and preliminary estimates for 1990 showed that no progress toward deficit reduction had been made (Khaled Sharif, *AI*, 7/30/90:10). Mexico began an assault on its deficits in 1985 and continued it throughout the rest of the decade (Urzúa, 5/90). The relatively low ratio of public enterprise sector deficit to GDP is a well-established feature of the economy, dating back at least to 1970 (Casar and Peres, 1988:95). Turkey simply held steady from the mid-1980s, neither reducing nor increasing its deficits, while India, entering its Eighth Five Year Plan period, was experiencing rising deficits in both domains. In both India and Mexico, the public enterprise sector, by the late 1980s, showed net profits, generated almost exclusively in

90

Bald comparisons

Table 3.8. *Value of SOE goods and services to GDP in EIMT*

Country	Year	Share
Egypt	1986	40.0
India	1988/89	22.2
Mexico	1988	12.0
Turkey	1987	19.0

Sources: Egypt: World Bank (1987). India: BPE (1990), 11. Mexico: unpublished data, World Bank (5/89). Turkey: Yüksek Denetleme Kurulu, *KIT Genel Raporu* (1988).

the petroleum sector, but the investment budgets of both SOE sectors were of such magnitude that their overall balances were in deficit. The four countries under examination could reduce their primary deficits by between a third and a half if they could eliminate their public enterprise deficits.[12]

In their survey of public enterprise in developing countries, Jones and Mason (1982:23) note a surprising uniformity of the value of SOE goods and services in GDP, for the most part falling in the range 7%–15%. However, Mary Shirley (1983:95) shows how wide the range is for a sample of thirty-six developing countries (shares of GDP at factor cost) in the late 1970s: Algeria heads the list with 66%, while the Philippines is at the bottom with 1.7%. Table 3.8, using more recent data, shows that the four countries, with the exception of Mexico, all fall well beyond the upper limit of the range proposed by Jones and Mason, and even Mexico is close to the upper limit.

2.2. The Four among themselves

Here we shall try to come to grips with the combined quantitative and qualitative indicators of public enterprise strength by examining the value of assets, the range of undertakings, the share in investment and value-added, and the share in employment of the SOE sectors.

It is very hard to generate simple aggregate figures of the value of assets in the four SOE sectors. The basic measure appears to be "invested capital," consisting in fixed assets plus working capital. The problems begin with what is included in the public sector. Alongside fully- or majority-owned SOEs there may be many firms in which the state has a controlling minority interest. There are also public banks and holding companies that in turn may own majority or controlling interests in

91

Exposed to innumerable delusions

Table 3.9. *The value of SOE assets in EIMT ($U.S. billions, current)*

Countries	1986-89
Egypt	
Nonfinancial SOEs	46 (14)
SOEs and public authorities	98 (49)
India	
Central government SOEs	51
State-level SOEs	22
Mexico	
Majority-owned SOEs with PEMEX	123
Majority-owned SOEs without PEMEX	86
Turkey	
Nonfinancial SOEs	41

Notes: All conversions to dollars were made at the exchange rate prevailing in the year of observation. All four countries have devalued; Mexico and Turkey repeatedly so. Egypt maintains multiple exchange rates. The first observation was made at the Central Bank rate, and that grossly overvalued rate was used for all subsequent observations. The figures in parenthesis show the dollar valuation at the "street" rate. India devalued in the late 1980s, which explains the unchanging value of state-level enterprise.

Sources: Egypt: Handoussa (1986); INP (1988); CAPMAS (1984); *AI* (5/7/90), 13. India: BPE (1990), 2–3; *Economic Times* (2/11/88); World Bank (1989), 299; Mishra and Ravishankar (1985), 136–49. Mexico: Rey Romay (1987), 80; Tamayo (1988), 677; World Bank (1989), 15. Turkey: Wålstedt (1980), 100–01; Yüksek Denetleme Kurulu (1988), Ek.3.

several *de jure* private enterprises. Sometimes only nonfinancial enterprises are included in asset valuation. By and large, the figures I have assembled in Table 3.9 appear to be conservative estimates of asset value. They are drawn from the period 1986–89.

These figures must be taken as representing gross relative magnitudes. Inflation, devaluation, and different accounting procedures obviate any possibility of precise comparison. Single industries can make an enormous difference in these estimates. For example, PEMEX is one of the world's largest corporations, with net assets in 1987 of $36.8 billion, putting it at the top of the *South* 500. The Comisión Federal de Electricidad in the same year had $16 billion in assets. By contrast, Egypt's incomplete figures probably undervalue its SOE assets. The most recent figure refers only to nonfinancial public companies. Alongside them, however, are several authorities such as the Egyptian Petroleum Authority (the func-

92

tional equivalent in Egypt of PEMEX), the Suez Canal, Alexandria Port, Cairo Public Transport, and so forth. The $98 billion figure for 1986 (converted at the overvalued Central Bank rate) includes everything from the Suez Canal to the Aswan High Dam.

More telling than figures are the kinds of activities in which SOEs are involved. All four countries through their SOEs, public authorities, and departmental undertakings, maintain a significant if not dominant position in the following list of activities:[13]

power generation	textiles	banking and
railroads	iron and steel	insurance
port administration	aluminum, copper	agricultural credit
highways	petrochemicals	industrial credit
urban	fertilizers	small business credit
transportation	petroleum products	crop purchasing
telephone and	machine tools	retail and wholesale
telegraph	heavy engineering	trade
radio and	consumer durables	foreign trade
television	consumer	railroad rolling
media and book	nondurables	stock
publishing	food and beverages	mining (iron,
agricultural	electronics	copper, coal, etc.)
extension	cars, trucks, buses,	defense industries
irrigation perimeters	tractors	airlines, shipping
construction		hotels

There is no major sector except agricultural production that the state has left to private enterprise, and in several sectors the SOEs enjoy a monopolistic or oligopolistic position. Predictably Egypt's SOEs dwarf the private sector except in agriculture. In value, 60% of industrial production, 100% of petroleum and gas, 100% of electricity, 65% of transport and communications, 75% of construction, and 51% of services are contributed by public entities (World Bank, 3/87:6). In the mid-1980s, fifty-seven manufacturing concerns were monopolies. The SOE sectors of the other three countries, with much larger private sectors, do not enjoy the same weight as Egypt's in total manufacturing, but they are dominant in energy, mining, and basic metals, and are the largest producers of capital goods and intermediate goods crucial to the rest of the economy. Table 3.10 indicates some magnitudes of provision and production for a certain number of sectors.

I had difficulty in locating estimates of the SOE sector share of gross fixed capital formation (GFCF) in the four countries. Either that datum was not recently reported, as was the case for Turkey, or was highly

Table 3.10. *SOE shares in production in EIMT, mid-1980s (%)*

Sector	Egypt	India	Mexico	Turkey
Mining	100	..	88	..
Coal	100	98	..	100
Crude petroleum	100	100	100	49
Basic Metals				
Iron and steel	100	55	59	69
Copper	..	100	..	100
Aluminum	100	48	..	..
Manufacturing	60	..	16	..
Sugar	100	..	53	73
Tobacco	100	..	..	100
Petrochemicals	100	..	100	100
Textiles	60	..	..	17
Paper	100	..	..	66
Chemical fertilizers	90	46	..	24
Transport equipment	100	..	51	..

Sources: Egypt: World Bank (3/87), 6. India: BPE (1990), 5. Mexico: Machado, Peres, Delgado (1986), 123–25; Casar and Peres (1988), 45; Tamayo (1988), 686. Turkey: Yüksek Denetleme Kurulu (1988), 24–25.

inconsistent, as for Mexico. In the late 1970s the average ratio for all LDCs was 27% (Short, 1984). With the possible exception of Mexico, all four countries' public enterprise sector account for a considerably larger share of GFCF. According to Wålstedt (1980:236), in Turkey the average for the period 1968–72 was 48% and all other indicators would suggest that such a ratio increased in the 1980s, rising as high as 58% in 1986 (TÜSIAD, 1988a:9). A number of sources put the Indian SOE share at over 50% (Montek Ahluwalia, 1986:table 9; Ministry of Finance, 1990; Nagaraj, 12/14/91:2877). In Egypt the ratio is probably around 70%. The Mexican estimates are peculiar in that they vary within the same source. Tamayo (1988:654, 728) advances an average for the period 1975 to 1983 of 27% (p. 728), whereas on p. 660 he offers an average of 45%. It could be that one set of figures contains PEMEX and enterprises with minority state shares and that the other does not, but that is not stated. Casar and Peres (1988:92) offer three estimates for the period 1976–80 (i.e., corresponding to the petroleum boom): 21%

Table 3.11. *Public sector investment: Shares of total investment and of GDP in EIMT*

	Year	Share of total investment %	Year	Share of GDP %
Egypt	1965/66	93	1976	15.0
	1974/81	80	1980/81	22.0
	1983/86	77	1982/83	20.0
India	1970/75	41		7.5
	1975/80	45		9.9
	1980/86	45		11.1
Mexico	1959/70	36	1965/70	6.5
	1971/77	38	1971/76	8.2
	1978/81	46		6.3
	1982/85	41		2.7
Turkey	1963/67	55[a]		..
	1975	49[a]	1977	12.3
	1981	62[b]	1980	10.8
	1985	61[b]	1985	11.6
	1987	53[b]		..
	1988	48[b]	1988	11.6

[a]Manufacturing and mining.
[b]Entire public sector.

Sources: Egypt: INP (1988); World Bank (3/87); AI (5/18/87), 33. India: Boillot (1989), 539. Mexico: Tamayo (1988), 658; World Bank (1989), 64; Basáñez (1990), 166. Turkey: Wålstedt (1980), 235; TÜSIAD (1989), 11; Öniş and Riedel (1990), 31.

generated by manufacturing enterprises not including petrochemicals; 52% including petrochemicals; 68% including all the preceding plus PEMEX and the Comisión Federal de Electricidad. Again, whatever the discrepancies, the hegemonic position of the state sector can hardly be questioned in any of the four countries.

In terms of the data presented in Table 3.11, the pairing is Egypt and Turkey with the largest investment shares, and Mexico and India, whose shares are considerably smaller. What must be at work here are the relative strengths of the private sectors. We should not be surprised that Mexico's and India's shoulder a relatively large proportion of the investment burden, nor that Egypt's does not. Rather, it is the continued predominance of Turkish public investment well into the 1980s that s:sArises. Turkey's private sector may be the most powerful in the Middle East, but one may speculate that it is not yet as mature as Mexico's (see Chapter 8).

The state sectors of the four countries employ a varying but substantial proportion of the nonagricultural work force. They are the single largest employers in their respective economies, and they have a corner, as it were, on the white-collar and skilled blue-collar work force. In Egypt the state sector has acted for nearly three decades as the employer of last resort for university graduates (Waterbury, 1983:241–46). Combined with external migration, it has in the last decade provided 90% of all new employment opportunities for job aspirants (Handoussa, 9/88:6).

Table 3.12 provides some relative magnitudes of public sector employment. In the mid-1980s total government employment in LDCs accounted on average for 25% of nonagricultural employment (Africa: 33%; Asia: 22%; Latin America: 20%; World Bank, *WDR*, 1983:102). Once again Egypt is in another realm altogether with 53% of the nonagricultural work force on public payroll, while the other three fall much closer to the LDC average. Nonetheless, as Nayar points out (1989:366–67), in India, if one singles out those firms employing ten or more persons, the administration and SOE sector in 1984 accounted for nearly 70% of such employment.

Finally, we see in Table 3.13 that the wages paid in the SOE sector of the four countries vary widely from 10% of GDP in Egypt to 1.3% in post–oil boom Mexico. It proved harder to estimate the share of total public sector wages in GDP as it was not clear whether or not state-level employees were included, as well as schoolteachers, police, and the like. Still, in the mid-1980s crude estimates yield 23% for Egypt, 9% for India, 6% for Mexico, and 9.4% for Turkey. Similarly, the SOE sectors' value-added (i.e., net sales revenues minus cash production cost other than labor) as a proportion of GDP ranges from 20% in Egypt to 6.4% in India. The only figure I could find for Mexico is for 1978–79, when oil prices were rising.

We must be careful not to confuse size and weight of public sector activity with strength and effectiveness. Big does not necessarily mean strong, and in the case of Egypt almost certainly does not. Regulatory regimes cannot be captured by quantitative indexes, and in India they have been a particularly important component of public sector dominance.

Table 3.12. *The size and share in nonagricultural employment of the public sector and SOE sector work force in EIMT (in '000)*

	Year	1. Non-SOE public work force	2. SOE work force	3. Total	4. Non-agricultural work force	2:4 %	3:4 %
Egypt	1976	1,550	1,109	2,659	..	..	..
	1984	2,819	1,347	4,166	7,700	17.5	54.0
	1988	3,200	1,742[a]	4,942	..	..	..
India	1979	..	1,703	..	..	..	..
	1984	17,500	2,284	19,784	93,000[b]	2.5	21.2
Mexico	1970	..	411	..	..	..	..
	1980	..	879	..	..	..	..
	1985	4,260	963	5,223	20,000	5.0	26.0
Turkey	1980	1,381	541	1,922	10,300	5.2	19.0
	1987	1,647	728	2,375	12,000	6.0	19.0

The 1988 Egyptian figure includes 450,000 employees in public authorities.
5,000,000 in "organized" sector.

Sources: Egypt: Handoussa (1988); Nabil Sabbagh, *AI* (1988); INP (1988), 15. India: CMIE (1983); PE (1989). Mexico: Carrillo Castro and Garcia Ramirez (1983); Tamayo (1988), 664–73; Jose añon (1989), 25, gives a figure of 1,405 million employees in the SOE sector. Turkey: T. C. Maliye Gümrük Bakanliği, *1988 Mali Yili Bütçe Gerekçesi*, Yüksek Denetleme Kurulu, *KIT Genel Raporu* 988). For none of the countries are figures for armed forces and police included. Nonagricultural ırk force figures are from ILO, *Yearbook of Labour Statistics*, Geneva (1988).

With these caveats in mind, it is still interesting to compare the size of the four public sectors by means of a weighted index for 1985. The index consists of government shares in total expenditures and consumption, the budget deficit as a proportion of GDP, the share of SOE sales of goods and services of total sales, the SOE share in total value-added, the public sector share of total investment, and the public sector share in total nonagricultural employment. Using Egypt as the benchmark, we can situate the size of the four public sectors (in the broad sense) relative to one another:

Egypt	100	Mexico	42
India	66	Turkey	63

Table 3.13. *SOE shares in GDP represented by value-added and wages in EIMT*

	Value-added/GDP %		SOE wages/GDP %	
Egypt	20.0	(1985/86)	10.0	(1985)
India	6.4		10.0	(1988/89)
Mexico	15.4	(1985)	14.8	(1985)
Turkey	14.0	(1986)	5.0	(1986)

Sources: Egypt: Handoussa (1988). India: BPE (1990). Mexico: Hill (1984), 362; Villareal, Rocio, and René Villareal (1980); Centro de Análisis e Investigación Económica (CAIE), *Informe Mensual sobre la Economía Mexicana* (1988), vol. 6, no. 10, 21. Turkey: Celâsun and Rodrik (1987); Yüksek Denetleme Kurulu, *KIT Genel Raporu* (1988).

This is only a snapshot, and the variables and weights used are somewhat arbitrary. It would be useful to be able to show trends over time, but I was unable to find consistent data with which to do so.

2.3. Growth of the SOE sector

The primary mode of SOE development has been the direct founding and development by the state itself. When not seizing the commanding heights, EIMT have been mounding them up, especially in steel, petrochemicals, heavy engineering, and defense-related industries. In the name of equity, all four moved into direct public ownership of services and agencies to regulate markets and control foreign trade. Early on they realized the crucial importance of controlling investment flows and thus created a range of financial institutions, such as Mexico's NAFINSA or Turkey's Sümer and Eti banks to promote sectoral development. Finally, all four have taken over failing private enterprises, especially those heavily indebted to the public financial institutions just mentioned.

There has been planned growth, improvised growth, and inertial growth. The 1970s in all four countries witnessed a major expansion of SOEs as cheap external public or commercial credit became available, coupled in the cases of Mexico and Egypt with a growth in petroleum earnings. This surge came simultaneously with a growing commitment to the promotion of the private sector and the use of market mechanisms to guide the public sector. The SOEs were already under heavy criticism even on the part of their creators, but the fact that oil rents and foreign loans passed first into state hands meant that SOE demands would be

98

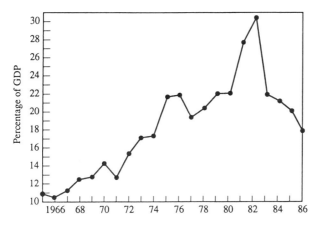

Figure 3.5. Noninterest expenditures of the Mexican public sector. Source: Adapted from the World Bank data.

satisfied regardless of the prevailing policy mood. This phenomenon lends credence to Margaret Levi's (1988) proposition that states are first and foremost revenue maximizers, even at the expense of their proclaimed ideological preferences.

The profile of Mexican expenditures in Figure 3.5 is typical of all four countries although in India and Egypt there was no sharp tailing off in the 1980s.

Nowhere is this anomaly more striking than in Egypt. Its public enterprise sector is divided into commercial companies, the most important of which are controlled by the Ministry of Industry, and various authorities responsible for municipal transport, the Suez Canal, the Aswan High Dam, petroleum marketing and production, and so on. Despite the formal launching of the "open-door policy" in 1974 to encourage foreign private investment and local private sector development, the SOE sector continued to claim the lion's share of public investment. The private sector did grow more rapidly than the public, so that there was a modest shift in overall public–private balances, but the ability of the public sector to protect its claims on new public resources was striking. Over the period 1975–85, the public sector financed 68% of all investment, and if public investment in joint ventures designated as private is included, the figure rises to 78%. More striking is that some 43 public domestic trading companies, with 4,800 branches, accounted in value for nearly 90% of all wholesale and retail trade (INP, 5/88:30, 56). Moreover, in the 1980s when petroleum revenues fell off sharply and economic growth rates

Table 3.14. *India: Central SOE shares in total production*

Sector	1968/69 %	1988/89 %
Coal	18	98
Lignite	100	100
Petroleum	51	100
Steel ingots	57	61
Saleable steel	56	54
Aluminum	..	48
Copper	..	100
Primary lead	100	100
Zinc	81	80
Nitrogenous fertilizer	74	46
Phosphate fertilizer	25	30

Source: BPE (1990), 5. For the decline in the share of SOE nitrogenous fertilizer production, see Levy (1988).

dropped proportionately, the public sector inertially maintained its grip on public resources (Rifaʿat, 7/30/90:9).

At the beginning of India's First Five Year Plan in 1950 there were only 5 SOEs, but by the end of the third plan the number had risen to 74. During the 1970s, despite the failure of the monsoons at the beginning of the decade, the oil shocks of the middle and end, and the war with Pakistan that gave rise to the founding of Bangladesh, the SOE sector grew to 186 enterprises; by 1985 to 214; and by 1989 to 239 with assets valued at $62.5 billion (see CMIE, 1983; BPE, 1984, 1990). The six largest corporations in India were all in the public sector and the top ten accounted for 55% of all invested public sector capital. The Steel Authority of India Ltd. and the Oil and Natural Gas Commission alone had net assets valued at more than the net assets of the large-scale private sector put together.

The level of market concentration of the central SOEs is very high. There are twenty firms in the energy sector that are monopolies; twenty-three more are monopolies in telecommunications, shipbuilding, nonferrous metals, aircraft, steel, and mining. Over one hundred manufacturing SOEs compete with the private sector but still control more than 60% of their markets (World Bank, 10/88). Table 3.14 shows the growth in market concentration over time.

Alongside the central public enterprise sector are some seven hundred

Table 3.15. *Mexico: State participation in gross industrial production by type of goods (%)*

Type of goods	1970	1975	1978	1981	1983
Nondurable consumer	2.0	2.5	4.3	4.7	5.5
Durable consumer	7.3	9.4	9.5	11.4	4.4
Nonpetroleum intermediates	10.9	11.4	11.8	14.7	15.2
Capital	5.9	5.9	5.4	6.7	8.3
Nonpetroleum subtotal	5.5	6.1	7.3	8.9	8.6
Refining, petrochemicals	94.2	96.4	94.8	94.1	95.8
Total state industry	10.0	11.3	11.4	12.7	16.2

Source: Adapted from Machado et al. (1986), 124.

state-level SOEs. In 1950 they numbered only fifty. They are poorly monitored, notoriously overstaffed and riddled with corruption, and are important cogs in state-level patronage machines. They are chronic loss makers, especially the state electricity boards and the state transport companies, and financially sick in that their debts are in excess of their net worth. These enterprises own net assets roughly equivalent to those of the central SOE sector with a total work force on the order of 2 million (see Mishra and Ravishankar, 1985:136–49; T. L. Sankar and J. S. Sarma, 1986, vol. 2:95–119; World Bank, 10/88, vol. 2; and T. L. Sankar et al., 2/25/89).

In Mexico between 1934 and 1946, 19 SOEs were founded including PEMEX (petroleum), Altos Hornos (steel), FERTIMEX (fertilizers), and CFE (electricity). The SOE sector grew steadily thereafter until 1970, when, under Echeverría, 160 new enterprises were founded or taken over. The period 1976–82 witnessed the addition of another 98 enterprises (Casar and Peres, 1988:34–36). On the eve of the 1982 crisis there were some 1,155 SOEs, about half of which were in the industrial sector. Moreover, public sector banks owned controlling shares in many enterprises both public and private. For instance, in 1984, NAFINSA's industrial group owned assets worth $11 billion (at the 1/1/85 exchange rate), generated sales of $360 million, and employed 157,000 (Tamayo, 1988:697).

The Mexican SOEs concentrated in intermediate goods but were dominant in no branch except petroleum and basic petrochemicals. However, with the 1982 bank nationalizations, the SOE sector became dominant in banking, social security, and health insurance (see Table 3.15). The administration of the Federal District of Mexico City was one of the largest entities. In addition the state owned the national lottery, monopolized telephone and telegraph services (Teléfonos de México, or TELMEX), power and light for Mexico City, two airlines, and the major trading company in agricultural products, Compañía Nacional de Subsistencias Populares (CONASUPO – see Urzúa, 1990).

In Turkey electoral politics have supplemented the inertial momentum of public sector expansion. As noted, even during the 1950s, when the Demokrat Party pledged itself to privatization, the politicians could not relinquish their grip on the SOEs or even slow their rate of creation. In the 1960s, the military deepened the public enterprise sector in industry to prepare Turkey for entry into the European Common Market (EC), while the politicians of the Justice Party continued the practices of their Demokrat forerunners. The 1970s witnessed electorally driven SOE expansion coupled with heavy external borrowing that produced the debt crisis of 1978–79.

As Turkey entered the 1980s it had some 32 large holding companies, designated as commercial state economic enterprises (SEEs), and another 10 conglomerates, known as public economic institutions, that were and are official monopolies or provide basic services to the Turkish people.[14] Altogether these holding companies and institutions owned 105 companies and another 40 subsidiaries. In 1985 the industrial SEEs accounted for 45% of the production of the top 500 firms, 27% of total industrial value-added and 45% of total industrial investment. Table 3.16 gives sectoral product shares of SOE undertakings.[15]

The SOE sectors of EIMT have all grown to some extent by the acquisition of failing private sector enterprises, or what the Indians call "sick" industries. In India this has become a political art form in which the state practically invites private entrepreneurs to run down their assets and to disinvest with the assurance that the state will take them over in the name of social equity. By the mid-1980s, the Indian government had tried to put a halt to the absorption of sick firms that contributed significantly to the overall SOE deficit, but counterpressures were substantial. In 1987, it was estimated there were 1,119 large-scale enterprises with negative net worth and debts outstanding on the order of $18 billion (in rupees equivalent), and more than 200,000 small-scale units similarly "sick," with outstanding debts of about $12 billion (Rangachari, 4/30/90).

State planners and politicians in EIMT have shared an interest in the expansion of the SOE sector. So too have state bankers. Specialized lending, especially in the industrial sector, has led over time to the conversion of private debt to public equity. We have already cited the example of NAFINSA in Mexico. To it should be added the take-over in the late 1970s, of SOMEX Bank (Sociedad Mexicana de Crédito Indus-

Bald comparisons

Table 3.16. *The share of Turkish SOEs in sectoral production, 1986*

Sector	SOE shares %
Minerals	90
Food, alcoholic beverages, tobacco	57
Textiles	15
Forest products	14
Paper	56
Petroleum, chemicals, rubber, plastic	68
Cement	21
Basic metals	49
Mineral products	15
Automotive industry	10
Electricity	91

Source: Turkish Republic, Yüksek Denetleme Kurulu (1987), 150.

trial), which itself controlled a large portfolio of private firms, and the banks nationalized in 1982 along with their enterprise portfolios, which, however, became immediate candidates for reprivatization under de la Madrid. The Mexican institution of *fideicomisos* (public funds or endowments) have been vehicles for funding and then bringing into the public sector a wide range of commercial activities. During the construction of the steel complex at Las Truchas (see Chapter 4), a special *fideicomiso* was set up to develop bakeries, laundries, and hotels at the site. Once in the grip of the *fideicomiso* and its bureaucracy, they could not be relinquished (Rey Romay, 1987:73–74).[16]

In Turkey, the government, through its financial intermediaries, especially the State Industrial Development Bank (DESIYAB), had large interests in thirty-five major private industrial firms. The state shares in equity ranged from 14% to 53%. These equity stakes were initiated by the Demokrat government in the 1950s as a kind of substitute for its unfulfilled promise of privatization. Similarly in India, the large public sector financial institutions owned from 15% to 50% of the equity in the top twenty-five private industrial firms, including 42% of India's most famous private enterprise, Tata Iron and Steel Corporation, or TISCO (see Nayar, 1989:373).

At a minimum, the countries of EIMT have asserted control over financial intermediation through their central banks combined with spe-

103

cialized investment banks for the domestic economy and for foreign trade. At various times, all four have extended public banking much further than that. India, until 1969, and Mexico, until 1982 (and once again after 1990), allowed considerable scope for private banking. Egypt and to a lesser extent Turkey brought most banking and insurance within the public sector. Even after fifteen years of the open-door policy in Egypt, the four major public sector banks held deposits six times greater than those of the 73 private deposit banks. In Turkey public sector banks controlled 51% of all deposits. Turkey's largest (and oldest, founded in 1865) bank is the Agricultural Bank, but the Iş Bank, founded by Atatürk and legally private, should probably be added to the public sector as it is 76% owned by the Treasury, the Atatürk Estate, and the Employees Pension and Mutual Aid Fund. In 1985 it had assets worth $4.6 billion and equity in more than 126 firms.

All four governments are heavily involved in agricultural commodities trade and the distribution of food products. The Food Corporation of India, established in 1965 after the monsoon failures, handles in excess of 10 million tons of grain every year. It is engaged in food processing and the maintenance of national buffer stocks. It sells food products at subsidized rates to Indian consumers, and its annual sales are second only to those of the Indian Oil Corporation. Of equal weight in the Mexican economy is CONASUPO, which trades in basic foods destined largely for low-income consumers. In the mid-1980s it distributed 39% of the beans, 19% of the corn, 44% of the wheat flour, and 21% of the rice consumed in the country. Egypt's Ministry of Supply and Primary Bank for Agricultural Credit, and Turkey's Soils Products Office (TMO) undertake similar operations in rural markets.

Such public agencies have supremely political tasks: Through administered prices they skim surplus from the agrarian sector for investment elsewhere while at the same time supplying a range of subsidized goods, primarily fertilizer, and credit to rural producers. The object is to lock in rural support for, or at least acquiescence to, the central authorities while providing wage goods to urban consumers and constituents.

The defense sectors of Egypt, India, and Turkey (but not Mexico) have in many ways been the anchor of public enterprise. The military from the outset saw heavy industry as an integral component of national security, and when senior officers such as Atatürk or Nasser became heads of state, defense and industrialization became two sides of the same coin. In India in 1962, after the disastrous military engagement with the PRC, Nehru lent all his weight to the promotion of defense industries and military research and development (Bernard, 1985:219–21). Today some of India's most technologically advanced industries are in the public defense sector.[17]

Turkey and Egypt also boast large military-industrial complexes that manufacture, frequently under license from foreign suppliers, a wide range of advanced weapons, aircraft, vehicles, and electronic surveillance systems. Both countries have become significant arms exporters, and during the Iran–Iraq war, Egypt found a multibillion-dollar customer in Iraq (*AI*, 4/25/88:22). Both defense establishments have invaded the civilian sectors of their societies. In the late 1980s in Egypt, defense industries were selling civilian goods, from refrigerators to heavy turbines, worth some £E450 million annually. Through the National Service Projects Organization, the military have entered into food production and infrastructure maintenance (see Springborg, 1989:95–134). In Turkey, the Armed Forces Mutual Support Fund (OYAK) was founded in the early 1960s as a pension fund for the officer corps. It has taken large equity stakes in a number of private and public enterprises, as well as joint ventures with foreign partners such as Renault (Ayres, 1983; Karaspan, 1987; Richards and Waterbury, 1990:chap. 13).

International donors and commercial creditors for years helped finance SOE expansion in EIMT and elsewhere (Babai, 1988) in the developing world. After all, the SOE sector constituted a large market the borrowings of which were almost invariably guaranteed by the state treasury. Even as the policy tide turned against SOE expansion, there were inertial forces at work here as well. For example, a Japanese consortium and the International Finance Corporation (IFC) helped fund the construction of the Dukhaila Sponge Iron project in Egypt's public sector. This project has external obligations of $600 million (*AI*, 2/29/88). In India it is a striking fact that between 1978 and 1988 the World Bank extended eleven credits and twenty-one loans to eleven Indian SOEs (including chronic loss makers such as Coal India and some state electricity boards) totaling more than $7 billion (World Bank, 1988, 7294-IN).

3. CONCLUSION

Although Egypt is in a realm of its own, all four countries' public sectors control substantial strategic resources in their economies. These resources can be used to promote desired development patterns, to dominate the political arena, and to fuel patronage networks and rent seeking. The sheer size of what is held should make it proportionately difficult to ease the state's grip on it (although Eastern Europe has shown that under certain circumstances this may not be the case). Moreover, political leaders of whatever stripe may be very reluctant to give up the leverage and control that the existing pattern of ownership provides them, even though such a course may make economic "sense" or even long-term political sense (see Chapters 6 through 9).

While ISI and public enterprise need not be theoretically or practically joined, in EIMT and many other developing countries they have been. The link is one between a strategy of growth and a prime instrument for implementing the strategy. In EIMT, the private sector and foreign capital were eschewed as instruments for the implementation of ISI in favor of state enterprise and the occupation of the commanding heights. Flaws in the strategy resulting from deficit financing, inflation, overvalued exchange rates, trade imbalances, and mounting debt were exacerbated by the chosen instrument, SOEs, which at the firm or sectoral level tended to replicate the malfunctioning of the state. Given their capital-intensive, import-hungry nature, their impact on all other imbalances of the macroeconomy proved to be particularly devastating. Until the strategy itself changed, the "system" generated few incentives to discipline the SOE sector.

4

Principals and agents: The characteristics of public enterprise performance

There is no evidence in EIMT that would challenge the proposition that SOE sectors are inherently less efficient in financial and economic terms than private enterprises. Each country can offer a few, oft-cited, exceptions in the SOE sector, but, as suggested in Chapter 1, there would not have been public enterprise in the first place had financial and economic profitability determined the state's investment priorities. This chapter examines the patterns of incentives and controls that drive SOE performance, and the evidence available comparing public and private enterprise performance in EIMT. We stress, once again, the interaction of these instruments of state strategy with the ISI strategy itself.

The starting point is the multiple missions assigned to the SOEs. Typically they have been called upon to promote industrialization, to raise the living standards of "backward" areas by locating in them, to carry out infrastructural development by building their own rail links and power plants, to generate employment whether needed or not, to yield financial surpluses for the state treasury, to absorb or develop new technologies, to supply cheap goods to poor populations, and eventually to compete with foreign suppliers of similar goods and services.[1]

It cannot and could not be done without the SOEs becoming a net drain on public resources. It is surprising this was not recognized at the outset, but as James Wilkie has shown (1990), in Latin America public enterprises were initially given great legal autonomy precisely because it was feared that the politicos would cannibalize what was predicted to be their high level of profits. The combination of high protective tariffs, oligopolized or monopolized sectors, and soft budget constraints *over time* produced the pathologically poor economic performance of SOEs. Initially, however, protection and oligopoly, coupled with the entry of the state into heavy industry, yielded in EIMT fairly high rates of growth.

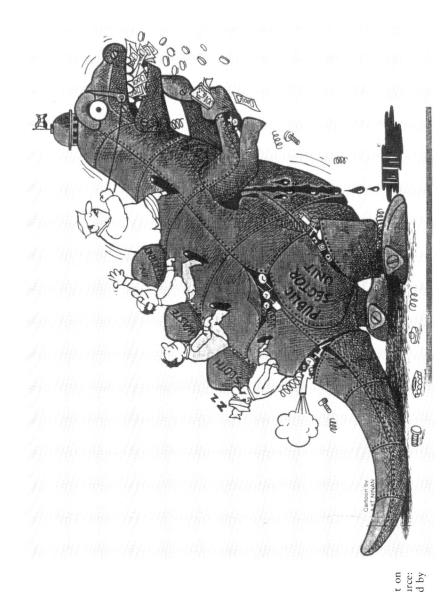

An Indian view of the assault on the commanding heights. Source: *India Today*, 9/15/91:64. Used by permission.

This is not, then, a story of consistent poor performance, or of laziness, corruption, or greed, but is, rather, one of the structure of tasks and incentives. Put another way, all the principals and agents involved – state supervisors and auditors, management, labor, suppliers, and creditors – have behaved in perfectly rational ways, maximizing their utilities within the structure of rewards and punishments offered them.[2]

Thus, when we try to understand who the principals are in the development and management of public assets, we should think not of profit-maximizing owners of capital but, rather, of a coalition of principals, including planners, state financiers and bankers, those who define national security interests, patronage politicians, and international creditors (see Aharoni, 1986:223). Each component of the coalition wants the SOE sector to serve different, and not always compatible, ends. The agents in this drama have to answer to many different masters who do not speak with one voice.

1. GOVERNMENT SUPERVISION AND CONTROL

In theory the taxpayers are the owners (principals) of the SOE sector. In terms of operational control taxpayers cannot effectively exercise their ownership rights and thus delegate them to the government. In systems with effective legislatures, the elected representatives of the citizenry hold the government accountable for the management of public property. It is safe to say that in EIMT only in India has there been such a legislature, and to a lesser extent in Turkey.[3] But the fact that all four countries have exhibited similar pathologies of SOE performance leads one to conclude that the problems inherent in public ownership overwhelm mechanisms of legislative monitoring.

We can learn a good deal about principal–agent issues from the experience of the command economies of Eastern Europe. Stripped of ideological baggage, these economies functioned according to three principles: production by plan, consumption by entitlement, and distribution by state prebends. In EIMT the market has had a much larger role in all three domains, but for policy makers the market was seen, at least initially, as more of a hindrance than as a tool. Although automaticity in economic transactions was at a minimum, the plan itself was frequently more an elaborate bargain arrived at by various government claimants than a rational blueprint for coherent public intervention. Planners acted as brokers among sectoral lobbies, driven by the power of lobbies and by the depth of systemic emergencies, yielding to the most powerful until the resulting crises in other sectors required emergency treatment.

One way to satisfy everyone was to give in to expansion in all domains.

Economic failure had no meaning for principals or agents so there was insatiable investment hunger. The state sector became both capital and labor intensive. Because there was no meaningful exit option for failing firms, the SOE sector tended to accumulate over time a mix of state-of-the-art enterprises alongside technological dinosaurs burdened with immobile labor. These command economies were characterized by chronic shortages of goods owing essentially to the unlimited demand of public firms. These were then met by massive imports of raw materials and technology that had little to do with any search for comparative advantage in international markets (Kornai, 9/10/81:966–69; Przeworski, 1991:chap. 4).[4]

There are many layers of principals and agents in the typical SOE sector, and depending on location any given official may play both roles. There is nothing neatly hierarchical about where one is located in this system. Hazim Beblawi, chairman of Egypt's EXIM Bank, lamented (*AI*, 1/1/90:24) that "despite the fact I am one of the specialists of economic policy in Egypt, I do not know where this policy is made. Is it the Central Bank, or the Minister of Economy, or the Council of Ministers?"

In Egypt and India in particular, what binds the actors are complex rules, premised on the expectation that in their absence public agents will abuse their power. By one account, Egypt has 58,000 acts, laws, and decrees that regulate economic transactions for the economy as a whole (*AI*, 3/22/91:7). Controls in India can be broken down as follows: a priori on all senior appointments and investments; *directives*, reflecting immediate governmental concerns; *circulars*, which are highly detailed and unilateral; *reviews*, monthly, trimonthly, and annual; *auditing*, through three separate auditing bodies; *investigation*, carried out by the Central Bureau of Investigation to detect criminal activities. All of these are contained in a two-volume, 1,200-page compendium (BPE, 1985; for Egypt, see Tawfik, Majeed, and Obeid, 1977). These are systems of controls without corresponding incentives in which sins of commission weigh more heavily than those of omission, although neither counts for much. It has been estimated that in India the typical project proposal of an SOE requires 637 days to move through the approval procedure. Key supervisory bodies that can block any investment include the Public Investment Board, the budget division of the Ministry of Finance, the National Planning Commission, the Foreign Investment Board, and the Reserve Bank of India. The labyrinthine approval procedures lead to large cost overruns. For 133 projects surveyed by the World Bank (10/88) overruns averaged 100% of the original estimated costs. In such a context, entrepreneurial behavior by an SOE manager would seem foolhardy at best, especially when appointments to the position of CEO are for a maximum of two years with the possibility of renewal.

At least one analyst (Ramamurti, 1987:880) has tried to delineate the Indian coalition of principals that controls the SOE sector. It consists of 7–10 ministers, 30–40 senior bureaucrats, 20–30 people in the media, 10–20 union leaders, and 20 members of the Lok Sabha (parliamentarians). None of these have a direct stake in the economic performance of the SOEs they influence, but all may have constituency or political agendas that they seek to pursue through the SOEs. India's Bureau of Public Enterprises was initially set up to protect the SOEs from excessive particularistic interference, but under Rajiv Gandhi the BPE was captured by the Ministry of Finance, which used it to assert financial control over them.

A former chief executive officer (CEO), Dr. N. C. B. Nath, laid out for me (interview, 5/14/86) "Nath's Laws" of Indian public enterprise. First, SOEs have no corporate culture of their own. Each CMD (chairman and managing director) has mixed political, economic, and administrative goals. Management will espouse whichever one is perceived to be dominant and then drop it when the CMD leaves. Second, ownership and control are never voluntarily separated. Instead, every SOE is governed by a troika of the minister, the secretary, and the CMD. The troika is inherently unstable. All three may have different agendas leading to paralysis. Two may ally against one, but ministers and CMDs change positions frequently. Nath suggested that perhaps the upper echelons of the civil service should be politicized so that they too would change frequently. Finally, every CMD wants to become a secretary or join the National Planning Commission with the rank of minister. The CMD-ship has little value in itself.

To Nath's Laws the following may be added. If there are weak penalties for poor managerial performance, or such performance can be masked by attributing it to failures in other parts of the SOE sector (e.g., power outages, poor-quality raw materials, lack of foreign exchange, administered prices, etc.), then profit maximization or total factor productivity maximization will figure low among managerial priorities, coming behind maneuvering for the next post, perk seeking, and personal aggrandizement.

Looking at all four countries, the formal structure of ownership and monitoring includes about five principal bodies: the planning ministry or agency, the treasury or ministry of finance, the council of ministers or some ministerial committee drawn from it, the direct supervisory ministry for a particular group of SOEs, an auditing agency, and the legislature to which the auditing agency typically presents its annual report.

2. SOFT BUDGETS AND NO-EXIT

Until very recently in EIMT financial extravagance was virtually riskless for SOE management because treasury-guaranteed loans would simply be rolled over (or on occasion converted into public equity) and enterprises could not legally or practically be liquidated or sold. As long as other sectors of the economy could be taxed (agriculture, mineral exports, worker remittances) and money borrowed abroad, the growing SOE and public deficits could be financed.

In the mid-1970s Turkey's public spending, driven partially by electoral politics but also by the sharp increase in the price of imported petroleum, spun out of control. The public sector borrowing requirement (PSBR) as a proportion of GDP more than doubled between 1973 and 1977. The budget deficit actually declined in these years, but the financial deficits of the SOEs (whose prices were held down administratively) increased sharply, accounting for 65% of the PSBR in 1979. Despite the reform efforts after 1980, by the end of the decade budgetary transfers to the SOEs began to grow again, and the Central Bank and the Treasury signed a protocol in March 1989 that was designed to tie the hands of the Treasury in extending credit to the SOEs and in funding the deficit. By 1991 there was evidence that the protocol was breaking down, owing in part to the Gulf War, but also to public sector salary increases and growing SOE borrowing.

Mexico's public deficit (*déficit de caja*) reached 16% of GDP in 1982, declined to 7% in 1984 and surged again to 14% in 1987. During the 1980s the SOE sector was squeezed by maintaining low prices during periods of high inflation and paying higher interest rates on its mounting debts. Despite the growing claims of the SOEs on credit and budget transfers, their contribution to the public deficit remained modest. Manufacturing SOEs accounted for only 5%–7% of the public deficit, whereas PEMEX, even as oil prices fell, generated a surplus. The entities that contributed the most to the public deficit were CFE (electricity) and CONASUPO (food products). The soft budget constraint in Mexico has applied less to the SOEs than to the federal government, which year in and year out generates more than 90% of the public deficit (Casar and Peres, 1988:96–97; Tamayo, 1988:729–31; Urzúa, 1990:table 1).

Between 1970 and 1989 India manifested an interesting trend: The external debt shrank as a proportion of GDP from 15% to 7%, whereas the domestic debt rose from 30% to 56%. Indian financial authorities began to lose their grip on borrowing and money supply in the mid-1980s. During the Seventh Five Year Plan, 1984–90, the domestic debt as a proportion of GDP grew from 42% to 56%. Bhattacharya and Guha

(4/14/90:781) note that the net worth of the Indian government's physical and financial assets was about equivalent to its total liabilities.

At the beginning of the seventh plan, Rajiv Gandhi announced what amounted to a hard budget constraint. The SOEs were expected to finance the bulk of their investment out of operating surpluses and commercial borrowing. SOE operating surpluses were forecast to be 354 billion rupees or $25 billion over the plan period, but as the Ministry of Finance's *Economic Survey* (1989/90:7; see also *Mainstream,* 1/6/90) noted, the "contribution of public enterprise fell short of projections by a significant amount." In fact, 66 of 244 central SOEs posted losses for three consecutive years up to 1990, and SOE defaults on loans from public sector banks contributed in a major way to the increase in domestic debt (Bhattacharya and Guha, 4/14/90:784 and *India Today,* 5/31/91:69). In general, instead of funding two-thirds of their needs out of their own resources, the SOEs funded only about a third, a level inferior to what had been achieved in the previous plan period (Gupta, 1988:2697; BPE, 1989:table 1.24; *The Statesman,* 4/30/90:8).

Egyptian SOEs borrowed, until 1991, at preferential rates 5% below the market rates available to the private sector. Most of the borrowing came from the National Investment Bank, under the supervision of the Ministry of Planning. Moreover, most SOE borrowing has been unsecured. In 1988 unsecured loans totaled £E 2.6 billion in the manufacturing sector against £E 716 million in secured loans (USAID, 1990:26).[5]

The Egyptian government, aside from the war of attrition years from 1967 to 1972, has seldom been able to exercise any self-restraint. For example, in the budget year 1987–88 government expenditures were projected to be £E 23 billion; the gross public deficit to be £E 4.9 billion, and the net deficit £E 680 million. The actual figures were £E 33 billion, £E 14.4 billion, and £E 5 billion (*AI,* 12/24/90:19).

The soft budget constraint contributes directly to the capital intensity of SOEs noted at the beginning of this section. It also burdens the SOEs with heavy debt-servicing requirements, at least in theory. This is particularly serious for new enterprises with large sunk costs and unproven competitiveness. Mexico's last large public steel complex, Siderúrgica Lázaro Cárdenas (SICARTSA), started life with $766 million in sunk costs and $1.5 billion in liabilities (Maza, 2/10/86:8). Even nationalized industries present similar financial profiles. In 1987–88, Coal India's principal and interest payments due were 4.7 billion rupees, of which it managed to pay only 10%. The World Bank has estimated that if market-clearing interest rates were charged in Egypt on loans to SOEs, most would go bankrupt.[6] If, by contrast, SOE debts are nonperforming, public sector banks will operate in the red.

113

In various ways SOEs are indebted to one another. They accumulate substantial arrears in payments for goods and services from other SOEs. The railroads are often victimized by those firms for which they haul goods or move passengers. There can be a kind of imploding chain of missed payments. The railroads may be denied financing for expansion. They delay payment to engineering firms or to iron and steel complexes for goods contracted and delivered. The latter may in turn postpone payment to the electricity authority for power used. In Egypt cumulative arrears in payments among SOEs reached 2% of GDP in 1990 (Sharif, 10/15/90:19). No SOE in Egypt has ever stopped trading with another for payment failure. More likely is the arrangement worked out between the notorious loss maker, Misr Dairy, and the armed forces. Misr Dairy sells the army perishable and defective milk products for which there is no domestic market, while the armed forces give Misr Dairy IOUs. This produces a variant on the old saw: They pretend to sell us usable goods; we pretend to pay them.[7]

When one nets out petroleum exports and rent-generating assets like the Suez Canal, the SOE sector in EIMT constitutes a net drain on foreign exchange. Egyptian SOEs in the late 1980s had foreign-exchange needs (capital and imports) of more than $4 billion, whereas they generated only $300 million in exports (Sharif, 1989; USAID, 1990:table 1.3). Similarly, Turkey's public sector net trade balance in 1989 was −$2.7 billion whereas the private sector's was +$996 million (TÜSIAD, 1990:111). In recent years more than half of Turkey's SOE financing needs have come from foreign credits. Mexican exports in 1985 totaled $21.8 billion. The private sector accounted for $7 billion, the petroleum sector for $14 billion, and the rest of the SOEs for $700 million (Casar and Peres, 1988:101).

Until the liquidation of Fundidora de Monterrey in 1986, there was no example in EIMT of a major SOE being shut down for insolvency. In Egypt it has been illegal to liquidate an SOE, although that has changed since 1991. In India the guiding principle was that SOEs enjoying high market concentration would have to set their prices within a certain range of the CIF cost of similar imported goods. If the SOE could not earn a profit in such an environment it could (1) be liquidated or (2) be given tariff protection. The World Bank notes laconically (10/88): "The first solution has never been used."[8] In Turkey in 1950 a commission of experts, chaired by Professor Abraham Hirsch of Istanbul University, was constituted to draft plans for the transfer of SOEs to the private sector. "No act of conversion by the Commission was ever registered" (Aysan and Özmen, 1981:53).

No-exit exacerbates the financial drain of SOEs on public resources. Budgetary protection and bailouts of the weak effectively discourage new entrants into certain sectors. Resources are diverted to the crippled, lead-ing eventually to the crippling of the healthy. Finally, the no-exit policy discourages technological innovation, as SOEs are under no competitive pressure to raise productivity nor to enter new markets with new products.[9]

3. PROFITS AND LOSSES

The decision to set up a public sector is, therefore, congruent with the decision not to maximize profits. To create a public sector and then to ask it to do what the private sector would have done is like going to the cinema to try to sleep rather than see the movie (Amartya Sen, 1975, as cited in Ramamurti, 1987:892).

The petroleum sectors of EIMT have earned steady profits since the early 1970s, and the volume of their profitable operations has been suf-ficient to offset the losses run up in most of the remaining SOEs. By whatever measure – profits to net assets, profits to sales, and so on – the SOE sectors have generated extraordinarily low returns. The debate then turns on the issue of the opportunity costs for public investments as against the welfare gains in job creation, technological innovation, and national security.[10]

Over the period 1973–87, the net rate of return on capital invested in Egypt's public sector fell from 5.2% in the first year, to 1.9% in 1982–83, and then to 1.7% in the last year (USAID, 1990:table 1.2). In the period 1985–89 the cumulative losses of public authorities reached £E 1.3 billion (these include the railroads, construction, land reclamation, Damietta Port [Qadi, 8/3/87]), and those of the industrial SOEs £E 1.2 billion, concentrated in textiles and electronics (*AI*, 9/8/89:27; Sharif, 9/11/89).

India's Bureau of Public Enterprises, in its 1989 survey, looked at 164 SOEs not in the petroleum sector, which has been a consistent profit maker, and not in the pool of sick industrial loss makers taken over by the state. The survey found that the rate of return on capital employed in the 164 firms was 1.7% in manufacturing and 1.9% in services (BPE, 1990:17). In the same year ten firms accounted for 73% of all SOE profits (Patil, 1989:271–74; BPE, 1990:14).

Some chronic loss makers, such as SAIL (steel), moved into the black, however briefly, at the end of the 1980s, but for the most part the loss makers were all too well known. By 1990 the state electricity boards had cumulative losses equivalent to $2 billion, and they ran up $7 billion in debts during the seventh plan period. The return on their invested capital has declined to − 10% (World Bank, 3/90:39; *India Today*, 9/30/90:67). Also at the state level, the road transport corporations and irrigation projects have contributed substantially to the losses (Sankar, Mishra, and

Nandgopal, 1991). At the central level Coal India has cumulative losses equivalent to $1.3 billion; the National Textile Corporation (comprising many sick units), nearly $900 million; and the Fertilizer Corporation of India, about $700 million. The cumulative losses of the Delhi Transport Corporation were twice its paid-up capital. Fifty-five other SOEs had cumulative losses that exceeded their paid-up capital as of March 1987 (Sarma, 4/90:9).

In Mexico a similar picture emerges, except not until the early 1980s was the petroleum sector able to compensate for the losses of the other sectors. After-tax losses in the industrial SOEs, including PEMEX, averaged 1.4% of GDP between 1970 and 1975, 2.3% between 1976 and 1980, and 3.6% in 1981–82. Only in 1983–84, when petroleum before-tax earnings reached 10% of GDP, did the entire industrial sector move into the black with net profits of 1% of GDP (Casar and Peres, 1998:97). However, as already noted, the major public sector loss makers are outside industry: the railroads, CONASUPO, and CFE. In the manufacturing sector, SICARTSA (steel) and FERTIMEX (fertilizers) have registered continuous losses. By contrast, the bulk of medium and small-scale SOEs operating in competitive markets have posted consistent albeit modest profits (World Bank, 5/22/89:9).

The crisis that began to build in Turkey in the late 1970s was fueled by the need to finance the growing deficits of the SOEs. These had been obliged to take on unneeded employment and electorally driven wage increases during a period of rapidly rising costs of imported energy. In these years the SOEs were permitted no significant price increases. Only three SOEs registered profits in those years: the Turkish Electricity Corporation (TEK), Sümerbank, and the Sugar Corporation (Hale, 1981:198–99). From 1975 through 1978 the entire SOE sector operated heavily in the red (Kepenek: 1990:91).

A major facet of the policy shifts following the military take-over of 1980 was allowing the SOEs to raise their prices. This they did regularly throughout the 1980s, with two very large increases in 1983 and following the elections in 1987–88. The increases generally outstripped inflation and clearly contributed to it. This was part of a demand management strategy that freed up intermediate goods from the domestic economy at large and made them available to the export sector. At a stroke (or two) the SOE sector was transformed into a generator of profits. Nonetheless, in the second half of the 1980s the ratio of profits to sales of the SOEs has steadily declined from 9% in 1985 to 1.8% in 1989. Preliminary estimates for 1990 indicate that some twenty-two of fifty-four SOEs registered losses, including the railroads, Turkish Hard Coal Company, the Turkish Cellulose and Paper Corporation (SEKA), and Turkish Electricity. The eight largest loss makers in 1990 totaled more than $1 billion

116

in losses (*The Turkish Times*, 6/1/91; see also Istanbul Chamber of Commerce, 1990:65).[11]

4. PRODUCTIVITY AND COSTS OF PRODUCTION

Every facet of an SOE's costs can be determined administratively. On the plus side, SOEs typically borrow at preferential rates, purchase foreign exchange at an overvalued exchange rate, and receive subsidized inputs and energy. On the negative side, they are often set up with unmanageable debt–equity ratios, are obliged to sell their goods and services at subsidized prices, tasked with developing extensive social infrastructure, and saddled with unwanted employees. Because so many SOEs dominate if not monopolize the markets in which they participate, some form of regulated pricing is inevitable.

Market concentration also means that price adjustments, without any change in the structural characteristics of the firm, can dramatically improve or harm its profitability and productivity. What little improvement there has been in Egypt's SOEs in recent years is probably because of administered price increases (*AI*, 2/5/90:38). The trade-offs are not simple. In Mexico from 1960 to 1983, SOE prices consistently lagged behind the general price index, but at the cost of mounting deficits (Casar and Peres, 1988:89). In Turkey, throughout most of the 1980s, SOE prices rose more rapidly than the general price index, thus fueling inflation.

Costs of production vary, of course, from industry to industry. Because the state can set general public sector wage levels, the price at which SOEs borrow, and the cost of raw materials, it is not very useful to compare costs within or among the SOE sectors of EIMT. For instance, India's Bureau of Public Enterprises surveyed costs for all of India's central SOEs. It found that *on average* raw materials and stocks accounted for 55% of total costs, wages about 10%, energy 6%, depreciation 6%, repairs and maintenance .5%, and interest 5% (BPE, 1990:9).[12]

The infamous Misr Dairy Company encapsulates all that inhibits increased productivity. Coincident with the opening of the Egyptian market to competition in dairy products, Misr Dairy had to absorb a 70% increase in the price of state-supplied sugar, yet it had also to hold down its prices. Simultaneously it lost its contract with the armed forces. The manager of the plant appealed to the head of the food-processing sectoral organization for relief suggesting three options: close the plant; renew the contract with the armed forces; raise prices. The matter eventually was bucked up to the Minister of Industry, who suggested that Misr Dairy undertake an advertising campaign. There is more than a little irony in this as Misr Dairy at that point in time did not accept checks, had no proper accounts, and no telex. £E2 million later, sales continued to decline while perishable inventories mounted. The plant started to reduce the amount of milk in plastic containers without changing the price. The plant contracted to import cheap powdered milk, but the shipment was impounded by customs officials who found the powdered milk to contain high levels of radiation. The manager of the plant was then "retired" by the Minister of Industry. The source of this vignette visited the plant on numerous occasions and found that the staff and workers were relieved that some outsider had come to see just how bad the situation had become.

In critiques of SOEs, excess labor is often given pride of place, but the Indian data would indicate that it is in the use of raw materials rather than labor that savings can be made. More than the cost of labor, it is low productivity that may drag down specific SOEs. For example, in the mid-1970s, Hindustan Steel Ltd. (HSL) produced 57 tons of steel per worker-year, whereas in the USSR the rate was 170 tons, in the United States, 220 tons, and in Japan, 280 tons (Gupta, 1977:131). In the main plant of Egypt's spinning and weaving complex at Mehallah al-Kubra, the 35,000 workers in the mid-1970s achieved rates of kilograms spun per person-hour that were 40% of Tunisia's level and 15% of the Common Market's (USAID, 6/76).[13]

One measure frequently used in assessing productivity in SOEs is total factor productivity (TFP). By this measure Handoussa, Nishimizu, and Page (1986:67–69) found that Egypt's SOE sector showed marked improvement in the period 1973–79 even though its financial balances had deteriorated. They speculated that the improvement was because of better capacity utilization, which had been very low following the 1967 military defeat. A subsequent World Bank report (3/87) bore them out. By 1987, TFP was in decline and the financial balances continued to worsen. After 1973, at the cost of heavy deficit financing and external borrowing, Egypt managed to overcome some of the capital and raw materials obstacles that had plagued the SOEs after 1967. Nothing, however, was done to change their management performance, technology, quality control, and market orientation. The gains from higher capacity utilization could not be sustained.

In the past fifteen years, particularly after the expansionary 1970s during which SOEs borrowed heavily, the interest component of overall costs has taken on major proportions. This merely reflects the increasing debt-servicing component in overall public expenditures. From the outset, SOEs have been capital intensive and, as we noted for India, often start off life with heavy debts. It was assumed that they would produce their way out of debt, but for a host of reasons that was seldom the case. Start-up cost overruns were the rule, economies of scale were long in being reached owing to limited markets, and capacity utilization was

118

typically low. This meant that capital was used very inefficiently. The World Bank estimated that the incremental capital output ratio in India increased from 4 in the 1950s to 10 in the 1960s and 1970s. The estimate for Egypt in the 1980s was 9. The investment needs of inefficient SOEs were met by rolling over loans and extending new lines of public credit. The end of the expansionary phase in the early 1980s saw a sharp increase in borrowing rates coupled with severe capital shortage.

In this vein, Turkey can stand as proxy for the other three countries. Between 1984 and 1988, servicing on the domestic and external debt rose from 12% to 23% of total budgetary outlays or from 3.4% to 8% of GDP (Öniş, 1989:75). With respect to the SOEs, the share of interest payments in value-added rose from 23% in 1982 to 50% in 1988. The share of wages declined from 66% to 35%, while the share of profits fell in a range between 44% (due to price increases in 1984) and 14% in 1988 (Yüksek Denetleme Kurulu, 1988:33).

For the reasons to which Sen cryptically alluded at the beginning of this section, it is generally the case in EIMT that according to most standard measures, private enterprise outperforms public. As noted in Chapter 1, there is no theoretic reason why this need be so. The costs of monitoring public enterprises are likely to be less than those of monitoring the private sector. What Shapiro and Willig call informational rents (1990:82) are also likely to be lower.[14] If credit and product markets are competitive, and if firms are allowed to fail, then public enterprises should perform as well as private.

Sometimes they do. But the conditions mentioned above seldom apply: Credit is subsidized, markets protected, and SOEs prohibited from exit. Because policy makers have structured the competition in this manner, they could also structure it in radically different ways, but they do not. Outside of Taiwan and South Korea, policy makers have perpetuated regimes that sustain political coalitions but damage productivity. Indeed, a significant part of the private sector is drawn into the regime and comes to thrive on privilege rather than on competition.

Evidence from India is telling. Subsidies and tariff protection have sheltered both public and private enterprise. Some twenty-one sectors are highly protected, and they pay wages 70% higher and use five times as much capital on average as firms in less protected sectors. Moreover, India's monopoly laws have had the perverse effect of restricting entry to oligopolized sectors. More than half of the country's industrial sectors have four-firm concentration ratios between 80% and 100% (*The Economist*, 5/4/91:11).

Whether or not their regulatory regimes are the same, empirical studies tend to show systematic differences in performance between public and private enterprise. Picot and Kaulmann (1989) compared the performance of public and private firms in the Fortune 500 that were exposed to domestic and international competition in credit, product, and management markets. The results showed that public firms exhibited lower rates of labor productivity, returns on assets, profits, and equity to assets ratios (see also Ayub and Hegsted, 1/87:84–85; and Aharoni, 1986:176–79; Nayar, 1991). There is no contrary evidence from EIMT.

The evidence, however, is not consistent across countries, sectors, and time. We have already emphasized the impact of administered price changes on every aspect of performance. Because many of the largest SOEs are capital intensive and technologically advanced, they may exhibit significantly higher rates of labor productivity than the private sector. Over the decade 1975 to 1985 labor productivity in Mexico's manufacturing sector (without PEMEX) was consistently higher in the public than in the private sector (Tamayo, 1988:667).[15] This has also been the case for the Turkish chemical and petroleum sectors, but in textiles, paper, and metallic products private sector labor is more productive than public (Karataş, 1989: Table 10:5; see also Özmucur and Karataş, 1990:299). Table 4.1 shows for Turkey what the impact of an administered increase in SOE prices can do to relative performance indicators. A major increase went through in 1983 with smaller ones in subsequent years. Although the private sector outperformed the public over the seven-year period, by 1985 the SOE profits–sales ratio had surged past the private.[16] In all other areas the private sector maintained a clearly superior position.

5. NET FLOWS BETWEEN PRINCIPALS AND AGENTS

At their inceptions, the SOE sectors of EIMT were expected to generate a steady surplus for the state treasury through taxes and shares in profits. Moreover, with the exception of enterprises providing basic services, they were expected to finance most of their own investment needs. Of course, these expectations turned out to be wildly optimistic outside the petroleum sector. It has been argued here that the political logic of the public property regime will lead to the breakdown of financial discipline, but the rate at which that occurs varies considerably.

India and Egypt experienced the malaise early on: during India's Second Five Year Plan and in Egypt by the end of the first plan. Turkey and Mexico offer contrasting examples. From 1939 to 1963, Turkish SOEs financed 73% of their own investment needs, and they paid in cumulative taxes a third more than their total investment (Rockwell's comments on, and in, Land, 1971:86). The 1970s, for reasons already set forth, saw the SOEs come to constitute a net drain on the treasury and a major contributor to the economic crisis at the end of the decade (see Table 4.2; Kepenek, 1990:82).

Public enterprise performance

Table 4.1. *Productivity and rate of profit in 500 largest firms in Turkey*

		Profit Sales (%)	Profit Equity (%)	Profit Total assets (%)	Value-added per worker ('000 TL)	Value-added Total assets (%)
1980						
	Public (79)	4.80	16.16		2179.1[a]	..
	Private (421)	10.47	50.69		3054.6[a]	..
1981						
	Public (64)	3.81	22.04		3477.8[a]	..
	Private (431)	8.22	42.87		4831.8[a]	..
1982						
	Public (64)	5.49	25.28	4.79	1581.7	23.04
	Private (431)	6.47	37.55	9.38	2102.2	39.08
1983						
	Public (74)	4.44	25.62	4.24	1156.6	14.47
	Private (426)	6.88	48.98	10.48	2467.7	35.43
1984						
	Public (84)	6.45	26.23	8.25	2495.7	20.11
	Private (416)	6.99	37.83	9.99	3943.2	33.24
1985						
	Public (94)	10.77	34.57	10.80	3853.0	17.40
	Private (406)	6.05	41.06	9.46	5699.9	33.71
1986						
	Public (91)	7.80	25.58	7.32	7831.3	27.06
	Private (409)	6.09	39.93	9.02	9245.9	35.59

[a]Sales from production/number of workers.

Source: Öniş and Özmucur (1988b), 72.

Table 4.2. *Consolidated budget of Turkey, 1973–89 (TL billions, current)*

Year	Budget deficit (A)	Financial requirements of SOEs (B)	Budget transfers to SOEs (C)	Public sector borrowing requirement (A+B-C)	Financial requirements of SOEs/GNP %
1973	5.1	14.2	6.1	13.2	4.6
1974	7.4	22.3	7.2	22.5	5.2
1975	8.5	30.6	10.3	28.8	5.7
1976	13.6	47.8	16.2	45.2	7.1
1977	53.1	58.3	27.8	83.0	6.7
1978	37.1	86.3	39.5	83.9	6.7
1979	87.1	186.1	83.4	189.8	8.5
1980	171.6	264.1	152.9	282.8	6.4
1981	112.8	434.7	229.5	318.0	4.8
1982	197.2	464.7	191.4	470.5	5.0
1983	344.2	594.7	278.1	660.8	6.0
1984	902.2	753.3	238.8	1416.7	7.7
1985	635.0	968.6	171.0	1432.6	5.0
1986	1073.0	1008.0	140.0	1941.0	5.0
1987	2598.0	1821.0	446.0	3973.0	6.8
1988	3440.0	3064.1	1007.5	5496.6	5.5
1989	9404.0	3415.8	1108.2	8799.6	5.0

Note: Public sector borrowing requirement: budget deficit + financial requirements of SOEs – budget transfers.

Sources: State Planning Organization, Ministry of Finance, as presented in Öniş and Özmucur, *The Role of the Financial System* (1988a); Central Bank of the Republic of Turkey, *Annual Report: 1988* (1989); Istanbul Chamber of Commerce, *Economic Report* (1990), 56–57, 66.

Similarly in Mexico, SOEs financed three quarters of their investment programs over the period 1939–60. The proportion fell moderately to 68% during the 1960s (Hansen, 1974:46–47). It was during the 1970s that fiscal discipline broke down in both countries. By 1980 in Mexico, budget transfers to the nonfinancial SOEs reached 5% of GDP (PEMEX included in the calculation), but with the austerity measures after 1983, the level tapered off to between 2.3% and 3% of GDP for the rest of the decade (Urzúa, 1990:45). The details of this deterioration are presented in Table 4.3.

The economic crises that Mexico and Turkey experienced in the 1980s led to marked reductions in public investment outlays. In Turkey public investment in industry was sharply curtailed, and the State Investment

Table 4.3. *Financial indicators of SOEs in federal budget (excluding PEMEX) (in constant 1978 Mexican $ '000 million)*

	1978	1979	1980	1981	1982	1983	1984	1985	1986
Net sales revenues	174.9	185.4	192.0	201.9	221.0	198.9	244.1	228.3	219.9
Wages	64.9	68.8	72.5	84.1	95.1	73.8	69.9	69.3	61.9
Other direct costs	112.7	109.9	128.9	161.5	146.5	161.7	189.8	161.4	152.8
Gross margin (before interest)	-2.7	6.8	-9.4	-43.7	-20.6	-36.5	-15.6	-2.4	5.2
Interest	15.5	18.7	23.4	26.7	37.8	57.4	62.1	53.8	38.2
Internal cash generation	-18.2	-11.9	-32.8	-70.5	-58.4	-93.9	-77.7	-56.2	-33.0
Investment	55.5	72.0	91.7	84.6	80.4	57.0	55.2	54.1	48.1
Financial gap (before net debt flows and govt. transfer)	-73.8	-83.9	-124.5	-155.0	-138.8	-150.9	-132.8	-110.3	-81.1
Government transfers	52.3	60.2	86.0	101.3	114.7	117.0	104.5	97.6	76.5
Cash available for debt amortization (i.e. principal)	-21.5	-23.7	-38.6	-53.7	-24.1	-33.9	-28.3	-12.6	-4.5
Gross mrgn/net sales (%)	-1.6	3.7	-4.9	-21.6	-9.3	-18.4	-6.4	-1.1	2.4
Financ. gap/net sales (%)	-42.2	-45.3	-64.9	-76.8	-62.8	-75.9	-54.4	-48.3	-36.9

Source: Compiled from World Bank data.

Bank, which had been the primary source of industrial credits, was converted into an Export–Import Bank (EXIM). The SOEs continued to receive about 45% of a very much reduced public investment program. This did not mean they were starved for funds. They went into international capital markets for project credits. By the late 1980s well over half the financial needs of the SOEs were obtained through foreign sources, while about a third came through direct budget transfers. The SOEs, in 1989, held about $4 billion in medium- and long-term foreign debt (Kepenek, 1990:86; TÜSIAD, 1/90:43, 115). Similarly, Mexican SOEs in the same year held $25 billion in foreign debt, $14 billion of which was held by PEMEX alone (*Uno Mas Uno,* 1/18/89:13).

There are several instruments through which the state can channel resources to the SOEs that do not show up in estimates of net resource flows. In Egypt, for example, the subsidy element in the provision of electrical power and fuel has been enormous, and rates and prices have systematically favored the public sector. The Nag Hammadi aluminum complex consumes more than 50% of the entire electrical output of the Aswan High Dam at a price per kilowatt hour (kwh) that is only a third of its marginal cost. The subsidy for one year's energy consumption at Nag Hammadi was about $45 million in 1989 ('Iz al-Din, 10/30/89:70–74). Industry in general consumes about a third of Egypt's total annual energy supply, and in 1989 the implicit subsidy for industrial energy consumption was £E 2.8 billion or 5% of GDP (Sharif, 1990b/:31; *Financial Times,* 6/24/91).

Credit subsidies on rapidly increasing SOE debt (not to mention treasury guarantees on SOE foreign debt) reduce the volume of payments from the SOEs to the government. If such subsidies are taken into account, the modest Turkish SOE profits registered after 1983 are turned into significant losses. In addition, off-budget funds are an important source of loans to SOEs, and in India finance more than 40% of central public enterprise investment needs. The sources include the Steel Development Fund, the Oil Industry Development Board, commercial borrowing from public sector banks, guaranteed bond issues, and inter-SOE deposits. About 12% of Indian SOE financial requirements come through foreign project credits (Gupta, 1988:2698).

It is common for governments to pay compensation to SOEs that suffer losses because of administered pricing arrangements. In Turkey, so-called duty losses are calculated as the difference between costs and administered prices plus 10% of the difference. In the 1950s duty loss payments did not exceed 1% of the state budget, but in the period 1974–85 they rose to 8%. Despite the sharp increases in SOE prices and profits in the mid-1980s, duty loss payments did not decline until 1987 (Kepenek, 1990:128–29; Yüksek Denetleme Kurulu, 1990:82).

Public enterprise performance

When measuring the net flow of resources as the difference between SOE profit shares and tax payments to the treasury, and budget transfer and direct subsidies to the SOEs, with the exception of brief periods the flow has been in favor of the SOEs when the petroleum sector is excluded. The net flow in India in the late 1980s has averaged well over $2 billion per annum in favor of the central SOEs (the flow at the state level is much greater; World Bank, 10/88:table 2.3; BPE, 1990:table 1.25).

Egypt's and Turkey's SOEs were the beneficiaries of net flows of public resources throughout the 1970s and into the early 1980s. Turkish SOEs reversed the flow after 1980 in favor of the treasury by higher profits (and hence higher corporate tax payments and shared profits) through administered price increases. Budget transfers have grown slowly, and State Investment Bank loans were completely terminated in 1988. The result was that in 1987, SOEs paid the treasury over TL 4 trillion while receiving TL 715 billion from the treasury (Kepenek, 1990:88). Egypt's Ministry of Industry (4/90:5) claims a similar situation for its 117 companies, which purportedly made a net transfer to the treasury in 1988–89 of £E 2.8 billion.[17]

In both Turkey and Egypt what has occurred is growing recourse to borrowing to finance SOE investment. The reliance of Turkish SOEs on external credits has already been noted. Egyptian SOEs are notorious for unsecured borrowing, and the government has seemed powerless (or unwilling) to stop it. (G'awini, 10/19/87). It is estimated that between 1980 and 1990 Egyptian SOEs borrowed £E 33 billion, primarily from the National Investment Bank, and contracted foreign loans worth $15 billion (al-Wafd, 8/2/90; see also Sharif, 7/30/90:10). Thus, while the treasury may have unburdened itself to some extent of a heavy drain on its resources, the load has been shifted (not reduced) to SOE debt and debt servicing – both ultimately guaranteed by the state.

Although the delegated owner of the SOEs, the state does not have a single view of the sector. Rather, its vision is fragmented by the various administrative agencies that engage the SOEs in specific programs and for specific purposes. The recognition that subsidies, budget transfers, nonperforming loans, and unsecured borrowing yield a deadweight loss for the public sector as a whole has seldom, until recently, been enunciated. The state would rather cook its own data to prove false net positive transfers to the treasury than to tighten up fiscal and credit controls. In the final analysis, it appears that the treasury or ministry of finance would rather have a captive and predictable tax base at suboptimal rates of tax generation than to allow public sector units to be liquidated, thereby reducing the deficit, or to be transferred to the private sector where they might yield more in corporate profits tax.

6. MANAGING LABOR

One of the basic missions of SOEs has been to generate employment. Some redundancy in work force was considered an acceptable cost so long as growth was not impaired. It is moot in EIMT whether high levels of redundancy have been a major factor in the poor productivity performance of SOEs, but that performance, sustained over years, has focused attention on excess labor. Documentation on all four countries frequently indicates levels of redundancy running between a quarter and a third of the entire public sector work force. India's coal sector alone may have 200,000 unneeded workers, and the World Bank estimates that additional wages paid to redundant labor in SOEs have been roughly equivalent to the firms' losses (World Bank, 3/90).

Specific industries present vivid evidence of common SOE employment practices. Aeronaves de México, as its debts and losses mounted in the 1980s, kept on a work force of nearly 11,000, or 284 for each of its aircraft. Eastern Airlines, no paragon of efficiency, had 146 (Carrera Cortes, 1989). Egypt's main telephone company, the Arab Republic of Egypt Telephone Organization (ARETO), over the period 1972–76 was obliged to take on more than 4,000 university graduates assigned to it and nearly 6,000 demobilized draftees from the armed forces. This was the equivalent of 25% of its entire work force (A.R.E. 4/30/78:Exhibit III–2). Turkey's Isdemir steel complex was designed for a work force of 8,000 and a capacity of 1 million tons. In 1979, it had a work force of 18,000 producing 250,000 tons (Munir, 11/9/79). In 1991, the new CEO of Sümerbank, Mr. Söylemezoğlu, announced that 10,000 of the firm's 47,000 employees were redundant.

Harvey Leibenstein (1989:1367) argues that in any enterprise labor and management are in a prisoner's dilemma whereby employees exert no more effort than is required to maximize their individual welfare, and the firm minimizes pay to the greatest extent possible. Leibenstein's is a more formal statement of the *boutade* "They pretend to pay us, we pretend to work." The two strategies produce suboptimal results for both parties. This abstract argument bears some resemblance to reality, although in some SOEs pay is frequently higher than in large parts of the private sector. Leibenstein's game model assumes managers effectively concerned by costs. The assumption is not robust. India's giant Heavy Engineering Corporation at Ranchi, a backward area, was designed to be the "mother" of some twenty-five steel complexes that India projected at the beginning of its industrialization drive. The continuous expansion of the public steel sector, HEC's only customer, did not occur. Even though it operated for years at far below capacity and accumulated heavy losses, its work force of 21,300 did not fall and its wage bill grew well in excess of the rate of inflation. Managers' pay grew more rapidly than that of workers. Person-days lost to strikes and other causes at the HEC were three times the average for the SOE sector as a whole (Singh, 1985; *The Statesman*, 5/10/86; *India Today*, 11/30/91:58).

Measuring labor costs is not a simple function of the wage bill. Frequently, wages constitute no more than half of effective take-home pay, the rest coming in the form of special allowances, automatic bonuses, free or subsidized services, and, even for chronic loss makers, shares in nonexistent profits. The nonwage payments are not taxed, an advantage of particular importance to senior management. Because wage levels are fixed by the government and are uniform across entire sectors, management can reward performance only through the manipulation of nonwage emoluments over which the managers have some independent control. A widely practiced company subterfuge is to budget positions well in excess of available personnel. Egypt's ARETO had nearly 54,000 budgeted posts but only 46,000 employees; a similar situation is reported for PEMEX (Ernesto Marcos, interview, 11/14/89).

7. SUCCESSFUL PUBLIC ENTREPRENEURS

Successful entrepreneurship among SOE managers is dependent upon three elements that probably must occur in combination. He (I ran across no female SOE entrepreneurs) must be self-motivated as the system in which he operates will provide few if any rewards for his behavior. He must be technically competent in some major facet of the firm he is running, and, third, he must be a gifted political maneuverer, able to obtain those privileges that will enhance the success of his firm. All SOE managers in EIMT must obey two logics, one dictated by their market position and the other by their political bosses and the coalition of principals that set enterprise tasks. The second logic is far more powerful than the first. The SOE entrepreneur, however, is one who is proactive in both domains. He lobbies successfully to strengthen his firm's market position (tariff protection, prices of inputs, access to foreign exchange, guaranteed market share, etc.) *and* undertakes those firm-level reforms and innovations that will allow his enterprise to maximize returns from the policy advantages he has been able to secure.

On occasion he may benefit from a special charter that endows his firm with more autonomy and flexibility than is generally the case in the rest of the SOE sector. The truly successful SOE entrepreneur will build a corporate culture that will survive his departure and sustain the firm under new management.

In the latter respect, the example of Bharat Heavy Electrical Corporation is telling. BHEL was rescued by V. Krishnamurthy after 1967 and consolidated by K. L. Puri. Krishnamurthy came to the job of CMD with training in engineering and great managerial success in turning round one of BHEL's units. He built BHEL into the world's twelfth largest manufacturer of heavy electrical equipment, with 75,000 employees and, in 1985, $1.4 billion in sales. It had a partially captive market in the state electricity boards, the oil sector, the fertilizer sector, and the railroads, but it was increasing its exports significantly. It is not sure that BHEL can weather the relaxation of import controls in India, but it has the corporate tradition to react creatively and aggressively.[18]

Hindustan Machine Tools (HMT) offers the example of a similar firm and manager, Sam Patil, who, like Krishnamurthy, was both a successful politician and public entrepreneur. He lobbied ministers and secretaries for licenses and foreign exchange, introduced new product lines, and built a corporate tradition of success. His most famous innovation, at a time when the company's traditional products were losing market share, was to launch the HMT wristwatch, which became a standard consumer item throughout India.[19]

In 1984, Erkan Tapan was brought in from the private sector to manage Turkey's Sümerbank, the flagship of the SOE sector with 41 manufacturing units, mainly in textiles, 44 bank branches, 466 retail outlets, and 50,000 employees. Tapan changed product lines, launched an aggressive advertising campaign, and improved retail services. The conglomerate's sales and profits performance improved dramatically. But Tapan lost the political battle. Although he had taken on this job with the strong backing of P. M. Özal, the shares of Sümerbank were nonetheless transferred after 1986 to the Mass Housing and Public Participation Fund in anticipation of privatization. Tapan complained that he had not saved Sümerbank only to sell it off, but his complaints were not heeded, and he resigned.

Another successful entrepreneurial manager facing privatization was Emilio Ocampo, managing director of Mexico's Cananea Copper Company. He had improved the company's performance in the mid-1980s, although rising world copper prices helped a great deal, and he prepared the entity for a sale that ultimately collapsed. He then took the perhaps foolhardy step of trying to engineer a management buy-out of Cananea financed by a consortium of Swiss banks. Shortly thereafter he was fired, arrested, and jailed on charges of corruption and embezzlement. Had his management buy-out succeeded, it surely would have been a first in the annals of privatization in LDCs, but, like Tapan, he had not carried out the necessary political groundwork.[20]

Sometimes the firm-level entrepreneur moves on to the sectoral level and performs for it the same functions. In the mid-1980s, Krishna-

128

murthy became the chairman of the Steel Authority of India (SAIL) and responsible for all India's public SOEs in steel. SAIL had been a chronic loss maker, but Krishnamurthy turned it around in a few years. The reasons for his success indicate the various elements the successful SOE manager must master. First, he had strong backing from Rajiv Gandhi and the minister of steel. Second, he was able to obtain a series of price increases for SAIL's products. Third, he drastically reduced and then ended the large overtime payments that had become an institutional practice in SAIL's units. He insisted upon punctual fulfillment of contracts, strict quality control, and penalty payments for delivery of defective products. SAIL is not yet, and may never be, internationally competitive. Indeed, it is still outperformed by Tata Iron and Steel in India's private sector. But Krishnamurthy did bring about basic changes in corporate practices and traditions that had built up since the 1950s.

Whether promoted out of the corps of SOE managers, or parachuted in from some other part of the public sector, we find in EIMT figures who are simultaneously principal and agent, promoting the fortunes of some large component of the public enterprise sector. The model here is Enrico Mattei, the creator of Ente Nazionale Idrocarburi (ENI), Italy's large public holding company in the petroleum sector (Aharoni, 1986:115–16). In Egypt, ʿAziz Sidqi, the first minister of industry after 1957, was the architect of the industrial public sector and negotiated the country's first Soviet industrial credits. He served as minister for nearly a decade. Chapter 2 has noted the seminal role of S. Mohan Kumaramangalam in the second phase of SOE industrial expansion in India under Indira Gandhi, and Mexico offers Adolfo Prieto, the driving force behind the founding of Altos Hornos de México (AHMSA) and the public steel sector. These men seldom concerned themselves with management issues per se but, rather, with capturing resources and launching projects. They were the prime actors of the exuberant phase of SOE expansion, and, had they known about the concept, apostles of Hirschman's theory of the "hiding hand" (1967:13).

We must finally note that some firms were successful in the absence of sectoral or firm-level entrepreneurs. They too are rare, and they follow a similar pattern. They combine unusual legal autonomy, conferring on their managers greater discretion than is common in the SOE sector, and their management procedures are taken straight from those practiced by foreign contractors who set up the firm in the first place. Erdemir Steel and the Turkish Petroleum Corporation (TPAO), and Madras Fertilizers of India, all enjoy a reputation for good management, good performance, and a certain insulation from political interference in corporate affairs.

8. STEEL STORIES

Among the most compelling illusions that all four countries shared was their faith that a large scale iron and steel sector, under public ownership, would lead their economies into economically viable industrialization, economic sovereignty, and, for three of them, military preparedness. All four used steel complexes to develop backward areas or to act as new regional growth poles.[21] Because of the centrality of the steel sector to the assault on the commanding heights, it is useful to review some of EIMT's experiences.[22]

In India the Ministry of Steel has acted as principal and SAIL as agent. SAIL, with its four large blast-furnace steel complexes, competes with the TISCO, the only private firm with similar technology, the mini–steel sector using electric arc reduction, and a limited amount of imported steel. In 1964 the Joint Plant Committee was founded to establish prices for steel products and to allocate output to various plants. The JPC grouped representatives of the producers and of major consumers such as the railroads.

When SAIL was created as the holding company for the public steel sector, the JPC's power was greatly diminished. SAIL, in conjunction or collusion with TISCO, tried to absorb the pricing and market planning functions of the JPC, reducing the latter, and its economic research unit, to the role of provider of technical information. Over time the Ministry of Steel came to accept the eclipse of the JPC but contested SAIL in setting prices. With SAIL controlling 40% (and a projected 60% if all planned expansion goes ahead) of the markets for most steel products, it could, with the help of TISCO, engage in predatory pricing against the mini–steel producers. The Ministry of Steel has tried to protect that sector, but it finds that SAIL has a relative monopoly on the information that is needed to set prices and allocate production. SAIL has cornered what Shapiro and Willig (1990) call contractible information; only the JPC remains as a feeble hedge against the high informational rents SAIL is able to extract. This situation, in which the SOE agent is able to circum-scribe severely the information available to the principal, is more the rule than the exception in the countries under examination.

Before and even during the tenure of Krishnamurthy at SAIL, the holding company engaged in "tied" sales. That is, in a context of limited supply, rising demand, and few imports, SAIL could oblige its customers to buy certain amounts of its inventory of low-demand products along with the products the customer really wanted. The customer in turn would sell off the unwanted products to retailers who, in combination with the products of the mini–steel sector, always had available a wide range of products for which they could guarantee prompt delivery. Thus, although SAIL was able to cartelize part of its market, it lost control of another part through the practice of tied buying.[23]

Although a given sector may receive priority attention, what projects are selected with what partners and what structure of financing will be the outcome of competition among agents and among principals. Foreign suppliers and investors, and private domestic competitors, can try to reenforce movement in a certain direction, or block it in others, but they seldom can initiate or determine the outcome of the process. This is demonstrated in the remarkable study of SICARTSA by Rainer Schüking (1982).

First adumbrated in 1947 was the idea of a large public steel complex on Mexico's central Pacific coast at Las Truchas, an underdeveloped region with large, unexploited iron ore deposits. The plant was not commissioned until 1969, and did not enter into production until 1971. By 1990 it had been judged economically unviable and was designated for privatization.

Both the Mexican private sector, particularly Fundidora de Monterrey, and the public sector – especially Altos Hornos (AHMSA), which in 1953 overtook Fundidora in production – were interested in the new project. But it was former president Lázaro Cárdenas who led a crusade for it that spanned nearly two decades. He was determined that Las Truchas be developed by the public sector and that U.S. partners, especially Bethlehem Steel, be excluded from it. Cárdenas solicited the technical advice of Friedrich Krupp Industriebau in 1955 (Krupp was simultaneously collaborating with the Egyptian government in the design and construction of Helwan Iron and Steel), and in 1957 he won the support of NAFINSA for funding the project.

Initially NAFINSA, in alliance with Altos Hornos in which it had an equity stake, tried to block Las Truchas as unwanted capacity and competition. In fact NAFINSA had interested Crédit Lyonnais in financing an alternative project at Mazanillo using the same iron ore. NAFINSA's allies were the Bánco de Mexico, the Mines Ministry (Fomento Minero), and probably President Ruiz Cortines. Cárdenas was convinced that NAFINSA was in league with U.S. steel interests.

Cárdenas's allies were the Comisión Federal de Electricidad, because of the large and costly hydropower station Las Truchas would require, the Ports Ministry (Secretaría de Marina) because of the port that would have to be built, and Krupp. In a maneuver that Schüking (p. 82) is not able to explain, Cárdenas was able to have the Las Truchas iron deposits put under the sole authority of a commission (Comisión de Tepalcatepe) that he himself had founded. That maneuver effectively checkmated the rival coalition.

After 1958, during the *sexenio* of López Mateos, the project languished

131

during the period of nationalization of foreign electricity companies, the recognition of Castro's Cuba, and a general souring of the regime's relations with the private sector. The minister of industry and commerce, Raúl Salinas (the father of Carlos Salinas de Gortari), assured Cárdenas of his support for Las Truchas. It was not until the *sexenio* of Díaz Ordaz, whose harsh repression of the students in 1968 Cárdenas supported, that Las Truchas was finally approved. Lázaro Cárdenas died in October 1970 before the plant entered into production. His son, Cuauhtémoc, was made subdirector of the plant.[24]

In 1978, SICARTSA was transferred to the newly created public holding company, Siderúrgica Mexicana (SIDERMEX). It is significant that in the 1970s the World Bank was urging the federal government to play an active role in expanding steel production, and forecast a rise in the SOE sector's share from 36% in 1975 to 60% by 1985 (Schüking, 1982:180–81). The World Bank was in step with a long phase of state expansion that began with Cárdenas's nationalization of the petroleum sector before World War II, López Mateos's nationalization of electricity, and the thrust into the steel sector engineered by López Portillo.

Fifteen years later, the World Bank (5/22/89:9) criticized SICARTSA severely, along with CFE, Ferrocarriles Nacionales, or FERRONALES (the railroads), and FERTIMEX, for the fact that in the first half of the 1980s "their cumulative value-added (i.e., net sales revenues minus cash production cost other than labor) was negative." In early 1990 the Mexican government announced that it would privatize SICARTSA and AHMSA, which between them, true to the Bank's earlier predictions, accounted for 60% of domestic steel production (*Latin American Monitor*, 4/90:763).[25]

9. CONCLUSION

The one conclusion that holds good for all underdeveloped countries is that public enterprise has an essential role to play in the developmental process. In stating such an obvious truth, however, we are far from assuming that public enterprise is necessarily more efficient than private. (Hanson, 1959:203)

The public property regime ensures that neither principals (if they can be identified) nor agents have any incentive to minimize costs of production or avoid the risk of unmanageable debt. Until the money almost literally ran out – for Turkey and Mexico in the early 1980s, for Egypt and India in the early 1990s – the soft budget constraint applied. Firms could not fail and thus did not exit. Over time the SOE sector became a kind of grab bag of "green grass" projects, sick industry take-overs and nationalized units both foreign and domestic, exhibiting every level of technology imaginable. Everyone conspired to promote the expansion

132

● موسم الجرد ●

كيان

ــ حريق متعمد ، لأنها فتشت بنطلون بابا وأخدت الفلوس اللى فيه !

SOE inventories and accounts: An Egyptian view. Higazi of *Ruz al-Yussef* comments on a spreading form of corruption in Egypt. Fires mysteriously break out in public sector warehouses just before annual inventory and all the contents are declared lost. The suspicion is that the contents have been turned over to the black market. The little boy explains to his sister, "Arson; because mama found some money in papa's pants and took it." Source: *Ruz al-Yussef* 2421, November 4, 1974.

of the SOE sector – heads of state, budget-hungry bureaucrats, politicians, the military, the managers, organized labor, and the international donor and commercial banking communities.

The inefficiencies associated with the property regime manifest themselves at the microlevel as well. Among agents and principals information is hoarded and data cooked, and because no one has any incentive to engage seriously in monitoring, the theoretic informational advantages of public ownership are in practice lost. By the same token, the rationality of planned expansion, which the creators of the SOE sectors assumed would guide them, was also lost to the bargaining culture that quickly developed. The state became the arena for a constant search for privilege, resource advantage, and market rents that were determined by policy makers wielding institutionally defined power. Although all may have had an interest in SOE expansion, each rival unit or agency had a specific set of preferences for the ways in which expansion would be pursued. The principals were generally grouped in unstable coalitions that in turn required a constant process of renegotiating bargains with the agents.

The wise manager would devote more time and ingenuity to building protective relations with his coalitional masters than in promoting firm-level improvements. Normally his tenure was such that reforms undertaken in the firm would be credited to his successor anyway. Nonetheless, he could not totally ignore firm productivity and performance in the market place. As Kornai (1989) suggests, coping with both bureaucratic politics and market forces is generally beyond the capacity of normally endowed managers.

Yet it is undeniable that in Turkey and Mexico at least, the SOE sector performed well for three decades, generating high levels of self-financing and tax payments to the state. The self-imposed restraints the state had exercised in both countries were abandoned in the 1970s, and the rapid deterioration of SOE finances contributed directly to the profound crises that shook both economies after 1979. The interesting question is, How was the state able to control itself in its use of the SOEs in those first three decades? How were all the diverse interests that subsequently nearly cannibalized the SOE sector held at bay? In Egypt the restraints broke down in the first few years of the First Five Year Plan; in India the process took a little longer and was briefly interrupted by the state of emergency. Part of the answer may lie in the Turkish military intervention of 1960, which ended for a time the pork barrel era of the Demokrat decade. In Mexico, perhaps the smaller relative weight of the SOE sector in the economy made its abuse of less economic consequence until the era of heavy foreign borrowing and the influx of oil rents.

The SOE sector does represent a captive tax base, and even as the SOEs run at a loss and seek financing abroad, they still generate a predictable source of taxes and compulsory payments to various fiscal agencies. The idea that some other mix of public and private enterprise might increase the general level of economic activity and hence of tax revenues is seldom explicitly considered.[26] There is no principal who has a vision of the entire public sector, who can see the suboptimality of certain arrangements for the sector as a whole. What passes for global policy is the summation of thousands of particularistic deals that most often honor the practice of robbing Peter to pay Paul. If commodity, credit, and managerial markets determined these deals to a greater extent than they typically have, then perhaps an optimizing hidden hand would come into play. However, such a development would threaten all the other, noneconomic logics that gave rise to state enterprise in the first place.

5

Reform and divestiture

What concerns us in this chapter is a reform sequence. It begins with the attempt to remake the context in which SOEs operate, that is, to reform the various axes linking principals and agents laid out in Chapter 4. Not infrequently the effort involves tinkering with existing arrangements, and it seldom involves serious efforts to change relationships *within* firms. For reasons to be explained in the sections that follow, when these contextual reforms fail to bring about significant change in SOE performance, more radical reform efforts are discussed, if not launched, and these may include privatization and liquidation. The first phase is carried out in the spirit of the founding of the public sector. All the old symbols and legitimizing themes are invoked to explain what is going on. In the second phase, the old ethos itself is called into question. A more or less sharp ideological break accompanies the policy break. Finally, the sequence from reform to privatization is paralleled by one in which political leadership initially adjusts costs and benefits *within* existing coalitions and then moves to attempts to reconstitute the coalitions themselves (see Chapter 7).

Within a decade or so of the state's capturing the commanding heights of the economy in EIMT, the major shortcomings in performance had been identified and to some extent made public. In all four countries, the first domestic questioning of the assumptions of state-led ISI was formulated in the middle 1960s (see, for example, V. V. Ramanadham, 1963; Fishlow, 1990). The first phase of contextual reform and tinkering then began. The attempts gained urgency as the economies were subjected to external shocks in the 1970s and early 1980s. It is important to note that reform of public enterprise was never approached in isolation from a broader effort at structural adjustment, and the timing of structural adjustment was determined by external shocks (see Bienen and Waterbury, 1989).

It is within the framework of structural adjustment that the contribution of SOEs to the financial deficit of the state became such an important issue. As we saw in Chapter 3, state economic entities in LDCs account for a larger share of the deficit than do those of the industrialized nations. When privatization finally becomes a priority policy issue, it has been and is primarily because it is seen as a quick way to reduce the public deficit. Increasingly, privatization was and is also seen as a vehicle for generating new flows of investment that states, undergoing the financial rigors of adjustment, cannot generate themselves.

The shift from phase one to phase two reforms is of enormous import for this study because it portends the disruption if not dissolution of existing political coalitions and economic entitlements. It is not surprising, therefore, that Egypt and India, until very recently never moved beyond the first phase of tinkering. Reform has been aimed at system maintenance. It is also not very surprising that after three years of military rule, the new civilian government in Turkey inherited an enabling environment in which to move to phase two. Mexico, however, has plunged further into phase two than the other three countries, defying a great deal of political logic in the process. Both Turkey and Mexico have pursued system transformation.

1. THE FUTILITY OF REFORM?

Why do phase one reforms so regularly fail to produce the desired results? Is it the result of a lack of political will, of an incoherent policy package, or of effective blocking strategies on the part of those likely to be hurt in the process? Despite the few success stories mentioned in Chapter 4, I will argue that individual SOEs can be turned around but not an entire SOE sector. The reason why these SOE successes cannot spread to entire SOE sectors is that that would defeat the logic of the system as a whole. The managers of turnarounds all cite four factors as crucial to success: autonomy from political interference, elimination of redundant personnel among workers and managers, pay differentials tied to productivity, and the ability to generate profits. The SOEs are what they are precisely because they are subjected to political control. Their objectives and the criteria by which they are judged must remain politically determined, otherwise there would be no compelling reason to retain them under public ownership. Likewise, if profits, or some other indicator of real returns to factors, were the predominant measure of success, it would be better to encourage the activity through private enterprise, or at least through contracting with private providers. Finally, shaping the work force in terms of real markets, and structuring salaries and wages to reflect productivity, would cut deeply into the social equity goals typically assigned to SOEs. It would also, of course, cut deeply into many of the entitlements that have accreted over time. Finally, such reforms would limit the latitude of political authorities to use the SOEs as vehicles for compensatory payments to select constituents in times of adjustment (see Waterbury, 1992).

The major interests represented in dominant coalitions do not set out to block reforms (although they may well try do that, too). Rather, they contribute to the failure of phase one reforms through their tendency to free-ride on the reform effort (a collective bad), hoping that others will pay its price. All concerned may recognize the economic logic of structural adjustment and public sector reform but be incapable of coalescing to promote either. Similarly, narrow self-interest may prevent them from coalescing to block either.

In this sense, the private sector behaves in the face of structural adjustment and public sector reform little differently from the managers of the public sector. The growth of the SOE sectors outlined in Chapter 3 led to the partial "deprivatization" of the private sector itself as it learned to play the same games as the SOEs in obtaining foreign exchange, credit, raw materials, licenses, and market shares from the agencies and financial institutions of the state sector. As the fiscal crises associated with ISI deepened, the rational goal of the private sector firm was to seek greater macroeconomic efficiency in all sectors while preserving for itself all the special deals and risk-reducing devices that had cushioned *it* against the costs of greater firm-level efficiency. If every firm, public or private, pursued its narrow interests, macroefficiency could not be achieved.

In sum, public sector managers, private owners, and organized labor, although more or less cognizant of the macroinefficiencies holding back the economy, have had a second-best preference for the status quo that protects their acquired privileges and deals. The logic of this argument conforms to that of the "new political economy" and the perverse effects of state intervention (see Chapter 1). Reform of SOEs will, more often than not, fall victim to free-riding coalitional interests rather than to "blocking" coalitions that actively oppose the reforms.

2. COALITIONS

The leaders of ISI experiments were generally successful in organizing coalitional support for them. Most of their success lay in the fact that ISI created many jobs, it was redistributive in its effects (leaving aside the rural sector), and inclusivist in that it could promise benefits to a wide range of interests.

Unlike the ISI experiment, the new strategies are not likely in the medium term to improve income distribution, to create many new jobs, or to appeal to a broad range of functional interests in society. To the contrary, they are and will continue to be based on narrow coalitions. If we were not dealing with developing countries, then some form of "popular capitalism" that presumably has kept the Conservative Party in power in the United Kingdom could broaden the base. But given levels of income and savings in developing countries, popular capitalism, that is, expanding the ranks of the small investor, is not yet on.[1]

What political leadership has going for it in the sequential shift is hesitancy and disarray among the members of old coalitions and a general mood of disillusion and cynicism among the populace at large. This is leadership's window of opportunity. In it, new, narrow coalitions can be formed. Parts of the private sector, especially in the export sector, will benefit from macropolicies and from targeted credit and tax breaks. The commercial agricultural sector, especially that part engaged in exports, may well benefit. Migrant workers will enhance the local value of their foreign earnings through devaluation. Parts of the small-scale and informal sectors may benefit from deregulation. The list is short, and the interests of these groups are by no means convergent.

Under these circumstances, the reforms will live or die by their ability to deliver some real growth. If there is growth, as there has been in Turkey since the early 1980s, and in Mexico since 1990, then the state can engage in selective compensation for some of the many victims of curtailed public expenditures, layoffs, and inflation. Growth also allows a stream of benefits to flow to new coalitional interests that will be called upon to respond to the signals emitted by the reform policies (see Waterbury, 1989, 1992).[2]

In the climate of recession and curtailed public investment that generally leads into phase two, the political feasibility of privatizing or liquidating certain SOEs has paradoxically been enhanced. As the state reneged on many components of its welfare commitments, the sanctity of public enterprise could be violated at relatively low political cost. In a sense, those costs were lost in the broader trauma of system transformation. Moreover, public officialdom lost its commitment to or faith in its ability to turn the SOE sector around. The Mexican crisis of the mid-1980s so traumatized Mexican society and so sapped the confidence of the stewards of the public sector that every facet of the old arrangements could be criticized and potentially discarded.

3. SYSTEM MAINTENANCE

3.1. Egypt

When public enterprise reform first appears on the policy agenda, the focus has typically been on restructuring principal–agent relations rather than on firm-level improvements. The ideal invoked is the separation of management from ownership; that is, the search for that magical balance between political supervision of the SOE, and firm-level autonomy and managerial responsibility. The search has generally involved tinkering at the juncture of the supervisory apparatus (i.e., the level at which the state exercises its ownership rights) with aggregates of firms.

When Egypt's SOE sector first took shape, after the nationalization of British and French interests in the wake of the 1956 Suez War, public firms were grouped under a holding company known as the Egyptian Development Organization. It was modeled explicitly after Italy's Instituto per la Ricostruzione Industriale (IRI), which influenced many other LDCs, including Turkey (on IRI, see Ayub and Hegstad, 1986:36). Within three years Egypt added another two holding companies, this time with firms taken over from the Egyptian private sector or created by the state itself. The unique feature of these holding companies was the diversity of their assets and the expectation that they would compete with one another.

Between 1961 and 1963, however, as Egypt's self-proclaimed socialist transformation reached its apogee, the system was entirely overhauled. The public sector had been greatly expanded after the extensive nationalizations of July 1961 (the so-called Socialist Decrees) followed by smaller take-overs in the next three years. The new arrangement was to organize SOEs by sector. Each sector became homogeneous in its product or service (e.g., textiles, metals, engineering, chemicals, food processing, trade, etc.), and each sector was put under the supervision of a General Organization that in turn answered to a specific ministry (industry, agriculture, supply, defense, etc.). The four large nationalized banks were attached to specific sectors. The General Organizations were charged with preparing sectoral plans, developing budget projections, procuring raw materials and financing, and identifying senior management.

There was no competition among them as each sector constituted a quasi-monopoly with only partially overlapping markets. Their investment and production strategies were to be worked out in conjunction with the five-year plan. All of this "rationalization" was accompanied by unified payscales and personnel procedures, and promotion by seniority. Needless to say, the whole structure was shielded by high tariff walls and quantitative trade restrictions.

Although substantial GNP growth was achieved over the first plan period, 1960–65, Egypt's trade imbalance had grown alarmingly and external financing depended on the goodwill of the Soviet Union and of the United States. The culprit was the SOE sector with its demands for imports, high-cost production, and inability to export. Moreover, it was seen that the General Organizations had begun to interfere in all aspects

139

of firm management so that the managers shoved most decisions up to the General Organization level and awaited orders. If none were forthcoming, they did nothing. The situation became so serious that in October 1965 the prime minister called a meeting of all top SOE management to find solutions. This yielded a law (#32) in 1966 to restrict the interference of the General Organizations in company affairs (Farid, 1/70:36–37).

This kind of tinkering had little impact, and in a sweeping move in 1975 (Law 111), the General Organizations were abolished. It was said the company heads would now be free to act like entrepreneurs. The supervisory ministries would set broad targets and help with financing but otherwise leave the companies (some 350 of them by this time) to their own devices, subject only to post hoc review. This move came one year after President Sadat launched the "open-door policy" (*al-infitah*) to encourage foreign investment and to force the public sector to compete for domestic markets.[3]

Neither enhanced performance nor a more competitive market was fully achieved. Foreign investment flowed primarily into tourism and banking, while the ministries absorbed all the tasks of the General Organizations without relinquishing the right to interfere in day-to-day management of the firms. Successful managers were those who pursued joint ventures with foreign investors, in some ways gutting their own SOEs in the process. Due primarily to the objections of organized labor, the initial surge in the formation of joint ventures petered out by 1980.[4]

In 1983, Egypt came nearly full circle in its reform efforts. Law 97 of that year essentially restored the sectoral General Organizations, now called Authorities. Sectoral homogeneity and noncompetitivity were maintained. What had changed most significantly in the intervening years was that the nationalized banks had been freed from their obligations to specific sectors, and in 1981 the National Bank for Investment was created to undertake SOE financing in conformity with the national plan. At the same time, the SOE budgets were taken off the state budget, thus artificially reducing the budget deficit.[5]

Other reform initiatives seem to have followed a one-step-forward, one-step-backward pattern. In 1978 and 1979, for example, SOE managers were given some latitude in setting wage levels and incentives. In addition, SOEs were no longer obliged to take on university graduates to whom the state owed employment. After 1979 the SOE work force ceased to grow at the rates of the preceding twenty years, and most managers stopped replacing employees once they retired. The level of direct state subsidies to the SOEs has been reduced significantly since the early 1980s, but indirect subsidies through cheap energy still amount to billions of Egyptian pounds each year (USAID, 1990:20).

Against these steps were other measures that inhibited the liquidation of SOEs, the reduction of the public equity share in any SOE, the recruitment of top-level outside management because fifteen years of experience in the SOE sector is required for any CEO, and the establishment of joint ventures. These restrictions can be gotten around, but they do represent the reluctance of an interlocking set of state-dependent interests to concede anything except under extreme duress.

Egypt has moved since the mid-1960s from an espousal of state socialism to an ineffective form of state capitalism. The goal is to preserve the state sector, but relegitimize it by making it profitable and responsive to the demands of consumers. Two documents capture this spirit and identify the interests involved. In 1982, the presidentially appointed National Specialized Councils issued a two-volume report on the public sector (National Specialized Councils, 1982). Its recommendations were of two kinds. First, it sought legal equality for SOEs with companies set up under Law 43 (see note 4 to this chapter). Regarding tariffs, the report recommended that high walls be maintained for locally produced goods, that tariffs on capital and intermediate goods not be higher than on finished products, and that the state purchase goods and services from the SOEs at their real cost and compensate consumers through subsidies. Second, it urged the reestablishment of sectoral holding companies and got its wish in 1983. At the same time, it invoked the need to encourage the real autonomy of firm managers, and to link wages to productivity. Such invocations have a nearly liturgical quality to them.

In all of this, the open-door policy was mentioned only insofar as it could impede the flourishing of the SOEs. This report was a tract written by the managerial class. Its tone was unsparing toward labor, which would be subjected to flexible hiring and productivity-linked wages, toward the bureaucrats who would have their monitoring powers curtailed, and toward the private sector depicted as the source of unfair competition. Eight years later, the Institute of National Planning issued its own investigations of the SOE sector, and its recommendations followed closely on those of the National Specialized Councils (INP, 5/88).[6]

Since 1987, Egypt's economic crisis has deepened. Falling petroleum revenues (until the Gulf crisis of the summer of 1990) and worker remittances were coupled with continued huge public deficits, high inflation, and accumulating arrears on more than $40 billion in external debt. The pressure from the donor community focused primarily on interest rates, consumer subsidies, and energy pricing, but there was an accompanying urging to move toward privatization.

For a time, Egyptian policy makers in essence stalled. There was no obvious public support for any of the reform measures being urged. The cabinet contained only one figure, the minister of tourism, who openly advocated privatization. There was no technocratic team in place to pursue the reform agenda, and the president was decidedly ambivalent about the whole process, as his remarks in 1987 indicate (as cited in Palmer, Leila, and Yassin, 1988:17–18):

I wonder about those who advocate selling the public sector, because this would be a dangerous step taken at the cost of the simple citizen, because the private sector operates according to the needs of the market, and its prices are high. So what is the simple citizen to do? Frankly, he will starve . . . The public sector regulates the private one, thus offering goods to the public at reasonable prices, because state control is a must. Selling the public sector would create a socioeconomic problem. I am careful to maintain social peace and balance.

The net result, up until 1991, was some marginal adjustments both in terms of SOE reforms and of privatization (Richards, 1992).

Until the spring of 1990 the most persistent pressure for privatization came from the international donor community. USAID in particular tried to use its project-funding leverage to promote the sale of public assets. In order to skirt the issue of direct sales to non-Egyptians or to an "irresponsible" private sector, USAID promoted and financed an employee stock ownership program (ESOP) between Egypt's Transport and Engineering Company (TRENCO) and Pirelli of Italy in a new joint-venture company to manufacture radial tires. Workers and management would hold about 30% of the equity of the new company. One Egyptian official stated that ESOPs constitute "the summit of socialism" (see Zayida, 1/1/90).

Other quasi privatizations may take place through sales of government equity in private companies (perhaps the equivalent of $1 billion), or through the sales of the equity held by public sector banks in public sector companies (about $3 billion equivalent – see *AI*, 5/31/90:15; Ministry of Industry, 4/90; Sharif, 7/30/90:33). The state holds a majority interest in some twenty firms whose paid-up capital in 1989 was $300 million. All future capital expansion in these firms will be through public share offerings.

The Gulf crisis and war of 1990–91 provided the United States and other Western and Arab creditors an opportunity to write off half of Egypt's external debt and, through the Paris Club, to reschedule the rest in conjunction with a stringent economic reform program. That such moves would be required had been clear for a couple of years before the war as Egypt's 1987 standby with the IMF collapsed and arrears on its debt accumulated. Egypt's participation in the war against Iraq provided a plausible excuse for forgiveness.

The implications of the reform program are far-reaching. The public deficit, running at more than 20% of GDP, is to be reduced to 6% in two years. Taxes, particularly a sales tax, are to raise revenues while consumer and energy subsidies are to be gradually reduced. A unified, market-determined exchange rate is to be introduced within one year, and positive interest rates on bank accounts and bank lending are to be applied. The government is to end the decades-old practice of guaranteeing employment to university graduates. As part of the effort to reduce the deficit, a program of selling of up to 49% of equity to the public and perhaps foreign investors has been adumbrated.[7] Harking back to the era of the three holding companies of the late 1950s, Egypt has now created sectoral holding companies that legally own the state shares of the companies under their jurisdiction.

It is significant that President Mubarak chose to announce the program and the understanding with the IMF during his May Day speech of 1991 to Egyptian organized labor. He described Egypt as being in "a crisis of terrifying, frightful proportions," brought on by what he called Egypt's most intractable problem: rapid population growth. But when he came to discuss the SOEs, some of the customary ambivalence came through (*AI, 5/6/91*:14):

We have very big companies like Mahallah, Kafr al-Dawar, Vestia, Iron and Steel, Aluminum ... In some of these huge companies we will liberate management in order to increase production and increase returns. It's not like what the working people are saying, that we are going to sell [them] ... no ... no. What are we going to sell?! Are we going to sit here and liquidate the workers or what?! We are not going to liquidate the country. There are big companies that need to be reformed so that their production will remain large and outstanding; and we have to remove the obstacles before other companies by public share offerings to the citizens ... the large companies are the property of the government, that is of the people, not of anyone else, and we are looking into the laws governing economic activity so that they conform with the spirit and goals of liberation.

Even though Egypt's hour of reckoning, postponed since 1977, seemed to be at hand, Mubarak made no changes among his top economic ministers. By mid-1992 no change team had been put into place.

3.2. India

Despite the importance of the state-level SOEs in India, I shall focus here on the 239 federal, or central-level SOEs. In general, the evolution of the SOEs has followed a calendar closely resembling Egypt's. Three five-year plans carried Indian public enterprise into the mid-1960s, when the inefficiencies in factor utilization became manifest. These were coupled with severe balance of payments problems that led to a devaluation of the rupee in 1966. The following year, the Administrative Reform Commission stressed that central SOEs are legally commercial entities and that

143

the government of India should measure their performance as such (World Bank, 10/88).

What distinguishes India most strikingly from Egypt and many other LDCs that followed ISI strategies is the prudence with which it managed its monetary and fiscal policies and its external accounts. Government spending, until the mid-1980s, was carefully controlled, inflation remained low, the rupee was not significantly overvalued, and the external debt and the balance of payments remained within tolerable limits. The monsoon failures of the mid-1960s and early 1970s, the military confrontations with the People's Republic of China (PRC) and Pakistan, and the second oil shock provoked crises that seem mild compared to those of the other three countries. Consequently, until about 1990 the depth of economic crisis was not such as to push Indian policy makers or politicians to call into question the strategy they had followed for nearly four decades.

Indira Gandhi, who took responsibility for the 1966 devaluation, did not follow consistent policies in dealing with the public sector. On the one hand, she promoted its expansion through the nationalization of most private banks in 1969, the nationalization of the coal sector, and the take-over of numerous sick private enterprises, especially in the textile sector. On the other hand, during the Emergency of 1975–77 she cracked down hard on strikes and agitation among organized labor, and India briefly entered a phase of authoritarian state capitalism. It was not, however, until her return to power in 1980 that public sector reform and economic liberalization were given real prominence (in general, see Nayar, 1989; Kohli, 1989, 1990; RoyChowdhury, 4/92).

A leading figure in this effort, and a close advisor to the prime minister, was L. K. Jha, a career civil servant and economic generalist who achieved prominence as an advisor to Prime Minister Shastri in 1964. He became the driving force behind the liberalization measures launched by Indira Gandhi and continued, after 1984, by her son Rajiv Gandhi. The broad lines of what Jha set out to achieve are contained in his 1980 book, and he recruited a younger group of economists and technocrats to work out detailed plans. While Congress remained in power, a change team was in place, although Rajiv Gandhi's attention was increasingly drawn elsewhere.

The groundwork was done between 1980 and 1984, but the liberalization program really took off in 1984–85 in the run up to the Seventh Five Year Plan. The main thrust was the easing of the highly restrictive regulatory regime of private enterprise in place since the mid-1950s, but strengthened under Indira Gandhi through the Monopoly and Restrictive Trade Practices law. Deregulation opened up restricted sectors of the economy to private investment, raised investment levels that required

144

licensing, delicensed some twenty-five industries, and allowed for certain kinds of capacity expansion and the introduction of new production lines without official approval. The asset limit above which MRTP legislation would be applicable was raised substantially. In addition, the importation of about a thousand items, mostly not produced locally, was delicensed. In order to encourage exports, the rupee was allowed to devalue over the seventh plan period by 40% (World Bank, 3/90). The Janata Dal government, elected in early 1990, continued the liberalization measures through easing restrictions on foreign investment and the importation of new technologies (*India Today*, 6/30/90:44).

During these same years a great deal of attention was focused on improving the performance of the SOEs. Significantly, two of the major high-level reviews were never made public. The first report was produced by a committee set up in September 1984 and chaired by Arjun Sen Gupta, special secretary to the prime minister. The Sen Gupta report was built around two familiar themes. First, it sought to increase firm-level managerial autonomy by setting up holding companies.[8] The government ministries would undertake overall strategic planning. Through the holding companies memoranda of understanding would be drawn up with individual companies as well as between the holding companies and the ministries. A third theme was peculiar to India: to wit, that parliamentary prying into the affairs of SOEs should be limited, as is the case in the United Kingdom, by a "self-denying ordinance" (report summarized and critiqued in Trivedi, 5/30/87). The Sen Gupta report did not address the issue of privatization.

A few years later another high-level committee drafted a white paper on the SOE sector. After two years of review and amending, it finally reached the cabinet in late 1988 (*India Today*, 4/30/89:67). This report was in most respects an extension of the Sen Gupta document. It too stressed managerial autonomy, and the authorization of corporate and sectoral planning by companies or holding companies. The draft white paper went beyond the earlier report in suggesting that some unviable firms be liquidated or sold and that SOEs float public share offerings with priority for workers.[9]

The white paper aroused some opposition in the cabinet, and Rajiv Gandhi, who supported it, was persuaded to hold it in abeyance until after the elections. Congress lost the elections, and the white paper has not been disinterred. K. Rangachari (4/30/90) subsequently remarked: "There is no more talk of privatization not only because there are few takers for the long neglected or mismanaged units but also due to the political unacceptability of the idea."

Although generalized contextual reform was thus stymied, some remedial measures were adopted. As noted in Chapter 4, at the beginning

An Indian view of memoranda of understanding. Source: *India Today*, 8/15/88:81 (cartoon by Ajit Ninan). Used by permission.

of the Seventh Five Year Plan, Rajiv Gandhi recognized an impending fiscal crisis by announcing that the SOEs would have to generate most of their own investment resources, either through commercial borrowing or retained earnings. Some SOEs, such as the National Thermal Power Corporation (NTPC), were authorized to issue bonds and debentures, but the public response was not encouraging. By the end of the plan period, it was clear that SOEs in general continued to make heavy claims on budgetary transfers.

Toward the end of the plan period, the Indian government instituted the use of memoranda of understanding on a fairly broad scale. These were inspired by the French experience since the mid-1960s with *contrats plans*. The object is to draw up multiyear performance contracts between the government and the firm by which the government commits specified levels of financing and prices in exchange for the firm's achieving targets in production or delivery of services within agreed-upon cost parameters. The contract framework would thus liberate firm management to pursue its targets with considerable flexibility.

In India the memorandum of understanding implies something less binding on the two parties. The object is not so much to realize specific targets as it is to develop, firm by firm, a set of performance indicators and performance signals to guide the level of resources provided by the government. Management is granted greater latitude in committing funds and making strategic decisions. The first two memoranda were signed with SAIL and the Oil and Natural Gas Commission, and by 1990 had been extended to eighteen other SOEs.

The memoranda have revealed several drawbacks. They are drawn up yearly and stipulate that firms provide quarterly reports on performance. Several managers, such as S. P. Wahi of ONGC, feel that they have not really changed anything and amount to no more than a new procedure for ratifying the annual company budget (*Economic Times*, 1/20/88). In India, as elsewhere, there are no clear consequences for the failure of either party to meet its obligations, but the problem is particularly difficult if the government reneges on commitments. In Mexico, where similar memoranda have been used for some years, a manager remarked to the author that they are a device by which managers and government officials lie to each other.[10]

India illustrates perhaps better than any of the other three the cleavage between the upper-level civil administration and the management of the SOEs. The Indian bureaucrats (pejoratively known as the "babus") are those who exercise ownership rights through financing, taxing, regulating, pricing, monitoring, auditing, and planning. One of the primary instruments of interference has been the Bureau of Public Enterprises. Until 1986 the BPE was part of the Ministry of Finance and clearly saw its role as watchdog. After 1986 it was lodged in the Ministry of Heavy Industry, where it was supposed to promote and facilitate the activities of the SOEs. Some would like to see it as an autonomous agency, like the Planning Commission, directly under the prime minister's office.

The migration of the BPE should be seen primarily as another example of tinkering with various facets of principal–agent relations. None of these moves has overcome the basic problem. The civil service elite, as well as the politicians, have little interest in promoting the autonomy of the SOEs, which would reduce the need for monitoring and the possibility of political interference. Neither support the dilution of SOE equity through public share offerings, which might lead to challenges to government representatives on SOE boards. The memoranda of understanding are attractive to the administration because they are designed by the Bureau of Public Enterprises, which remains largely under "babu" control.[11] Privatization is the least desirable reform because it reduces, perhaps irreversibly, the scope of administrative controls.

To date, India's policies of economic liberalization have not included any significant steps toward privatization. At the same time tariff protection for both public and private enterprise has remained high. As the World Bank noted (3/90:51), "the import substitution bias of the trade regime has actually increased." In contrast to the other three countries, new SOEs are being added to the public sector at both the state and federal levels on a regular basis.

Nonetheless, a number of avenues toward divestiture are being explored. For years even staunch supporters of the state sector have advocated liquidating some white elephants like the Heavy Engineering Corporation at Ranchi or the brand-new Haldia Petrochemical complex. As in Egypt, the formation of new joint venture companies with foreign partners may offer an opportunity for public share offerings. The Abid Hussain Committee in early 1989 recommended that those SOEs operating in competitive markets sell 25% of their equity to the public. There is a general consensus that the government should sell many of the sick industries it has taken over in the last twenty years and use the proceeds to invest in viable SOEs. Finally, some privatizations have occurred at the state level, such as the sale of the Lucknow SOE, Scooters Ltd., to the private sector Bajaj Auto Ltd.

As India closed out the 1980s and entered the 1990s, Congress lost and regained (minority) control of parliament, and two interim governments fell. Under the circumstances it was hard to develop, no less implement, a coherent set of macroeconomic policies. During the crucial period 1989–91, the public deficit grew rapidly, inflation moved to more than 20% per annum, both the domestic and external debts grew alarmingly, and the trade balance deteriorated. A decade later than Egypt, Mexico, and Turkey, India began to show all the symptoms of a profound structural crisis. As in 1966, it was compelled to seek relief from the IMF, and the new Congress prime minister, Narasimha Rao, committed his government to ambitious reforms (*India Today*, 5/31/91:66–70; *The Economist*, 6/8/91:78).

Nonetheless, it is unclear whether or not the current crisis is of a depth and intensity such that the older patterns of resource utilization and their beneficiaries will be substantially discredited. The inertial force of Indian economic strategy, the cushioning effect of its huge domestic market, and a minority government operate against any sharp break with past policies. However, Prime Minister Rao has, under Finance Minister Manmohan Singh, the embryo of a change team, and the defenders of the status quo have unquestionably been put on the defensive.

4. SYSTEM TRANSFORMATION

Privatization or liquidation of SOEs will be pursued as the result of a combination of factors involving unsatisfactory attempts at improving SOE performance, the need to reduce the public deficit and generate new investment quickly, and the longer-term objective of reducing the state's responsibilities for setting the standards of and safeguarding the socioeconomic welfare of the bulk of the citizenry. If it is sustained, it will be part of a major strategic shift from ISI to a market-oriented growth strategy founded on private enterprise. It will entail a major overhaul of coalitional alignments (see Chapter 7).

4.1. Turkey

Under this rubric, Turkey is a pioneer, not only because its strategic shift was begun in 1980 but because of the failed effort at divestiture in the 1950s. In the 1960s and 1970s, Turkey undertook a number of high-level reviews of the SOE sector, yielding recommendations similar to those already discussed with respect to Egypt and India (Wålstedt, 1980; Karataş, 1986; Waterbury, 1992). Beginning in 1964, a select committee met over a four-year period on SOE reform but produced few concrete results. As Turkey entered its crisis in the late 1970s, a four-year reform program was drawn up but never applied because of the military take-over. According to its terms, all SOEs were to be put under sectoral directorates, supplemented by specialized sectoral banks, which would set targets for production and investment and determine marketing strategy. The SOE sector as a whole would enjoy a uniform set of legal arrangements and standardized employment and wage practices. There would be a sectoral division of labor, guided by the State Planning Organization and the State Investment Bank (Ekzen, 1981). This broad formula is an almost exact replica of that devised in Egypt in the early 1960s.

The last SOE reform proposals came in 1982, when Turgut Özal, Turkey's current president, was briefly out of power. In that year, the Ulusu government enacted Law 2929 (based loosely on recommendations of a committee headed by Professor Mustafa Aysan) establishing thirty-one sectoral holding companies, with each sector to report to the High Control Board (Yüksek Denetleme Kurulu, or YDK) and to the Grand National Assembly. When Özal returned to the prime ministry in 1983, he ignored the recommended reforms and replaced Law 2929 with Decree 233, which, as had occurred in Egypt in 1975, abolished the sectoral holding companies and brought ministers back into direct involvement in the management issues of individual firms (Karataş, 1986).[12] The new decree divided Turkish SOEs into two groups: those delivering basic goods and services and thus not evaluated according to commercial criteria, and those that competed in the marketplace and would be allowed to set their own prices.

Simultaneous with the promulgation of Decree 233, Özal launched Turkey's privatization drive. He called in foreign consultants, including Morgan Bank, which drew up a privatization master plan in 1986 (State Planning Organization/Morgan Bank, 1986; Leeds, 1988). He recruited a small change team of Turkish economists, mainly with foreign training, to design the export and privatization strategies. He put them in charge of the Central Bank, the State Planning Organization, and the Mass Housing and Public Participation Fund which was to be the lead agency for privatization. Özal claimed authorship frequently and publicly for the changes under way.

The privatization drive was part of the more far-reaching shift toward deregulation, trade liberalization, and export-led growth. With something on the order of $12 billion in fresh funds from 1979 to the mid 1980s, Turkey was able to pursue its new strategy without sacrificing real growth in the economy. It was this level of funding, both multi- and bilateral, more than the policy of constant real devaluation of the Turkish lira, that enabled Turkey to increase the value of its exports sixfold during the 1980s (Celâsun and Rodrik, 11/87). The principal instruments for the export drive were large private conglomerates in manufacturing and engineering, represented by trading houses fashioned on the Korean model (Öniş, 10/89). The drive was fueled by export tax rebates, duty-free imports of inputs for manufactured exports, and subsidized credits. The SOEs, as noted in Chapter 4, played only a minor role in the drive.

The economic cost of Turkey's strategy was in the form of high rates of inflation resulting from high levels of public outlays and from the price effects of devaluation, and a growing external debt representing more than half of GDP. As long as real growth in the economy was maintained, there were sufficient resources to invest and redistribute on a selective basis. As long as the export drive continued, Turkey could continue to borrow abroad.

The abrupt strategic shift after 1980 was engineered in the wake of the military coup. The generals leading the coup justified their action on the grounds that Turkey was slipping into political anarchy, if not civil war, and that national security required that the military act. But the generals wasted little time in launching the policies that constituted the export drive, and their principal advisor was Turgut Özal, a civilian engineer with experience in the World Bank. During the period of military rule, old political parties were banned, militant trade unions shut down and their leaders arrested, and the universities purged of radical professors on both the left and the right. The fragile and costly coalitions that had dominated the 1970s were smashed so that opposition to the economic reforms was minimal. Moreover, the Turkish people themselves were relieved that the growing political violence and economic disarray of the late 1970s had come to an end.

Özal's newly created Motherland Party (ANAP) won the first post-coup elections in 1983, and he became prime minister. It became clear that Özal would not devote much effort to reforming the SOE sector. He undertook three initiatives with different objectives. The first was to

The rescue of Turkish SOEs by privatization. Source: *Milliyet*, 5/22/88. Used by permission.

have the Treasury absorb a good portion of the SOEs' debt. The second was to allow the firms to raise their prices substantially. Large price increases occurred in 1983 and 1988. Through these two measures the SOEs wiped out their deficits and restructured their debt–equity ratios. Price increases were passed on to consumers. Farmers, for instance, saw the price of fertilizers go up fourfold. The third initiative was to begin the gradual conversion of the 200,000 or so white-collar administrators of the SOEs to the status of contract personnel. On the one hand, such conversion might entail higher salaries but at the same time would be based on one-year contracts that could be easily terminated. Moreover, contract personnel were forbidden to join unions or engage in strikes.

While the quasi-monopolistic SOEs were no longer a net drain on the budget, and their management less secure in its tenure, nothing had been done at the firm level (with the exception of Sümerbank) to improve performance. Indeed over the period 1985 to 1989, SOE labor productivity declined, and the ratio of net profits to sales fell from 9% to 1.8% (ICOC, 1990:65).

By 1986 several SOEs had been nominated for privatization, and an order of priority established, and in May of that year Law 3291 on privatization was issued. It provided for the transfer of the shares in targeted SOEs to the off-budget entity, the Mass Housing and Public Participation Fund (MHPPF). Whatever its long-term objective, this fund has become one of Turkey's largest holding companies, and its director serves at the behest of the prime minister. It not only held the controlling equity in dozens of SOEs but was empowered to change management and restructure the finances and operations of SOEs being prepared for privatization. Most important, it could retain in any privatized SOE a "golden share" that would allow it to veto any decisions taken by the board. Here we have a prime example of the orthodox paradox (Kahler, 1990), with the added dimension of the discretionary use of recentralized power.[13]

Not until February 1988 was the first privatization carried out. Ironically it involved a firm, Teletaş, for the manufacture of telephone equipment, which was already legally private. The MHPPF sold 22% of the equity that was publicly held (Karataş, 1989, and Leeds, 1988) through a general share offering.

The authorities may have eschewed further public share offerings given the size of the larger units coming up on the schedule and the shallowness of the Turkish capital market. The next privatization involved five productive units of Çitosan, the public sector cement firm. Ninety percent of the equity in the five units was sold to Société Ciment Français. As part of the deal, the French purchaser committed itself to a $75 million investment program spread over four years. The French company pledged that after three years 39% of the equity would be offered to the public. A similar deal was being prepared with Scandinavian Airlines for the purchase of USAŞ, a catering service for Turkish Airlines.

These moves were challenged by Özal's principal rivals, the True Path Party (Doğru Yol Partisi, or DYP) and the Social Democratic Party. They went to court to block the Çitosan and USAŞ deals. The Sixth District Court of Ankara, in late 1989, suspended the sales, on the grounds that they were in violation of decrees of the Higher Planning Council and of the MHPPF that stipulated that privatization would take place through share offerings to the workers in SOEs, small savers, expatriate labor, and the people in general (see Hazama, 1990, and *Cumhuriyet*, 2/21/90).

Reform and divestiture

The Motherland government promised that no block sales to foreign interests would be contemplated. That meant turning to Turks in the private sector. It was proposed that privately held (i.e., nontraded) Turkish firms swap shares for shares in the SOEs. This would have the double effect of bringing family firms into the capital market, thereby deepening it, and providing an incentive for the acquisition of the SOEs. Private buyers could form consortia with foreign interests to carry out the swaps. The swaps would be mediated by the MHPPF (*Cumhuriyet*, 11/28/89).[14]

Eventually the legal obstacles to block sales, foreign buyers, and secret bidding were overcome. In 1991 more cement companies were sold, minority government holdings in a number of private companies divested, and sales prospectuses drawn up for the major public petrochemical firm. By 1992, the government was legally enabled to plunge ahead. The real question was, would it do so.

The adjustment and reform efforts of the early 1980s began to lose steam after 1988. Özal's Motherland Party suffered a heavy defeat in municipal and local elections in March 1989, partially because of continued high rates of inflation. New parliamentary elections in October 1991 led to the defeat of Özal's party, although he continued on as president, a post to which the Grand National Assembly elected him in 1989. In recent years his attention had moved away from the privatization agenda to the maintenance of the fractious coalition within his own party. The team of young technocrats, with the exception of the governor of the Central Bank and the head of the State Planning Organization, has not been stable, and its immediate political bosses have changed rapidly. It has also become clear with time that the process of privatization is complex and ties up the energies of a limited number of technocrats for long periods. There is a high opportunity cost for this deployment of scarce talent.

The electoral coalition that kept the Motherland Party in power did not in any direct sense benefit from the economic reforms. Many agricultural producers and small-scale manufacturers have been hurt by trade liberalization, high prices for SOE-supplied inputs, and high interest rates. The large scale private sector generally adopts a stance of political neutrality. Economic growth and compensatory payments to select constituents allowed Özal to maintain a narrow, center–right coalition for nearly a decade.[15]

The True Path Party (DYP), also center right and the direct lineal descendant of the Demokrat Party that had governed Turkey during the 1950s, came to power in late 1991, in coalition with the Social Democratic Party, the lineal descendant of the former Republican People's Party. The incipient populism that Özal had begun to manifest was more

153

sharply put in focus by the new government, although it reaffirmed a commitment to public enterprise reform and privatization (Oyan, 2/92; Sanver, 3/92).

4.2. Mexico

Mexico presents the greatest challenge to conventional understandings of what produces change within seemingly stable political systems. It illustrates the process by which pragmatic damage-control efforts can escalate in the hands of a programmatically guided change team into policies that, if sustained, would transform the system profoundly. The collapse of petroleum prices and Mexico's inability to service its external debt drove Miguel de la Madrid in the early 1980s to a series of pragmatic reforms that involved reductions in public outlays, layoffs of public personnel, liquidation and consolidation of several rather minor SOEs. De la Madrid was the product of a system in place since the late 1930s. His object was to reform it so that it could continue to be viable economically and politically.[16]

The SOE sector had grown greatly and incoherently during the 1970s within the *sexenios* of Luis Echeverría and José López Portillo. Failing private sector firms were taken over, myriad special funds (*fideicomisos*) founded, and new lumpy assets added to the public domain. In the late 1970s, with the oil boom, PEMEX came to constitute a kind of economic state within the state, controlled in large part by the Petroleum Workers Union (SNTPRM; see Chapter 9). The period of wildcat SOE expansion culminated in the nationalization of several large private banks in 1982, ostensibly to stem the capital hemorrhage under way at the time.

In 1977 there was an attempt to structure the SOEs into homogeneous sectors with "coordinators" at the head of each and responsible to the key ministries (Secretarías Globalizadoras: see del Carmen Pardo, 1986:238; Cuadernos de Renovación Nacional, 1988:17–18). With the advent of de la Madrid after 1982, there were further efforts at rationalization, all within the long-prevailing philosophy of the *rectoría del estado* espoused by the president at least until the mid-1980s.

In 1986 a new Law for Parastatal Entities was drawn up in order to define more explicitly managerial autonomy (in the words of del Carmen Pardo [1986:244], "reduce the bureaucratic spider web"); to specify the purview of the three controlling ministries (Finance and Public Credit; Planning and Budgeting; and Auditing [*Controlaría*]); and to redefine the principal sectors. Simultaneously, the government absorbed the heavy debts of several SOEs equivalent to $12 billion (Castrejon, 1989a:11; Cuadernos de Renovación Nacional, 1988:98–108). In return, the SOEs signed performance contracts (*convenios de rehabilitación financiera y cambio estructural*), designed to promote technological upgrading, price reform, and a reduction in idle capacity and in the work force.

It was perhaps unrealistic to expect such measures to have much effect when the economy as a whole was registering negative per capita rates of growth and when the SOEs were faced with declining demand and massive debt-servicing obligations contracted in the late 1970s and early 1980s. As important, however, was the conclusion in December 1987 of the Pact of Economic Solidarity among the government, labor, and business. It put in place a negotiated system of price and wage controls, accompanied by a crawling-peg devaluation of the peso.[17] The pact succeeded in reducing domestic inflation drastically, but it meant that SOEs lost autonomy in adjusting the prices of their goods and services. The pact has been renegotiated periodically since 1987, and its maintenance ironically may vitiate the effect of a Public Enterprise Reform Loan (PERL) agreed to by the World Bank and Mexico in 1989. It sought to put teeth in the performance contracts so that good performance is rewarded and mediocre performance penalized particularly through hard budget constraints.

The sequence from public sector reform to divestiture was telescoped in Mexico so that by 1986 both processes were going on simultaneously but with key technocratic skills being devoted to divestiture. The qualitative shift came in 1985–86 when Mexico joined the GATT, reduced its tariffs to a degree perhaps unprecedented in the developing world, and also liquidated Fundidora de Monterrey. The impatience with gradualism and systemic tinkering grew as a result of inflation running at 180% per annum in 1987–88 and no growth in the economy. The government had no funds to invest, and the private sector was unwilling to borrow or to bring back flight capital.

There were, then, three major elements that spurred on the privatization drive: deficit reduction, the search for new investment, and, peculiar to Mexico, the overriding concern to establish some modicum of confidence between the private sector and the government. The willingness to pursue noncosmetic privatization was signaled by the preparation of the Cananea Copper Company for sale. Cananea occupied a hallowed place in Mexican nationalist history, and the government's determination to sell it showed it was prepared to meet strong criticism.

By the summer of 1988 some 722 SOEs out of a total of 1,216 were in the process of liquidation or sale. Although estimates differ, the units involved may have produced as much as 25% of the SOE sector's gross product, excluding PEMEX (Pichardo Pagaza, 7/88:26; Cuardernos de Renovación Nacional, 1988:91). After 1988 and the accession to the presidency of Carlos Salinas de Gortari, the process was accelerated. Salinas had headed Planning and Budget under de la Madrid and had designed the sharp cuts in government outlays. He entrusted the Ministry of Finance and Public Credit, which had primary responsibility for privatization, to Pedro Aspe, a professor of economics. He in turn recruited a team of very young, highly trained economists who espoused, like Aspe, a coherent package of neoclassical reforms for the economy. In another instance of the orthodox paradox, the Office of Privatization, to which shares of companies slated for privatization were transferred, was itself detached from the Ministry of Energy and Mines and put under the control of Pedro Aspe's ministry (*Latin American Monitor*, 10/90:823).

Facing a time frame of six years, or effectively five, in which to set in motion irreversible policy changes, the team pushed forward at breakneck speed. Salinas appeared to be right along with them, and certainly took some spectacular initiatives of his own. In 1989, he took on the Petroleum Workers Union by jailing its leader on charges of tax fraud. The signal to other unions was unmistakable, and the fact that there was no groundswell of support for the jailed leader sent an equally clear message. This was a major triumph for Salinas. It complemented less spectacular moves toward Aeroméxico and Cananea, both of which were declared bankrupt so that their labor contracts were nullified, allowing major layoffs, and so that new management could be brought in before privatization.

It became clear that hardly anything in the SOE sector was off limits to the Aspe team. TELMEX, the huge state telephone and telegraph company worth about $7 billion, was partially sold on condition that the purchasers undertake a major investment program.[18] The state holding company for steel, SIDERMEX, a chronic loss maker, was also targeted, and it appeared likely that over time everything owned by PEMEX in refining and secondary petrochemicals would be sold off, leaving only the extraction facilities (*Financial Times*, 5/31/91). Easily the most important move was the announcement in May 1990 that the government would privatize the nineteen commercial banks it had taken over in 1982. This move required a modification of the constitution achieved by a voting alliance with the Partido de Acción Nacional (PAN), a rightist, probusiness party long anathema to the dominant Partido Revolucionario Institucional (PRI). This move led to the restoration of a considerable measure of government–business confidence. In the space of three years the Mexican government had sold $22 billion in assets, eliminating about 200,000 public sector jobs in the process (*Latin America Monitor*, 1–2/92:978)

Real growth returned to the Mexican economy in 1989, private investment picked up, flight capital began to return, and the drive in nontraditional exports continued to show positive results. The Brady Plan (named after Treasury Secretary Nicholas Brady) for debt reduction, combined with a growing volume of debt–equity swaps, reduced the external debt substantially. After nearly a decade of severe depression, inflation, and falling standards of living, the modest upturn may generate enough hope and goodwill to allow Salinas and his team to push ahead.

By 1994 the result could be an SOE sector built around the oil fields, the railroads, atomic energy, the post office, and the social security administration. The mines, heavy industry, vehicle assembly, shipping, airlines, agricultural marketing, petrochemicals, sugar refineries, and banks will be under private ownership. The place of foreign capital throughout the economy is likely to grow, especially if a free-trade agreement with the United States is worked out. The PRI, for the first time, might retain power having won less than half of the national vote (see note 15 to this chapter), and as its cooperation with the PAN suggests, it will move its center of gravity to the center right. No single factor accounts for this extraordinary shift. Rather, it has been a combination of the depth of Mexico's crisis with concomitant discrediting of the defenders of old arrangements, the need for new investment and to restore good relations with the private sector, the assembly of a competent, coherent, and determined change team closely identified with the president, and the time constraints of the *sexenio* itself that have produced the phenomenon of cascading change.

5. CONCLUSION

In their bright beginnings, it was assumed that SOEs would produce their way out of their initial debt and generate a surplus that would permit their continuous technological upgrading. Instead, debt crippled them, they generated little surplus and fell into technological obsolescence. Now the state treasuries have no resources for investment and overhaul, and international capital markets provide relief for only a chosen few. In this light, privatization or liquidation of SOEs is not really an alternative but a necessity.

In the empirical evidence adduced in this chapter, there are some important but puzzling lessons to be drawn. The reform of large, old state enterprise sectors is both difficult and perhaps doomed to failure. In what I have called phase one reform efforts, the objective has been to maintain existing systems. The reason for failure, however, is not because powerful vested interests block reform, but rather because the reforms, if successful and carried to their logical ends, would vitiate the SOE sector of its ability to fulfill the non- and quasi-economic objectives for which it was created. Moreover, the partial reform and liberation of SOEs may bestow upon their managers the worst of both worlds; that is, the need to adjust to markets, all the while adjusting to continued bureaucratic determination of investment, supply of inputs and of foreign exchange (Kornai, 1989). From the same evidence we also see that vested interests turn out to be paper tigers, unable to ally with one another or to mobilize their very

157

substantial organizational and financial resources to resist both phase one and phase two reforms.

These generalizations pertain to both phase one and phase two reforms, although the two, I have argued, are qualitatively different. The passage from one to the other is not so much a function of crumbling blocking coalitions as it is the depth of economic crisis that disarms the defenders of the status quo and numbs the populace at large to the specific hardships engendered by specific reforms. This combination of privileged interests beggaring their neighbors in the quest to preserve specific entitlements and the underprivileged consumed by the challenge of day-to-day survival affords the leaders of phase two reforms an opportunity to force through change even in the absence of organized political support.

The transition from phase one to phase two, at both the macrolevel and the level of the SOEs, will be characterized by an accelerating reform effort on all fronts. The gradualism and careful sequencing of reforms in phase one that allowed the maintenance of older coalitional arrangements yields, through crisis, to an assault on existing entitlements. The task will be facilitated if the leaders have come from outside old coalitional arrangements, as in Turkey after 1980, but the Mexican crisis of the early and mid-1980s was of sufficient depth to provide Carlos Salinas, a product of old coalitional arrangements, an opportunity to undo them.

It is far too early in EIMT and elsewhere to know how far phase two reforms can or will go, no less whether or not they can be sustained. Even in Mexico there is likely to be a substantial residual public enterprise sector. There are two principal ways by which policy makers can approach the remaining SOE sectors. The first is to recognize that most SOEs will continue to be saddled with several, contradictory objectives that will undermine economic and financial efficiency. These objectives will continue to be politically determined and will have a social welfare component (subsidized products and services, job creation, development of backward regions, etc.). Public outlays specific to the SOEs and to the public sector in general will be used to compensate on a selective basis sectors of society particularly hurt by the adjustment process, and to maintain the support of strategic interests that constitute fairly narrow political coalitions. The best the government or the taxpayer can hope for is to contain costs, to subject the SOEs to a fair amount of scrutiny, and to use gimmicks such as memoranda of understanding to keep management from falling asleep on the job. This, I suspect, will be the "formula" that India will follow. Of its 239 SOEs only about 90 are not structurally unviable or in noncompetitive markets and hence salable. The rest will have to be kept alive or liquidated. Because of the size of India's domestic economy, it can afford the attendant inefficiencies.

The second way out is to seek a kind of mercantilist equilibrium along the lines of South Korea or Taiwan. The components of the equilibrium would be the key economic ministries and public banks, the SOEs, and the large-scale private sector. The goal would be state-supported capitalism (with or without an export orientation) in which public agencies intervene in the economy to support large-scale enterprise both public and private. There is an x factor here, however: The willingness of bureaucrats, managers, and politicians to forgo large-scale rent seeking and to refrain from devouring the units the state seeks to support. It supposes that there will be an equitable use of credit and investment such that SOEs do not crowd out the private sector. This is the direction in which Turkey was moving in the early 1980s, but predatory and rent-seeking instincts may have derailed the process.

Privatization, on the other hand, is equally problematic. It is part of a broader process whereby fiscally constrained states unburden themselves of parts of the social welfare agenda. It is an implicit call upon the private sector to accept responsibility for meeting the needs of the work force for jobs and an acceptable standard of living. It is an implicit admission that bureaucratic decision making allocates resources in suboptimal ways and that partially regulated markets are likely to do a better job.

Privatization, then, places assets somewhat beyond the reach of the state, thereby reducing the temptation of officials and politicians to use them for venal ends. It is a step toward making the public authorities referees in factor markets where the actors are juridically private. If this is to work, then the private sector itself must, in a way, be privatized – that is, denied subsidized credit, energy and inputs, licenses and quotas, award of contracts through noncompetitive bidding, and so forth.

No state in a developing country, however, can remain passive in the face of unemployment, inflation, and business failures. Privatization will make economies more vulnerable to business cycles, and if it is associated as in Mexico and Turkey with a shift toward export-led growth, the economy will be exposed to contractionary shocks in international markets. This may mean that even bold experiments such as Mexico's may, in some of their major facets, be reversible. The state could be compelled to save failing banks and enterprises, regulate markets, reintroduce price controls or wage indexing, all paid for by a new surge in deficit financing and borrowing. The collapse of socialist experiments around the globe may mean that a return to the radical statist projects of India, Egypt, or Mexico, when they first adopted ISI, is highly unlikely. But those who believe in the perverse effects of state intervention and regulation are probably right to the extent that once bureaucrats and politicians gain control over resources they are reluctant to give them up.

6

Managerial careers and interests

The pool of senior managers in the SOE sector in EIMT is examined in this chapter from two angles: First, limited descriptive data has been marshaled to delineate typical career patterns and strategies for success; second, we assess the extent to which this pool may have taken on some corporate if not class identity with the passage of time.

We shall see that despite considerable variation among EIMT, top-level managers are by and large well trained and have had long experience in the area of their expertise. In this sense they are professional. But professionalism, cronyism, and rent seeking are not incompatible (except in the strictly legal sense). The extent of the latter also varies by country and over time. In the SOE sector there are few performance-based rewards, so that scrupulous execution of one's mandate, as well as acting in a truly entrepreneurial manner, are temporary phenomena and dependent upon a high level of self-motivation. Such comportment is rare and difficult to sustain over time. Once again I argue that the property regime, with its peculiar principal–agent relations, in which the SOE managers find themselves tends to overwhelm degrees of technical competency and career stability as factors influencing performance and survival.

1. GENERAL CONSIDERATIONS

There is a debate about what makes the average public sector manager tick, and what the aggregate effects are of the individual behavior of managers. The debate resembles the one over the perverse or benevolent nature of state intervention in economic transactions. There are those, such as Niskanen or Srinivasan, who predict that administered market interventions and complex regulatory regimes will produce a general tendency toward rent seeking (among bureaucrats and between the bureaucracy and private actors) with "directly unproductive" consequences

160

for the economy as a whole. By contrast, an older public administration ethos avers that a more or less selfless bureaucrat, whose private agenda will correspond to his or her charge to serve the public good, is not only possible but, with proper incentives, can become the norm. These generalizations apply to all public officials, not simply to the state enterprise managers, although insofar as the logic of arguments for or against the public-spirited civil servant are concerned there is no reason to single out the managers.

John P. Lewis (1989, 1990) puts forth a nuanced case for the benevolent, public-spirited bureaucrat. In his study of major shifts in Indian macroeconomic policy in the 1960s, he identifies a set of senior officials spread across several ministries and agencies, concerned with reshaping agricultural policy. "These" writes Lewis, "were not the cautious, literalist, risk-averse bureaucrats of legend. They were a gifted and experienced set of risk-takers committed to the reform strategy and capable of some creative improvisation" (1990, chap. 4:44).

Much of the literature on Taiwan and South Korea has stressed the role of powerful bureaucrats who guide private economic activity according to priorities set by the state, and they do this without succumbing to the rent seeking that their power could afford them, or to the collusions with private actors that regulation elsewhere seems to produce (Evans, 1989, 1992; Wade, 1990).

To this debate I would, at this time, add only two points. First, bureaucracies and their occupants, to the extent that they have corporate characteristics, change over time. The determined, can-do technocrats that John Lewis witnessed in India in the 1960s may well be the jaded senior "babus" whom I interviewed two decades later. Second, like "irrational" voters who continue to go to the polls even though their individual vote cannot change the results, most bureaucrats most of the time do their jobs according to the rules (except, as we shall see, where moonlighting is concerned). Managers of state enterprises not infrequently go well beyond what is required of them to move peacefully through their careers. If we adopt Akerloff's lemon principle, it should be the case that if there are no penalties for mediocre performance and no material rewards for good performance, all public enterprises should cluster around a mediocre mean. Yet, as we have seen in Chapters 4 and 5, they do not.

Indeed, there are penalties for public entrepreneurship, and performance success may prove a liability to the manager. Successful senior managers noted that good economic performance of SOEs would almost inevitably trigger whispering campaigns suggesting malfeasance and creative bookkeeping. The less successful managers would collude with publicity-hungry politicos to smear the true public entrepreneur. Of the dozen or so SOE entrepreneurs whom I identified in EIMT, none had escaped smear campaigns. Emilio Ocampo, CEO of Cananea Copper, wound up in jail, and P. C. Sen, the CMD of Burns Std. Ltd. in Calcutta, was driven into the private sector. This is not to say that these and other successful managers had nothing to hide; it is hard to imagine how success could be achieved if serpentine rules had not been broken.[1]

Most managers simultaneously denounce yet take comfort in the invasive practices of the coalition of principals that dominates them. As long as real managerial autonomy is denied them, and politicians in the name of the people look over their shoulders, they can obscure the causes for poor performance. The impetus for efforts at restructuring principal–agent relations examined in Chapter 5 seldom come from the corps of SOE managers. If there were rewards for success, managers might welcome real control over their firms, but such is not the case. Rather, in interviews with successful managers they stated without exception that the only incentive for aggressive firm management is successfully meeting self-imposed challenges and the personal satisfaction derived therefrom.[2]

At senior managerial levels, the career is political and unpredictable. Appointments are almost never made exclusively in light of what the "owners" think will be best for the firm but, rather, in light of loyalty to particular ministers, as payoffs to politicians, or because it is somebody's turn. New members of the coalition of principals will often want to clear out all the clients of a departing member regardless of their managerial competence. Top-level private sector managers may also be subject to frequent change, but the reasons for moving up, down or out presumably will be based on the performance of the firm. Good managers will be bid for by other firms, but, as Kornai observes, there is no genuine job market for public managers (1989:40; see also Aharoni, 1986:194).

Senior managers in public enterprise are often depicted as conforming to two types: the tecnicos and the politicos. The first, frequently drawn from the corps of engineers, evince a high level of firm or sectoral loyalty, advance on the strength of their technical expertise, and seldom move laterally out of their area of specialization. If they move to the level of CEO, they had better develop political skills quickly or be ground up in patronage politics. At the uppermost levels of the SOE sector the distinction between politico and tecnico loses much of its meaning. V. Krishnamurthy in India and Taha Zaki in Egypt started as tecnicos and wound up as accomplished politicos.

For the politico, "a firm is a season in a political career" (Escobar, 1982; see also Kautsky, 1969; Camp, 7/72; Jacome and Cabrera, 1987:104).[3] The entire public sector is the arena for the politico and a specific firm is a stepping stone to something higher. As Nath's Laws posit, every Indian CMD wants ultimately to become a secretary or join

162

the Planning Commission. But tecnicos and politicos need each other; the tecnicos can make the politico look good, thus allowing him or her to move up; the politico can extract the resources and privileged deals that allow the tecnico to do the job more effectively. This dichotomy is heuristic; in practice these roles are not always neatly separated, nor are politicos absent from the private sector in highly regulated business environments.

Interviews with managers, and evidence from secondary sources, reveal a set of conventional concerns about performance and the logic of public enterprise. The coalition of principals has always contained figures who, sincerely or otherwise, have insisted on the transformative role of the SOEs and their obligation to promote social equity. Even during periods in which the "socialist" vocation of the SOEs was stressed by political leadership, the managers seldom joined the chorus. Instead they talked of rational management practices, increasing labor productivity, generating profits, and competing effectively. Sooner or later political leadership in EIMT came to share these concerns (Ramamurti, 1987:865). In March 1967, President Nasser met with all Egypt's public company heads and emphasized that there was no difference between socialist and capitalist management, only a difference in the ownership of the means of production and the use of the profits. In both systems, he said, wages must be linked to productivity. Taha Zaki put it more bluntly (to the author, 2/7/74, as cited in Waterbury, 1983:252): "All these debates between capitalism and communism can be reduced to one thing – who gets the money. I don't care about the debates. The question is to get some money first, otherwise the debates are about nothing."

There are at least three ways in which political criteria come to bear on the selection and removal of SOE managers: (1) power consolidation on the part of principals, (2) electoral swings with attendant payoffs, (3) political and ideological correctness.[4]

The first criterion is the most common of the three. Powerful, and hence vulnerable, figures at the apex of the policy-making apparatus want to assure themselves of loyal agents. Loyalty without competence is not of much use; both are needed to protect the power of the patron or to raise him to new heights (Grindle, 1977). In general all senior SOE positions are appointive, including division heads, managing directors, chief executives and all board-level officers. Within the firm, this means that a CEO cannot choose his own closest associates. As Erten (1969:148) notes for Turkey, "The formation of a cooperative team becomes a matter of coincidence." Within the public sector as a whole, a single shift at the apex of the appointive pyramid has far-reaching effects. Between 1973 and 1987, India had twelve ministers and eight secretaries in the Steel Ministry. The chairman of SAIL was changed six times during the same period, while the CMD of the Indian Iron and Steel Co. was changed fourteen times (*Business India*, 8/16–23/87:50).

In 1978, 'Issa Shahin became minister of industry in Egypt. In what became known as the massacre of company heads, Shahin fired 21 of the 112 CEOs under his jurisdiction, and 90 of their board members. Law 60 of 1971 empowered ministers to appoint and dismiss CEOs after consultation with the company boards. Whether or not any such consultation took place is moot. What is particularly ironic about this episode is that it came on the heels of Law 111, which was designed to endow company heads with greater insulation from political interference (see Chapter 5 and Waterbury, 1983:120).

Because this phenomenon of power consolidation through appointments is ubiquitous, it is not surprising to find similar sorts of informal institutions in place to allow managers (and other civil servants) to cope with it. In Mexico, the *camarilla* (or cooking pot) is a small group of similarly situated officials (*camarillas* occur outside the government as well), and nominally loyal to a particular patron (*gallo*). While they may occasionally display shared ideals and preferences, they are essentially instrumental and personalistic (Smith, 1979:550–51; Camp, 1980:18–19; Centeno, 1990:225). In Egypt, similar knots of cronies, known as *shilal*, are important to the survival of midlevel managers in line for promotion by appointment. The fortunes of each of the group's members do not wax and wane in parallel so that the more fortunate can help out the less fortunate. There is nothing peculiarly Mexican or Egyptian about these devices other than their names.

Elections have traditionally provided the winners with the opportunity to reward their supporters and to build a coalition of interests that may see them through new confrontations at the polls. So anemic has been Egypt's electoral system since 1952 that it will not figure into this discussion. By contrast, although the PRI in Mexico has won all national-level elections since 1940, a combination of shifting factions within the PRI and the principle of non-reelection has meant that turnover at the top of Mexico's governmental structure is enormous. According to Peter Smith (1979:163), "during each presidential term, approximately two-thirds of the high national offices have been held by complete newcomers to elite circles." In an earlier study, Frank Brandenburg estimated that with each *sexenio* 18,000 elected and 25,000 appointed positions changed hands (as cited in Hansen, 1974:178; see also Rey Romay, 1987:93).

One Mexican manager claimed to the author that since the *sexenio* of López Portillo the continuity in senior appointments has actually diminished. When he took over a major SOE in 1976, he changed only five senior managers. The same firm, during the *sexenio* of de la Madrid, saw two hundred of its senior managers changed. This informant wittingly or unwittingly neglected to mention that since 1970, and the advent of Echeverría, the percentage of *re*appointments throughout the government has steadily declined, falling from 50% to 37% in that *sexenio*, then to 20% under López Portillo and de la Madrid.

India has experienced four changes of party control through elections, but only one, that following the victory of the Janata Party over Congress in 1977, has been of sufficient duration to permit analysis. Two others have restored the Congress Party to power. In 1977, for the first time in thirty years, there was the possibility for a new coalition of interests to redistribute the spoils of state. Sharad Marathe was secretary of industry at that time and served on the Public Enterprise Selection Board (PESB) responsible for nominating all senior SOE managers and board members. The composition of the PESB was not changed by the new government. Although the politicos wanted to distribute SOE positions to their allies, Prime Minister Morarji Desai adamantly opposed any such distribution. He was, according to Marathe, far more scrupulous than Mrs. Gandhi in this respect (interview, 4/24/86).

Turkey experienced a similar shift in electoral fortunes in 1950 when the Demokrat Party replaced the Republican People's Party in power. The new incumbents tried to remake the upper echelons of the government and state enterprise sector through appointments, but the Conseil d'Etat threw out some 1,400 appointment decrees (Heper, 1985:92). After 1965 and the restoration of civilian rule, the Justice Party pushed out senior officials identified with the RPP into "advisory" positions or onto ineffective boards. But it was in the period 1973–80 that electoral politics and coalitions led to rampant political payoffs. When Demirel's Justice Party replaced Ecevit's RPP coalition in 1979, 90% of top-level SOE managers were changed (Wålstedt, 1980:190). Demirel was merely continuing established practice. Between 1973 and 1980 the average tenure of an SOE general manager dropped from 3.5 to 1.7 years. Iskenderun Steel Co. saw 16 plant managers come and go over the same period (Hale, 1981:200; Heper, 1985:115).

The third type of managerial instability to be considered is that resulting from political purges, that is, ideologically driven rewards and punishments. Only Egypt and Turkey have experienced purges. Curiously, in Egypt they came under Anwar Sadat more than under Nasser. As the public sector was built after 1956, and as nationalized firms were added to the public patrimony over the ensuing ten years, much of the incumbent management was kept on, although individual managers may well have been unsympathetic to the regime and to socialism (Qassem, 1967; Farid, 1/70; Ayubi, 1989a:173). The general practice was to leave in place the general manager and to put someone politically trustworthy in as chairman of the board. Salah Farid was himself such a holdover. As the general managers retired they were replaced by the "sons of the revolution," but whether new or old, managers in the public sector increasingly found themselves watched over by "commissars" from the Arab Socialist Union who were often little more than glorified police informants (Salmy, 1979:137).

When Sadat succeeded Nasser to the presidency in 1970, he anticipated a challenge from what could loosely be called the left wing of the Nasserist regime, an alliance including the head of the ASU, the minister of interior, and a number of senior military officers. The challenge came in May 1971, and Sadat outmaneuvered his adversaries. For the rest of the decade, but especially in 1974 when he dismissed 37 SOE managers and 104 board members, Sadat removed those associated with the defeated coalition of leftists ('Adil Hussein, 1982, 2:490–91).[5]

The military coups of 1960 and 1980 in Turkey were followed by widespread purges of top government and state sector leadership. Within hours of taking power in 1960 the military abolished all SOE boards thereby removing in one fell swoop all the Demokrat cronies as well as competent managers that had survived the 1950s (Cihat Iren in Economic and Social Studies Conference Board, 1969:77). After that the SOE sector became a favored dumping ground for purged or retired officers in the armed forces (Bayart and Vaner, 1981:60). When the armed forces intervened again in 1980 they removed or arrested 18,000 civil servants in the first year. They dismissed 32 SOE managers including the CEOs of Turkish Radio and Television, the Turkish Petroleum Corporation (TPAO), TEK, the State Airports Authority, the Turkish Cellulose and Paper Corporation (SEKA), and the Deniz (Maritime) bank. Retired officers were moved in (*The Middle East*, 5/81:30; Heper, 1985:138).

2. DESCRIPTIVE CHARACTERISTICS

Not much biographical data is available on the senior managers of the public enterprise sectors of EIMT. Through various registries, surveys, and "Who's Who" compilations, I was able to sketch rough profiles for the senior managers of Egypt, India, and Mexico. I was unable to do so for Turkey, as existing surveys did not yield the kind of information I needed (see Roos and Roos, 1971; Szyliowicz, 1971; and Heper, 1977). For the other three countries very imperfect data were available, allowing only limited comparisons across them. For that reason, I have not tried to generate tables that would compare the three in terms of specific variables.

With what sort of universe might we be dealing? In Egypt, the pool of public sector managers subject to discretionary appointment in 1984 totaled some 35,000 to 40,000, of which 5,819 were at the most senior level (CAOA, 6/84). Of this latter group, 1,441 were to retire between 1983 and 1987, which would indicate they began their careers before or just after the 1952 revolution, and almost certainly in the private sector.[6] In India, in 1984, there were 5,136 senior managers, for 179 SOEs, in the discretionary pool. The total managerial pool was more than 100,000 (BPE, 1984). At the level of the board of directors, managing directors, and chairmen of the board there were about 450 officials, the filling of whose positions was the result of nominations by the Public Enterprise Selection Board (PESB) and confirmation by concerned ministers (Billimoria, 1985). I am unable to provide comparable figures for Mexico or Turkey.

By and large the top-level SOE managers are well educated. An exhaustive compilation of top executives in the Indian public sector in 1987 (SCOPE, 1987) revealed that of the 819 most senior officials, there were 27 Ph.D.s, 533 masters or its equivalent, 254 bachelors of arts or sciences, and only five below that level.[7] In Mexico a 1982 Who's Who (Dirección General de Comunicación Social, 1982) showed that at least 25 of 79 CEOs had advanced degrees and had engaged in professional teaching. All 79 had some university training. Perhaps more than in any of the other three countries, high-ranking Mexicans go abroad – principally to the United States, followed by France and the United Kingdom – for advanced education. In recent years, a new Mexican tribe has been born – the ITAMITES, or those who have graduated from ITAM and then gone on to MIT for a master's or a Ph.D.

Other Mexican surveys of the entire governmental sector confirm the high levels of education. One such survey (Presidencia de la República, 1987) found that of 1,156 top-level officials, 1,129 had finished university studies and 555 had gone on to graduate work. Of those, 333 had gone abroad to study (20 to Stanford, 18 to Harvard, 19 to the Université de Paris, 13 to the London School of Economics, and only 1 to Princeton). An analysis of Mexico's "power elite" of 500 personages, including 50 public sector CEOs (Jacome and Cabrera, 1987:140) showed that 15% had earned a doctorate and 34% a master's or its equivalent.

By contrast, Egypt's SOE elite shows a wider range of educational achievement. Recent data on educational levels among public enterprise managers was not available, but an older survey (CAPMAS, 10/74), of more than 34,000 high-ranking administrators in the SOEs and public authorities showed that 58% had a high school or university degree,[8] while 1.2% had advanced degrees, including 57 doctorates. What is somewhat surprising is that 34% had not received schooling beyond the "preparatory," or pre–high school level. Later, but not very reliable, information on 96 CEOs (General Organization for Information, 1989) yielded 57 with undergraduate degrees, 5 with master's, and 34 with Ph.D.s; 23 had studied abroad.

In all four countries, the era of public enterprise has corresponded to the era of the engineer. With the partial exception of Mexico the managers of state enterprises have been drawn heavily from the engineering profession. Only recently, now that financial management and marketing have taken on new importance in public firms, do we see the gradual rise to prominence of a generation of managers with business training. This is not surprising given that the mission initially bestowed upon public enterprises was production. This was the major goal, especially for the newly created industries in iron and steel, and chemicals. The managerial task was built around construction, installation, and operation of complex industrial processes. Equally important was state ownership and management of ports, shipyards, airports and airlines, railroads, dams, power grids, and construction companies. Rapid expansion along all these fronts called forth the engineers who became the captains of public enterprise. They have measured their own performance by quantitative production targets rather than returns to factors.[9]

If we conceive of engineers basically as tecnicos, then they constitute the single largest group of SOE managers. Ayubi (1989a:173) noted that in 1973 engineers made up 88% of the boards of directors of 275 Egyptian companies and authorities. The 1989 nonrandom sample of an older cohort of senior managers revealed that 30 of 96 had been trained as engineers (General Organization for Information, 1989). In India in 1979–80, 48% of the senior management pool and 58% of chief executives were engineers. The SCOPE (1987) survey gave information on the educational background of 750 managers; of these, 458 were engineers. In the 1950s and 1960s, Indian Railroads, Tata Iron and Steel, and the state electricity boards were raided for engineers by the rapidly expanding SOE sector. One can infer a similar process in Turkey. The corps of trained engineers there grew from 15,500 in 1960 to 120,000 in 1984, and they were concentrated in the public sector (Göle, 1986:200).

The Mexican state and the "Revolutionary Family" have traditionally been the province of lawyers, drawn mainly from the national university, Universidad Nacional Autónoma de México (UNAM) (Camp, 7/72, 1980; Smith, 1979). But beginning with the *sexenio* of Echeverría in 1970, the governmental elite and the state sector became heavily peopled with engineers and economists. Of the 1,156 prominent government officials surveyed in 1986 (Presidencia de la República, 1987), 21% were engineers, while 25% were lawyers and 16% economists. Figures on 79 CEOs in 1982 indicate that 26 were engineers and 50 were lawyers. In

1987, of 97 managers surveyed, 40 were engineers, 11 were lawyers, and 18 were economists.[10]

It is common for SOEs to run their own training institutes, such as Egypt's Kima Institute of Technology, attached to the Kima Fertilizer Company of Aswan, one of Egypt's earliest SOEs. Several of Kima's senior managers were products of that institute, and several others went on to head other SOEs. When the public sector pays for specialized training or education, the beneficiary is generally required to serve out a bond period before being allowed to seek employment outside the public sector.

All four countries have either established or contemplated establishing special schools for training public sector managers and senior civil servants. In Egypt, the Ford Foundation helped set up the National Institute for Higher Administration and Development, whose training functions have now been absorbed by the Sadat Academy. In India in 1983 the Advanced Management Program, run in conjunction with the four Indian Institutes of Management, was begun, and the establishment of a National Academy for Public Enterprises adumbrated. Nothing in Turkey has superseded the old Mülkiye school that dates back to the *tanzimat* period of the late Ottoman Empire. Mexico's National Institute of Public Administration (INAP), run by Raúl Salinas, father of the president, was designed to produce a stream of competent senior managers for the public sector.

In the three countries for which I have data, the average age of senior managers is predictably around fifty-five. Because the bulk of the managerial career is determined by seniority, few can rise to the top at an early age. At the same time, statutory retirement is at sixty in Egypt and sixty-two in India.[11] In Mexico the compass of discretionary appointment is so great that the governmental and managerial elites tend to be somewhat younger than in India or Egypt. The average age of 79 CEOs surveyed in 1982 (Dirección General, 1982) was forty-seven. The average age of Miguel de la Madrid's cabinet was forty-nine (Rodríguez, 1987:12). The 1987 compilation of 97 senior managers gave an average age of fifty. Only the Egyptian biographies (Ministry of Information, 1989), which included retirees, deviated from the mean significantly, with an average age of sixty-three.

Women make scarcely any appearance in these elites. In 1974, of 34,208 senior managers in Egypt's public sector, only 1,450 were women; of 316 CEOs, only 3 were women. Of the 96 senior managers listed in the 1989 collection of biographies, only one was a women.[12] In India, in 1985, there was one woman among 230 company heads. Mexican surveys of 1982 and 1987 uncovered no women among the top-level SOE managers, whereas the 1987 survey of the Mexican government

Exposed to innumerable delusions

found that of 1,156 high-ranking officials, 52 were women (see also Jacome and Cabrera, 1987:137).

One assumption that has guided my research from the outset is that because the public sectors of EIMT are relatively old, one would have a good opportunity to observe the effects of well-institutionalized careers on the esprit de corps of the senior managers. It may be, however, that the inherent instability that characterizes the posts open to discretionary appointment overwhelms all the career predictability that structured the manager's life in its first two decades. That said, it is still the case that Egypt offers the most structured and "professional" context for the managerial career, and Mexico the least. In India, electoral politics and the hegemonic quest of the Indian Administrative Service (IAS) have led to high levels of instability among senior managers, and in Turkey the combination of elections and purges has produced the same result.

Much of the following analysis is based on the various surveys just cited. It is important to remember that they include only the survivors. We do not have comparable career information on those who, for one reason or another, may have been driven from the corps of managers. Thus, the elements of career stability are overemphasized. Nonetheless, as a kind of benchmark, we can compare data here with those of Britain's twenty largest companies. In Britain the average age of the CEO was fifty-eight, the years served in the company, twenty-eight, and the years served as CEO, six (*The Economist*, 3/5/88:65).

It has already been noted that as Egypt built its SOE sector, it held over a significant group of managers from the nationalized firms. The 1974 CAPMAS survey found that nearly a third of the 34,208 managers in the sample had started their careers in the private sector before the nationalizations (see Chapter 2). By 1984 many of these individuals had made their way to the highest-level positions in the state enterprises.

However Egyptian managers may have begun their careers, once in the public sector they have followed model paths of rational advancement and sectoral specialization. Successful Egyptian managers have started young, have been hired in the area of their educational specialization, and have tended to serve out their careers in closely related fields (see USAID, 6/76). These are the characteristics of the true tecnico. In its exaggerated simplicity, the career of Mohammed al-Fiqqi, CEO for thirty years of TRENCO is instructive.[13] In a surprisingly Weberian fashion, it is the case that 42% of the 1974 group of 34,208 managers were hired by responding to public announcements in the newspapers. Presumably, appropriate training and merit had more to do with these hirings than knowing the right people.

The individual biographies of 97 senior managers (published in General Organization for Information, 1989) bear out these generalizations. A

170

couple of summaries will give the contours typical of the sample as a whole. Tawfiq Zaghlul was born in 1938 in Gharbia governorate and earned a bachelor's degree in science at Cairo University in 1966. He then worked as a chemist in the Tanta Oils and Soap Company, eventually being made head of its quality control section. He was also active in the plant-level union. In 1988 he was president and chairman of the board of the company. He was also a member of the council of Gharbia governorate, as well as a member of parliament since 1976, serving as deputy president of the industry committee. He has been a lecturer at the Institute of Workers' Culture.

Hilmy ʿAmr was born in Cairo in 1929. He earned a bachelor of science degree in chemical engineering from Cairo University in 1952. He was recruited to the Kima Fertilizer Company in Aswan and soon became director of production. He served on the administrative board of Kima from 1958 to 1970. He then became director of the Nasr Coke Company (part of the Helwan Iron and Steel complex) from 1970 to 1976, president of the board of the Egyptian Chemicals Company from 1976 to 1978, president of the board of the Nasr Coke Company from 1978 to 1983, and then for several years president of the board of the Chemical Industries Authority, set up after 1983 to fill the void left by the abolition of the sectoral authorities in 1975 (see Chapter 5).

Recruitment to senior management positions in Egypt's industrial SOEs has traditionally been carried out by the General Organization for Industrialization (GOFI), itself headed for many years by a single individual. GOFI experts, in consultation with sectoral and company heads, would identify younger managers with leadership potential and begin to maneuver them into tracks that would lead them to the top in light of anticipated retirements and transfers (interview with Hadi al-Ennara, 10/85). It was very rare that a senior manager moved laterally from some other SOE sector or from some other part of the public administration.

In Mexico a general consensus holds that there is not a structured, professionalized corps of senior managers or a typical career. Continuity at senior levels is strictly bounded by the *sexenio*. In the 1982 survey (Dirección General, 1982) 51 of 79 CEOs had been appointed at the beginning of de la Madrid's *sexenio*. The data presented in Presidencia de la República (1987) show that for 65 managers for whom there was information, 62 had been appointed during the same *sexenio* (see also Schneider, 5/89).

Perhaps conforming to the somewhat dated image of Mexico's rule by lawyers, there is a tradition of the senior generalist, called upon to ride several horses. About half the managers surveyed in 1987 had been recruited from the civil service and several others from unrelated sectors. The director general of SIDERMEX, appointed in 1982, had come from the National Association of Brewers. The pattern that prevailed until the 1980s is well exemplified in the trajectory of Jesús Reyes Heroles. He took a law degree at UNAM in 1944. He then became an advisor to the secretary of labor, then mayor of Tuxpan, then director of the Mexican Book Institute, then subdirector of the Mexican Institute of Social Security (IMSS), then deputy in the National Assembly from Veracruz, then, between 1964 and 1970, the director general of PEMEX, then head of the industrial complex at Sahagún, and finally, in 1975, director general of IMSS. Reyes Heroles is the personification of the politico (see also Camp, 1980:139–41, on Victor Villaseñor).

Despite the prevalence of lateral movements at the summit, a kind of engineering technocracy has been slowly emerging over the years. In steel, PEMEX, the railroads, and the power sector, the real, day-to-day senior management functions are handled by persons with specialized knowledge and expertise. No CEO parachuted in from outside could afford to lose them without, at the same time, harming his own chances for further advancement. This is but an example of politicos needing tecnicos and vice-versa.

In India the senior management career is a function of a triangular relationship between the civil service elite (the IAS and ministerial secretaries), politicians, and professional managers. The fundamental tension is between the IAS and the professional managers whose only organized representation comes through SCOPE (see section 2 of this chapter). The IAS is an elite corps of administrative, nominally apolitical, civil servants. The origins of the IAS can be traced as far back as 1833, when the Indian Civil Service was chartered. At independence the ICS had 1,500 members, half of whom were British. Renamed the IAS, this corps was gradually expanded to 3,000 in the 1970s and then to 6,000 in the 1980s. The total civil service is more than 10 million. Recruitment to the IAS is through a fiercely competitive examination, and only about 600 are inducted each year. They are trained at the Lal Bahadur Shastri National Academy of Administration (see Hardgrave, 1980:72; "Babu Power," 4/29–5/5/90).

Members of the IAS are generally assigned to state cadres, although they can serve anywhere in the public administration of the republic. They constitute a fairly tightly knit administrative caste, conscious of their status, their training, and their brains. They are the vanguard, as it were, of a larger stratum of some 60,000 senior bureaucrats who more often than not are the sons and daughters of civil servants (Malyanov, 1983:291–94). At the time of independence, members of the IAS were thrust together in the setting up of the public sector with technical personnel recruited from the railroads, state-level enterprises, and the private sector. The tension between the specialists and the generalists was immediate and has persisted to this day. The specialists belonged to no national cadre but, rather, to the firm. For them, the IAS generalists were "birds of passage" without any real stake in the firm per se. Moreover, it was widely believed by the tecnicos that the recruitment of senior managers was the product of collusion between the senior civil servants who made up the Empaneling Committee and the IAS. Howard Erdman reports (1978) that the entire top management of the Fertilizer Corporation of India resigned in late 1972 in protest at the Empaneling Committee's rejection of the professional managers' recommendations for senior appointments.

Even the bureaucrats had come to realize that Indian public enterprise needed a professional corps of senior managers with technical expertise, and there were eminently successful exemplars, such as V. Krishnamurthy and Sam Patil, to remind them of that fact. Thus, in 1957 an Industrial Management Pool was constituted with seven grades and pay scales superior to those of the IAS. About two hundred serving managers joined the pool (Khera, 1964). For reasons that are not altogether clear, this pool did not perform its task of identifying and training senior and technical managers, and it was wound up in the late 1977. Hiten Bhaya, one of its products who went on to be CMD at Hindustan Steel, claimed that the IAS had scuttled the experiment (interview, 3/21/86). Nonetheless, the practice of deputation from other branches of government and the IAS was gradually discontinued in favor of promotion from within the ranks of company management. By the early 1980s any civil servant joining the ranks of SOE managers would have to resign from his or her cadre or home ministry. It was the case in 1986, however, that twenty-eight SOEs were still headed by deputed civil servants (SCOPE, 12/89).

Much of the resentment of the technocratic managers focuses on the Public Enterprise Selection Board, which makes all board-level appointments in the central SOEs. The PESB was founded in 1974 and grew out of the Empaneling Committee. In the early 1980s the PESB nominated (but did not have the authority to appoint) candidates for some 405 positions, about a third of which would turn over in any one year. Its recommendations are not always respected as ministers and secretaries jockey to consolidate their positions with loyal supporters. It is often the case that senior SOE positions go unfilled for months or years, or are occupied by interim appointees (Billimoria, 1985).

The PESB has generally been staffed by senior civil servants rather than technical managers. This is still a source of aggravation to SCOPE, which has recommended that the PESB be headed by a retired private sector CEO, assisted by one retired and two serving SOE heads, and three government representatives.[14] SCOPE has also opposed the establishment of an Indian Management Services, as the functional equivalent of the

IAS, as it would create all its clubby evils, and propagate "a civil service culture" that would destroy the SOEs' business orientation (SCOPE, 12/89).

It is true that deputations have dropped markedly. The 1984 BPE survey noted only 199 deputed managers out of 5,136 positions covered. The most prominent deputed manager was P.C. Jain, from the IAS, and CEO of the National Textile Corporation. Of 819 senior managers identified in the 1987 SCOPE survey, 52 were deputed, but only 30 of the deputations were from the civil service; the rest were from other companies, the railroads, or the state electricity boards.

Over the years, then, the Indian managerial elite has become more professionalized with service increasingly confined to sectors of specialization. But in the most senior posts, instability still prevails. First, each firm head is appointed for a probationary period of one or two years, with the presumption of serving five. Many managers find this process demeaning and that it places too much discretionary power in the hands of senior civil servants. The incumbency of the heads of SOEs tends to be relatively short, often because they are appointed just before statutory retirement. Of the 110 CEOs identified in the 1987 survey, 45 had been appointed in 1986–87 and 31 in 1985. More than half of them had come from some other firm or agency, while for the entire group of 819, 28% had made lateral moves to their current positions. There are exceptions. Not surprisingly, one comes from BHEL, a firm with its own distinct culture and reputation for success. K. L. Puri, with a bachelor of science degree in electrical and mechanical engineering, joined BHEL as assistant works manager in 1965 and rose to the position of CMD in which he served for several years. His successor, B. S. Samat, joined BHEL in 1959 as an engineer trainee.

An important question in EIMT is the amount of movement between the public and private sectors. We shall have a good deal more to say about this in Chapter 8. If, in Egypt, we leave aside those managers that survived nationalizations, there has been very little movement from the private to the public sector. There is a major barrier to any such movement: A CEO must have had fifteen years' experience in the public sector before acceding to his post. As in the other three countries, after retirement, SOE managers frequently do migrate to the private sector in some capacity.

The evidence from India is mixed. In 1973, Laxmi Narain published a survey of 663 managers of both state and central SOEs in Hyderabad state. Of these managers, 244 had come from the private sector, and job security was a major factor in explaining their move. By contrast, Narain found movement in the opposite direction to be minimal, involving mainly accountants and design engineers (1973:99–103). At the national level, the PESB has encouraged private sector managers to make themselves available for SOE appointments. (The Tata family, beginning with the patriarch J.R.D., have established something of a tradition in this respect, especially with regard to Air India, founded by J.R.D. and then nationalized.) R. P. Billimoria hoped, in fact, that some managers from the private sector could be attracted to the public by the sheer size of the mess to be cleaned up. Those hopes notwithstanding, the number of board-level appointments involving migrants from the private sector declined from 11% in 1974 to 1% in 1985.

The 1987 Mexican survey of 97 top-level managers indicated that 29 had had some, generally very brief, experience in the private sector. Of these, several had had foreign training and worked for foreign firms in Mexico, but most of the rest were holdovers from private sector companies and banks nationalized in 1982.[15] Most observers depict the Mexican governmental and business elites as two relatively self-contained entities. More than half of the governmental elite are from Mexico City and come from professional or civil service families (511 power wielders of 1,156). Only 163 of these power wielders come from families engaged in commerce or business (Presidencia de la República, 1987:table 16; also DeRossi, 1971:202; Smith, 1979:102; Jacome and Cabrera, 1987:140). The years of expansion of the state sector under Echeverría as well as the years of public austerity after 1982 served to constrict the movement of people in either direction (Jacome and Cabrera, 1987:153).

In none of the EIMT countries has the SOE sector become a dumping ground for troublesome or retired military officers. Defense industries are generally run by military personnel with proper technical qualifications. For example, in India, among the 819 senior managers surveyed in 1987, 39 came from military backgrounds and nearly all were employed in the military sector industries, shipyards, and ports. The most famous military figure outside the defense sector has been Colonel S. P. Wahi, with a bachelor of science degree in mechanical and electrical engineering, who for many years headed the Oil and Natural Gas Commission. The 1987 Mexican survey turned up 3 out of 97 senior managers with military experience. In Egypt, in the late 1950s and early 1960s, there was a greater tendency to put senior officers in watchdog positions or sinecures than in the other three countries. A quarter of all Egyptians in elite managerial civil service positions in the mid-1960s were drawn from the military (Qassem, 1967). Ayubi (1980:347–53) estimates that in the mid-1970s, 8% of all chairmen of boards and 3% of all senior SOE management came from the military. The sample of 97 top managers compiled in 1989 produced 15 with some military background.

In Turkey, civil servants are not allowed to affiliate openly with political parties; thus we have no clear idea of their political preferences. I was unable to find any information on the political affiliations of India's senior managers. In Egypt and Mexico there is evidence of affiliation with the dominant party: either the PRI in Mexico or the Arab Socialist Union (1962–75) and the National Democratic Party in Egypt.

It is expected in both countries that senior managers and bureaucrats will support the party. Information on Mexican managers was volunteered by respondents and may understate the true extent of political activism. In the 1982 survey, 13 of 79 CEOs mentioned being active in the PRI or in the PRI's Institute of Political and Economic Studies (IEPES). They tend to rub elbows with powerful political patrons. Carlos Salinas joined IEPES in 1971, then headed it during de la Madrid's campaign. He was succeeded by Pedro Aspe. The data pertaining to 97 senior managers in 1987 produced 70 who had militated in the PRI, in IEPES, or the Instituto de Capacitación Política.

Egypt's parliamentary committees, whether under the single-party regime of the period 1953 to 1974, or the single-party dominant regime prevailing ever since, have had a special place for state enterprise managers. The party in Egypt has in large measure simply been an extension of the state bureaucratic and enterprise sectors, and the elite of both have rather perfunctorily acted out their designated political roles.

We know precious little about the attitudes of senior civil servants in EIMT, let alone SOE managers, toward their work and the public sector in general.[16] More important, there is no direct evidence of their sense of corporate identity or consciousness of shared interests. We will have to get at that important question through indirect means in the next section.

3. A STATE BOURGEOISIE?

Before the domain of the state came under general assault in scores of developing countries, it was possible to envisage, as suggested in Chapter 1, a self-perpetuating system in which the state and its highest officials controlled the evolution of mixed economies with subordinate private sectors (inter alia, Duvall and Freeman, 1983:573). The relative autonomy of the state from *control* by class forces was and is founded on the existence of a coherent set of interests and the institutionalized power of the state elites themselves. They need not be hostile to the private sector in order to try to maintain the state's lock on significant national resources and decisive leverage over their allocation.

If there is or was a state bourgeoisie in EIMT, the crucial questions that need to be answered are: (1) do its members stand in relation to the means of production in a roughly similar way and do they enjoy the same access to material wealth? (2) are its members conscious of shared interests and do they go about promoting and defending them as a class? (3) does this putative class have a strategy for reproducing itself? On all three counts, the state bourgeoisie in EIMT is not a class but merely bourgeois.

For many, however, the answer to these questions is affirmative. Max Thornburg (no Marxist he) saw Turkey in these terms years ago (Thornburg, 1949:195):

The main support for Etatism arose originally, and still flows, not from foreign infiltration, and not even from native conviction, but rather from a ruling class of government bureaucrats who are indifferent to theory but have become so dependent on the existing system that they will oppose its retrenchment.

We are concerned mainly with the managers of state enterprise who control significant means of production, allocation of resources, and the shaping of consumption patterns (see Richards and Waterbury, 1990:188–91; and Waterbury, 1991). But Thornburg and others extend the concept of the state bourgeoisie to include virtually all senior officialdom. In 1970, Alonso Aguilar identified 6,000 to 10,000 members of the Mexican state bourgeoisie, of whom he said (as cited in Smith, 1979:194), that

if one could speak of a bureaucratic or governmental bourgeoisie, it would contain the numerous current and former public functionaries who have made great fortunes through their offices and who have sizable investments in farms and ranches, in urban real estate, in luxurious homes, in national and foreign banks and in businesses of the most varied kinds, but who are fundamentally considered to be politicians. To this sector would belong well-known ex-Presidents of the Republic, prominent cabinet members, directors of national institutions and state-supported companies, high military officials, governors, deputies, senators, many municipal presidents, and not a few labor leaders.

For others that state class spreads across state boundaries to constitute part of the private and foreign business sector. In his study of Peru's mining technocracy, David Becker attributes to it "an undeniable class character" and labels it "the national manageriat" (1983:210–11).

That a state bourgeoisie could come into existence is generally seen as the result of a kind of class vacuum brought about by a feeble private entrepreneurial class, a tiny proletariat, and a dispersed peasantry. Such a class structure "can give rise to *state capitalism* [emphasis in original] as the political and economic project of a 'national state-bureaucratic class'; reformist and anti-imperialist even if integration into the world capitalist economy is not questioned as such" (Fitzgerald, 1979:37). This project, John Freeman argues, is pursued by the state managers in a relatively enlightened and disinterested manner. They are not immune to self-seeking behavior, but they do not heavily discount the future and thus serve the basic interests of future generations (1989:93–94, 120).

There may have been a time in EIMT when the captains of public enterprise were selfless in their task, but in the course of systemic crisis their altruism gave way to cynicism and nest feathering at the expense of future generations. By running down state assets, the managers put at risk the very base on which their identity was founded. For some this indicates a peculiar self-destructive urge as a class; for me it indicates that the managers may never have been a class in the first place.

If any of the four countries could have produced such a class, it would have been Turkey. The evolution of the Ottoman bureaucracy in the nineteenth century and its absorption into the republic's development efforts, the absence of an indigenous bourgeoisie, and the bureaucracy's reliance on a smallholder agricultural sector for its revenues, all conspired to imbue the Turkish higher civil service with a strong ethos and the relative power to command the fate of the nation.

The Tanzimat reforms had as one of their consequences the abolition of the sultanic practice of confiscating the privately held wealth of public officials. With that abolition, a true administrative oligarchy developed, against which the Young Turks (or the CUP) positioned themselves at the end of the nineteenth century (Mardin, 1969:261). Both Young Turks and older administrative power wielders were drawn from the trainees of the Mülkiye school, founded in 1859 to emulate the French model for creating the *grands corps d'état*.

The CUP also positioned itself against a nascent, essentially non-Turkish bourgeoisie, and sought to stimulate the formation of a Muslim Turkish capitalist class, but one that would remain subordinate to the central state apparatus (see Chapter 2). The partial collapse of that class in the 1930s left the civil service and the growing ranks of the state managers as uncontested masters of the economy. Drawing their revenues from rural tribute, high officialdom could, in Keyder's judgment, act as a class for itself. As token of such action, state revenues in the 1930s grew from 11% to 18% of GDP (Keyder, 1987:26–27, 77).

The Turkish state elite has had well-defined interests and has always felt comfortable with its role as guardian of a normative social order. The Turkish intelligentsia, by and large, has been an extension of this elite, and even the radical review of the 1930s, *Kadro*, was produced by state-employed intellectuals. Ismet Inönü, in his years as prime minister, subordinated the RPP to the state class by making the minister of the interior secretary general of the party and provincial governors regional chairmen of party branches. According to Chambers (1964:325–26), the administrative elite came to dominate the Grand National Assembly, the cabinet, and the provincial governorships.

After World War II, the state elite tried unsuccessfully to thwart the quest for power of the bourgeoisie that had grown in strength during the war years. During the period of Demokrat Party rule, it had to fight a rearguard action (such as the Conseil d'Etat throwing out many of the proposed changes of public sector managers proposed by the Menderes government). In 1960 it reclaimed its hegemony as it allied with the military and the civilian intelligentsia to put an end to the Demokrat experiment. The electoral wars and patronage politics of the 1970s weakened it, and Özal's moves toward privatization in the 1980s kept it on the defensive. Boratav (1989) laments the erosion of the older, rule-bound, uncorrupt, rationalistic senior civil service, and its replacement with patrimonialism and profiteering. Nonetheless, some of my Turkish interlocutors still discerned a hard Mülkiye core, deeply entrenched in the state apparatus.

The principal advocate of the Turkish state elite as class is Çağlar Keyder, and he sees its class interests rising and falling with its ability to tax the Turkish peasantry.[17] But what Keyder fails to note is that the civil service at all levels is itself heavily taxed while at the same time being especially victimized by inflation. Between 1972 and 1979 the real wages of workers rose by 36% while that of government employees fell by 26% (Okyar, 1983:547). In 1980 two-thirds of all income taxes were paid by wage and salary earners, whereas farmers, small businessmen, and the liberal professions paid virtually no income tax (World Bank, 1982). Such taxing policies do not seem to reflect the interests of a putatively powerful state class.

Egypt's managerial elites have not boasted the historical depth of Turkey's, but in the last thirty years have enjoyed the most coherent, "rational" careers. Over time key ministers and heads of authorities (such as Petroleum and the High Dam) were recruited from the senior managers within the organizations themselves. The question of who would be minister of industry became one of which branch would supply him: traditionally textiles (the infantry of the SOE sector), but perhaps automotive or chemicals (the functional equivalent of air force and armor). In short, principals and agents have tended to come from the same professional pool.

Despite the fact that career patterns, a high degree of professional specialization, and institutional interests would seemingly foster an *esprit de classe* in Egypt, most (but not all: Zaalouk, 1989:41) students of the manageriat have concluded that it has fallen far short of that (Ghun'aim, 1968; Waterbury, 1983:247–60; Ayubi, 1989b:178).

Unsurprisingly, neither Mexico nor India offer compelling evidence of a managerial class for itself. In Mexico, the Porfiriato produced the state technocrats known as the *científicos*,[18] a handful of whom survived into

Principal and agent: President Anwar al-Sadat and Osman Ahmad Osman. Osman Ahmad Osman, CEO of Egypt's SOE, the Arab Contractors Ltd., and former minister of housing and reconstruction, is Egypt's most famous state capitalist. His son married President Sadat's daughter. Source: Osman Ahmad Osman, *Pages from My Experience* (Cairo: Modern Egyptian Library, 1981). Used by permission.

the era of Calles and Cárdenas in the banking sector (Anderson, 1968:114). Otherwise the managerial elites of the revolution were formed principally during and after the *sexenio* of Alemán (Reyes Esparza, 1973). There is sharp disagreement on the character of these elites. Scholars such as Cockcroft (1983:216), and Reyes Esparza (1973) see the state bourgeoisie as part of a state that is a product of class struggle and of the control of the dominant class made up of the private bourgeoisie and monopoly capital. By contrast, Rivera Ríos (1987:173) argues that the state bourgeoisie enjoys considerable margin of maneuver to direct the development of capitalism, while Miguel Basáñez, in quite a different vein,

180

Managerial careers and interests

portrays the same managers as dependent creatures of the president (Basáñez, 1983; also Schneider, 5/89:16). Centeno, finally, argues that networks of *camarillas* are, for the bureaucratic elite, more important than class position (1990:225). This lack of consensus is typical of the analysis of the state bourgeoisie. We can agree that it looks like a duck but not that it waddles like one, no less that it is one. In an extensive treatment of Indian "state capitalism," the Soviet analyst, Malyanov (1983:291–94), makes no mention of a state bourgeoisie in the SOE sector at all. Rather, he argues that the real state class lies in the ranks of the 59,000 gazetted upper-level bureaucrats (including, of course, the IAS), over half of whom were the sons or daughters of high-ranking bureaucrats.

Other students of Indian political economy have discerned a more broadly construed state class, but one that conflates the managers with the civil service in general. Bardhan (1/21/89:156) is representative:

If the other two ruling classes [private industrial capital and the agrarian bourgeoisie: Bardhan, 1984] had their way, they would have preferred an economic regime in which the state is much less predominant. In some sense the state *has* captured the commanding heights of the economy, and sections of the professional class which run this gigantic machinery have thereby acquired powers which are not just of a junior partner in the ruling coalition. (Emphasis in original)

There is a loose consensus that if the Congress Party has become the bastion of the petite bourgeoisie, then the state-dependent class was dominated by Brahmins and other upper castes (Malyanov, 1983:294; Bardhan, 1984:52; Rudra, 1/21/89:145). To the extent this is accepted it weakens the popular, but largely unsubstantiated argument that India's is an "intermediate regime" dominated by the petite bourgeoisie in its various forms (Raj, 7/7/73; Prem Jha, 1980; Nayar, 1989).

3.1. Mentalities

SOE managers are, by and large, a reflective lot, and I had the privilege of interviewing several of them in each of the four countries. None ever talked to me, except in the most perfunctory way, about the socialist mission of the public sector. None held any particular brief for public ownership. Several recognized that their societies were confronted with enormous distributional and equity challenges, but none saw public enterprise as the key to meeting these challenges.

In fact, the only kinds of ideological statements I encountered came from senior bureaucrats, planners, and ministers, people like Egypt's former minister of industry, ʿAziz Sidqi, or former members of India's Planning Commission, like R. C. Dutt. It is perhaps that these officials saw themselves as the architects of a new order, and as its attainment receded over the horizon, could not bring themselves to question or reject

181

their vision.[19] The managers, by contrast, depict themselves in ideologically neutral terms. If they had not actually read John Kenneth Galbraith on the new technostructure of modern economies, they fell naturally onto a similar vocabulary. The issue was and is to get the job done; issues of property designation are important only insofar as they promote or impede this goal.

There is an annual conference of the Association of Graduates of the National Institute for Higher Administration and Development in Egypt, most of whose members are SOE managers. I was able to consult its annual report and recommendations over the period 1964–88.[20] The titles of the reports often reflected macropolitical trends in the polity such as Arab socialism or the open-door policy, but as Maghraoui (1990) noted, in the reports themselves, adjectives like "revolutionary" were frequently affixed to recommendations on administrative reorganization. Maghraoui goes on to say:

[The Association] seems to have made a conscious effort to maintain a certain autonomy from the political authorities. As long as the economy could run in an efficient, disciplined and rational manner, the managers were willing to work and cooperate. They never made any normative statements about either capitalism or socialism.

The themes the managers in EIMT frequently sounded had to do with efficient management and whether or not the private or public sectors better rewarded it. There was not much consensus on that score as the public managers shared a somewhat disparaging view of private sector capabilities, especially in family-owned firms where nepotism was and is allegedly rife. The managers, the bulk of whom were engineers, stressed aspects of physical production in assessing their own successes and failures. They had been able to do what all the outside advisors and former colonialists had said they could never do: produce steel, chemicals, vehicles, electronic and engineering equipment, run the Suez Canal, or test a nuclear device. In an era in which the SOEs have come in for heavy criticism for low or negative returns on assets, poor quality of products, and the inability to export, the senior managers, who brought the SOEs to life, feel that what they were able to accomplish, against extraordinary odds, is unappreciated if not forgotten (cf. Kenz, 1987:320–21).

Munir Ezz al-Din, the CEO of Egypt's SOE Wooltex, reflected over his career in the following terms (interview 11/6/85):

We were young technicians in the 1960s, given tremendous challenges at a time when the cost of living was low. We loved our enterprises and we built them. They were our babies. Money was not important. We replaced foreigners and had to show we could do it. Then we moved to other companies and our attachment lessened; but there were always the national tasks, the national challenges. But life grew more expensive, our families larger, and we discovered that problems we solved gave rise to ten we didn't anticipate, [among which] the misuse of the labor force. We began to feel thwarted by the system; we lost the feeling that we had it in our ability to solve our own problems.

The allure of the early years had begun to fade in EIMT in no more than a decade after the first big thrusts into state-owned enterprise. The 34,000 managers surveyed in 1973–74 in Egypt (CAPMAS, 10/74) were asked to rank professions by their importance. The highest-ranked profession was university professor (!). CEO of a public enterprise was ranked sixth.

By the mid-1980s, it is safe to say morale among senior managers was poor. Their accomplishments were overlooked while they were saddled, explicitly or implicitly, with the blame for the malfunctioning of public enterprise. As privatization loomed on the horizon or became a reality, senior managers did not know what their task was – simply to run a holding operation before sale or liquidation? They felt themselves moving from the soft budget constraint to a situation in which no new investment might be available. The senior managers could at least look forward to comfortable retirement; middle management faced far bleaker prospects.

3.2. Managers' lobbies

If the managers are in any sense a class, one would expect them to organize in some fairly formal way. It turned out, however, that in EIMT there were no strong managerial associations and no formal lobbies. In Turkey such associations are illegal, but in other countries, where they are legal, they are nonetheless weak or, as in Mexico, nonexistent.

At least on paper, India has the most developed agencies for the representation of senior SOE management. The Standing Committee on Public Enterprises (SCOPE) is the designated vehicle, and it is impressively housed in an enormous complex in New Delhi with office space allotted to individual SOEs. It holds meetings, sponsors special studies (a number of which are cited in the bibliography), and annually presents recommendations to the prime minister. But its director and the moving force behind it, Waris Kidwai, acknowledged to the author (5/14/86) that it has little power and is not taken very seriously by the senior managers themselves.

It is significant that the most vocal protests to public criticisms of Indian SOEs and to the threat of privatization were voiced by the National Confederation of Officers' Associations of Central Public Undertakings. In February 1988 it called upon Rajiv Gandhi to denounce the unwarranted criticisms of the public sector and to place their confederation and SCOPE on an equal legal footing with private business associations like the Associated Chambers of Commerce and Industry of India (AS-

SOCHAM) and FICCI (*Economic Times*, 2/23/88). In 1990, Waris Kidwai told the author that he was not very familiar with the confederation but that he thought that it mainly represented managers below board level.

In Turkey managers at whatever level are not allowed to unionize. However, as part of a "social entente" negotiated between the Ecevit government and the main trade union confederation, Türk-İş, public sector managers were allowed to organize employers unions at the firm and sectoral level. The legal difference appears to be that at the firm and sectoral level managers form part of the union as corporate entities rather than as individuals. They thus have become the functional equivalent (again on paper) of the private sector employers' associations grouped in the Turkish Confederation of Employers' Unions (TISK) (Kepenek, 1990:109). It is not clear how active these unions have been in recent years, although they have been encouraged since 1983. At least one assessment sees them as devices by which public sector managers can bargain directly with organized labor to force down wages.[21]

Other manifestations of lobbying and collective action are likely to be seen at the sectoral or firm level, or involving specific kinds of public sector managers. For example the 40,000 lawyers employed in Egypt's SOE sector protested vehemently against a proposed business law that would have placed them under the control of the boards of directors of individual companies and authorities, thus effectively ending their putative "independence," and perhaps their careers. Similarly, senior managers in India's SAIL initiated for themselves the SAIL Executives' Legal Forum to express their grievances against the abuses of managerial prerogatives (presumably exercised by the very top managers including Krishnamurthy) granted in the name of firm autonomy (*Financial Express*, 4/22/90). Once again we find that middle management may have a very different set of concerns than those at the pinnacle.

Specialized training institutes for the managers might also be an indicator of class formation. Such institutes not only would provide camaraderie and group identification through shared education but would be the selector through which the class reproduces itself. Once again, however, we find nothing resembling the *grandes écoles* of France. India has no specialized institutes for public sector managers. Egypt's National Institute for Higher Administration and Development once had pretentions to *grande école* status. In 1957 it was attached to the Economic Development Organization, the first public sector holding company, to train its managers, and after 1960 the Ford Foundation supported its training programs. Its graduates' association, as we have seen, has been the only organized forum for Egypt's managers, but its training functions have now been absorbed into the none too illustrious Sadat Academy of Management (Salmy, 1979:237).

The National Institute of Public Administration in Mexico (directed by Raúl Salinas, the father of Carlos Salinas) was founded during the period of public sector expansion and was designed to be the seedbed for professional managers. It had hardly tried its wings before the liquidation of the SOE sector had begun. One SOE manager uncharitably referred to it as the "archaeological museum." In 1975 in Turkey, under the auspices of UNIDO, the Industrial Management Training Center (SEGAM by its Turkish acronym) was set up, but, as in Mexico, its function in life was questioned almost as soon as it had gotten under way.

In sum, we find scant traces in EIMT of any concerted effort on the part of a state class to organize and represent itself or to create those educational institutions that would allow it to reproduce itself as a class. The promotion or defense of interests are pursued not collectively but, rather, in one-on-one bargaining with the various principals who control the fate of enterprises. Beggar-thy-SOE-neighbor tactics often result. The same could be said for private enterprises that strive to drive one another out of business. But more often than not, the latter also develop powerful representative bodies through which they can protect their class interests as a whole (see Chapter 8). SOE managers have not followed suit, perhaps because they have no collective sense of what is at stake.

3.3. Class action

The period covered in this book encompasses phases of SOE expansion, restrained growth, and actual contraction. Is it possible to observe linkages between the collective behavior of managers and the fortunes of their enterprises and sectors in any of these phases?

When resources are relatively plentiful, managers are skilled at laying claim to them, but they seldom do so collectively. During the 1970s, when petroleum rents rolled into state coffers or cheap commercial credit was available in international markets, the state sectors in many LDCs, and in each of EIMT, expanded significantly. The private sectors in these countries were not able to lay commensurate claims to the resources being channeled through state treasuries and central banks.

In addition, the aggregate effect of individual managers protecting their prerogatives was to maintain for some time the soft budget constraint, so that SOEs did not have to compete intensely for resources. At the same time, managers were granted perquisites unmatched elsewhere in the public sector. For the topmost managers in Egypt, supplementary allowances as a percent of base salary reached 190% in the mid-1980s, while in the rest of the public sector the maximum was 94% (USAID, 1984:47). Hansen (1974:126), citing Brandenberg, lists the "goods" a Mexican cabinet minister or SOE director could hope to acquire over his tenure in office. In 1960s prices the "goods" could easily reach $300,000, and some twenty-five officials were able to leave office with fifteen times that amount in cash. Despite low base salaries, SOE managers seldom suffer financially, and their opportunities to cash in on their positions are legion. However, these individual perquisites did not come through collective lobbying; rather, they either were built into the system at the outset in order to attract scarce talent, or were bestowed by benevolent principals in periods of abundant public resources.

By the same token, we find that principals quite often ignore the managerial corps, even regarding decisions that directly affect their enterprises. Reorganizations, personnel shifts, new projects, and closures may be handed down by decree without any managerial input (Dicle, 1978). Another close observer of Turkey's corporate life, Özer Ertuna, told the author (6/14/88) that managers do as they are told and willingly defer to state authorities. It is, he said, another example of the old Ottoman *devlet baba* (the Father State) mentality.

What then happens when the SOE sector is under attack? What does not occur is any coherent, collective defense. Rather there is a general *sauve qui peut*, which, *in aggregate*, can amount to a sort of defense. Analytically it presents all the problems of capital flight or foot dragging among peasants: Are we witnessing a group strategy or individual utility maximization (or, for that matter, damage control)?

Kornai (1989) tells us that bureaucrats will not implement programs leading to their own demise; but rather than block such programs, they may carry them out zealously, earn them a bad name, and then recentralize. So far as SOE reform and privatization are concerned, there is no evidence of such a strategy in EIMT. On the other hand, there are isolated cases of policy sabotage, such as a Turkish SOE, scheduled for privatization, whose managers contracted substantial new debt rendering the company unattractive. Another gambit is to sell off or liquidate losing branch operations of a firm in order to protect the core and improve the company's overall performance. In this way SOE managers behave like most other interest groups in the polities of LDCs: They react to policy initiatives rather than try to block them or advance their own. As Tony Killick points out (1989), if the principals signal policy shifts well in advance (or deny themselves the element of surprise) economic agents will anticipate the changes, and their anticipatory actions will effectively neutralize the policies. In Mexico, in any case, that has not been the case since 1986.

Managerial careers and interests

Like private capitalist classes, the putative state class is riven with internal rivalries. When times are good, they can take the form of the infighting that surrounds project selection, as in the case of the Mexican steel complex at Las Truchas (see Chapter 4). A proposed joint venture between the Egyptian SOE, Nasr Automotive, and General Motors for the assembly of private automobiles was eventually scuttled, after cabinet approval, by a complex alliance of senior managers, bureaucrats, senior military officers, and rival foreign investors.[22] Similarly, it may take good times to allow something like Egypt's Aluminum Complex at Nag Hammadi to consume more than half the power output of the Aswan High Dam at a price equivalent to only a third of its cost. The Electricity Authority has to carry on its books the enormous losses this policy entails, while the giant textile sector, among others, suffers from frequent power outages.

The quest for these privileges and deals, negotiated along vertical lines of the principal–agent hierarchy, becomes even more intense during hard times. Beggar-thy-SOE-neighbor runs rampant (Savas, 1987:30–31). We do not find the kind of back scratching in the face of shortages and credit squeezes that Nove (1977) sees as characteristic of Soviet managers. Indeed, given the fairly rapid turnover of senior managers in all but Egypt, the expectation of reciprocity might be ill-founded. Instead, like the Indian manager of a steel plant who advocated the privatization of Coal India because it provided such poor-quality coke, we should expect managers to try to look good at the expense of others in, or connected to, their sectors.

4. CONCLUSION

In EIMT there have been two extraordinary collapses of seemingly powerful, highly organized state interests that may yield some clues as to what drives the state managers. Cárdenas in Mexico began the process of domesticating the Mexican military establishment, and aside from General Cedillo's brief and unsuccessful challenge, the military meekly watched their budgets and privileges erode over subsequent *sexenios*. In Egypt, in 1975, President Sadat effectively abolished the Arab Socialist Union, the single political organization that had monopolized political life since 1962. Among the thousands who had built careers in the ASU, there was not a single note of protest. As a sign of the times, the ASU headquarters in Cairo was turned over to the Faisal Islamic Bank.

The lesson, it seems to me, is that we should not confuse institutional interests – in these cases the military establishment and the single party – with individual interests. The key to compliance in both instances was that important players were given attractive options of golden handshakes

187

and reappointment to other lucrative or powerful positions. The rank and file of the ASU were for the most part officials seconded from ministries and the police. The ASU was their secondary residence. A class must be defined in terms of control over, or at least in its relation to, power resources and means of production. As with the power wielders in the Mexican military and the ASU, what really may be at stake is an assured way of life, a bourgeois standard of living and consumption.[23]

The property of the state managers is not their enterprises but their skills and competence. It is intellectual property, and it is movable. Specialized skills are particularly scarce in LDCs, so that, unlike the great sea of civil servants, SOE managers can generally avail themselves of good jobs in the private or international sector. Early retirement may provide them both a pension and several years of private employment.

One of the shortcomings of this study is that I did not interview much middle management in the course of my research. Depending on their skills and training, middle managers may not enjoy the mobility of their bosses and may therefore be more firmly wedded to the public firms to which they are attached. I have no firm evidence of this, but it is not implausible.

In addition to the lateral mobility of skilled managers, in the most senior posts they are creatures of political power with no enforceable claims to their positions and no organic links to their enterprises (the occasional Mohammed al-Fiqqi notwithstanding). What they need to defend in order to survive is not public property but their links to powerful patrons.

If intellectual property is the hallmark of the state class, we would expect it to exclude others from access to the same educational facilities. Here the evidence is mixed. In India, Mexico, and Egypt there is good evidence that managers and other high-ranking officials are disproportionately the offspring of professionals and public officials. The technocracy has been a refuge to some extent for the scions of families of private wealth faced with the radicalizing experiments discussed in Chapter 2. Yet in all four countries, higher specialized education has been opened to a remarkable degree and has provided avenues for upward mobility. The state technocracy has no lock on the educational institutions that produced it.

At the same time, it is clear that few of the children of the senior managers in EIMT will follow their fathers into the public sector. Not only will there be little intergenerational transfer of formal employment, many of the offspring have left or will leave their countries altogether. We are thus witnessing the reproduction of a standard of living but not of a class.

Thus, in answer to the three questions posed at the beginning of this chapter's section 3, there is an observable group of managers who share common positions of institutional power and material wealth. They do not, however, exhibit any consciousness of shared interests, especially when resources are scarce. To the extent they can guarantee access for their children to high quality, advanced education, they are able to pass on intellectual property and the ability to maintain a high standard of living, but not access to or control of the public sector itself.

If the managers will not defend the SOE sector, and indeed have no class-based interest to do so, who will undertake the defense? Two interests are the likely candidates: organized labor (treated in Chapter 9) and senior bureaucrats. Senior civil servants do not have the possibilities for lateral moves into the private sector enjoyed by senior management; for many, their positions depend on the continued existence, if not expansion, of the public sector. The survey of top-ranking Mexican government officials carried out in the mid-1980s (Presidencia de la República, 1987) shows that about 46% are situated in ministries and agencies that supervise or control SOEs. Ramamurti (1987:880) estimates a somewhat more restrained set of senior Indian bureaucrats similarly dependent on the public sector. Whether through foot dragging and sabotage, or policy advocacy, *if* there is to be a defense of the SOE sector, it will come from the senior administrators and not the managers.[24]

7

Coalitions and state-owned enterprises

Because of the enormous resources that flow through the SOE sector, including its banks and other financial intermediaries, it has become the linchpin of coalition maintenance in all four countries. Although the soft budget constraint has operated within the SOE sector, it has also operated between that sector and all the public and private constituencies that have come to depend on it for jobs, contracts, loans, and inputs. Chapters 8 and 9 will look in some detail at two important constituencies – the corporate private sector and organized labor – parts of which are generally within the older coalitional base associated with ISI. A shift away from that strategy necessarily entails a recasting of the coalition during a time in which public resources are extremely limited (in general, see Nelson et al., 1989). This latter task is best undertaken by new political leadership with different, if not less demanding, allies. This was the situation in which Özal (prime minister of Turkey 1983–89; president after 1989) found himself after 1983. The task is or will be far harder for the incumbent presidents Salinas and Mubarak, and only slightly less so for the (6/91) Congress prime minister, Narasimha Rao.

Analysis of coalitions provides a bridge between instrumental approaches to the state and state sectors and those emphasizing state autonomy. All systems of rule have coalitional underpinnings, and they typically contain constituents that spread across formal state agencies and dependencies into civil society. Sometimes certain coalition members may have preponderant influence over the state apparatus and policies, such as the military or corporate business. Sometimes the coalition is dominated by state actors themselves, including, once again, the military, state-dependent labor unions, or senior civil servants.

Public resources are used to maintain these coalitions and hence to ensure political survival. Some coalitions may enhance the overall productivity of the economy, such as the wedding of smallholder farmers, corporate *chaebols,* and the military in South Korea. A productive econ-

190

omy, as Japan has demonstrated over four decades, can sustain basic coalitional arrangements for a long time (Calder, 1989); stagnant or declining economies cannot. In the latter instances, the dynamic of distributional coalitions analyzed by Olson (1982) appears to be at work. An accumulation of increasingly exclusive interests maximize their own utilities at the expense of the economy and society as a whole. They tend to lead to the sacrifice of investment, technological change, and growth for the immediate gratification of group consumption.

One does not need to be a neoclassical economist to arrive at the same conclusion. K. N. Raj, India's leading leftist proponent of intermediate regime approaches, observed (7/7/73:1192):

> Since intermediate regimes are dominated by (or are in partial alliance with) numerous social groups who could secure considerable gains in the process, they are invariably under pressure – sometimes from one group, sometimes from another – to follow price policies which in effect subsidize one segment or the other of the ruling class and its main allies. Such subsidization is in fact the main method available to these regimes for retaining support of this somewhat heterogeneous mass.

Sobhan and Ahmad (1980) concur and point out that this servicing of allies can defeat the basic project of the "intermediate regime" that is to substitute for a weak bourgeoisie.

In that same vein Pranab Bardhan has chalked up India's slow industrial growth to a broad-based and "motley" alliance of industrial and agrarian capital with the elites of the state. "When," he says, "none of them is individually strong enough to dominate the process of resource allocation, one predictable outcome is the proliferation of subsidies and grants to placate all of them, with the consequent reduction in available surplus for public capital formation" (1984:61). What Indians have come to call "the license raj" of rampant exploitation of regulations for rents, lay, claims Sharad Marathe (1986:89), at the heart of a nonproductive alliance of politicians, bureaucrats, and businessmen.[1]

The process of maintaining or restructuring coalitions will depend on how the privileges of their constituent parts were first acquired. In corporatist systems privileges were often bestowed upon rather than won by the beneficiaries. The most striking case in point was Nasser's proclamation after 1962 that henceforth workers and peasants would have at least 50% representation in all the republic's elected bodies. The principle was not the result of any pressure generated by the peasants or workers themselves. Similarly, under structural adjustment, investment incentives, tax breaks, and deregulation that benefit private agents may not be the result of their organizational strength. I posit that those who have not won their acquired rights through organizational trials of strength will probably not be effective in defending what they have been granted.

Nonetheless, they may be more powerful than any combination of potential rivals. In the shift from ISI toward market-oriented reforms under conditions of resource scarcity, incumbent political elites will have to deal with older distributional coalitions with legitimized and institutionally anchored claims to resources as against potential but as yet unorganized allies who will benefit from the new policies. Political death may lie between these two stools. If, as in Eastern Europe, the existing coalitions and their claims have been thoroughly delegitimized, political leadership may face little resistance in thrusting them aside. But that kind of discrediting of older arrangements has not proceeded as far in EIMT, even in Mexico and Turkey. Economic crisis has left old coalitions in disarray and unsure of how to organize their defenses, but it has not stripped them of their banners.

Some observers have placed the problem of restructuring coalitions in the context of democracy versus authoritarianism, arguing that restructuring will fall victim to the politicians' needs to mobilize alliances of voters. Kohli (1989:324) believed that Rajiv Gandhi's efforts after 1984 to liberalize the Indian economy would ultimately fail for those reasons. My view is that the challenge is enormous under any set of political arrangements. The corporate claims of coalition allies in single-party Mexico or authoritarian Egypt have been as pressing as the electorally driven ones of Turkey and India. It is similarly argued that the major impetus toward redistributive polices in India and Turkey has come through the electoral process, but in most respects redistribution went further in Egypt, under what amounted to a military dictatorship in the 1960s, than in any of the other three countries.

Much coalitional analysis, to some extent including my own, assumes that the economic niches in which coalition members find themselves tell most of what we need to know about their interests and how they will react to changes in economic strategy. For example, Wellisz and Findlay (1984:151) examine different economic interests in terms of specific kinds of rent-seeking behavior, Robert Bates (1981) explains antirural coalitions, and Ronald Rogowski (1989), coalitions of capital, labor, and land that determine the willingness of economies to trade or protect. But, as Haggard and Kaufman warn (1992), in practical terms, because individuals are associated with a range of economic institutions (household, firm, private sector, public sector, etc.) simultaneously, categories are seldom watertight and the costs and benefits of any set of policies are very hard to measure.

In addition, coalition members are not always exclusively or mainly defined by economic interests, no matter how heterogeneous. In Turkey there are both secular and ideological constituents, such as the social democrats associated with the RPP or the proto-fascists grouped under the now defunct National Action Party. Parties have competed for the allegiance of Sunni or Alevi Muslims, and the latter briefly had their own political party. The coalitional mosaic is, of course, even more complex in India, where specific castes, and ethnic and lingual groups, lay claim to public resources and legal privileges. With respect to Mexico, Zermeño (5/87:35) discerns clear ideological "outlooks" associated with coalition partners ranging from the communitarian ethos of *campesino* groups to the democratic centralism of the Revolutionary Family. It is probably in Egypt that one can most easily read political behavior and demands from economic position.

1. WHEN TIMES WERE GOOD

In EIMT, ISI strategies were associated with implicit social contracts; in Egypt and Mexico welfare guarantees for strategic groups such as organized labor, the intelligentsia, and some private enterprise were traded for a certain amount of political quiescence.[2] In India and Turkey, where elections played a much more prominent role, commitments to welfare established critical vote banks from which rural constituents, among others, drew considerable benefits. As long as economies were growing, could borrow abroad, and had some surplus to redistribute, the guiding policy was that, felicitously coined by Bent Hansen (1972:72–73) for Egypt, of "the line of least popular dissatisfaction." To tread it demanded exuberant use of public resources.

Coalition maintenance led to heavy discounting of the future. Leopoldo Solís (1976:87) recalls that in 1971 Echeverría discovered that the Central Bank and some commercial banks had been carrying reserves above their legal requirements, thereby restricting the flow of new investment. The president was furious and a spending spree ensued: "Speed became the sole constraint on spending . . . Swiftness in program preparation was the key to larger shares of the budget." By 1973 the deficit had doubled to 5% of GDP and "inflation exploded." Hacienda (Finance) then had to step in to cool off the economy. The government, faced with the threat of strikes, fostered an accord between capital and labor for wage restraints, which Echeverría subsequently tried to formalize into a Tripartite Commission (Basáñez, 1983:89–90; Luna, 1987:460). In Egypt, the shock upon the regime of the cost-of-living riots of January 1977 led to the abandonment of all efforts at structural adjustment and to a consumption binge that did not end until 1986.

193

1.1. Constituent parts

Throughout the preceding chapters I have touched upon some of the principal beneficiaries of the ISI political formulas, and because private capital and labor will be treated in the following two chapters, only a brief reprise is required here. The essential point is that older coalitions were broad-based and diverse; and when conflicts emerged within them, the solution was to throw money at them.

Outside of Mexico, the claims of the military have seldom been denied. Its growing weight in the civilian sector of the other three economies has profound implications for coalition maintenance. On the one hand, the military has generally been allied with SOE managers in that the SOEs are seen as providing strategic strength for the nation as well as direct production of matériel for the military itself. Moreover, in recent decades the SOEs and trading companies set up under the auspices of the military have led to close collaboration with foreign and private local capital. Generally both sorts have shared with the military a preference for high tariffs and protected markets, but the basic point is that rather than playing the role of an autonomous guardian of the nation's borders and internal security, the military have become allies of important economic actors. Chapter 5 has noted the joint ventures between Turkey's officers' pension fund (OYAK) and both private local and multinational capital. Since 1985 the trend has been reenforced by the establishment of an off-budget fund, the Defense Industry Support Fund, with dedicated tax and tariff revenues totaling anywhere from $600 million to $1.5 billion annually, to finance arms procurement and investment in military industry. On its board are public officials, military officers, and prominent private businessmen like Sakip Sabanci (*Middle East Economic Digest,* 11/23/ 85:44; *Turkish Almanac,* 1989:199). Ayres (1983:816) summarizes the resulting situation in these terms:

> Not only does the military have an interest in preserving the status quo but the financial oligarchy see the military as the guardian of the system. From the late 1960s, the growing strength of the labour movement, with its revolutionary demands, could only be held in check ultimately through the power of the military, and the fortunes of capitalists became linked to those of the military officers.

In India similar trends are under way, especially in advanced electronics, military applications of computers, aeronautics, telecommunications, lasers, and so forth. Joint ventures between private local and foreign providers of such technologies will become increasingly common. In Egypt we saw the Military Industrial Organization come forth with a Korean partner to bid for a project to manufacture passenger cars. But in both

194

India and Egypt, a segment of the senior officers corps still depends on Soviet equipment as well as on the trading companies that both countries set up to finance the payments arising out of Soviet project aid and military deliveries (Waterbury, 1983:395–99). Given the changes in the former Soviet Union and in Eastern Europe, this segment of the officers corps may not be able to defend its entitlements.

The intelligentsia in EIMT comprises virtually all those with advanced degrees. Its two faces are the civil service and state technocracy on the one hand, and the free professions on the other, with schoolteachers somewhere in between. It is both the foundation and the focus of an important subcoalition of parents, students, teachers, professors, education bureaucrats, and politicians. Until after World War I, literacy and numeracy, not to mention more advanced training, were restricted to very small elites within EIMT, and in India and Egypt that fact was attributed to colonial policies that, the nationalists promised, would be reversed. They were.

The impact of these commitments and the entitlements that flowed from them is best illustrated in Egypt. All levels of public education were made free. Then it was decided that any student who successfully passed the secondary school exam could go on to university. When the military government tried to reverse this in 1957, it faced one of the few parliamentary revolts of the period. Then, in 1964, the state committed itself to providing a public job to anyone graduating from university or from technical training institutes. Between 1977 and 1987 the number of graduates of universities and technical colleges doubled from 185,000 to 376,000. Given the preponderance of the SOE sector in the economy, the task of absorption of these hundreds of thousands of bearers of "advanced" degrees fell upon it. The pool of redundant managers grew as quickly as the pool of redundant workers in the SOEs until some relief was provided in 1979 (see Sharaf El-Din, 1982:7; Waterbury, 1983:234–46; Handoussa, 9/88). In 1991, as part of its commitments to the IMF stabilization program, Egypt pledged to end the state's role as legal employer of last resort.[3]

None of the other three countries has been quite so profligate as Egypt in delivering educational services to its citizens, and in Mexico the proportion of those going on from high school to university is relatively small. But whether out of guilt, moral indignation, or ideological commitment, the intelligentsia itself has generally lobbied hard for mass higher education and for the obligation of the state to protect the future of the educated. When the proposition comes to the surface that markets for skilled personnel should significantly affect the size and composition of university output, the intelligentsia is directly threatened. It can rally

Mubarak's happy coalition. Source: *al-Ahram al-Iqtisadi*, 5/6/91:12. Used by permission.

its numerous troops through ideological denunciations of the state's sur-render to markets and capitalist needs. Mobilized students, with *relatively* little to lose, can make regimes tremble.

Organized labor, frequently concentrated in the SOE sector, for years benefited from wage levels and supplementary allowances that in no way reflected their scarcity value. In the decade of intense electoral competition between the Justice and RPP in Turkey, labor was consistently rewarded. Between 1974 and 1978 real public sector wages increased 58%, em-ployment 28%, while value-added per worker declined 20% (Boratav, 1986:136). Over the entire decade the SOE work force doubled in size from 362,000 to 646,000. In good or bad times, political leaders may segment their public sector constituents in terms of rewards. During roughly the same period, the real wages and salaries of government employees fell by 26% (Okyar, 1983:547). We find the same phenom-

196

enon in Egypt, where the wage and salary index for the SOEs increased from 100 in 1978 to 122 in 1984–85 while declining for central government employees from 100 to 72 (Handoussa, 9/88:57).[4]

Another indicator of relative rewards is the rate of pay increases relative to rises in the cost-of-living index. It was generally the case in times of freer resources that public sector and civil service payscales rose much more rapidly than the CPI and actually contributed to overall inflation. In India, after the emergency, the CPI increased 275% between 1978 and 1988, while public sector pay increased 370% (*India Today*, 4/15/89:55).

Packages of bonuses, wage supplements, and profit shares became routine in EIMT. In an Orwellian announcement Egypt's Ministry of Industry in 1988 set the shares of profits for workers in twenty-six loss-making SOEs. Egypt's "social bonus," paid out annually, serves to fill the gap between increases in real wages and the rate of inflation. In 1988 the bonus represented 15% of gross wage, and in negotiations between the minister of labor and the president of the General Confederation of Trade Unions, the same bonus was extended to 3.5 million private sector workers (*AI*, 7/15/88).

Until recently, the corporate private sector has not played an overt political role in the dominant coalitions, but parts of it have been integrated into the economic rewards that flow from tariff protection, state licensing, and subsidized credit. The aptly named "alliance for profits" that Clark Reynolds (1970) coined for Mexico applies in the other three countries. In all four countries, moreover, the fair weather coalition has included capitalist farmers. These can be the large-scale, export-oriented farmers of Mexico and Turkey, benefiting from cheap credit and publicly provided irrigation, to the smaller-scale farmers of India and Egypt, selling predominantly to the domestic market and enjoying subsidized machinery, power, and fuels. In India, representatives of what the Rudolphs (1987) have called "bullock capitalists" have come to dominate state legislative assemblies and are important in the Lok Sabha. They and their clients represent an interest-defined swing vote that drove Indira Gandhi from power and a decade later helped bring V. P. Singh in. No leader will casually tamper with their claims to cheap electricity, fuel, and fertilizers.

1.2. Discretion and compensation

So far, we have examined direct, material rewards to identifiable coalition members. There is, however, a much more diffuse set of interests that must be taken into account in successful coalition maintenance. Significant segments of the population must be neutralized, if not co-opted,

Exposed to innumerable delusions

Table 7.1. *India: Shares of subsidy items in total subsidy outlay, 1975/76–1989/90*

Year	Food (%)	Fertilizer (%)	Export promotion (%)	Other[a] (%)	Total rupees bn
1976/77	53	..	34	13	4.7
1977/78	53	..	28	18	9.5
1978/79	37	21	25	17	12.9
1979/80	39	23	25	13	14.7
1980/81	33	33	20	14	18.2
1981/82	34	26	21	19	19.1
1982/83	36	19	24	20	19.5
1983/84	31	26	21	22	23.0
1984/85	29	36	16	19	28.8
1985/86	25	41	11	22	44.2
1986/87	33	42	12	12	49.2
1987/88	37	41	12	10	55.7
1988/89	28	41	18	12	77.3
1989/90	23	43	19	14	106.7

[a]Includes interest rate subsidies.

Source: Economic Times (3/12/86); Sarma (1990), 11.

through less targeted disbursements. The three types I consider here are inertially growing consumer and producer subsidy programs, off-budget funds, and electorally driven disbursements. All are part of what I think are best seen as compensatory flows and payments that *partially* offset the surplus extracted from poor populations through direct or inflation taxes, differential pricing for agricultural products, and inadequate public services.

In Table 7.1, the growth in India's basic subsidy programs for the period 1975 to 1990 is set out. The expansion was dramatic, and by the end of the period totaled some $7 billion in rupees equivalent. These figures do not include energy subsidies and a host of others that government economists estimated in 1990 at more than five times the total in Table 7.1 (*India Today*, 3/15/91:54). One should remember that when Indira Gandhi nationalized the main banks in 1969, she instructed them, as part of her war on poverty, to greatly expand their loan portfolios to the "weaker sectors," especially among the rural poor. The banks did so, even employing loan *melas* at which cheap credit was hawked to potential borrowers (inter alia, CMIE, 1983).

Egypt's subsidy bill underwent a similar explosion in the 1970s, and in 1977 the first modest efforts to rein it in provoked the January cost-of-living riots. As mentioned in preceding chapters, the bottom of Egypt's subsidy iceberg lay in subsidies to the major consumers of fuels and electrical power. Despite some whittling away at direct consumer subsidies during the 1980s, the outlays were still enormous at the end of the decade. Direct and implicit (through an overvalued exchange rate or domestic prices for fuel relative to international ones) subsidies on food and energy totaled nearly £E 10 billion or about a fifth of GDP (World Bank, 2/90:13, 49).

In Mexico, food products, fuels, and fertilizers have been heavily subsidized, and as inflation took off in the 1980s, interest rate subsidies also took on growing weight, reaching 6.6% of GDP in 1983, but tapering off to 1.8% by 1987 (Brothers, 1990:297). In 1982 various price subsidies reached about 7% of GDP, while fiscal incentives, credit subsidies, and expenditure subsidies raised the total to 14% (World Bank, 1986:10). By the end of the decade price subsidies on basic food items alone totaled $2.3 billion in pesos equivalent (*El Financiero*, 11/10/89).

Top leaders in EIMT and elsewhere have a natural inclination to protect or expand their range of discretionary action. In this respect both the automaticity in economic transactions advocated by the international donor community, and the entitled access to resources asserted by coalition members, have been and will be resisted. No one in EIMT has been more ingenious in this respect than Turgut Özal. His favored mechanism has been the off-budget fund. These have a long history in Turkey, dating back at least until 1941. In the 1950s another nine were added followed by twenty-three between 1964 and 1980, leading one observer to term Turkey's as "a fund economy" (Oyan, 1987:96). Özal took the model and ran with it, adding thirty-five new funds after 1983, including the one already mentioned, the Defense Industry Support Fund, as well as the Mass Housing and Public Participation Fund, the Municipalities Fund, the Resource Utilization Support Fund, the Social Solidarity Fund, and so on.

The funds receive their revenues from dedicated tax and tariff sources, and their aggregate weight in the economy has been growing. In 1988 the World Bank estimated their revenues at the equivalent of 20% of all government revenues (World Bank, 4/88:17). Oyan, by contrast, advanced an estimate of 42% equivalent of total tax revenues in 1986 and 6.2% of GDP (1987).

The funds are audited, and they are required to present final accounts to the Grand National Assembly, but their operations are not subject to any prior legislative approval. They can be seen as discretionary tools of governmental policy that can direct scarce public resources toward sectors of the population that need relief or coddling. Moreover, because many of their operations are interest free, they create a favorable image among Turkey's practicing Muslims. The donor community, however, sees them as a threat to the coherence of adjustment programs (World Bank, 4/88:98–99).[5]

During the 1970s in Mexico the special funds, known as *fideicomisos*, proliferated, but they had already become an important part of coalition maintenance.[6] They were used both to stimulate growth in specific sectors and to compensate specific groups (Anderson, 1968:174). Typical of them was INFONAVIT, the Institute for the Development of Workers' Housing, founded in 1971, destined to provide limited housing for unionized blue- and white-collar employees. Delivery was run according to a lottery system that is often associated with compensatory schemes. In this instance there were about 4 million eligible people, of whom only 600,000 were to receive housing. A computer-based allotment system was ended in 1978, thereby increasing the discretion of union bosses in determining beneficiaries (Díaz Cayeros, 1989).

Of a different stripe was the creation in 1983 of FICORCA (Fideicomiso para la Cobertura de Riesgos Cambiarios), which was set up to absorb $11 billion in dollar-denominated debt held by the Mexican private sector, the servicing of which was seriously jeopardized by the devaluation of the peso. In exchange for the dollar debt, FICORCA issued discounted peso debt instruments. Some twenty firms accounted for 80% of the absorbed debt, and these firms are said to be part of a group of private entrepreneurs close to Salinas.

The number of off-budget funds and special financial intermediaries in Egypt is very large, although the resources available to them appear to be less than in Turkey or Mexico. One favored path to discretionary funds is to set up a "cooperative" and then apply for subsidized credit from one of several institutions that lend to cooperatives. Much middle-class housing has been developed through bogus housing cooperatives. In addition, there are funds on the Turkish model, such as the Fund for Services and Local Development, in Cairo governorate, which the opposition accused of using its resources to support the official party (the NDP) in the 1984 elections. The resources available to all funds in 1985 was estimated at £E 1 billion (or about $1 billion at the prevailing exchange rate), and their use was nominally under the supervision of the Ministry of Finance (*al-Wafd*, 9/12/85:3).

There have been contested elections uninterruptedly in India since 1947 and sporadically in Turkey since 1950. Contestation in Mexico until 1988 has been nominal at best. Egypt moved between 1976 and 1984

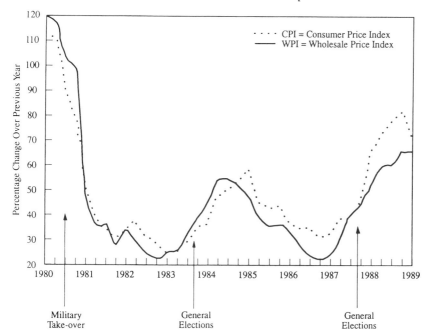

Figure 7.1. Inflation rates and general elections in Turkey, 1980–89. Source: Dani Rodrik (1991), "Premature Liberalization, Incomplete Stabilization: The Özal Decade in Turkey," in Michael Bruno et al., eds., *Lessons of Economic Stabilization and Its Aftermath* (Cambridge, Mass.: MIT Press), Figure 9.2, © 1991 Massachusetts Institute of Technology. Used by permission.

from a plebiscitary dictatorship to something resembling the long-standing Mexican system of single-party dominance. All four countries are subject to electoral spending cycles, but they are much more evident in Turkey and India than in Mexico and Egypt.

I have referred several times to the "election factories" that became prominent in Turkish politics in the 1950s. By the 1970s, with their fragile coalition governments, all partners, regardless of ideological coloring, were at one in promoting the expansion of the SOE sector.[7] The military take-over put an end to electoral-cycle spending, but with the general elections of 1983 and 1987, the cycle took hold once again (see Figure 7.1). Just before the fall elections of 1987, agricultural purchase prices were raised sharply, putting about $2 billion into the rural economy, whereas SOEs were not allowed any price increases until a few months after the elections.

The real political power of the public sector can be gauged by Indira Gandhi's preparations for the 1984 elections. She nationalized thirteen "sick" textile mills, gave a 25% wage increase to 500,000 coal miners, and sponsored nationwide loan fairs (*melas*) through public sector banks. In April 1990 a panel of eminent Indian economists and pundits reviewed the evidence from the preceding decade. They noted that in the election years of 1984–85 and 1989–90 public expenditures grew by 25% and then fell back to their more normal growth rates of 15% to 18% per annum. In these years public agencies were allowed to spend well over authorized levels.[8] The Janata Dal Party, which had triumphed over the Congress Party in the 1990 elections, had already committed itself to writing off about $650 million in rupees equivalent of rural debt. Raja Chelliah lamented, "The Government is a prisoner of the system," while Prem Jha seconded the assessment: "Our whole economic framework is irrational. We have made only marginal changes in arrangements that are thirty years old."

2. COALITION BUILDING AND MAINTENANCE IN HARD TIMES

The hard times have come to all four countries, and the old ISI coalitions are unlikely to withstand the shock. Mexico and Turkey are nearly a decade into the process of refashioning coalitions while pursuing economic adjustment, and it is on them that I focus in this section. But even in India and Egypt, the heads of state have admitted that the crisis is at hand. As early as December 1987, Rajiv Gandhi told Congress workers in Madras that India "could no longer afford socialism" (*The Statesman*, 12/23/87), and in his May Day speech of 1991, President Mubarak simply described Egypt's economic situation as "terrifying" (*AI*, 5/6/91:13).

As I have argued throughout this book, Carlos Salinas has gone furthest in restructuring both the SOE sector and the coalition that grew up around it. Carlos Ramírez caught the mood of the new *sexenio* accurately (Ramírez, 1/9/89:24): "It is a question of the retreat of the state, not of a new equilibrium within a mixed economy." In his first state of the union address (El Informe de Gobierno, 11/1/89), Salinas sent a warning to his erstwhile allies:

This decade of crisis has devastated the level of living of the population in an unprecedented manner and has destroyed the myths jealously guarded by a minority benefiting from state gigantism for whom the fate of millions of compatriots, the stifling of social initiative, and the bureaucratization of the political task are of no importance.

What the economic crisis had done to erode the coalition, Salinas continued through public policy. In Turkey, the military used martial law for the same purpose, clearing the political arena for Özal to attempt to fashion a new governing alliance. Rajiv Gandhi flirted with a radical departure in 1985, but the economic crisis was so muted and the Congress Party so entrenched that he had almost immediately to retreat (Kohli, 1990:317–20). Until the summer of 1991, Husni Mubarak did nothing to shake his coalitional pillars, although inflation, a kind of universal political solvent, had over several years weakened their foundations.

I must stress that the use of the terms "coalition" and "alliance" connote something a great deal more positive and activist than is generally the case in EIMT. These are not alliances spontaneously entered into but, rather, are clusters of constituents, separable and separate, called into existence and sustained by political authorities. They can block, but they seldom attack. When a part of the coalition blocks, the other parts generally stand by and watch. The state that creates their costly and conflicting entitlements, and tolerates the webs of rent seeking that holds them together, is not so much malevolent as incompetent. When parallel economies reduce the state's ability to tax, and when domestic and foreign creditors will lend no more, the game is over.

The costs of restructuring the economy are both concentrated and dispersed. Devaluation, curtailed public expenditures, and stagflation will affect the bulk of the population,[9] while the costs of SOE reform and privatization will fall primarily on the shoulders of organized labor and SOE management. The initial benefits of structural reforms will be highly concentrated, confined to agents primarily in the export sector. Demand management policies will at best contain inflation, as devaluation, rising interest rates, and SOE price increases will push the price index upward.

In an intuitive manner, political authorities grope for strategies and tactics to allow them to survive this process. One effort is to maintain as much concentrated, discretionary power in the hands of the executive as possible in order to direct resources to trouble spots with the minimum amount of fuss. The risk to the reform process is that the concentration of power may foster new forms of rent seeking. A second tactic is to increase the lottery aspect of compensatory programs. These will be touted as addressing the needs of broad categories of economically deprived citizens, but in fact, given the limited public resources available for them, the beneficiaries will be determined by lot or by clientelism.

Finally, the political leadership will redefine the corporate coalition. In the good days of ISI, the corps were defined in terms of what their members did and do economically: They were workers, peasants, capitalists, professionals, and the like. As these economic functions come under stress, those who fill the corps must be redefined essentially as consumers. The redefinition helps the leadership in two ways. First, consumers have generally been victimized by the old regulatory and protective institutions of ISI. It is the case that in EIMT the decades of state-led growth did produce a large middle class straddling the public and

203

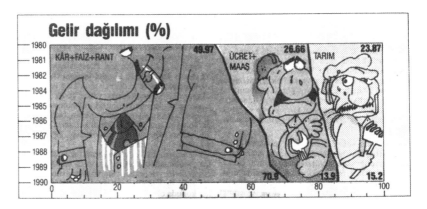

Gelir dağılımı (%)

The winners and losers in Turkish adjustment income distribution, 1980–90. The three panels measure the shares of profits, interest, and rents (49.9%–71%), wages and salaries (26.6%–13.9%), and agricultural income (23.8%–15.2%) as shares of national income. Source: *Cumhuriyet*, 11/28/89. Used by permission.

private sectors and commercial and professional activities (Zermeño, 5/87; Kohli, 1990:328–29). Appeals to the middle class, including portions of organized labor, may strike a responsive chord. Second, the aspirations of consumers tend to be more uniform across groups, whereas the interests of the old functionally defined corps may be at odds with one another. The reform program holds out the hope (but seldom the reality) that consumer aspirations can be satisfied, while their negative implications for the old corporatist coalition is all too clear.[10]

The indicators of a distributive crisis in EIMT are unmistakable. In all but India real wages have dropped significantly over the decade of the 1980s: in Mexico by 40%, in Egypt by 33%, and in Turkey by 25%. The years of nongrowth in Mexico witnessed, according to the source, the elimination of 2 million to 4 million jobs with a commensurate increase in open unemployment. De la Madrid terminated more than 200,000 public sector jobs, and at the end of the decade the most entitled work force of all, that of PEMEX, shed 63,000 of a total of 213,000 jobs (on Mexico, see Carr, 1983; *La Jornada*, 10/1/89; Lustig, 1990:1331). In all four countries the share of wages in national income declined precipitously. Rodrik (1991), for example, estimated the share of wages and salaries in Turkish national income in 1980 at 27%, while in 1988 it had declined to 16%. In the same year agriculture accounted for 14%, and rents, profits, and interest, for 70% of national income.

Rather than differential rewards and entitlements, the hard times dictated differential cushioning of economic blows. Thus we find in Turkey that the wage base of SOE workers declined less rapidly than that of

ـ سمعت إن المصلحة ح تدينا علاوتين أو كيلو لحمة أيها أفضل

Compensating the salariat. "I heard the division will give us two bonuses or a kilo of meat, whichever is more." The sign over the bureaucrat's desk reads "Patience." Source: *al-Ahram al-Iqtisadi*, 6/15/87:15 (cartoon by Nagi). Used by permission.

white-collar civil servants or of private sector workers (World Bank, 8/ 88:74). Within the ranks of SOE white-collar employees and managers, real wages increased substantially while some 40,000 positions were eliminated (Yüksek Denetleme Kurulu, 1988:44–45).

Although wages may be repressed or lagged behind inflation, some compensatory resources will flow back to workers in their capacity as consumers, residents of certain regions, squatters in search of legal title, and so forth. It helps, as in Turkey, to have an economy that is growing so that some of the growth can be used for compensation. Özal's gov-

205

ernment innovated a number of compensatory programs. It sold revenue-sharing certificates in bridges and power plants that, in fact, bore guaranteed interest rates in excess of the rate of inflation. This was the petty capitalist appeal. A rebate system on the value-added tax was initiated that, according to one's income range, could pay back 5% to 20% of one's monthly expenditures. The appeal was to consumers, and one of the effects was to ensure that VAT was applied and reported. Municipalities were given greater control over tax revenues, which could then be used for targeted public works. The appeal here was to specific urban residents. Titles were granted to a range of squatters, who could then begin to buy and sell urban real estate. The appeal here, once again, was to the petty capitalist (Boratav and Yalman, 10/89).[11]

For a time Özal described his Motherland Party as the central column (*orta direk*) of a new kind of corporatist structure of all those lower-middle-class and burgeoning informal sector interests abused by the years of etatism (Parla, 1986:158–59). In that spirit, Özal launched one of his most famous *boutades:* "Prices are set by God" (*Günaydin*, 2/22/87). Not the hidden hand but the divine hand replaces administered pricing.

The private sector has undergone far-reaching changes as restructuring unfolds. The era of the coupon clipper dawns, especially in Mexico and Turkey where positive interest rates on a host of short-term financial instruments have created a new, but somewhat hidden, class of savers (Akyüz, 1990; Boratav, 1990a).

In India, the hesitant reforms of the Rajiv Gandhi years triggered a boom on the Bombay Exchange. In 1988–89 alone new stock issues raised some $2 billion in rupees equivalent. Some estimates put the pool of beneficiaries at about 100 million, which in India is only 15% of the population (Ghosh, 10/21/89:2349). Nonresident Indians, investing in the exchange, have come to form part of the emerging coalition in support of market-oriented reforms.

The private export sector becomes a privileged target of discretionary measures in shaping a new coalition. The role of FICORCA in Mexico was instrumental in this respect, and there, as well as in Turkey and India, tax rebates, duty-free imports of inputs for export industries, and subsidized credit are used to move private agents into the export economy. Import duties may be maintained on a discretionary basis to protect private firms moving from domestic to export markets (Baysan and Blitzer, 1990; Rodrik, 1991). Akyüz summarizes the discretionary practices thus (1990:110–11):

It is difficult to give an accurate picture of credit costs in the 1980s. Almost every single loan has had a different effective rate applied to it for a number of reasons

206

including the persistence of a great variety of lending rates on preferential and non-preferential loans, different rates of interest rate subsidies from and contributions to the Interest Rate Rebate Fund, and the practice of blocking part of loan proceeds at different rates for different borrowers.

Enterprise life and death could be determined by the terms of loans extended through public intermediaries. A famous case was that of Halit Narin, a prominent textile manufacturer whom many believed was punished for his association with the True Path Party. As his holding company hovered on the brink of bankruptcy, one of his external accountants advised him to get on his hands and knees to Yusuf Özal (Turgut Özal's brother and minister of state for the economy) and beg for a deal.

Social contracts must be renegotiated. In Mexico this has been an explicit process, one founded on the precedent of the pacts negotiated in better times. In December 1987, as inflation spun out of control, the Pact of Economic Solidarity (PSE) was negotiated to establish agreement between labor and capital on price and wage restraints. It was replaced by the Pact of Stability and Economic Growth (PECE) with the same general purpose. These pacts have endured several years, inflation has been brought down, and real growth restored to the economy. The private sector has had to observe price ceilings (as have the SOEs, thereby jeopardizing the implementation of performance contracts), and organized labor has bargained essentially over the rate at which real wages continue to fall (*Latin American Monitor*, 9/90:809). The return of flight capital, private debt–equity swaps, export incentives, and the availability of short-term, high-interest-rate instruments have all contributed to growing profits for parts of the private sector. Greatly reduced tariff protection, depressed markets, and high interest rates have clearly hurt other parts.

There is little doubt that during his *sexenio* Salinas wants to remake the foundations of the PRI. Its older entitled groups in white- and blue-collar unions, in the protected private sector, and in the *ejidal* agricultural sector will no longer receive favored treatment. The gamble is that they have no credible rival party to which they can turn. Some substantial portion of them will absorb the enduring hardship while hoping that the PRI can lead them to better times. Simultaneously, Salinas is trying to firm up the PRI's relations with the private sector, especially with the new exporters and with elements coaxed away from the PAN. The re-privatization of the banks and the sale of large SOEs to consortia including established Mexican firms are tokens of the government's willingness to legitimize the large-scale private sector. There is, finally, a potential constituency to be found among the popular organizations that emerged in Mexico City in the aftermath of the earthquake, as well as in the nonorganized small-scale and informal sectors. In all of this refashioning, one cannot turn a blind eye to the persisting violence, especially at the state and local levels, used by the PRI to deal with its opponents (Bazdresch, 5/88; CAIE, 11/88; Gomez and Bailey, 1990; *Latin American Monitor*, 9/90:1; Dresser, 1991).

The donor community, especially the World Bank, recognizes that the social strains caused by these processes of economic adjustment and political restructuring may provoke social outbursts that could, as in Egypt in 1977, bring both processes to a halt. Thus, in a number of countries social solidarity funds have been established and have become major vehicles for compensatory transfers to affected segments of the population. Turkey's Social Solidarity Fund and Mexico's National Solidarity Program (PRONASOL), created in 1988, have been set up to deal with a broad range of antipoverty measures, ranging from job creation and training to rural works programs. In Mexico and Turkey, funding has been appropriated out of domestic resources. PRONASOL, for instance, was initially funded at more than $200 million and has been greatly expanded since then (*Latin American Monitor*, 12/90:844; Dresser, 1991). PRONASOL has become the favored instrument for reaching the new PRI constituencies already mentioned, and some see it as displacing the PRI altogether. It has become the embodiment of Salinas's "neo-liberal populism" (Dresser, 1991).[12]

As Egypt entered into agreement with the IMF and the World Bank for stabilization and structural adjustment programs, it too set up a social fund with about $400 million coming mainly from the World Bank and other donors. The fund is directed to undertake job creation, retraining of workers and returning worker migrants, and loans to small-scale enterprise. Given the scale of the social dislocations with which they must cope, and the modest level of the resources at their disposal, these funds will have to be run according to the lottery principle, or, as likely, to buy votes.

3. CONCLUSION

If we review the origins of ISI in EIMT, we find that economic strategy choices were the catalyst to interest formation and coalition building. The one existing interest that welcomed ISI, and sometimes lobbied for it, was the indigenous private sector, but in none of the four countries was it a fully legitimized coalition ally. When the ISI strategy produced macroeconomic results that made the strategy untenable, the move, under conditions of crisis, to market-oriented strategies once again dictated state encouragement of new interests (exporters, commercial farmers, small-scale enterprise) and the formation of new coalitions. The process is too new in EIMT to predict with any confidence what the composition and relative weights of constituent elements of the coalition will be. If the transitions are successful, South Korea may offer a reasonable facsimile of the future.

What is clear is that the constrained states of EIMT are retreating not only from planning, regulation, and the ownership of assets, but also from the responsibility of guaranteeing the welfare of the citizenry. State authorities no longer want, nor can the state afford, to be the major employer and creator of new jobs, the determining power in setting wage and salary levels, the almost exclusive provider of education and health services, and the owner and manager of most utilities and mass transportation facilities. State authorities want the private sector, and individuals through their savings, to take on some of this burden. The counterpart to asking the private sector to share in the risks of development is to ask it to share responsibility for the social costs.

In late 1989, the Salinas government tried to bring the Teachers' Union under control. It removed the long-standing head of the union and granted members a 25% pay raise. The rank and file would have none of it. For days, tens of thousands of *maestros* flocked from the provinces into downtown Mexico City, tying up traffic and filling the Zocalo, and demanding a 100% pay increase. To concede it would have effectively scuttled the PECE. To repress the demonstrators would have turned public opinion against the government. The long-term solution is to decentralize the issue, making each state responsible for working out accords with the teachers' unions (*Latin America Monitor*, 12/91:964). At the time, however, the massing of state-dependent protesters in the Zocalo, directly in front of the Ministry of Finance with its revolutionary Diego Rivera murals, was both the symbol and the substance of the government's costly social contract.

When he was head of the Turkish Confederation of Employers' Unions (TISK), Halit Narin recognized the same dilemma. He commented on a strike in the paper products SOE, SEKA, saying that it was politically dangerous for the government to be an employer. "It is one thing for the newspapers to write that Halit Narin is a bad guy, and quite another when the government is the target" (*Cumhuriyet*, 12/7/88). But after the disastrous 1989 municipal elections, in which ANAP came in third, and with the GNP growth rate slowing to little more than 1% while inflation remained at 70%, the Turkish government found itself forced to ease the social strain. Agricultural purchase prices were raised, as were pensions as well as wages and salaries for both blue- and white-collar workers. Money supply doubled, and longer-term financial and structural reforms were put at risk. These two examples highlight the need for state authorities to divest themselves of some of the social agenda.

The new coalitions will be much more narrow than those formed under

Dengeli cumhurbaşkanı

Turkey's fragile coalition: The presidency (Özal) balanced on the prime ministry, balanced on the Motherland Party. Source: *Cumhuriyet*, 2/26/90. Used by permission.

ISI. They will also be looser in the sense that the constituent parts will not always have the organizational underpinnings of the corporatist period. Indeed, the kind of "debilitating pluralism" that Bianchi (1984) attributed to Turkey in the 1960s may come to prevail: myriad small, weakly organized interests, associations, and unions that can be co-opted and dropped by the incumbent political authorities according to electoral considerations and available resources. The appeal to these groups will be on the basis of their material interests, and the state will have to deliver on some of its promises some of the time. That will not be possible without growth in the economy. It is likely, therefore, that the new coalitions will be volatile, and subject to collapse if the economy performs poorly. On the one hand, then, the more narrow and less costly coalitions may prevent the accretion of new entitlements to public resources, but, on the other, they may provide no or little support in the inevitable periods of economic crisis.

8

The public–private symbiosis

In the wake of the failure of state-led growth strategies, the private sector in EIMT is being invited by somewhat sullen state leaders to provide the dynamism and to stimulate the growth that their economies lack. Whatever the practical realities of this invitation, the rhetorical challenge is formidable. The indigenous private sector over the years has been labeled as weak, parasitic, exploitative, shortsighted, monopolistic, and antinational. At no time to date in any of the four countries has the private sector been granted the keys to the political kingdom. When public criticism and suspicion has periodically abated, political authorities have suggested that this has not been because the private sector can be trusted but, rather, because it has been beaten into submission. The private sector has learned its place.

State paternalism toward the private sector runs deep; Deepak Lal traces its origins in India to the Moghul period and to the reforms introduced by Cornwallis in the East India Company (1988:106–7). Onto this foundation was laid the amalgam of Nehru's Fabian socialism and Brahmin contempt for the trading castes. Even as his grandson, Rajiv Gandhi, tried to liberalize the economy, the reactions were nearly stereotypical. In 1985, the National Institute of Public Finance and Policy, a dependency of the Ministry of Finance, issued a report on "black money" (mainly tax evasion), which it explained as stemming from the actions of private agents to escape complex and onerous regulations as well as to obtain the resources needed to bribe officials and politicians. K. N. Kabra and N.S. Jagannathan assaulted the report in the following terms (1985:9):

What is implied is that it is the scheme of government controls and taxation and general laws [that are at fault] rather than anything connected with origins, nature, historical experience, the morals, motivation and social standing of those who flout and violate these laws.

212

The public–private symbiosis

Kabra and Jagannathan do not deny the illogic of many of the regulations, but their maintenance is a lesser price to pay then that of unchaining the private beast. All the more ominous would be turning over public assets to private owners. A senior manager of Mexico's NAFINSA, Benito Rey Romay, predicted (1987:115) that if privatization goes forward, "Assuredly the economy will be irremediably more monopolized and more externalized, and society and political life less developed and less democratic. Is it possible to think otherwise?" Similarly, Dr. ʿAli Nassar, reflecting on the course of the open-door policy in Egypt, warned (INP, 5/88:117), "I think we have nearly crossed the red line, socially speaking, in the concessions which have been given to local and to parasitic capital."

For the intelligentsia and the civil servants, profit was a dirty word. Prakash Tandon, who started his career in the private Hindustan Lever, in 1961 became a board member of the SOE Hindustan Steel Ltd. He later recalled (Tandon, 1980:125): "Profit honestly earned was as much frowned upon as that dishonestly come by . . . in Hindustan Steel I had felt sad because we made no profits; in Hindustan Lever I was sad because we made profits."

For some, careers in the private business sector were equally dirty. In 1959, a sample of more than a thousand Turkish *lycée* students were asked to state which careers they most respected: 49% indicated the free professions, 22% government and the military, while 2% indicated business and trade (as cited in Roos and Roos, 1971:84). Güvenç Alpander (1968:235) explained the general outlook:

In Turkey, the notion of business is misunderstood. Often, the business man is viewed as a speculator, if not a thief. Business in general, and retailing and wholesaling in particular for a long time were downgraded and looked upon as occupations no respectable Turk would enter . . . No great business heroes have emerged in Turkey, no entrepreneur has gained social recognition, and no business leader has ever held public office.[1]

Flogging the private sector is generally good politics. The bank nationalizations in India in 1969 and in Mexico in 1982 were highly popular, and in 1986, when the then finance minister, V. P. Singh, launched a series of raids against businesses suspected of tax evasion, 75% of a nationwide middle-income sample approved of the action (*Illustrated Weekly*, 4/20/86:11). Although Echeverría cut deals with private sector figures throughout his *sexenio,* he scored points with public opinion, as in October 1976, when he attacked the Monterrey capitalists as "profoundly reactionary and enemies of the people" (Basáñez, 1990:54). It was, however, in Egypt that punitive measures went far beyond tongue-

213

lashings. Nasser told one of his officer colleagues that Lenin had made a mistake in cooperating with the Russian bourgeoisie. As for Egypt's, Nasser said (as cited in Ansari, 1986:88), "We have no other alternative but to liquidate them by arresting all of them and putting them in Wadi al-Jadid [a desert concentration camp]."

1. THE SEPARATION OF THE ECONOMIC AND POLITICAL REALMS

A near explicit understanding has underlain the public–private symbiosis in EIMT, and its terms have been largely determined by the political leadership (cf. Hirschman, 1968:29). It is that the private sector will be allowed to seek profits in the economic realm, subject to state regulation, but it will not be granted any overt, legitimate role in formal politics. In two instances that understanding has been imperfectly observed. Since the 1930s the PAN in Mexico has openly championed business interests and has challenged the PRI in elections, while during the 1960s in India the Swatantra Party challenged the Congress. Its poor showing in the 1967 elections sounded the death knell of the party. Far more typical, however, is the studied partisan neutrality of business leaders, supplemented by campaign contributions to likely winners, or even to all horses in the field.

Denied political legitimacy and frequently the target of official opprobrium, the business sector has benefited from many of the privileges associated with state-led growth. It has enjoyed tariff protection and oligopolized markets, cheap inputs from the SOEs, government contracts, and preferential credit. Weak private sectors in EIMT, struggling with the consequences of two world wars and the Great Depression, to some extent welcomed greater state intervention because its immediate effect was to absorb risk stemming from competition and world prices that the private sector would otherwise have born alone (inter alia, Tignor, 1984:110). Moreover, through its commitment to the social contract, the state in effect tamed labor though corporatist measures and held down wage levels through consumer subsidies and welfare programs (Maxfield, 1988?:2). For the members of political elites, few of whom had any background in the private sector, the toleration of private initiative enhanced economic productivity and growth while affording the possibility of skimming private earnings (Hansen, 1974:xxviii).

In India, Turkey, and Egypt the compartmentalization of private economic and public political spheres was rooted in the fact that the trading and merchant communities were mainly drawn from minorities or trading castes. In India, the old "managing agency system" that spread scarce managerial skills around the growing number of private companies founded in this century (see Brimmer, 1955) was dominated by Parsis, Marwaris, Jains, Chettiars, and Gujaratis (Kochanek, 1971:869; Hardgrave, 1980:133). Similarly in Turkey and Egypt, at the turn of the century, Jews, Armenians, Greeks, and Syro-Lebanese were the most dynamic local entrepreneurs as well as the intermediaries between European capital and local markets.

In India these minorities have safeguarded their economic privileges up to the present time, but in Turkey the upheavals of the period 1908–23, and in Egypt the nationalizations of 1956 and 1961–64, led to their virtual elimination. In Turkey, the republican state was able to set about constructing an entrepreneurial bourgeoisie out of returning Turkish émigrés from the lost provinces of the empire, especially the Crimea, who were given properties and enterprises left by departing or deceased Armenians and Greeks (Keyder, 1987:69). The new Turkish Muslim business class thus started life fully subordinate to the state class and asserted some autonomy only after 1950. Some argue that the subordination and compartmentalization of the Turkish bourgeoisie has persisted to the present time (Buğra, 1989, 1990a). After 1974, the Egyptian state, without ever dissociating itself from the crushing of the large-scale private sector in the 1950s and 1960s, tried to lure back capitalists who had fled abroad as well as to create through policy measures a new indigenous private sector. Nonetheless, since 1956 no private business person has ever been a member of the Egyptian cabinet.

In informal ways private sector actors have, of course, played a political role, but, like that of SOE managers, influence has been individualized and not the result of organizational representation. The Birlas in India have always remained close to Congress. Nehru consulted frequently with the "red" businessman from Madras, T. T. Krishnamachari, while Rajiv Gandhi drew criticism for his close contact with Dhirubhai Ambani, who, in fifteen years, turned Reliance Textiles into one of India's largest firms. Luis Echeverría for a time dealt closely with Eugenio Garza Sada, the major figure in the Monterrey industrial group (Basáñez, 1983:90), and the families of Anwar Sadat and of Ahmad Osman, the head of the Arab Contractors, were joined by marriage. From these particular associations, one cannot read a structured alliance of interests.[2] Rather, they were instances of friendship or tactical deals in a context of mutual suspicion and private sector subordination.

As the electoral systems of EIMT become more contested, the open support for heretofore dominant parties, extended by businessmen like the Birlas to Congress, or Vehbi Koç for a time to the RPP in Turkey, may fade into cautious neutrality.[3] Direct opposition to predominant political forces, or alignment with a losing party, can be costly, as Halit

Narin learned in Turkey. Until the mid-1980s the resources controlled by dominant state systems were simply too important for business groups to risk confrontation. Large segments of the entrepreneurial classes have, in fact, been created by public policy and favors, and, it is alleged, a profound dependency mentality dominates their conduct (Rubio, 1988:35; Loaeza, 4/89:7–8). Buğra recounts (1989) that in 1988, TÜSIAD, the Turkish Industrialists' and Businessmen's Association, issued a report severely criticizing the government's economic programs and handling of inflation. A prominent member of the government came to TÜSIAD to debate the report. The president of TÜSIAD, Ömer Dinçkok, reiterated the critique, but in the subsequent debate none of the other members of the association dared engage, no less criticize, the government representative. Dinçkok resigned as president shortly thereafter.

The combination of market-oriented reforms and the tacit abandonment of social contracts will inevitably mean that private interests will be formally represented in the political realm. Turkish governments since 1983 have contained several ministers from the private sector, although they tend to come from medium-size firms rather than from the large holding companies. In addition, the Motherland Party has used businessmen as organizers at the local level (Arat, 4/87). Similarly, in Mexico the national legislature now contains thirty-five deputies from the business sector, and at the national and state levels private sector finance committees for the PRI have been set up (Rodríguez Reyna, 1/92). As responsibility for the social contract is shifted partially onto the shoulders of the private sector, and as the state divests itself of some of its risk-absorbing functions, the private sector will speak with a louder collective voice and will be openly heeded by political authorities concerned with the success of market-oriented reforms.

2. MUTUAL SUPPORT AND CONFRONTATION

It is very difficult to know which protagonist has drawn the greatest benefits from the public–private symbiosis. The analytic challenge is similar to measuring net flows between SOEs and the government – what the government gives with its right hand, it takes away with its left. The private sector at various points in time in EIMT has complained bitterly about the hostile policies and general intrusiveness of the government, while the intelligentsia, citing the steady growth in private activity, has tended to depict the public authorities as the willing accomplices of private interests. Depending on the evidence, both claims can be substantiated.

216

The babus and the license raj (an Indian view of rent seeking). MRTP = Monopolies and Restrictive Trade Practice, RBI = Reserve Bank of India. Source: *India Today*, 4/10/91:55. Used by permission.

2.1. Support

"Etatism clearly promoted capital accumulation by the Turkish bourgeoisie" (Pamuk, 1/81:27; see also Eralp, 1990). That is undoubtedly true, and to some extent that was the explicit intent of etatism. In India similar charges have been made with the suggestion that the enrichment of the bourgeoisie was likewise the goal of public policy. India's license raj is a telling case in point. The MRTP and FERA (Foreign Exchange Regulation Act) regulations were put in place ostensibly to curb monopolies, lower prices, ration foreign exchange, and generally police the large-scale private sector. Yet, as even the conservative publication *The Economist* (5/4/91:11) pointed out, two decades later the net effect was to discourage entry of new competitors into already oligopolized markets. In more than half of India's major industrial sectors, the four-firm concentration ratio is between 80% and 100%.

Does it follow that the consequences of MRTP were intended by those who designed it? Clearly not. The intent was, and remained until the early 1990s, to restrain firm concentration and monopoly profits. The policies were badly designed to do that, and not even the most ferocious of the guardians of Indian socialism could do much to alter that fact.

217

Far more effective in breaking up private sector oligopolies were Nasser's blanket nationalizations of 1961–64, which some Egyptian observers have nonetheless seen as promoting capitalism. The general point is that policies benefiting the private sector may be the result not of the assertion of private sector power but, rather, of the independent judgment of government policy makers, and some benefits will be the result of the unintended consequences of other public policies. There is, of course, a third possibility – that the private sector gets what it wants – but in EIMT to date that has been fairly rare.

In Mexico the statist experiments gave rise to a protected, medium-scale private sector that was hostile to foreign capital, tolerant of corporatized labor, and politically supportive of the regime. Not a few of the members of the Revolutionary Family were, like General Aarón Sáenz in the sugar sector, rewarded with control of private firms (Purcell, 1/81:217). Members of this new entrepreneurial class urged nationalization of the foreign-owned power sector in 1960, and López Mateos obliged. The greatly enlarged federal electricity company (CFE) that resulted from the nationalizations supplied electricity at subsidized rates to private sector users (Wionczek, 1964).

In the other three countries the medium-scale enterprise sector, selling to the domestic market, has generally cooperated closely with public authorities inasmuch as public policy has crucially shaped its rates of profitability. Protection against imports is of paramount concern, for even if the SOEs raise the prices of inputs, steep tariff walls will still protect access to local markets. But this populous enterprise sector has neither the moguls who can bargain directly with ministers nor much organizational strength as its professional bodies tend to be controlled by the political authorities. It is a policy taker. For example, in 1966 when Egypt found itself in severe balance of payments problems, Nasser encouraged a range of small scale manufacturers to enter into exports to the Soviet Union and Eastern Europe. Guaranteed markets for their goods were negotiated annually between Egyptian and Soviet officials. Ten years later, Sadat suspended payments on Egypt's debt to the Soviet Union and terminated the bilateral trade agreements that had been the instrument for debt servicing. In one abrupt move the private sector lost its markets. In gaining access to those markets, and in their subsequent loss, the private sector was the creature of public policy.

The public sector is a major purchaser of goods and services, and although SOEs generally are obliged to give preference to one another in such purchases, private suppliers can enter into long-term, lucrative arrangements (although governments are frequently delinquent in payments). Arçelik of the Koç Group in Turkey manufactures consumer durables and steel office furniture. The Turkish government has a minority equity position in the firm and buys much of its office furniture from it (Sönmez, 1988:122). However, the most lucrative contracts lie in the construction sector, where private firms can bid on the capital-intensive projects of the state in infrastructure and heavy industry. An oft-cited statistic is that during Egypt's First Five Year Plan, 40% of all outlays went to pay subcontractors in the construction sector. But large SOEs are important subcontractors in their own right. The large public textile complex at Mehallah al-Kubra in Egypt comprises 30 plants that in turn supply yarn to, and buy cheap "popular" cloth from, some 1,600 small-scale weaving businesses.

A division of labor develops between the public and private sectors. The public concentrates in the strategic supply and energy sectors and sells intermediate goods to the private sector. The prices of the public sector goods are held down even as production costs rise. Thus, private production is subsidized and private producers may be able to sell in relatively unregulated markets. If, as in Turkey, this means that private firms price themselves out of depressed domestic markets, there is a vent for surplus and export.

The public sector, as outlined in Chapters 3 and 4, has taken over failing private enterprises so as not to aggravate unemployment. On occasion this practice has invited private owners to cannibalize existing investments in order to move into more profitable ventures, leaving the hulk of the original firm to the public sector. At the same time, it is important to note that administered pricing schemes, as in India's inte-grated textile mills or Mexico's sugar refineries, have driven the private firms into sickness and take-over.

Section 6 of this chapter deals with the question of public finance of private enterprise, but I introduce here the question of those companies in which the government and its banking institutions take minority po-sitions. This is a kind of intermediate zone between the public and private sectors, or what the Indians call the "joint sector." The firms within it are joint in the sense that either private shareholders have a stake in an SOE or the government owns equity in a private sector firm.

Egypt has some of both. When the SOE sector was first expanded in the 1950s, the government encouraged private participation in the equity of new public firms. There were and are fifty such firms, including the Helwan Iron and Steel Company. Private shareholders played no role whatsoever in monitoring the performance of these firms, and their shares had no traded value.[4] By contrast, after the issuance of the investment code (Law 43) of 1974 that encouraged joint ventures between SOEs and foreign investors or companies, public sector banks, insurance com-panies, and construction firms invested in nearly 250 joint ventures and provided more than 50% of all the paid up capital of the Egyptian

219

partners (Sa'id, 1986:191; INP, 5/88:74). As noted in Chapter 5, privatization in Egypt may consist initially in selling off the government's stake in the Law 43 firms.

The Indian government, through its specialized development banks, also owns substantial proportions of several private firms. The Tata Iron and Steel Corporation is 40% owned by the government, and government representatives sit on its board. According to Howard Erdman (1987, 1988) no fertilizer company in India can be considered truly private. Some Indian reformers saw the joint sector as a staging zone for privatization. Through share offerings and ESOPs in wholly- or majority-owned SOEs, these could be transferred gradually to private ownership, transiting through the joint sector on the way. In Mexico, NAFINSA by itself managed an extensive joint sector, and, with the nationalization of the major banks in 1982, the Mexican joint sector expanded prodigiously. Reprivatization of the banks will entail a major return of assets to majority private ownership.

Kepenek argues (1990:120) that in Turkey the government has bankrolled the joint sector to the decided advantage of the private owners. The number of companies in which the government had a minority position increased from 72 in 1962 to 306 in 1988. According to company law, paid-up capital in any firm must be at least 25% of nominal capital. In practice, this means that in joint ventures in which the government owns, say, 49% of the shares, it will pay up all its investment while private owners will pay up 25% of the remaining 51% equity. Having paid in only 12.5% of the capital, the private owners will receive 51% of the distributed profits. Kepenek estimates that in 1987 the government denied itself nearly $120 million (in Turkish lira equivalent) in profits.

In the 1990s, the governments of EIMT will channel resources to one subgroup within the private sector: exporters of manufactured goods. Mexico and Turkey have deployed an arsenal of supportive measures and have achieved remarkable success. In 1988, Mexico generated nearly $14 billion in total exports, two-thirds of which came from the manufacturing sector. Within that sector 243 Mexican private and 63 foreign private firms claimed equal shares in manufactured exports. The Foreign Trade Bank (Bancomext) lent about $8 billion to the manufacturing sector in 1988 (*Expansion*, 1989:37).

Turkey modeled its export drive on that of South Korea by encouraging the establishment of trading companies, which in turn were owned by the major private holding companies. In 1984 companies that had succeeded in exporting $30 million or more could apply to the Central Bank for subsidized export financing, receive foreign exchange from the Export Promotion Fund, special import permits for materials needed for exports, and export tax rebates up to 6% of the value of the exported goods.

The public–private symbiosis

About thirty export houses have come to dominate the field, and their share of total exports has risen from 6% in 1980 to 46% in 1988, or about $5.5 billion. Because of the tax rebates, exporters systematically over-invoiced their exports, giving rise to "fictitious exports" that may have averaged 11% of total exports (Öniş, 10/89:22; Rodrik, as cited in *Cumhuriyet, 12/8/88*). Baysan and Blitzer (1990:14) estimated that government subsidies to exporters of manufactured goods declined in value from 23% of total manufactured exports in 1983 to 16% in 1986.

2.2. Discriminatory policies

As a policy taker, the private sector has had to take the bad with the good. Aside from obvious assaults upon its position, such as bank nationalizations, tax raids, and punitive regulations, the private sector has had to deal with less overt public policy discrimination. The "award" of a greater share of the investment burden to the private sector by state planners in Egypt and India was greeted with decidedly ambivalent feelings. As both countries entered a new five-year plan in 1988 and 1986 respectively, the planners set a target growth rate, estimated the investment needed to achieve it, and simply assigned to the private sector the gap between available public investment and the target level. In neither case was the private sector consulted about its role, nor was any effort made to determine its real investment capacity.[5]

For every tax break or subsidy private actors receive there are tax rates and administered prices that put them at a disadvantage vis-à-vis the SOEs. In Turkey the private corporate tax rate has been considerably higher than that for SOEs. In Turkey and Egypt, SOEs can borrow at interest rates well below those available to the private sector (except when a discretionary deal is struck). In India, SOEs enjoy preferential status in all public sector tenders, and the very tariff walls that protect some private producers force others to buy high-cost goods from SOE suppliers. In Egypt, private textile producers pay more for Egyptian cotton than SOEs do. The standard justification for such discriminatory policies has been that they compensate for the higher social costs borne by SOEs, a claim that cannot always be empirically sustained.

None of this adds up to a coherent set of pricing, tax, and incentive policies for the two sectors, and sometimes the situation becomes nonsensical. In December 1985, Egypt's public sector spinning plants raised the price at which they sold yarn to the private sector by 60%. The owners and workers of some 720 small-scale weaving plants in Mehallah al-Kubra closed down in protest (*al-Wafd, 12/26/85*). The irony is that the yarn was in large measure for the production of "popular" cloth, destined for subsidized sale to low-income Egyptians. Like Sadat's ter-

221

mination of bilateral trade with the USSR in 1976, this unilateral price increase constituted a body blow to the petty bourgeois capitalists in whose interests, some believe, the Egyptian regime rules.

If SOE interests run directly counter to those of certain private actors, policy makers will protect the SOEs. In the early 1980s both Egypt and Turkey experienced a breakdown in their regulated foreign-exchange markets, accompanied by a blossoming of black market and quasi-legal foreign-exchange dealers. Egypt denied itself the option of devaluation, and as foreign-exchange earnings declined with the price of petroleum, there was a growing spread between the price formal banking institutions would pay for foreign exchange and that offered on the black market. The public sector faced a severe credit squeeze. The minister of economy, Mustafa Said, saw only one way out: to merge the official and black markets and to institute a politically determined queuing system (interview, 7/13/88). Had the merger worked, it would have given priority to the public sector for foreign exchange and effectively crowded out the private sector.

Turkey's solution was to keep foreign-exchange earnings expanding through continuous devaluation and the export drive, to channel foreign exchange to the export houses, and to allow private firms to control some of their foreign-exchange earnings as well as to borrow abroad. Egypt, by contrast, could not export and could not borrow abroad. With declining petroleum earnings the public and private sectors found themselves in a zero-sum situation, and Mustafa Said elected to protect the public sector SOEs and banks. There was no way, however, to force foreign-exchange earnings through the formal banking sector at an overvalued exchange rate and at low interest rates. By 1988, the problem Said had sought to remedy had reemerged full-blown. Public officials still rail at "unpatriotic" Egyptians who hold as much as $40 billion abroad.

Toward the private sector, the state is thus both supportive and invasive. Mexico's NAFINSA was established to support the development of private industry but consistently used its equity position to extend its control over private enterprises. In 1942 it promoted the AHMSA steel complex and by 1947 had so expanded its equity position that for all intents and purposes AHMSA became an SOE (Blair, 1964b:215–16). Similarly, by the middle 1970s, NAFINSA owned a third of Fundidora de Monterrey, and a controlling interest in Cananea Copper. Under Echeverría, NAFINSA became the lender of last resort and the eventual owner of many failing private enterprises. By that time close to 70% of its portfolio by value consisted of public sector ventures (Bennett and Sharpe, 1/80:177; Ramirez, 1986).

The Las Truchas steel complex promoted by Lázaro Cárdenas (see Chapter 4) was seen by most private steel producers as preempting their own potential markets and expansion. The years needed to gain approval for the project effectively paralyzed private sector development. Once production had actually begun, the decision to raise output at Las Truchas to 3 million tons per year was taken without consulting private producers (Schücking, 1982:186).

Similarly, in Turkey, Petkim, a large state holding company in the petroleum sector, founded Petlaş, a tire company utilizing obsolete Czech technology. It entered into competition with private sector joint ventures with Pirelli, Uniroyal, and Goodyear. Its main plant was located for political reasons in central Anatolia, where it was able to oligopolize the regional market for truck tires. It enjoyed preferential purchasing accords for raw materials and was able to use Petkim's extensive storage network.[6]

To summarize briefly, the basic dynamic of the public–private symbiosis has been that the public supports the private when such support has enhanced public sector performance and revenues. However, in instances when public and private interests have diverged, the private sector has had neither the economic nor the institutional strength to do more than cushion discriminatory blows. In the era of structural reform, this dynamic is changing.

The fundamental change taking place in the support granted by the state to the private sector in EIMT is that the latter is being moved center stage in the effort to revitalize the process of economic growth. For decades the SOE sector was accorded that role and the privileged claim on public resources to go with it. As government intervention becomes, as in East Asia, increasingly market supporting, rather than market thwarting, strategically placed actors within the private sector are likely to play a more proactive role in shaping the public policies that affect them.

3. THE FAMILY HOLDING COMPANY

The firm structure of preference for the large-scale private sector in EIMT is the family-owned holding company. It appears to be well adapted to cope with both economic and political risk. As in the public sector, there is little effective separation of management from ownership. To the extent that shareholders monitor firm performance, it is because the majority of shares is owned by the family itself. The most senior management positions are generally reserved for family members. These are not holding companies in the normal sense of the term, because, although they do hold controlling shares in a diverse portfolio of enterprises, they also involve themselves in the management of those firms. In India the old managing agency system formalized such direct managerial oversight, and the step to the family empires of the Birlas, Tatas, Modis, and others was an easy one (on Indian groups see Herdeck and Piramal, 1985). A Turkish manager within one such holding said that he was more like a steward of a rural estate than a corporate planner.

Nathaniel Leff, who has written extensively about the economic functions of such holdings, refers to them simply as *groups* (1978, 3/79). Drawing mainly on evidence from Brazil, he sees the *groups* as vertically integrated, multiproduct oligopolies that minimize competitive pressures from both clients and suppliers. They are, according to Leff, a response to failure in input markets including capital. Through diversification and operation in several markets, they spread risk. Through vertical integration, they avoid dealing with oligopolized supply markets. In turn, they are able to extract quasi rents from sales in imperfect input markets. The rents are generally used to further diversification at the expense of specialization and research and development. For maximum risk minimization, it is crucial that the group control its own banking institution. The bank nationalizations in Egypt, India and Mexico gutted scores of private groups, and in Turkey only a few entrepreneurs have launched their own banks.[7]

The top twenty or so business groups in Turkey conform closely to the Leff model, as Buğra has shown (1989, 1990a,b; see also Sönmez, 1988). However, she stresses two distinctive characteristics. Turkish groups sacrifice some vertical integration for an almost eclectic diversification of interests. Typically they are involved in domestic and export markets, trade and manufacturing, real estate speculation, and, for a few (Koç, Sabanci, Çukarova, and Yaşar), banking. Second, this diversification responds to the increased discretionary powers of the state, allowing the groups to profit from special deals in sector x that may not be applicable in sector y. Indeed, the plight of Halit Narin, to which I referred earlier, may have resulted from overspecialization in the textile sector.

Even when such groups go public through share offerings, the ownership of equity will generally remain highly concentrated (Ersel and Sak, 1987). That need not always be so. Although today Egypt boasts no private group to rival a Koç or a Tata, before the nationalizations of the 1960s it had one of the Middle East's most venerable holding companies, the Misr group. Its founder, Tala'at Harb, owned only 5,000 of some 500,000 shares, while other members of the indigenous oligarchy, like Abboud Pasha, held larger minority stakes. Hossam ʿIssa wrote (1970:330): "The Misr group was . . . the most anonymous form of the Egyptian bourgeoisie as a whole. It was, in a way, the collective property of that bourgeoisie."

The private groups are big by any standards. In Mexico, they are

The public–private symbiosis

concentrated in Monterrey, and in the hands of a few families like the Garza Sadas and Zembranos. In 1990 the ten largest Monterrey groups had sales of $10 billion and profits of $650 million, while employing 180,000 (*Financial Times*, 5/29/91:6; Chávez, 2/4/92; also Jacobs, 1981). The Tata group in India consists of seventeen major companies with $4 billion in sales and $160 million in profits in 1988 (*India Today*, 10/15/88:65). In Turkey, the Koç Holding registered $3 billion in sales while the Sabanci group accounted for $2.7 billion. One single Koç firm, Arçelik, registered nearly $500 million in sales in 1988 (*Dünya*, 7/3/89).

4. PRIVATE SECTOR REPRESENTATION AND CLASS ACTION

Powerful private entrepreneurs, like their public sector counterparts, transact important business with the state on a personal basis. Although they may participate in them, they do not really need professional business associations to promote their interests. Rather, such business leaders can use professional associations as the forum in which to define political and economic stances. For lesser members the associations serve to regulate the profession and help members through complex dealings with the bureaucracy.

In all four countries one finds several business associations that have been created or suborned by the state itself. In Egypt, the prerevolutionary Federation of Egyptian Industries was forced into a docile, supportive role within Nasser's corporatist system, and was seconded by the Union of Chambers of Commerce. Essentially these organizations became instruments by which the state communicated its priorities to the private sector, rather than bodies through which the private sector could communicate its needs to the government.

The open-door policies after 1974 stimulated a halting private sector renaissance, and in 1977 a group of businessmen, including several former public officials, registered themselves as a cultural organization with the Ministry of Social Affairs. Thus was born the Egyptian Businessmen's Association, and its first president was a former minister of supply. By 1984 it had 250 members, each of whom had to pay an entry fee of £E 1,000. Parallel to it, and with considerable shared membership, was the Union of Banks (including seven public sector banks), and the Egyptian–American Business Council. These organizations emphatically set themselves apart from the older, tame associations, and although confrontation with the government was *not* common, they lobbied proactively on bread-and-butter issues such as licensing, power rates, and the retention of foreign exchange. Ministers concerned with the economy met

225

regularly and publicly with the Businessmen's Association (Sa'id, 1986; Bianchi, 1989:172–78).

The same emergence of a proactive business association can be seen in Turkey. Throughout the first decades of the republic, commercial and business interests were represented through the Turkish Union of Chambers, while crafts and tradesmen had their own association. The Union of Chambers was made up largely of inward-oriented private firms, vulnerable to state policies on tariffs, input pricing, and licensing.

In 1971 the large holding companies broke away from the Union of Chambers and founded the Turkish Industrialists' and Businessmen's Association, TÜSIAD (Öncü, 1980:462). A division common to all four countries was cemented with this hiving-off of TÜSIAD. The Union of Chambers became the spokesperson for smaller-scale businesses dealing mainly with the domestic market and therefore alarmed by the prospects of trade liberalization, no less of Turkish membership in the Common Market, whereas TÜSIAD took up the cause of the *relatively* more outward-oriented holding companies for whom entry into the Common Market holds a certain appeal. Özal's political support in the private sector lies mainly in the numerically important Union of Chambers, while TÜSIAD carries more of the burden for the success of his economic policies.

In 1979, TÜSIAD publicly criticized the policies of the Ecevit government, and that stance was seen by some as presaging the military takeover in 1980 (inter alia, Boratav, 1989). However, TÜSIAD has also been strongly critical of Özal's economic policies, particularly of high interest rates and high inflation. In July 1990, the president of TÜSIAD, Cem Boyner, after more such criticism, was called into the state prosecutor's office to answer charges that TÜSIAD had violated its nonpolitical role. Boyner pointed out that TÜSIAD, after all, is not an association of canary lovers (Aybuk and Boduroğlu, 1/89; Buğra, 1989).

In India and Mexico there is a much older tradition of organized private interests criticizing government policies, and it was in keeping with that tradition that both countries saw the founding of business-oriented political parties. The most autonomous business association, formerly dominated by British interests and now by Indian capital in favor of trade liberalization, has been the Associated Chambers of Commerce and Industry (ASSOCHAM). Indian capital with an inward orientation has been represented through the medium-scale industries in the All India Manufacturers Organization and through the Federation of Indian Chambers of Commerce and Industry (FICCI). FICCI has been dominated by the Birlas and has generally cooperated closely with the Congress Party. The Birla family, which has promoted an alliance for profits and kept a low political profile, was studiedly cautious in its reaction to the bank nationalizations of 1969. J. R. D. Tata remained politically aloof, eschewing any association with FICCI or the Congress, and sponsoring the Forum for Free Enterprise to speak for the private sector. Whether confrontational, supportive, or neutral, Indian private interests have had little direct influence upon public policy until the 1980s. During the radical phases of Nehru's and Indira Gandhi's incumbencies (see Chapter 2), "business ... never succeeded in blocking or even modifying the introduction of a major redistributive policy" (Kochanek, 1971:882).

The interventionist reforms of both Calles and Cárdenas in Mexico provoked a sharp reaction in the Monterrey business community, which led to the founding in 1929 of COPARMEX (Confederación Patronal de la República Mexicana), and eventually to the PAN. COPARMEX brought together industrialists, merchants, capitalist farmers, and bankers in direct opposition to the state-led economic program of the late 1930s.

Beginning with Cárdenas, but especially during the *sexenio* of Alemán (1946–52), medium-scale industrial enterprises, benefiting from the increasing protection of the ISI formula, and representing a new class of beneficiaries of the revolution, took on considerable weight and regional concentration around Mexico City and in the valley of Mexico. Closely linked to the PRI, their primary association, the National Chamber of Transformation Industries (CANACINTRA), was founded in the early 1940s (Luna, Tirada, and Valdés, 1987).

During the 1950s and parts of the 1960s, all factions of the private sector shared in the remarkable growth of the Mexican economy, and by and large accepted the implicit deal of political quiescence for state-supported pursuit of profit. The government was always able to find allies of convenience even within the adversarial camp of COPARMEX. The state-owned BANOBRAS Bank, for instance, bailed out the Alfa Group, belonging to the Garza Sada family, in the late 1970s. Prominent private bankers sat on the board of the Bank of Mexico, and, until the bank nationalizations, business interests had good, informal access to policy makers in Hacienda (Finance) and the Bank of Mexico (Maxfield, 1988?, 1990).

There were, nonetheless, frequent instances of tension and hostility between the regime and elements of the private sector. López Mateos's nationalization of the foreign power sector, coupled with Mexico's recognition of revolutionary Cuba, was one such situation. Relations were hostile during the Echeverría *sexenio*. A restrictive foreign investment code, the devaluation of the peso, the expropriation of land in Sonora, and the prodigious expansion of the public enterprise sector appeared to parts of the private sector as a governmental renege on the basic understanding. The most disgruntled elements founded, in 1975, the Entrepreneurs' Coordinating Council (CCE) to voice their displeasure (Rubio, 1988:37; Basáñez, 1990:60). López Portillo succeeded in reestablishing some level of confidence with business interests. His government abandoned plans to bring Mexico into the GATT as even CANACINTRA openly opposed the move. But the bank nationalizations at the end of his *sexenio* opened a breach that Salinas is at present trying to overcome.

Given the depth of Mexico's economic crisis, it was perhaps inevitable that de la Madrid, no matter what he did to revivify market forces, would fail to win over all the private sector. He moved quickly to blunt the impact of the bank nationalizations through compensation and the extension of the right to buy back nonbank financial institutions such as brokerage firms and insurance companies. He removed Carlos Tello, the author of the nationalizations, from the Bank of Mexico and replaced him with Miguel Mancera, a figure far more palatable to the private sector.

Against this, however, de la Madrid decided to bring Mexico into the GATT, and this was done in typical unilateral fashion. According to Escobar Toledo (1987:772):

> The Mexican political system set the guidelines for reaching a decision that ultimately was the exclusive responsibility of the president. It did not proceed from consultation with the Ministry of Commerce or of any agreement among entrepreneurial organizations, much less from a democratic process.

De la Madrid's amendments to the constitution, including the incorporation into it of the bank nationalizations, have been variously interpreted. For Rubio (1988:38) they extended greater legitimacy to the private sector while safeguarding the primacy of the state in economic affairs. For COPARMEX, however, the amendments altered the very spirit of the 1917 constitution. It objected to the government's espousal of "revolutionary nationalism," the "social sector," and the extension of state ownership. The government denounced these criticisms as ideological and therefore exceeding "the limits for which these associations were created and, by the same reasoning, to overstep the legal framework which supports them" (as cited in Bravo Mena, 1987:100). In this respect the two market reformers, Özal and de la Madrid, had the same political reaction to the insubordination of the private sector.

Despite the taking of public, association-based positions, such as TÜSIAD's in 1979 or COPARMEX's in 1983, there is scarcely more evidence of the business classes of EIMT acting collectively than that offered by public sector managers. Like peasants, however, private interests can vote with their feet, or, more exactly with their money. The investment strike and capital flight are the most effective weapons of the rich. But it is difficult to know if they are wielded by a class at war or by individual

228

The public–private symbiosis

entrepreneurs maximizing their gains or limiting damage to their port-folios. The evidence for investment strikes in EIMT is weak to non-existent, and drops in private investment closely correspond to drops in public investment. By contrast, Mexico experienced severe capital flight for over a decade. Morgan Guaranty Bank estimated it at $84 billion over the period 1977 to 1987 (*Latin American Monitor*, 9/89:690). Car-rillo Aronte (1987:57) is convinced that this flight was a class action. The Egyptian government estimates that private Egyptian citizens hold about $45 billion abroad, although it is not clear if this is flight capital or accumulated earnings on assets owned abroad (*AI*, 6/5/89). Capital flight has not yet been a significant problem for either India or Turkey.

5. INVESTMENT AND FINANCE

The general trend in EIMT over the last decade has been for the total volume of investment to grow modestly in real terms (India, Egypt, and Turkey) or to decline (Mexico). In all cases the share of private investment has grown so that in Turkey it now exceeds public investment, in India the two sectors are in rough balance, while in Egypt the private sector, since 1974, has increased its share from 10% to 30% of the total.

Public financial institutions have been an important if not dominant source of private investment financing. At the same time, these institutions have been called upon to finance public investment as well. On balance, can one arrive at some estimate of the degree to which public borrowing requirements crowd out private? Bardhan sees no conflict because private investment is stimulated by public spending, or so Indian data would seem to indicate, and this positive relationship "tends to dominate any possible negative effect through competing for investible funds" (1984:25; see also Taylor, 1988:53). That conclusion may be too quickly reached.

Dwight Brothers (12/88) finds unambiguous evidence in Mexico to the contrary. When the public sector financial deficit grew from 7% to 12% of GDP in the early 1980s, 90% of it was financed through private sector savings. In 1986 alone, 85% of the public sector borrowing requirement was so financed. The phenomenon, while accentuated during the crisis of the 1980s, was by no means new as the figures in Table 8.1 show. Brothers points out that the resort to preferential lending to targeted clients also has the effect of crowding out potential borrowers, especially in the private sector. For example, interest subsidies on preferential credits to public sector borrowers over the period 1982–86 averaged nearly 4% of GDP.

There is similar evidence from Turkey, where the government has financed its deficit through the sale of treasury bills bearing high, tax-

Exposed to innumerable delusions

Table 8.1. *Mexico: Implicit private-to-public financial transfers, 1975–87 (annual % of GDP)*

1975-79	1979-82	1982-86	1987[a]
4.3	8.0	11.0	19.1

[a]Preliminary.

Source: Brothers (12/88), 44. Used by permission.

free, real rates of interest. Banks have mobilized private savings to purchase these T-bills, in turn exerting further pressure on interest rates. Private sector firms are faced with high-cost credit, while because of the high rates paid on T-bills private savings are diverted from the capital market. In fact, in early 1990, when the government lowered interest rates on one-year TL deposits, the trading volume on the Istanbul exchange quintupled. Beginning in 1991, Egypt likewise began to fund its government deficit through the sale of treasury bills.

The Indian public sector has likewise funded more than half its investment needs from private savings (CMIE, 1983), but as Barnett Rubin has shown (1986:99) most of this has come out of household savings rather than from the private corporate sector. The bank nationalizations of 1969 allowed the government to tap these savings more effectively and to channel them to preferred borrowers.

The evidence on the direction of bank lending is mixed. In Mexico, the banking sector, most of which was public after 1982, opted for low-risk lending to the government, and bank credit to the private sector fell from 19.5% of GDP in 1972 to 7% in 1988 (*Latin American Monitor*, 6/90:786). In Egypt and Turkey, quite the opposite appears to have occurred. In the former, between 1978 and 1984, the proportions of total credits extended by the banking sector to public and private lenders were reversed. At the beginning of the period the public sector claimed about two-thirds of all credits, while at the end the private sector claimed that same share (Moore, 1986:641).[8] Similarly in Turkey, over the period 1979 to 1986, the share of the private sector in total banking credit increased from 50% to 73%. Significantly, the sectoral distribution changed markedly: Industrial credits fell from 46% to 28% of the total, while the share of foreign trade grew from 4% to 16%, and that of construction and housing, from 3% to 12% (Akyüz, 1990:108, 115).

It is not implausible that private savings, in the sense used by Rubin, have gone to fund the public deficit, and that in the process many potential private borrowers have been squeezed out of credit markets. On the other

230

hand, the flows of discretionary public credits to private borrowers have been substantial, and the rescheduling or bailing-out of heavily indebted private firms a common feature of the public sector banking system. For instance, private firms hit hard by the currency reforms introduced by Mustafa Said in 1985 were bailed out by his successor in the Ministry of Economy, and the role of FICORCA in absorbing the foreign debts of many private Mexican firms has already been noted (Chapter 7; Rivera Ríos, 1987:121).

Four of India's largest financial intermediaries may own as much as 50% of the equity in the large-scale corporate sector ("Money Muscle," 9/30/89:67).[9] Nayar (1989:373) shows that the financial institutions own between a quarter and a half of the equity of each of India's twenty-five largest private firms. They lend at concessionary rates in coordination with the Ministry of Finance, and loan agreements provide for the conversion of debt to equity.[10]

However credit is being shared between public and private borrowers, it is increasingly scarce. In all four countries, the private sector is being urged or driven to use local capital markets to raise funds for investment. In India, Mexico, and Turkey the local stock exchanges are growing rapidly. Their market capitalization in 1990 was as follows (*IMF Survey*, 7/15/91:210):

India $38.6 billion
Mexico $32.7 billion
Turkey $19.1 billion

Egypt's Cairo and Alexandria exchanges are still tiny and stagnant. The volume of trade for 1988 was only £E 256 million (ca. $100 million). Under Egypt's new Business Sector Law of 1991, up to 49% of equity in SOEs can be sold to private investors. Depending on how public assets are valued, this could lead to a supply of shares worth billions of pounds to meet a very limited demand.[11]

If it is true that governmental pump priming is crucial to increasing levels of private investment, we should expect a decline in private investment as fiscal crisis forces states to retrench. Yet there is little evidence of that. Private borrowing and investment is increasing in all four countries, and the private sector is being encouraged to become the principal mobilizer of savings and investment.

6. BRINGING THE PRIVATE SECTOR BACK IN

Above all else, the acute shortage of investable capital has forced state policy makers to call upon indigenous and foreign private investors to fill the gap. Privatization and deregulation have been pursued with that

The toppling of La Quina and the Mexican private sector. In January 1989, President Salinas arrested "La Quina," the de facto head of the Petroleum Workers Federation and of PEMEX. La Quina's head is in the wastebasket and the Mexican private sector, opening the door to PEMEX, inquires, "May I come in?" (see also Chapter 10). Source: *El Financiero*, 1/13/89:53.

in mind. Contrary to those observers who minimized the significance of Mexico's bank nationalizations in 1982, it is clear that President Salinas concluded that reprivatization was the only way to restore confidence between the government and the private sector, and to stimulate substantial new investment and the return of flight capital. At the other end of the spectrum dealt with throughout this book, India, with the return of Congress to a fragile grip on power in the summer of 1991, has, under the guidance of the finance minister, Manmohan Singh, committed itself to stimulate the private sector and to relax barriers to foreign investment. Egypt, too, after reaching agreements with the IMF, the World Bank, and the Paris Club on economic reform and debt relief, has embarked on the same path.

At this juncture it is not at all clear whether these public authorities, by and large the same people who for years privileged the public sector, can effectively convince the private sector that a new era has dawned. All four executives retain enormous discretionary powers and, Mexico's bank reprivatization notwithstanding, control over financial intermediation. More than the transfer of assets back into private hands, what private sector actors in all four countries want most is a clear set of rules consistently applied and modified only after joint consultation. To date none of the four countries can boast such an arrangement.

The capacity of the private sector to respond to the new appeals is fairly strong in Mexico, India, and Turkey, but in Egypt a very weak private sector with unpleasant memories faces a bloated state that so far has only promised to go on a diet. Even Egypt's open-door policy after 1974 was a state project worked out with no more involvement of the private sector than had been the Socialist Decrees of 1961. As a result, the game since 1974 has been one of "You pretend to liberalize, we pretend to invest." Springborg (1989:11) rightly points out that if Egypt's socialism failed for want of socialists, its capitalism may fail for want of capitalists.

Not all of the private sectors of EIMT will benefit from the new era. Those entrepreneurs most dependent on state business favors, or on protection against foreign imports, will be hurt as trade barriers come down and public credit and investment dry up. The threatened private actors are numerically important and were the only private interests given some representation in older corporatist arrangements. It is estimated that in Mexico trade liberalization may have caused the failure of some 77,000 enterprises and the loss of 100,000 jobs between 1986 and 1991 (*Latin America Monitor*, 3/91:868). The hope of authorities reshaping older coalitions must be that these private interests have no political alternatives. A test of that assumption may well be run in Turkish and Indian elections where proto-fascist and religious parties may try to convert petty entrepreneurial discontent into votes.

Larger private corporate interests are not happy that they have been left naked before labor as the state allows publicly supported social pacts to crumble. A group of prominent Turkish businessmen chided the government for incoherent policies (likened to Turkish folk songs) that placed such heavy interest burdens on private investors, neither profits nor workers' wage levels could be protected. The business leaders felt themselves to be sitting on a time bomb (*Cumhuriyet*, 3/30/90).

The policy transition is an economic and political tightrope walk. Its economic success depends on favorable international trade conditions and availability of foreign credit, and the containment of inflation at home. The resuscitation of the private sector, buoyant capital markets notwithstanding, will be highly leveraged, and any major depression can cause the collapse of banking institutions that would then have to be reabsorbed into the public sector, if they ever left it in the first place. Inconsistent policies and overuse of discretionary powers could trigger new rounds of capital flight. For public authorities to deal with these risks and maintain political legitimacy will require real growth in the economy to afford partial compensation for sectors left out of the growth in relative terms. Governing with limited resources and narrow coalitions means that the incumbent's grip on power is always tenuous and dependent on adroit adjustments to sectoral crises.

It is easy for leaders to become so distracted with putting out brush fires that the longer-term strategy is lost from view. Hence, the temptation to let the market take over is politically as well as economically derived. Many public leaders realize that in the past they proved poor managers of economic and social relations, and they would like now to unburden themselves of some of the responsibility for growth and distribution. It is doubtful, however, that the electorate will let them.

9

Organized labor and the public enterprise sector

Organized labor has been a basic coalitional partner to the regimes that designed and implemented the ISI strategies in EIMT. Over time unions acquired a broad range of entitlements enjoyed by no other groups within the work force not boasting advanced education. Organized labor has come close to embodying all the deleterious effects attributed by Mancur Olson to distributional coalitions in general. It has promoted its own consumption at the expense of productivity and has impeded technological innovation in order to protect jobs. Society as a whole has had to pay for its privileges. Part of the price, as suggested by Colander and Olson (1984:124), has been significant amounts of involuntary unemployment in the nonorganized sectors of the work force, the existence of which has allowed the unions to control access to the privileged sectors. Finally, no other constituent part of the ISI coalition has felt as threatened by public sector reform and privatization as has organized labor. Reform implies raising productivity and stressing performance criteria rather than seniority in promotion and payscales. Privatization implies the elimination of jobs. For these reasons some have predicted that organized labor would put up fierce resistance to either set of policies (Aharoni, 1986:327), although that prediction has not yet materialized in EIMT.

There is no little irony in this casting of organized labor as a privileged elite pursuing its corporate interests at the expense of the economy and the less privileged. We should not lose sight of the paradox here. On the one hand, there is the image of a pampered labor force, brazenly defending low productivity, claiming bonuses when losses are made, perfecting the art of absenteeism, using contract labor to perform their jobs, and invoking their proletarianism to block constructive change. It is easy to become indignant. But these people are not at the beach or home watching TV. They still spend hours in crowded buses, hold down second and third jobs, live in teeming, substandard housing, spend revenue on unemployed relatives, and pay high prices for goods that their alleged

235

indolence makes more expensive. Organized labor cannot insulate itself from the costs of its privileges, nor, given the corporatist rules under which it has been allowed to function, can it adopt a role other than that of defending the material privileges granted it.

The irony is many-layered. In none of the four countries, with the possible exception of Mexico before 1917, was there any kind of organized industrial work force capable of threatening constituted governments on a scale to rival the labor movements of late-nineteenth-century Europe. In Egypt, Mexico, and Turkey, the men who led their countries into statist experiments also groped for rigid corporatist frameworks to contain fairly unthreatening labor forces. After all, the experiments arose because there was very little industry and not much of a bourgeoisie. By definition, there would not be much of a proletariate to contain, but Atatürk, Calles and Cárdenas, and Nasser acted as if worker-led class warfare were a real possibility. Only in India was the labor movement left relatively unfettered, although the simple fact that the public sector dominated the organized work force was leverage enough.

The basic formula has been for the state to create a single dominant, or even monopolistic, confederation of trade and labor unions with leaders carefully chosen by the state. The deal struck is that labor will not indulge in the familiar activities of strikes and confrontation – the hallmarks of labor autonomy and the fashioning of class solidarity – in exchange for a constant stream of material benefits and virtual inviolable job security. The labor leaders have enforced the deal among the rank and file, and as they became corrupted over time as distributors of the spoils, they could not credibly threaten the state with leading their wards into opposition. Public sector employment became the instrument by which the state could most expeditiously deliver the benefits. Note that in this sense, although labor was a far more legitimate member of the dominant coalition than the private sector, like the latter it was denied any overt political role. Only Turkey briefly tolerated a political party built around organized labor.

There is much at stake for organized labor in the economic reform process, yet despite its strong organizational underpinnings and location in the productive process. The reasons appear to be as follows. Organized labor is internally divided. Henley and Ereisha (1987), in a fine empirical study of a large Egyptian textile SOE, found that the seniority system by which all promotions of workers were guided, produced four age cohorts with very different maximizing strategies and no little friction among them. If the SOEs' promotion schemes had been determined by performance and productivity, one would have expected a curvilinear relationship between age and earnings, with the peak coming in that cohort combining experience and physical capacity, let us say in their thirties

236

and early forties. Instead, earnings were strictly linear with the oldest workers, who were the least fit physically and with the fewest family responsibilities earning the most (in some instances eight times the wages of the lowest paid), whereas those in their thirties and forties, capable of much higher productivity, were often obliged to carry one or more outside jobs in order to raise their young families. They punched the clock at the SOE and beat themselves senseless in more remunerative but less stable outside jobs. "They can sometimes be found asleep, exhausted, in obscure corners of the factory compound" (p. 514). The youngest workers had little experience, no marketable skills for second jobs, and the lowest earnings. They wanted to start families, but hard work got them nowhere. They were the most eager to leave the plant for migration abroad. The seniority system not only led to declining productivity and high turnover, but in fact inhibited worker solidarity and promoted inter-cohort resentment. I suspect that what Henley and Ereisha found in Egypt may have broad applicability.

A second reason why the public sector unionized work force may not be well equipped to resist reform and divestiture is because its privileges were not won in confrontation with private or public capital but, rather, were granted by the state. This is not to say that at specific times, and for specific unions, there have not been strikes, violence, and martyrs – in all four countries labor lore is replete with the culture of struggle. Nevertheless it would be hard to find examples of these actions truly driving the state to make significant concessions to labor. When organized labor has chosen to confront the state (examples are provided in the paragraphs that follow), it has almost invariably been smashed.

It is not uncommon for the rank and file to become alienated from their co-opted leadership. Mexico has borrowed from its own past the term *charro*, which refers to native work gang recruiters for colonial or foreign bosses, to describe these leaders (see the "CHARROL'S ROYCE" cartoon, p. 253). Dissident unions may form, such as Turkey's radical DISK confederation, and parallel, underground leadership may emerge. The state, on the one hand, funnels the benefits of the social pact exclu-sively through such leaders to the rank and file, but, on the other, seldom forgoes an opportunity to remind them of their lack of legitimacy. In September 1974, in official hearings on Egypt's political future, the regime consulted directly with organized labor during which "unidentified" voices from the floor questioned their leaders' right to speak in their name (Waterbury, 1983:358). Thus leaders who are political eunuchs are granted the sole right to distribute "the gains of the revolution." Dissi-dents, if not illegal and thus subject to arrest, get the police, vigilantes, arrests, disappearances, and martyrs – but no goods. Only in India, as we shall see, do these generalizations break down.

Were labor to look for effective allies in the dominant ISI coalition to resist reform, they would be found, if anywhere, among the senior civil servants. The senior SOE managers would not make common cause with labor. Indeed, in interviews and in secondary literature, it became apparent that organized labor was resented about equally with interfering bureaucrats by senior managers. Managers who had long promoted the public sector and endorsed its redistributive role welcomed the state's breaking of compacts with labor. For years management had followed the path of capitulation to labor, inasmuch as backing of tougher stances by management was seldom forthcoming from supervisory political authorities. Accommodation was the easiest course, but one that left a bitter taste in the mouths of many managers. Disciplinary measures inevitably tied management up in long and inconclusive litigation and arbitration; disciplinary reports, signed by the responsible official, often had to be made public, exposing the official to considerable danger (on Egypt, see Jones, 9/81, pt. 2:16–17).

A senior Mexican manager recounted to me that on the basis of his experience the power of organized labor had to be broken. While politically he sympathized with Cuauhtémoc Cárdenas, he supported Salinas's hard line toward the unions. He said that labor virtually owned the SOE of which he was head. Over time it had been able to bring most supervisory personnel into its fold so that all effective supervision disappeared. With Salinas's lead, he said, all collective agreements would be renegotiated and tough performance standards introduced. He predicted that because his firm was operating at 40% capacity, he would lay off some 700 workers.

Thus, while labor costs as a proportion of total operating costs of SOEs may be fairly low (and declining as interest charges grow), managers see a great deal of their time tied up in wrangles and disputes with unions and individual workers. In terms of the performance of SOEs, managers might more logically resent the banks that collect all the interest, or the principals who saddled the SOEs with all the debt in the first place. But in terms of the day-to-day life of the firm, managers see labor, in a sense, as the enemy, but one that the prevailing ideology until recently forbade them from acknowledging as such.

Labor leaders reciprocate in kind. As poor SOE performance was increasingly exposed to public scrutiny, labor leaders frequently laid the blame at the doorstep of incompetent management and also what they termed "disloyal" competition from private interests given favorable treatment by the state. In short, labor claimed it had to carry the can for lazy managers and crony capitalists.

In large measure the near mirror images labor and SOE managers came to hold of each other were accurate, and they were the product of the policies designed and implemented by the political managers of the public sector. Managers were not really allowed to manage in any autonomous fashion, labor was given few incentives to improve productivity, and the division of labor between public and private sectors often worked to show up SOE performance in a bad light. The viability of this system, built around an Akerloffian market for lemons, could be maintained only so long as deficit spending and foreign borrowing could be sustained. When that was no longer the case, the major protagonists blamed one another for the debacle, generally adding in the IMF and foreign creditors for good measure. The curious side to all this is that no one felt good about their own role. Time and again I heard from managers that when they were given the backing by their principals to try to improve firm performance, there was a general sense of relief on the part of both management and labor. This is what Krishnamurthy found in SAIL or the Egyptian investigator of the horrific state of the Egyptian Dairy Company. In some measure the protagonists felt they had been acting out a charade, and that their performance had increasingly earned them all bad reputations. When the state recast them, they were not in a good position to do more than feign indignation and resistance.

1. EGYPT

The Egyptian Trade Unions Federation (ETUF) has enjoyed a total legal monopoly on the representation of workers within Egypt's political system. In the late 1980s it claimed to speak for some 4 million workers, with the bulk concentrated in the textile and construction sectors. ETUF was the creation of the Nasserist state, and its influence was enhanced under Sadat and Mubarak.[1]

The military regime that took power in 1952 immediately showed its colors toward labor, crushing a strike at Kafr al-Dawwar and executing its Communist leaders. The junta then purged the ranks of organized labor and began a lengthy process of restructuring and corporatizing the unions. The basis for the deal of apoliticism in exchange for material benefits was laid in the 1950s and given final form in 1962 when the National Charter was issued (see Chapter 2). At that time the Nasserist regime bestowed upon labor and the peasantry the right to 50% representation in all elected bodies in the republic.

Labor was declared one of the pillars of the "alliance of working forces" embodied in the Arab Socialist Union. This new corporatist phase overlapped with Egypt's First Five Year Plan, during which an employment drive in the public sector was openly announced. Something like a million new jobs were created over the period 1960–65, and new industries were burdened with work forces that they could have used only after a long period of maturation. In order to maximize the numbers hired, overtime was restricted and the work week shortened.

In both the SOEs and the civil service over the period 1960–76, employment grew at a rate of 7.5% per annum, whereas the labor force as a whole grew at only 2.2% (Handoussa, 9/88). Labor productivity, which had grown modestly between 1937 and 1960, began to fall continuously thereafter. Absenteeism grew rapidly, as did the hiring of so-called nonoperatives, mainly white-collar contractees whose ranks became the dumping ground for graduates of technical institutes and the universities. In confirmation of Colander's and Olson's hypotheses, Sharaf El-Din (1982:108) concluded that the employment drive benefited a labor elite while driving down wages in the nonunionized work force. It reduced productivity uniformly in industries and sectors employing different technologies with different levels of capital intensity, and operating in different markets.

As Sadat moved toward some economic liberalization in the 1970s, and as he purged the regime of well-known Nasserists and some Marxists, he wanted to buy peace on the labor front. The social contract with organized labor was, if anything, strengthened under Sadat. Public sector employment continued to grow rapidly. Between 1975 and 1985 the work force employed in the SOEs grew from 945,000 to 1,258,000 (Handoussa, 9/88:36). Mubarak continued the same practices in the 1980s. Handoussa estimates that 90% of all new jobs created in the Egyptian economy between 1978 and 1988 came through either public sector employment or migration abroad (p. 6).

Although illegal in the public sector, there were periodic strikes, but nothing to rival the surges of labor unrest in Turkey in the late 1970s or in India just before the Emergency. After the June War of 1967, and especially after the lenient sentencing of senior officers implicated in the debacle, workers and students triggered two episodes of protest strikes in 1968. With the regime's legitimacy already badly frayed, Nasser had to respond with some cosmetic moves toward greater democracy in the ASU, but the confrontations were not of a regime-threatening kind. Under Sadat, strike activity was sporadic, and the participation of organized labor in the riots of January 1977 was relatively minor and totally unblessed by union leadership. Not until August 1989 did another major outburst occur when workers at Helwan Iron and Steel went on strike. Egypt was negotiating at the time with the IMF for an agreement that was not finally reached until 1991, and Mubarak sent in security forces who smashed the strike, leaving one worker dead (*Financial Times*, 8/7/89).

This denouement was characteristic of the slow unraveling of the social pact that had begun with the first attempt to apply austerity measures in 1977. The preceding year, a new president of ETUF, Sa'ad Muhammed Ahmad, had been put in place and was to remain there for the next eleven years. He negotiated with both Sadat and Mubarak to cushion the blows that would inevitably come from structural adjustment. His concern throughout was to protect existing jobs, even as wages declined, and to protect the SOEs, which he saw as the surest guarantors of job security. Real wages had begun to decline even before the oil price boom petered out, but between 1982 and 1987 they declined by 40% (World Bank, 2/ 90:16).

In addition, there was some modification of the labor laws of 1959 and 1961, which had set up the complicated procedures for handling worker–management disputes and sanctions of workers for negligence, repeated evidence of which constituted the only grounds for dismissal (Roy, 1980). Law 48 of 1978 granted management more flexibility in hiring (including refusing appointments of university graduates) and in promotion according to performance. Because the legislation provided no standards for evaluating performance, this latter remained a dead letter. Still, the upshot was that although SOE employment continued to grow, it grew at a much lower rate than in the 1960s and early 1970s. As idle capacity in SOEs was reduced, some labor productivity gains were registered. At the same time, many of the most skilled workers, especially in chemicals and textiles, had migrated to the Gulf.

In Bianchi's view (1986:438; see also Posusney, 10/91), with Saʿad Ahmad at its helm ETUF acquired a right of veto over certain aspects of macroeconomic policy. Its 1981 recommendations provide the flavor of its opposition to parts of the open-door policy, especially joint ventures between public and private firms that would, according to Law 43 of 1974, automatically be considered part of the private sector (ETUF, 1981:152–64). ETUF staked out its position in response to a set of proposals on the evolution of the SOEs prepared by Taha Zaki, at that time minister of industry. ETUF's basic points were:

- The public sector is the anchor of the national economy
- ETUF refuses the breaking up of public sector firms under any guise, as well as all joint ventures or sales to the private sector
- Worker shares in profits and participation in SOE administration are constitutional rights and cannot be altered
- ETUF opposes the establishment of multi-firm, sectoral holding companies
- ETUF opposes capital expansion through public share offerings[2]

It is widely alleged that some years later, ETUF was able to block the attempt to establish a joint venture between Nasr Automotive and General Motors that would have created a new, private vehicle assembly plant with a small work force, leaving behind the obsolete, overstaffed, and capital-starved Nasr Automotive to endure a lingering death in the

241

public domain. There were many other factors that led to the shelving of this project, but to the extent that ETUF played the role attributed to it (Kandil, 1989), it may have been its last hurrah.

Saʿad Muhammed Ahmad was dismissed in 1987 as head of ETUF with no explanation given. It is believed that President Mubarak and some of his key ministers had lost patience with his obstructionism. In 1987, Egypt once again tried to reach an understanding with the IMF, the implications of which were that major overhaul of the SOE sector would have to be begun. The standby of that year eventually collapsed, but the new head of ETUF, Ahmad al-ʿAmawy, was chosen to lead his unions into the new era.

In May 1989 there was a remarkable "Joint Declaration of Workers and Employers concerning the Push toward Greater Production and Productivity" (*AI,* 5/8/89 and 6/5/89:20–27). The actual signatories were al-ʿAmawy and ʿAdil Gazarin, former CEO of Nasr Automotive and president of the (tame) Federation of Egyptian Industries. Some of the recommendations were familiar: that is, separate management from ownership, and diminish ministerial interference. Others anticipated the Business Sector Law issued in 1991: that is, establish multi-firm holding companies, bridging sectors; create a deputy prime minister to oversee the public sector; allow firms to raise prices to cover costs of production. Public share offerings, and even liquidation of losing SOEs, were not ruled out. The declaration stated, "The private sector, as we see it, are the sons of this country who have saved their wealth from their own sweat and effort." The joint declaration provoked bitter criticism from the Egyptian left and from some dissident unions, but the reform effort moved glacially forward.

The Business Sector Law of 1991 embodied most of the changes that ETUF had declared unacceptable in 1981. Multi-firm holding companies, joint ventures, liquidations, and sales of equity are now not only to be possible but desirable. At the same time, it is not clear that management will have any greater control over the hiring and dismissal of labor, at least in firms in which the government retains a majority share. There are to be tripartite commissions of labor, management, and the government to review dismissals and sanctions. The wording of their powers indicates that the latter can be applied only in the event of negligence or willful errors, but not in response to downturns in business activities (Thabit, 7/29/91:18).

2. INDIA

The Indian government has never tried to force the country's highly fragmented labor movement into a rigid corporatist framework. In fact, there are thousands of legal unions and federations, many affiliated to political parties, at the national and state levels. In 1980 there were more than 36,000 registered unions (Nigam, 1990). The largest is the Indian National Trade Union Congress (INTUC), affiliated to the Congress Party, and claiming, in the mid-1980s, 3.5 million members. It has with rare exceptions been faithful to government policies when Congress has been in power, but it is no surprise that given India's complexity and the sheer size of INTUC, dissident movements have been frequent. Another ten unions claim some 8 million members. What has transpired is that more marginal unions, fighting for membership, have adopted confrontational stands in firms they share with INTUC, and have driven the establishment federations to adopt more militant stances than they would have otherwise. Thus, various governments, but especially those of Indira Gandhi, have tried to limit the proliferation of unions in the workplace by setting vote barriers in plantwide elections to eliminate all but the three top vote-getting unions.[3] Still, in comparison to the other three countries, labor management relations in India appear almost chaotic, fully in keeping with the variegation of the society itself.[4]

The size of the unionized work force is a matter of some debate, and it has varied over time. Before the Emergency there may have been about 9 million organized workers. That number dropped to about 7 million by the end of the Emergency, and has risen again to as much as 12 million. The total work force in the "organized" sector of the economy is between 25 million and 30 million, two-thirds of which is employed by the public sector (World Bank, 3/90:2).

The proliferation of unions, coupled with bidding wars for increased benefits packages, has produced high levels of agitation and strike activity. Sir Brian Mookerjee, the last private sector CEO of the Indian Iron and Steel Company at Burnpur in West Bengal, resigned his position in 1969 and laid the blame for the firm's poor performance squarely at labor's door. He noted that his work force of 22,000, for production of a million tons of steel per year, was three times international standards, and labor agitation constantly drove up the labor cost per ton of steel. "The result is," he said "that even after agreements have been arrived at between the management, the majority of the unions, and the State Labour Directorate, a single group of workmen, comprising of just a few men, such as locomotive or crane drivers, can at the behest of a particular political party create total stoppage of production" (*EPW*, 9/20/69:1534).[5] Mookerjee found unlikely and unsolicited support from none other than P. C. Mahalanobis, the leftist father of central planning and state-led industrialization (7/69:1121):

Our labor laws are probably the most highly protective of labour interests . . . in the world. There is practically no link between output and remuneration, and hiring and firing are highly restricted...protection of organized labour...operates as an obstacle to growth and also increases inequalities.

Phenomena common to all four countries became manifest in India by the mid-1960s. Labor productivity, which had grown at nearly 5% per annum in the early 1950s, declined to 3% per annum in the early 1960s, and then registered no growth at all in the mid-1970s (Krishnamurthy, 1985:132). The World Bank (10/88) estimated that nearly 15% of the public sector work force was redundant, and that its additional wage bill was the equivalent of the aggregate operating losses of several SOEs. Despite redundancy, Indian public and private enterprises had to resort to contract labor, outside collective bargaining agreements, to get essential tasks done. For example, at Durgapur Steel, in addition to the regular work force of 32,000 there were 6,000 contract laborers in 1986.

From the mid-1960s on, strike activity increased steadily, and the private sector was affected much more seriously than the public in terms of person-days lost (Vermeulen and Sethi, 1982). The total number of person-days lost rose from 7.7 million in 1964 to 40.2 million in 1975 on the eve of the Emergency (Lal, 1988:212). In 1979, with the Emergency over and the Janata Party in power, strike activity rose once again. West Bengal alone accounted for 18 million of the 43 million days lost in that year (Rudolph and Rudolph, 1987:262). As a BHEL personnel manager observed to me, "There are twenty-one states in India...and then there is West Bengal."

The creation of the Bureau of Public Enterprises in 1969 was partially designed to contain the escalation of labor demands and to impose standard agreements to protect the viability of the SOEs. During the emergency period, Indira Gandhi led India toward a subcontinental variant of bureaucratic authoritarianism. A major railroad strike in May 1974, "the first political challenge by a trade union to the central government at the national level" (Rudolph and Rudolph, 1987:274) was crushed in three weeks, and the number of person-days lost to strikes dropped precipitously to 12 million in 1976.

With the lifting of the emergency, strike activity, and also management lockouts (Nigam, 1990:9), increased gradually. By 1987 nearly 40 million person-days had been lost. The major strike in the post-Emergency years was the great textile strike in Bombay that lasted from January 1982 to the end of July 1983 and involved 180,000 regular and 40,000 contract workers. It was led by a maverick organizer from INTUC, Dr. Datta Samant, who had been jailed during the Emergency, and who gained national notoriety but few tangible gains for the strikers. This was for Indira Gandhi the equivalent of Thatcher's confrontation with the coal miners. At its end more than a third of the strikers had drifted away into other employment, and several units were closed down (*Business India,* 1986; Heuzé, 1989).[6]

Despite Rajiv Gandhi's liberalization policies, labor sought to broaden the scope of the social pact. In the coal sector, fully within the public sector, where labor costs averaged 65% of total operating costs, a major strike was called involving several hundred thousand workers. One of labor's demands was that each employee retiring from Coal India be allowed to designate one of his dependents to replace him, thus creating a kind of heritable guild system. In a similar vein, local unions militated for local hire at all levels of employment, according to the principle known as "sons of the soil" (Weiner, 10/83:45). Large SOEs, like BHEL, that had operations in several states and wanted to move skilled personnel and management among plants where they were most needed, found themselves in constant altercations with local unions who opposed all such shifting.

As in Egypt, some Indian unions openly opposed any moves toward privatization, the importation of job-displacing technology, and the entry of multinational capital. A symbolic public sector–wide strike was called for January 21, 1987, and although INTUC refused to endorse it, it was widely observed (*EPW,* 1/27/87). And again, as in Egypt, unions fought efforts to link wages to productivity and any moves away from promotion by seniority. Orwellian terminology is peppered throughout Indian labor–management negotiations. A public sector textile strike in November 1985 generated demands that the "statutory minimum bonus" be augmented by an additional "bonus." The government advised management to concede, in exchange for the acceptance by labor of the *concept* of "scientific work norms" (*Economic Times,* 3/28/86).

The economic reform program initiated in 1991 may put well established patterns of interaction between labor and public sector firms to the test. But the fact that the current Congress government is dependent on the votes of other parties in the Lok Sabha may weaken its will to confront labor constituencies that could be crucial in new rounds of elections. And it is precisely this aspect of labor's power that is unique to India. Unions are part of a contested electoral system. That fact has allowed dissident leaders to emerge and even thrive. The multiparty system, especially at the state level, allows them to ally with politicians and, in exchange for votes, distribute some benefits to their followers in the event of electoral victory. It is in large measure for this reason that state governments rush to take over sick industries within their states so as not to put labor in the street.

Thus, at no level does INTUC enjoy a monopoly of distribution of benefits to workers, and elections do implicate large flows of resources

The Indian working class and ESOPs. Source: *The Times of India*, 4/29/90. Used by permission.

so that there is room for a Datta Samant, or a George Fernandez or the Communist Party of West Bengal, to bargain votes for benefit packages. The social pact in India works in the sense that the central political authorities acquiesce in, if not encourage, a system of labor-politico spoils.

3. MEXICO

The structure of state labor relations in Mexico finds its origins in the aftermath of the revolution. The 1917 constitution went further than any of the other hallowed documents of EIMT to enshrine labor's rights in the new revolutionary society. Partly this emphasis simply recognized what had become in the early years of the century an aggressive and unruly labor movement; partly it reflected the ideological shift after the collapse of the Porfiriato. The upshot was that in Mexico the entire experience with state-led growth has been built on a close, cooperative alliance between organized labor and the state.

Labor never had the upper hand in this alliance, and from 1917 on state authorities tried with increasing success to co-opt labor leaders and drive unions into a state-imposed grid. The first effort came through the creation of the Regional Confederation of Mexican Workers (CROM), which, until the Cárdenas *sexenio,* developed a dominant position in labor representation. The first in a long succession of "bought" leaders, Luis Morones, began under Calles to build Mexico's unique corporatist variant. It has consisted in union control not only over benefit packages, but over seats in the assembly, in state legislatures, and in the Mexico City council; direct union ownership of productive assets; and regular representation at the ministerial level. Morones himself was appointed minister of industry, labor, and commerce under Calles. At the same time the Labor Law of 1931 vested broad rights in the state to undertake binding arbitration in labor disputes, and to authorize and supervise union activities.

After 1934, Cárdenas, in his struggle against Calles (see Chapter 2), sought to wrest control of the labor movement from the CROM, and toward this end created the Mexican Confederation of Workers (CTM), which, up to the present time, has remained the single most important peak labor organization. Cárdenas's political strategy to isolate and discredit Calles led him to take the side of labor in the incipient class war that he stimulated, while his economic strategy called for the strengthening of private capital in the development effort. He could not have it both ways, winding up with armed peasants and workers, dissidence in the armed forces, the founding of the PAN, and capital flight (Collier, 1982:69–71).

The period of labor mobilization and inclusionary policies under Cárdenas was followed by a tightening of corporatist controls and exclusionary policies that were imposed especially by Alemán (1946–52) and prevailed throughout the "stabilizing growth" period up to the *sexenio* of Luis Echeverría. The centerpiece of the control system became the CTM, and it in turn fell under the undisputed sway of Fidel Velázquez from 1940 on. He replaced Lombardo Toledano, Cárdenas's man at the head of the CTM, and has reigned supreme ever since. The basic pact that Alemán engineered included wage restraints and harassment of dissident labor leaders in exchange for a prebendal system of labor entitlements. As the Mexican economic "miracle" unfolded, labor registered real gains in income from the late 1950s up to 1974 (Hansen, 1974:114–15; Prevot-Schapira, 9/83).

The era of institutionalized *charrismo* had begun. It held organized labor in check in the wake of the painful devaluation of 1954, and allowed even left-of-center presidents like López Mateos to break strikes called by dissident leaders. In 1966 a loose, and relatively powerless, Congress of Labor (Congreso del Trabajo) was created to act as an umbrella organization for the CTM and other officially tolerated labor federations.

Mexican political leaders, beginning with the Industrial Labor Pact of 1945, have persistently pursued formal corporatist accords among labor, capital, and the state (Alonso, 1976:177; Escobar Toledo, 1987:6; Luna, 1987:460). The riots and demonstrations of 1968 marked a rupture in the political entente between, on the one hand, students, workers, white-collar labor, and the intelligentsia, and, on the other, the political leaders and the technocracy. In the following four *sexenios,* those of Echeverría, López Portillo, de la Madrid, and Salinas de Gortari, formal efforts were undertaken to fashion new ententes.

Under Echeverría, labor's prebends were expanded at the same time that leaders and unions tried repeatedly to break loose from the corporatist grip of the CTM and the Congress of Labor. The period was dubbed that of "shared growth." It meant in practical terms that the entire dominant coalition operated under the softest of budget constraints, with Echeverría placating both labor and the private sector. Some SOEs as well as public assets such as the port of Veracruz were under the more or less direct control of unions, and the state could not appoint management to them without labor's consent; this was the case especially in the railroads, PEMEX, and the social security institute (Carr, 1983:105). Under Echeverría, unions were granted a share of all public construction contracts, and the share of the petroleum workers was set at 40% (Solís, 1976:123). A quarter of all deputies in the assembly represented the unions.

Despite Fidel Velázquez's ability to expand the entitlement system, the 1970s witnessed an upsurge in dissident labor movements. Within the PRI, the *tendencia democratica* developed, while various unions broke away from the CTM. Not all by any means were leftist, and some, like the Revolutionary Confederation of Workers and Peasants (CROC), may have been quietly promoted by the regime to remind the CTM of its vulnerability.[7] In Diesel Nacionál (DINA), the large state truck manufacturer, the labor force broke from the CTM and launched strikes almost yearly throughout the 1970s. The firm's work force increased by 40% over those years. The union won the application of work norms stipulating that the level and quality of work would be governed by "custom," and that in the event an assembly line shut down for whatever reason,

248

workers could not be transferred to some other task. The last strike was in 1986, just before the firm's privatization.

Similar breakaways were occurring in mining and metals, the railroads, and in the automotive sector. On the left, the National Union of Education Workers (SNTE), with 750,000 members, was riven by a struggle between dissidents and the state-appointed leadership that, in various guises, has persisted until the present time. In 1972 the main union at Fundidora de Monterrey aligned itself with *tendencia democratica*. On the right, the anti-Communist, antiparty Independent Workers' Union, with some 250,000 members, made inroads in the automotive sector and in Aeroméxico.

López Portillo, cushioned by surging petroleum revenues, saw no reason to do more than tinker with the pact fashioned by Echeverría, although, as Carr points out, from 1974 on there was some erosion in the real wage. This was offset, however, by myriad benefits and bonuses, consumer subsidies, and disbursements of *fideicomisos*. López Portillo gave effective control of the housing fund, INFONAVIT, to the CTM. In this respect, Carr observes (1983:97),

What counts in Mexico is the social wage, i.e., money wages plus the package of non-wage benefits (*prestaciones*). These include such state-originated services as subsidized or free health insurance, subsidized food, transport, clothing and housing; and union- or employer-administered benefits in other areas.

Benefit packages in turn were frequently under the direct control of the major recognized unions under the Congress of Labor and its affiliates. The most powerful of them was the Federation of Unions in the Service of the State (FSTSE), with over 700,000 members, about the same size as the CTM, and the Federation of Workers of the Federal District (e.g., Mexico City; FTDF) with 300,000 (Prevot-Schapira, 9/83:95). In all, the Congress of Labor claimed more than 3 million of a total unionized work force of about 5 million. In what may have been its last hurrah, the Congress of Labor in 1978 called for the expansion of the public sector, the rededication of the rectorate of the state, and the resistance of the state to the offensive of oligarchical forces (Casar and Peres, 1988:117). It was, indeed, in similar terms that Miguel de la Madrid described the tasks of his *sexenio* in 1982, although his subsequent actions belied his words. The CTM tepidly endorsed his candidacy, but Velázquez had deep misgivings that he did not hide (see note 7 to this chapter).

The economic crisis after 1981 hit the Mexican working class, and the poor in general, harder than did the crises in the other three countries. Between 1981 and 1985 the wage share of national income fell from 43% to 31%, and open unemployment grew from 2.7 million to 4.6 million (Lustig, 1990:1332–34). Between 1981 and 1983, 1.2 million to

1.7 million jobs in the formal sector were eliminated (Carr, 1983:104). Labor was relatively quiescent during the long years of negative growth, and unions fought a rearguard action to preserve what they could. De la Madrid, however, began an assault on labor's entitlements. Fundidora de Monterrey, which had been plagued with labor disputes even as its economic viability declined, was declared bankrupt and liquidated. This became the preferred pattern as the declaration of bankruptcy automatically led to the suspension of collective labor agreements, and allowed the state to restructure the work force without effective union countermeasures. In subsequent years strikes at Aeroméxico, Cananea Copper, and the Las Truchas steel complex led to similar measures with privatization resulting for Cananea and Aeroméxico, and plans laid for it at Las Truchas.

In 1987, inflation accelerated rapidly and capital seeped out of the country. The Pact of Economic Solidarity negotiated in December of that year was a response not to labor's deteriorating position but, rather, to the need to stimulate the private sector. Velázquez endorsed the pact reluctantly, for what the wage and price controls introduced at that time meant was that the *rate* of decline of real wages would be slowed; in fact, between December 1987 and January 1989 real wages declined by 24%. Much of organized labor was openly or tacitly opposed to the candidacy of Carlos Salinas for the presidency because he had helped design the austerity measures that led to labor's relative decline.

Salinas disappointed no one, moving aggressively against the leaders of the Petroleum Workers and the Teachers' Union, breaking a strike at Cananea by force, seizing the port of Veracruz, which had virtually been the property of its seven hundred workers, and deregulating truck transport, thereby effectively destroying a rent-seeking monopoly of the truckers' union. At the same time, he sought to establish links between the PRI and the proliferating private voluntary organizations that had sprouted up in Mexico City and elsewhere, and that lay outside the formal union structure. He created PRONASOL as a discretionary fund to build new patronage networks with low-income constituencies. In all these ways he restricted the ability of the unions to control the disbursement of resources and benefits.

Unsurprisingly, not all unions knuckled under, and as Cuauhtémoc Cárdenas mounted his challenge to Salinas through the launching of the PRD, dissident unions rallied to his cause. Major strikes were held at the Modelo Brewery and at the Ford Motor Company. A new dissident federation was proclaimed, the United Front in Defense of the Workers and the Constitution, itself the creation of the CROC, which in the past had often cooperated with the government (*NYT*, 4/8/90; *Latin American Monitor*, 5/90:772). All these moves notwithstanding, the midterm assembly elections in August 1991 produced a resounding victory for the PRI. Growth had been restored to the economy, a labor movement too long mired in spoils discredited, and the one political challenger, Cárdenas, unable to convince the electorate that he had a viable program.

The crucial event in the changing state–labor equilibrium came on January 9, 1989, when Salinas ordered the arrest of Joaquín Hernández Galicia, known as "La Quina" (a diminutive of Joaquín) and the man who, since 1964, had formally headed or indirectly controlled the National Revolutionary Union of Petroleum Workers of the Mexican Republic (SNRTPRM). At the time of La Quina's arrest, the SNRTPRM had 120,000 regular members and itself employed another 80,000. PEMEX, for all intents and purposes was the union's fiefdom. Six days before his arrest, La Quina had issued the following warning (Albanán de Alba and Martinez, 1/12/89):

> The day the federal government seeks to take from us a millimeter or a centimeter of the petroleum industry, to put it in the hands of foreign or national private interests, the union will launch its first strike before the nation... For no reason will we accept that the property of Mexicans, that President Lázaro Cárdenas bestowed upon us, be transferred to private hands.

La Quina had openly opposed the nomination of Salinas for the presidency and had denied him the all-important "embrace" that loyal members of the Revolutionary Family give to demonstrate their fealty to the party's choice. It was rumored that the SNTPRM funneled financial support to Salinas's nearly successful challenger, Cuauhtémoc Cárdenas. Having scraped, perhaps fraudulently, his way to victory, it seemed unlikely that Salinas would do anything so foolhardy as to challenge the petroleum workers. They were reputedly armed and prepared to shut down the entire petroleum sector. The news of La Quina's arrest sent Mexicans flocking to gas stations to fill their tanks in anticipation of what even seasoned politicos (one of whom I was interviewing when the arrest was announced) thought might be civil war.

The court official who delivered the arrest warrant was shot by La Quina's bodyguards. Police and army immediately moved in to overwhelm La Quina's protection and to seize control of his house. Simultaneously the armed forces took control of key petroleum installations and began using military tanker trucks to bring petroleum products to the civilian market. There was no strike and no notable resistance by the SNRTPRM. There was considerable satisfaction that this *charro* of *charros* had been arrested. Not only that, Salinas had asserted control over the political system, showed strength and confidence, and in one stroke put his near defeat in the elections well behind him.

The formal charges against La Quina were tax evasion and illegal possession of arms. In the subsequent searches and investigations, these and many other accusations against La Quina were confirmed and widely publicized. He was found to own luxury residences outside Mexico (including one in a ski resort in Colorado) and to have enjoyed a life-style totally at odds with his beginnings as a welder. He truly was, for his fellow unionists, a *padrino:* a tough man willing to use violence against adversaries and dissidents, but a cornucopia of goods and services to loyal followers. He made no effort to hide the fact that he lived well; that was clearly part of the persona.[8]

Through the union, he had built an empire that could deliver goods; so much so that he was no longer dependent on the state for access to them. Here are some of the assets at the disposal of the SNRTPRM. It owned its own petroleum fleet (Petroflota), its own construction firm, and its own airline (Aerogolfo). It owned 27,000 hectares in commercial agricultural properties and 10,000 head of cattle. Its supermarket chain was the second largest in Mexico. It owned dress, furniture, and heavy machinery factories, and printing houses.

The union's prebends were so extensive that La Quina hired a businessman, Sergio Bolaños, to help manage them, and to set up fronts for the acquisition of new assets. It was through his Grupo Serbo that the Mexican government received a very large bid for the acquisition of one of the two national carriers, Méxicana. The true identity of the bidder was recognized, and although the highest, the bid was rejected. Had the bid gone through, a truly unique privatization would have occurred.

State authorities, before Salinas, had given up trying to control La Quina. He picked his successors at the head of the union, and controlled the selection of the managing directors of PEMEX. It is said that in 1984, de la Madrid began to make contingency plans for breaking the union and dealing with a strike. He consulted secretly with the top military officers about taking over the oil fields. A few days later La Quina is said to have met with de la Madrid and shown him accurate transcripts of the conversations, at which point de la Madrid backed down. Subsequently, de la Madrid appointed a reputedly tough and clean managing director of PEMEX, Mario Ramón Beteta, to wrest control of the SOE from La Quina. The ten loyal SNRTPRM deputies in the assembly then brought charges against Beteta, accusing him of fraud and embezzlement in the purchase of tankers for the PEMEX fleet.

Beyond its colorfulness, the La Quina saga points up at least two major characteristics of state–labor relations in Mexico, and to some extent in the other three countries. First, the utilization of unions to control the work force and to keep it apolitical was contingent not only on channeling benefits through them to the rank and file but also on allowing them to

EMBOTELLADA ■ Rocha

Salinas's appointment of Elba Esther Gordillo to replace Jongitud at the head of the National Union of Education Workers (SNTE). Sra. Gordillo had to face massive protest marches of her own rank and file in November 1989 that daily caused huge traffic jams in downtown Mexico City. Riding in her "CHARROL'S ROYCE," she is caught in one of them. Source: *La Jornada*, 11/10/89.

own assets in their own right.[9] All of the ISI coalition members to varying degrees obtained prebends from the state. Second, it is *as if* state leaders had deliberately set up labor leaders over decades of co-optation. Their ability to deliver public resources to a select few ultimately led to their own delegitimatization in the eyes of the broader public, and when episodes of confrontation occurred, they found themselves isolated and unable to appeal to a popular base beyond their own rank and file. Indeed, substantial parts of the rank and file may have bolted the stable long before. Thus, after La Quina, Salinas moved on the longtime boss of the teachers' union, Carlos Jongitud Barrios, many of whose members had long called for his removal. They got their wish – but not control of the union.

253

4. TURKEY

The new Turkish republic acted as if it faced a large, militant, organized industrial labor force. After having legalized union activity in 1924, it greatly restricted it in 1925. A 1936 labor law introduced bans on strikes in specific sectors, and a 1938 law on associations banned any organization based on social class (Işikli, 1987). In the 1930s, through the Republican People's Party, Atatürk introduced a strongly corporatist political system that made the tiny organized labor sector one of its pillars. When, in 1952, the major peak labor confederation, Türk-İş, was founded, its total membership was only 150,000.

Not until after the military take-over of 1960, and the issuance of the somewhat radical constitution of 1961, was organized labor given the legal possibility to expand significantly.[10] The period after 1961 also corresponded to one of sustained economic growth, rapid urbanization, and industrial deepening. One result was that unionized labor mushroomed to more than 2 million workers in the early 1970s.[11]

The center of organized labor was occupied by Türk-İş, and it in turn represented workers concentrated in the public sector.

Aided by the public sector's rapid adoption of automatic dues checkoffs and centralized collective bargaining, conservative unionists have come close to acquiring perfect representational monopolies over the state industrial workforce. Over 90 percent of the workers in state industry are now dues-paying union members, and about 80 percent of these belong to conservative unions (Bianchi, 1984:231).

Türk-İş was created during the period of the Demokrat Party incumbency, but in the years after 1960 it found ways to cooperate with all comers – with the military in 1960 and 1970, with its more probable ally in the Justice Party in the period after 1965, and with the various coalitions of the 1970s. It was the only union federation that was not dissolved by the military government after 1980, and under the leadership of Şevket Yilmaz, it has struck a modus vivendi with Turgut Özal and the Motherland Party not unlike that between Fidel Velázquez and de la Madrid or Salinas.

Despite Türk-İş's periodic denunciations of government wage policy, high inflation, and worsening income distribution, denunciations that may be theatrical, large segments of the labor movement have, since the early 1960s, tried to structure a more confrontational role for their unions. In 1961 the Turkish Labor Party was founded by the Marxist left, and it sought to aggregate the electoral weight of a more radical labor constituency. It was shut down by the military authorities after 1971. It won 300,000 votes and fifteen seats in the Grand National

Assembly in 1965, but its supporters appeared to be more drawn from the urban middle class, Kurds, and Alevis than from the ranks of organized labor per se (Shamim, 1985).

Strike activity increased during the 1960s with 409,000 person-days lost in 1966. There were wildcat strikes at the Zonguldak coal mines, which Türk-İş could not control (Roy, 1974), and at the Paşabahçe Glass factory, also an SOE, which led Türk-İş to suspend six unions (Margulies and Yildizoğlu, 2/84). In the following year, a new radical labor federation, DISK (the Federation of Revolutionary Workers' Unions), was founded and within a few years claimed to represent a million members.[12] It was initially close to the Turkish Labor Party, but after the party's banning in 1971, DISK moved closer to the RPP, which had become a social democratic party under the leadership of Bülent Ecevit. From 1975 on, strike activity increased greatly, rising from 1.1 million person-days lost in that year to 5.4 million in 1980, the year in which the military once again intervened. The most famous strikes were called by the Mining and Metal Workers' Union (Maden-İş) over an eight-month period in 1977. The strikes involved direct confrontation with the Mining and Metallurgy Industries Employers' Association, then headed by Turgut Özal. In the same year May Day demonstrations turned into violent clashes with police that left forty dead.

The military government dissolved DISK and put 306 of its leaders in jail. In 1983, Laws 2821 and 2822, severely restricting the right to organize and strike, were issued. They have been a bone of contention between Turkey and the European Common Market, which has seen them as not conforming to the freedoms granted European labor. The new Turkish constitution of 1983, in Article 52, stipulated that labor unions "shall not pursue a political cause, engage in political activity, receive support from political parties or give support to them, and shall not act jointly for these purposes with associations, public professional organizations, and foundations." The right to strike was denied to about half the organized work force, which is in sectors designated as "strategic," and the ban on union activity among civil servants and military personnel was continued (Sunar, 1987). As noted in Chapter 6, public sector managers were encouraged to form their own employers' associations and to "get tough" with labor. Similar to Youssef Cohen's findings among Brazilian organized labor under the generals (Cohen, 3/82), Turkish analysts found that a majority of Turkish workers approved of the military government's insistence on the apoliticism of unions and its restoration of law and order (Koç, 1986; Boratav and Yalman, 10/89).

The period after 1980 was, as in Mexico, one of austerity in which the real wages of workers, and the share of labor in value-added and national product, dropped sharply while the shares of profits and inter-

Table 9.1. *Real wage and salary index for Turkish work force, 1968–87 (1968 = 100)*

Year	Wages	Salaries
1968	100	100
1978	221	109
1979	196	106
1987	118	44

Source: Adapted from Kepenek (1990), 98.

est payments rose proportionately (Cevizoğlu, 1989:100; Kepenek, 1990:161). This followed several years in the mid- and late 1970s during which organized labor was the beneficiary of substantial income redistribution. In Table 9.1, it can be seen that real wages grew rapidly between 1968 and 1978 while salaries, concentrated in the nonunionized sector of the labor force, grew hardly at all. With the onset of the crisis and triple-digit inflation in 1979, declines in both wages and salaries commenced, but the rate of decline in the unionized, wage-earning sectors was much slower than in the nonunionized salary-earning sectors.

The significance of the redistribution of national wealth in favor of wage earners during the period 1974–80 is partially captured in Figure 9.1 measuring labor productivity and the real wage index. The rate of increase of the real wage far exceeded that of productivity during that period. By contrast, since mid-1981 productivity gains have substantially outpaced increases in the real wage, which by 1988 had only regained its mid-1975 level.

Although white-collar employees have absorbed relatively harder blows to their standard of living than unionized blue-collar labor, the 1980s was very hard on both. Declared unemployment over the decade hovered around 10% of the work force, or around 2 million people. As noted in Chapter 7, Özal's strategy was to compensate partially afflicted sectors, not as workers or employees, but as consumers and investors. Revenue-sharing certificates, rebates on the VAT, and legal title to squatter land were some of the devices employed. Wage- and salary-earners resorted to multiple jobs, family members who should have been in school might be in the informal labor sector, and, in specific crop sectors, the flow of income may have been reversed, moving from the countryside to beleaguered relatives in the city (Boratav and Yalman, 10/89). Remitt-

Organized labor and public enterprise

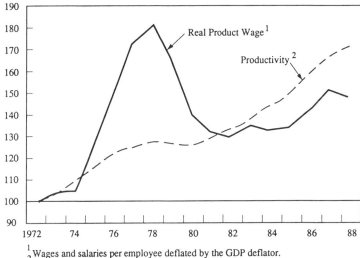

[1] Wages and salaries per employee deflated by the GDP deflator.
[2] Real output per employee.

Figure 9.1. Labor cost and productivity in Turkey (Index 1972 = 100). Source: *OECD Economic Surveys: Turkey* (1990), 30. Used by permission.

ances from the migrant labor force in Europe (more than $3 billion in 1990) remain crucial to family survival.

Despite all this family-based coping, there was a resurgence of organized labor activity in the second half of the 1980s. In 1987 nearly 2 million labor days were lost in strikes as compared with 5,000 in 1984 (Koç, 1986; *Dünya*, 6/22/88 and 7/1/89). Union membership recovered to about 2 million, of which 1.4 million were in Türk-İş. Hak-İş, loosely affiliated with the religious right, claimed 150,000 members, while the remnants of DISK filtered into recognized unions. One of DISK's most prominent leaders, Abdullah Baştürk, after release from prison, joined the Grand National Assembly in 1987 as a Social Democrat deputy.

By the end of the decade, persistent high inflation had begun to erode ANAP's political base and to weaken the effects of compensatory payments. In 1989 and again in 1991 the government was forced to concede very large collective wage and salary settlements to public sector employees, the real value of which, however, still lagged behind the rate of inflation.

The Turkish government has tried to segment the public sector work force. On the one hand, it has recognized the importance of maintaining a solid working relationship with Türk-İş, whose 1.4 million members occupy the center of the labor movement. The federation must be granted some control over the disbursement of public resources to the rank and

257

file. On the other, the ANAP governments have promoted the conversion of significant numbers of public employees to "contract personnel" status. Such status, provided for in Law 440 of 1964, was aimed at recruiting managers to the public sector on an exceptional basis and for specific tasks (Karataş, 1986:152; Kepenek, 1990:105).

In 1985, in the public sector, there were only 5,000 contract personnel; by 1989 the numbers had swelled to nearly 300,000 (*Cumhuriyet*, 12/28/89). Contract personnel cannot join unions, and they are not part of collective wage settlements. Contracts are normally for one year, subject to renewal. As the numbers of contract personnel rise, so too does the state's relative bargaining power toward labor and the salariat. The attraction for individual workers and managers has been the possibility of higher salaries or wages; the trade-off has been increased job insecurity. There is some evidence that the World Bank encouraged the Turkish government to follow this course (World Bank, 6/86:44).

The Social Democratic Party challenged the legality of the conversions of public employees to this status, and an Ankara court upheld the challenge, declaring the conversions unconstitutional on three counts: The status is supposed to be exceptional; those in it are not supposed to be "converted" from some other legal status; and adoption of the status is supposed to be purely voluntary. The government has drafted new legislation to define the status of contract personnel, but the main clauses appear to offer little change over the situation now declared unconstitutional (*Cumhuriyet*, 1/15/90).

The multistranded policies the Turkish government has implemented with respect to organized labor and the salariat reflects the sometimes contradictory exigencies of economic strategy and political survival. Turkey's market-oriented reforms of the 1980s lead in the direction of selling off public assets and ending social welfare entitlements for privileged elements of the labor force. By contrast, the need to control public resources for compensatory payments, coalition maintenance, and preelection pump priming dictates retention of public assets, the preemption of large segments of the organized work force from rival political forces, and continued government intervention in large collective wage settlements. As Japanese experience has shown, this kind of tension between economic strategy and political control can be sustained over long periods, so long as there is growth in the economy (Calder, 1989).

5. CONCLUSION

I have argued that of all the members of the ISI coalition, organized labor is the best equipped and the most highly motivated to resist the erosion or divestiture of the SOE sector. In relative terms that is true, but the evidence from EIMT suggests that resistance has so far been feeble. If maintenance of a certain standard of living and real wage level is the driving force behind much union activity, then labor, at least in Mexico and Turkey, lost the battle in the generalized economic crises of the early 1980s. Soaring unemployment, high inflation, and widespread layoffs across the private and public sectors left organized labor in disarray. Strikes in Mexico actually gave the government the pretext to suspend collective wage agreements, declare SOEs bankrupt, and to liquidate or sell them off. "Loyal" unions in Mexico and Turkey have used their privileged relations with the government mainly to limit damage.

Beyond the stunning impact of economy-wide crisis, two main factors explain the relative helplessness of organized labor to thwart the pace and direction of reform. First, many of the unions in the peak federations were and are corporatist shells rather than coherent organizations. The benefits of the social pacts had been granted without prior struggle. As Ellis Goldberg has argued for Egypt (1992), the preemptive granting of entitlements rendered union membership a burden; free riding prevailed, as did resentment of union leadership.

Second, the social pact was paid for, in part, by the operating losses of the SOEs. The insistence of the unions on benefits packages and work norms that, in essence, sapped the economic viability of public firms, simultaneously reduced labor's bargaining power. It is one thing to threaten to strike and paralyze a dynamic industry or sector, for the effects will be felt throughout the economy. It is quite another to threaten to strike in a sector of chronic loss-making industries whose goods and services have never been delivered on time and when delivered, have been substandard. To the extent that SOEs are not concerned with making profits, much of the threat posed by a strike to a firm's bottom line is lost. The Bombay textile strike was a monument to organized labor's conundrum.

There are key sectors – in petroleum, transportation, and power generation – where labor's threats to disrupt could have profound consequences, but the rout of La Quina and his petroleum workers in Mexico demonstrates that that threat may be more theoretical than real. For unions to bargain from strength, their members must be both skilled (i.e., not easily replaced) and strategically located. Those two conditions are rarely joined in EIMT.

10

Conclusion: The redefinition of state economic intervention

The illusions to which EIMT were exposed are not innumerable, and for many informed individuals, beyond the leadership of the respective countries, they were anything but illusions. Rather, they were plausible expectations, and in their essence went as follows. If exploitative private economic behavior, both indigenous and foreign, could be throttled or eliminated, if the proliferation of middlemen with their attendant usury, speculation, monopsonies, and short-time horizons could be halted, then a dynamic, carefully and rationally planned state enterprise sector could, as farsighted helmsman of the economy, mobilize scarce resources, stimulate markets, adopt new technologies, and rapidly lift the entire economy to a level of self-sustaining industrial growth. The longtime horizon of planners and managers would allow for an optimal combination of growth and equity. The social mission of public enterprise would not cripple it economically, because rational planning would reduce the high transaction costs associated with distorted private markets. The experiment would pay for itself and generate enough surplus to spill over into the "backward" sectors not directly associated with the modern industries and services of the state.

It followed that morale among workers and managers in the state sector would be high as the exploitation of labor by capital would not be a factor. The productivity of capital, if not of labor, where some redundancy was accepted as a given, would be correspondingly high. It was assumed that the state, in its parts or taken as a whole, would act coherently to promote the plan and the public good.

This is, of course, a bowdlerized condensation of understandings in EIMT that were far more subtle and cynical, but the belief in a kind of benevolent leviathan was shared by elites with a transforming mission as well as by a host of foreign advisors and creditors. That public officials and agencies would themselves become rent seekers, that morale would falter and labor–management relations become adversarial, that

260

labor productivity would be so low and costs so high, was simply not anticipated. That SOEs would be unable to produce their way out of debt, that they would become a net drain on public finances rather than a steady provider of fiscal surplus, also came as a surprise.

The first intellectual critiques of what had gone wrong tended to take two lines of attack. One, coming from the left, argued that the emerging crises were due either to the fact that foreign and domestic private interests were sabotaging the statist experiment, or to the logic of the experiment itself, which was to build a private capitalist class to which the commanding heights would gradually be ceded. Atatürk did have such a vision, which he partially abandoned in the 1930s. From the right, the argument was that a misconceived effort in socialist transformation had met its inevitable end. In contrast to both understandings, I have argued throughout that for the designers and the implementors of etatism, the economic arrangements they put in place, and their role in them, were to go on in perpetuity. As Pollock (1982), and later Freeman (1989), argued with respect to European state capitalism, the system was to be self-sustaining, not a stage in the evolution of a new set of economic and class relationships. In EIMT the future, like the present, was to be one of a mixed economy in which the private sector was politically and economically subordinated to the "rectorate" of the state. Change was to consist in a shift from an agrarian to an industrial mode, the building of national economic sovereignty, and the spread of broad-based prosperity for all citizens.

The four countries analyzed in this book were selected because their statist experiments have been both old and ideologically self-conscious. My assumption has been that this would enable one to see why it was the experiments were launched in the first place, what new economic and political actors were given a stake in the experiment, and how the redefinition of the state's intervention could be brought about. Economic and class structures, it was found, acted as retardants to processes of change but did not determine or cause them. Rather, narrowly based political leadership, assisted by insulated change teams, drove forward both the ISI strategy itself and the subsequent introduction of market-conforming policies and structural adjustment. In the first instance, leaders sought, with considerable success, to wrench the economic structures of agrarian societies into an industrial mode. In the second, leaders have tried to break the very interest structures the earlier experiment had created. The second restructuring will be the more difficult because it will not enjoy the populist support that nationalist and inclusivist ISI generated. Its constituency will be narrow, its resources limited, and its popular image mean-spirited.

261

Exposed to innumerable delusions

1. INSTITUTIONAL CULTURE AND PROPERTY REGIMES

The legal designation of property has had a profound impact on the functioning of the statist experiments. Public ownership of economic assets gave rise to an institutional culture that, over time, transformed the nature of state intervention from one of benevolent public-spiritedness to one of narrow pursuit of agency interests at the expense of society and in the absence of a sense of national purpose.

The essence of the institutional culture lies in the relations between principals and agents. The former, the legally designated owners of public assets, in fact turn out to be coalitions of interests often in conflict one with another. The multiple objectives assigned to public enterprise in turn produced an unwieldy and costly amalgam of dependent capitalists, organized labor, politicians, intellectuals, technocrats, senior civil servants, the military, and international donors, all of whom benefited from the SOE sector. There was no agreed-upon set of criteria by which to judge the performance of public assets, and no set of incentives among the principals to bring about effective monitoring of what they nominally owned.

The agents, or managers of the assets, quickly learned that they could not meet all or most of the multiple objectives assigned them, and that the lack of effective monitoring meant that their failure to do so bore little cost. At the same time, the typical pattern of the managerial career and the absence of any system of rewards for entrepreneurial behavior meant that the "rational" manager would increasingly pursue his own personal agenda. In this way, the presumed monitoring advantages of public principals and agents proved to be fictions as agents typically came to hide information from one another and from their monitoring units. The mechanisms for monitoring, rewarding, or sanctioning behavior among the managers proved to be such that the undeniable competence of most was largely wasted.

The institutional, property regime logic that failed to produce effective monitoring of public enterprise performance also failed to produce on the part of public authorities much resistance to the demands of the coalitional interests that grew up around the statist experiment. Indeed, that sort of discipline could only have come from the principals policing themselves. What this means is that some component of the coalition of principals has to impose discipline on the others. EIMT offers three examples of this: Chronologically they are Indira Gandhi's brief flirtation with authoritarian controls between 1975 and 1977; the Turkish generals' crackdown between 1980 and 1983; and Carlos Salinas's disciplining of labor after 1988.

262

The state enterprise sector, with its banks, factories, and services, was the center of the distribution system that developed to service the material needs of the coalition in all its parts. It hired the educated and maintained high wages for organized labor; it produced subsidized goods for low-income consumers; it funneled investment into backward areas; it supplied energy and inputs to the private sector and let contracts to private suppliers. It was thus the guarantor of social pacts, and its operating losses and mounting debts were covered by the treasury and by foreign debt. So difficult was it to resist these claims that even as the structural crises became manifest in the 1960s, all four countries (and scores other as well) expanded their state sectors significantly during the 1970s, exacerbating the fiscal and debt crises that brought them all to their knees over the next ten years.

2. COALITIONS AND RESISTANCE TO CHANGE

EIMT attempted to reform their state enterprise sectors, either trying to make a state capitalist experiment work better (as in Turkey or to a lesser extent in Mexico), or to move from market socialism to state capitalism (Egypt and to a lesser extent India). The reform efforts largely failed. There was no theoretic reason why public assets could not be made to perform like private assets *if* markets were competitive and exit the price of poor performance. Individual public enterprises in all four countries did achieve considerable market efficiency. The empirical reality has been, however, that the political logic that gave rise to the SOE sectors in the first place – the need to redistribute income, maintain the coalition, preempt resources from possible challengers outside the state, and build national security – would not yield to a market logic across the SOE sector as a whole. In the 1980s it became apparent to Turkish and Mexican policy makers that the only way to escape that political logic was to put most of the public sector beyond the reach of the state through privatization. A similar awareness appears to be taking hold in India and Egypt in the 1990s.

From this situation emerges an apparent paradox. The institutional culture of the public property regime, combined with the constellation of coalitional interests dependent on that regime, mean that successful reform is nearly impossible. At the same time, when fundamental restructuring is entered upon, none of the threatened interests appear capable of blocking the restructuring. The reasons for this, in my view, stem from their organizational weakness and their loss of legitimacy (if they ever had any in the first place) among the growing portions of society that did not directly benefit from the social pacts, such as many rural producers, those in the informal sector, and many middle-class consumers who have become particularly sensitive to deteriorating quality of services and products as well as to the erosion of their incomes through inflation.

As important as these factors is that defense of the old pact arrangements is a collective good – or, for the beneficiaries of the old arrangements, a collective bad – and no single entitled interest would have any incentive to contribute to it. Rather, these interests have tried to defend their particular entitlements, allowing determined change teams at the highest political levels to pick them off one at a time. Indeed, specific interests have tried to blame one another for the poor performance of the state sector. This kind of behavior is reenforced by the habits, formed over years, of cutting deals, firm by firm or interest by interest, up vertical hierarchies in the state system. Interests dependent on the state never developed habits of collective bargaining but, rather, relied on particularistic deal making. When threatened, these same interests resorted to particularistic damage control, repairing leaks in their vessel as the ebbing tide brought all ships down.

Somewhat surprisingly, SOE managers, at least the most senior of them, have faced the public sector bashing with equanimity. If they constitute the state bourgeoisie, they have exhibited little sense of their shared interests no less an awareness of being a dominant class. I have suggested that this is because their status and standard of living are not directly dependent on their continued control of the public means of production, and that their real property is professional expertise and managerial competence, both of which are in short supply and high demand throughout the public and private economies. By contrast, senior civil servants who monitor, audit, finance, and appoint staff to SOEs do not enjoy the same options. Their civil service functions depend on the continued existence of the SOE sector, and they may have more incentives to try to impede divestiture than the managers themselves. But even they, as retirement approaches, may have little reason to enter into collective defense of SOE turf, and may content themselves with foot dragging and occasional sabotage. In short, there is no state class that acts as such, and if any stratum of the state sector is reproducing itself, it is the great undifferentiated mass of the younger, petty employees with few or no marketable skills.

Organized labor has felt the most directly threatened by public sector reform and privatization. Public sector unions have not been swayed by economists' arguments that real jobs will be better paying and more secure than ersatz jobs in the public sector, and that the revenues freed up by divestiture can go to create real jobs. No union leader would act on this logic because the short-term loss of public sector jobs could cost him his power in the union or destroy the union itself. However, organized labor, although the best equipped and most motivated to defend the public sector, has so far, in EIMT at any rate, done little to halt the pace of change. First, as a corporate group it has in large measure been created by the state, not by struggle, and thus does not have the organizational history and sinew to block divestiture. Second, the collusions it has worked out with state elites over many years have left a general public impression of corrupt deals at the expense of the real working classes, outside the state economy and formal organizations. To resort to strikes and agitation to block reform or privatization of public firms whose losses may widely be perceived as stemming from labor's entitlements, could strip unions of all remaining legitimacy. Political leaders like Salinas have been able to break up labor fiefdoms or count on continued cooperation from co-opted leaders who would sink into oblivion were they to lead their unions into true opposition. Like other state interests they want to protect their immediate followers even though the entire labor movement may be in jeopardy.

3. THE NATURE OF CRISIS

Structural change has come in varying degrees to all four economies, and it has come as the result of systemic economic crises. I have argued that the crises were inherent in the strategies of state-led ISI and the peculiar public property regime it produced. There is no necessary link between ISI and the institutions of public enterprise, but empirically the two have frequently gone together. A change in strategy need not entail a change in property regime, or vice versa, but because a change in either will necessarily entail a change in coalitional arrangements, there will tend to be change in both. That has certainly been the case in EIMT.

It is very difficult to determine the weight of domestic and external factors in shaping the crises and the responses to them. There tend to be linkages over time between both sets of factors (world depression leads to ISI, ISI leads to inflation and debt, inflation and debt lead to payments crisis, payments crises lead to structural adjustment, etc.). However, I have privileged domestic factors because some countries, like South Korea, have managed large public sectors and ISI in such a manner as to avoid the payments crises. India, until the mid-1980s, and despite very modest growth rates, was similarly successful.

The four countries split into two groups in terms of the timing and the depth of crisis. Turkey and Mexico, between 1979 and 1982, were no longer able to contain inflation and service their external debts. For a time India was able to ignore the warning signals of growing inflation and rapidly mounting domestic and external debts. Egypt was able to ignore nearly deafening warning signals from 1977 on as it collected substantial strategic rents. By the early 1990s, however, both countries had run out of options for maintaining macroeconomic balances.

Nevertheless, within the confines of this study we have only two test cases of attempts at system transformation: Turkey and Mexico. In Turkey the process began with a sharp break in political continuity and the smashing of old coalitional arrangements through the military intervention of 1980. In Mexico no such break occurred, although by the end of the decade Mexico had proceeded much further than Turkey in remaking its economic system.

Neither class analytic nor rational actor models account well for structural change led by incumbents. The first would envisage change driven by the collapse of dominant interests and the insurgence of repressed and exploited segments of the population, while the second would predict stasis until some exogenous shock left the incumbents in disarray. Mexico's experience under Salinas defies both explanations, and if India and Egypt enter into system-transforming change in the 1990s under their present leaders, so too would they.

I have suggested that if the crisis itself is of sufficient severity, it provides the element of discontinuity that allows incumbents to restructure their power bases. I confess that to so state is to beg many questions. We may only know what is sufficient with hindsight. Crises may drag on for years and produce no change, and then, in some near magical way, as in Mexico in 1986, rattle a system to its foundations. Clearly, prolonged crisis numbs whole sectors of society at the same time that it delegitimizes the beneficiaries of the old order. It is then possible for determined incumbents, assisted by insulated change teams, to drive their agendas forward. Their major challengers will be found not so much in disaffected members of the old coalition, for they typically espouse more of the same, but rather among the long-standing critics who had heretofore been on the margin of the political system. Gorbachev in this sense, both in his significant achievements and in ultimate failure, may stand as a kind of paradigmatic incumbent reformer.

4. SYSTEM TRANSFORMATION AND SUSTAINABILITY

The example of Gorbachev raises the questions of sustainability and political survival. Both may hinge on generating some growth in the economy coupled with partial compensation of strategic allies and of those hardest hit by the reforms. Growth depends on the successful implementation of economic reforms, a task, I have argued, that may require a programmatically guided change team to carry out. The team may well espouse policies that would limit the government's discretionary powers and maximize automaticity in the application of public policy. Compensation, by contrast, will require discretionary policies. There is, then, an inevitable tension between the goals of the change team and the goals of supreme political leadership. Managing this tension is crucial to sustaining the change, and in Turkey, since 1987, we are witness to the failure of Turkish leadership to succeed in this task.

Although it is highly unlikely that political leaders will lead a retreat of the state from all the domains in which it has intervened over the last decades, they will have to unburden the state partially of the role of arbiter and ultimate guarantor of the material welfare of the bulk of the organized work force. A large part of that task will have to be passed on to a private sector that may be very reluctant to take it on. The organized private sector has benefited from the state's willingness to absorb risk for it in financial and commodity markets. Sustainability of system-transforming policies will depend in no small measure on the ability of the private sector to accept risk and to deal directly with the organized labor force. In short the organized private sector needs to be privatized (see Aspe, 1/92).

The old, costly corporatist structures of interest may fall victim to change. I have already argued that they may be unable to block it. Political leadership, in the phase of transformation, may be tempted to encourage what Bianchi (1984) has called "debilitating pluralism" (see Chapter 9) so as not to face in the future the well-organized constituents it had brought into being in the past. But if debilitating pluralism replaces state corporatism, political leaders may have nothing very coherent to lean upon if the reform process gets into trouble. The disarray in interest groups and lobbies that the crisis brought about and that allowed, in Mexico at least, the reform process to surge ahead, may in turn undermine the ability of the leadership to sustain the process.

5. INSTRUMENTS OF INTERVENTION

If the perfect market is about as utopian as the classless society, why has the former so fully captured the public imagination to the detriment of the latter? (Comisso, 1990:577)

No one has yet shown that the failure of government intervention *necessarily* outweighs market failure. (Fishlow, 1990:66; emphasis in original)

In terms of their economic experiments EIMT have come to similar situations, although they reached them over a decade's time. The message, it seems to me, is that different levels of national wealth, different rural–urban balances, and wildly different cultural traditions had relatively little to do with this outcome. That public sector pathologies and their impact on the macropolitical economy were so similar lends credence to the proposition that the crises were generated by the nature of the public sector itself, and the ways in which it shaped the use of public resources. It also suggests that the articulation of the public sector with the rest of the economy in the four countries was not sufficiently deep for the peculiar characteristics of each society to determine the nature of the crisis.

Was, then, state-led ISI a mistake, a strategy and practice that should have been avoided? To come to that conclusion would require arguing the counterfactual: that is, where would EIMT be today in the absence of ISI? It would also require a counterfactual argument in the sense that virtually all LDCs have resorted to ISI.

It may be more useful and more accurate to think of ISI as an important phase of development in which infrastructure was built, new industrial technologies transferred and absorbed, and labor and management trained. It is hard to think of another strategy or set of agencies that could have accomplished the same tasks. The process of state-led ISI contained the elements of its own collapse and obsolescence. But it made possible the coming, market-oriented phase. Indeed in Brazil, Korea, Taiwan, and Turkey, the public and private industries nurtured under ISI began the shift to a different competitive environment and toward exports. The same infrastructure, the same labor force and managerial corps, and, to a lesser extent, the same plant and financial intermediaries, can be put to new purposes in new institutional and market settings. Rules, regulations, and property rights will change, but the human and productive legacy of ISI is substantial.

There is no reason to think that the shifts in EIMT are linear in nature, that the moves toward markets and private sector growth are irreversible. The reforms may fail to deliver growth and a modicum of equity, leading to calls for their repeal. Economic actors may be ground into paralysis by the exigencies of markets and continued bureaucratic interference. Increasing involvement in world trade may require a reassertion of the state's mercantilist interventions. Economic success may tempt the state to reacquire assets; economic failure may oblige it to do so. Widespread collapse of export-oriented private firms, heavily indebted to public or private banks, could force state authorities to take over private assets in order to put them back on their feet. Once in the state domain, however, a dynamic may take over that would keep the assets under public ownership.

Turkey has shown that public sectors and statist strategies wax and wane. Turkey liberalized and tried to privatize in the 1950s, and in the 1960s rediscovered central planning and public ownership. Business cycles and market crises in relatively poor societies will always generate significant calls for state intervention. It will be some time, if ever, before private entrepreneurs enjoy the kind of legitimacy that would enable them to resist popular pressures for a reassertion of public controls on, if not the actual take-over of private assets. But history will not repeat itself or move in circular fashion, nor will it move linearly unless we can see beyond capitalism in all its forms. Perhaps in twenty years it will require the skills of an archaeologist to study SOEs, but they were and are merely the instruments states devised to mobilize resources and influence the competitive arenas in which they sought to survive. The challenges remain the same, although the instruments may change.

Notes

1. INTRODUCTION

1 On India's "giantism" as an independent variable, see John Lewis (1991).

2 In a cultural argument once removed, Myron Weiner partly accounts for Indian democracy as the result of British colonialism and presumably British cultural preferences (1989:78).

3 In a similar vein, Alfred Stepan (1978) has seen Latin American corporatism as springing from Roman law and traditions of the Catholic church, giving rise to what he calls "organic statism," but what he describes could quite easily be applied to, for instance, Turkey.

4 Ibn Khaldun, often described as the first sociologist, stressed the importance of *'asabiyya*, or group feeling defined by blood, as a kind of hidden hand in economic exchanges, allowing for cooperative outcomes and a division of labor. In today's jargon, it combated free riders and established norms of behavior. See Ibn Khaldun (1981:230) and Dieter Weiss (7/30/90:96–97).

5 That point would certainly be contested. For representative debates for proponents and critics of class-based explanations, see, for Egypt, Fu'ad Mursi (1976) versus John Waterbury (1983); for India, Pranab Bardhan (1984) versus Lloyd and Susanne Rudolph (1987); for Mexico, Nora Hamilton (1982) versus Peter Smith (1979); for Turkey, Çağlar Keyder (1987) versus Metin Heper (1985).

6 There is a vast literature on both, very partially referenced in Waterbury (1991).

7 Nayar (1989:244) points out that in India where the native bourgeoisie had considerable power, it is not conceivable that after having helped the Congress Party win independence, it would need a large public sector to advance its interests. An arrangement more like Meiji Japan would have been likely. Instead, the entrepreneurial bourgeoisie was significantly constrained by the Industrial Policy Resolution of 1956 that legally barred it from investing in strategic sectors of the economy (see Chapter 2).

8 Some of the most impressive evidence supporting the clairvoyant state thesis comes from the Far East. See, for example, Robert Wade (1990) on Taiwan, and the review article by Ziya Öniş (1991b) of the books by Chalmers Johnson, Alice Amsden, Fred Deyo, Bruce Cummings, and Robert Wade.

With respect to Europe, see Claus Offe (1975) and John Freeman (1989:39). Albert Hirschman (1968) shows that in some Latin American countries the state forced producers to develop backward linkages to local suppliers when such producers would have preferred to continue to rely on imported raw materials and intermediate goods.

9 In general see Hirschman (1982) and Maxfield and Nolt (1990). With respect to Egypt, see Harbison and Ibrahim (1958) and for Turkey, Max Thornburg (1949).

10 John Freeman, in his interesting analysis and advocacy of corporatist mixed political economies (e.g., Austria and Sweden) assumes, without ever demonstrating, that taxpayers as owners will exercise their ownership rights through the vote. He does not discuss their incentives for doing so (1989:117).

11 Throughout this book, SOE performance is to be judged in economic terms, although not necessarily in terms of profitability. Successful performance would consist in the SOE sector generating a consistent financial surplus for the state. Some state monopolies have been able to do that, but firms in anything approaching competitive markets have generally not (see Chapters 4 and 5). Once again, following Wade (1990:180), Taiwan offers a major exception.

12 There is also an ample literature that argues for the centrality of legal designation of property; see, inter alia, Hanke (1987); Kornai (1989); Savas (1987).

13 Khaled Sharif (10/15/90:19) notes that Egyptian SOEs typically have huge arrears in payments to other SOEs. He knows of no single instance in which an SOE, such as the Electricity Authority, terminated service to another SOE for failure to pay for past services.

14 In his theorem of "fundamental non-decentralizability" Stiglitz posits that efficient market allocations cannot be achieved without government intervention (1989:37).

15 It is instructive to read the analysis of Turkey's economy by the private industrialist Max Thornburg (1949), or of Egypt's by the public administration and economic development experts Harbison and Ibrahim (1958). They questioned the way in which the Turkish and Egyptian states intervened in the economy, not the logic of the intervention.

16 In general, see Hirschman (1987) and Killick (1989). Trimberger (1978), John Lewis (1962, chap. 4, and 1989), John Freeman (1989), and Wade (1990) all depict states in ways that emphasize their disinterested, benevolent capacities for intervention in the economy and in favor of the public good, or at least in favor of some project extending well beyond the servicing of their own material interests.

17 Marathe (1986:31) quotes Gandhi as characterizing the state as "violence in concentrated and organized form" and as "a soul-less machine which can never be weaned from the violence to which it owes its very existence." Bernard (1985:24) cites Gandhi as saying that states succeed at the cost of the destruction of the individual.

18 Margaret Levi elaborates on this theme, proposing a kind of iron law of revenue maximization (1988:173).

19 See Krueger (6/74); Bhagwati (1982); Colander, ed. (1984), Srinivasan (1985); North (1989). E. L. Jones (1988:187) argues that the transition from extensive (in which economic growth merely keeps pace with population growth) to intensive (in which per capita income rises rapidly) growth in

world history is largely determined by the extent of rent seeking in the economy.

20 If, however, bidding is oligopolized, as it frequently is, then some of the rents may be invested to increase production.

21 Samuels and Mercuro (1984:58–62) critique the rent-seeking literature for failing to note that the legal status quo is itself the product of lobbying for privilege. Policy does change the relative prices of factors, and hence it is both inevitable and legitimate that economic actors will seek to turn policy to their favor.

22 In a sophisticated critique of Niskanen's argument, Dunleavy (1991) disaggregates public officials and bureaus to show that different levels of officialdom and different types of bureaus follow very different logics in the pursuit of resources; for example, lower-ranking officials may be most concerned with budget maximization, whereas senior officials, who are best placed to obtain those resources, may be more concerned with maximizing status and prestige and shaping the nature of the tasks of the bureau.

23 Kornai, the leading analyst of Hungary's failure in socialist economics, attributed its basic course to the logic of its institutional regime for monitoring public assets rather than to any particular set of policies (1981:969; 1989:84).

24 These are very broad generalizations and vulnerable on those grounds; for example, on the highly qualified autonomy of the Mexican state, see Nora Hamilton (1982).

25 On the expectation that organized labor and SOE managers will oppose divestiture, see Olson (1982:111) and Aharoni (1986:327).

26 For critiques see Pryor (1984) and Cameron (1988). Japan can be seen as a dynamic, productive, and innovative economy that is shot through with distributional coalitions and collusions. See Kent Calder (1989).

27 An institution, in its broadest sense, is a well-recognized and embedded pattern of exchange behavior that provides predictability to the actors involved. In its more narrow sense, "institution" means a formally codified entity with specified goals and rules of behavior. Here, I am using "institution" in its more narrow sense.

28 For contrasting views, see Jeffrey Sachs (1985), Peter Evans (1989), and Gustav Ranis (1989). Cameron's argument (1988:597) that a country's "place in the world economy" is of overwhelming importance, cannot account for different responses to crises on the part of states that are similarly placed in the world economy.

29 I have in mind the incumbencies of Nasser of Egypt, Nehru in India, and Atatürk in Turkey. Calles and Cárdenas in Mexico were the architects of the public sector, but ISI, as a strategy, did not emerge until the 1940s. See Roldán (1988) and Robert Kaufman (1990).

30 Again, Mexico is somewhat exceptional. The Cárdenas *sexenio* was inclusivist, but it was not until the *sexenio* of Miguel Alemán that a coherent ISI project was launched, and it was accompanied by policies of exclusivism.

31 Interesting discussions of change teams in major policy shifts are to be found in John P. Lewis (1990), who analyzes the remaking of Indian agricultural policy in the mid-1960s, and Sylvia Maxfield (1990), who examines López Portillo's team of structuralists who engineered the nationalization of the Mexican banking sector in 1982.

32 Crisis is a necessary but not sufficient cause of change. It is hard to predict

ex ante when a crisis is of sufficient depth to promote change. Egypt has grappled with "crisis" since 1967 without undertaking system-transforming change. By contrast, many outside observers missed the depth of the crisis that led to the sudden collapse of Eastern European systems. The bluntness of crisis as a tool for predicting change is discussed in the introduction of Haggard and Kaufman (1992). See also Grindle and Thomas (1991:5, 7, 164–65). Jerry Hough (1989:41) provides an example of a leader consciously exacerbating a crisis thereby "making the status quo unthinkable."

2. THE WILL TO TRANSFORM

1 Inter alia, see Kalecki (1976); Petras (1977); Sobhan and Muzaffer (1980).
2 Although we shall return to them below, some of the major documents are the Mexican constitution of 1917, the six principles of the Kemalist republic, enshrined in the 1938 constitution, the Industrial Policy Resolution of 1956 and the texts of the Second and Third Five Year Plans in India, and the Socialist Decrees of 1961 and the National Charter of 1962 in Egypt.
3 It is somewhat curious that some Soviet analysts of the Khrushchev era (e.g., Georgi Mirskii) and several Western students of modernization (e.g., Manfred Halpern, 1963, and John Kautsky, 1969) independently concluded that the progressive, transformative regimes of several LDCs (Guinea, India, Burma, Egypt, Algeria, etc.) were so structurally unfettered that they could skip the capitalist stage and move directly to some form of state socialism. See Carrère d'Encausse (1975:159–67) and Waterbury (1991).
4 The degree of continuity between Atatürk's efforts and those launched by his Young Turk predecessors is a matter of some debate; those emphasizing continuity are Rustow (1964), Sugar (1964), and Mardin (1980). Hershlag (1988:23–24) stresses the break represented by Kemalist policies.
5 The best single account remains that of Bernard Lewis (1961). See also Kazancigil and Özbudun, eds. (1981).
6 An excellent summary is to be found in Mardin (1980).
7 Gökalp and others set the target as building a "national economy" (*milli iktisat*), a notion profoundly hostile to a liberal market economy and to free trade. In the 1930s the term evolved into "etatism" (*devletçilik*).
8 It was one of six fundamental principles qualifying the state as republican, secular, populist, nationalist, and revolutionary.
9 In general on the first statist era, see Derin (1940); Kerwin (1959); Hershlag (1968); Göymen (1976); Okyar (1976); Hale (1981); Aysan (1982); Boratav (1982); Insel (1984–85); Kuruç (1987); Kepenek (1990).
10 It is interesting to note that this model of assistance remained unique until the advent of Nikita Khrushchev, when it became generalized to all the Soviet Union's "progressive" clients in the developing world. The Five Year Plan itself met with the approval of a U.S. advisory mission led by W. D. Hines and the ubiquitous W. E. Kemmerer (Hershlag, 1968:75).
11 Kepenek calls this the era of the "new *étatism*" (1990:31); see also Kerwin (1951); Ahmad (1977); Hale (1981:81); and Pamuk (1/81:27).
12 The Thornburg mission was not at all disapproving of Turkey's ISI policies but merely felt that the private sector should receive equal treatment within it. Thornburg conceded that the private sector had not performed well, but pleaded that it should be given a new chance in conjunction with foreign capital (1949:28). See also Maxfield and Nolt (1990).

13 The National Action Party was led by Alparslan Türkeş, one of the leaders of the 1960 coup, and known at that time as a radical and a "Nasserist." Given his evolution as well as that of other officers, it is hard to know what these labels mean.

14 The Mexicans were acutely aware that their revolution and the Bolsheviks' were running in tandem. The Mexicans saw themselves and the Russians as leading the world into a century of profound transformation. The Mexican fascination with the Soviet experience was vividly represented in many of the murals of Diego Rivera, one of which is illustrated in this chapter.

15 The *sexenio* is indeed an institution that has acted as an independent variable, influencing every aspect of the conventional political and policy-making processes. It is predictable and shapes expectations, and behavior is adjusted and routinized in light of it. Whatever the structural resemblances between Mexico and other developing countries, the *sexenio* is a unique and extremely important institutional innovation.

16 The world depression hit Mexico harder than it did Turkey because Mexico was much more heavily involved in exports, especially minerals. This, however, does not seem to have much direct bearing on the radicalization of the Mexican experiment after 1934. In general see Wionczek (1964:40); Roldán (1988:19–20); Fuentes (3/13/88); Solís (1988:871–72).

17 Alemán also accelerated the process of moving state officials and members of the extended "revolutionary family" into private enterprise.

18 The fact that Nixon imposed a 10% surcharge on all imports into the United States in 1971 weakened the "special relation" between the United States and Mexico and pushed Echeverría along a more radical and confrontational course than might otherwise have been the case.

19 López Portillo earlier in his *sexenio* had promised to defend the peso "like a dog." After he was forced to devalue, it is said he was reluctant to appear in public, as such appearances would be greeted by woofs and howls from those who saw him.

20 The sectors were or are post and telegraph, satellite communication, printing of money, power generation, railroads, petroleum and basic petrochemicals, and, 1982–91, banking and credit.

21 The zamindars were a stratum of rural rent collectors who, over time, had acquired title to their right to collect as well as to substantial amounts of rural property.

22 John Lewis is not alone in noting that Nehru's bark was worse than his bite (1962, esp. chap. 4) but nonetheless concedes that Indian socialism was designed to provide economic security and equal opportunity, and to preempt private oligarchy (pp. 204–5).

23 Kohli (1987) sees Nehru's relatively gentle handling of the private sector as indicating a fundamental commonality of interests because capitalist activity, with state help, could raise the level of the depressed classes (p. 54). State industrialization was designed to support a capitalist pattern of development (pp. 64–65). This contrasts with the view of Nayar (1988:233–34) and my own, less informed, understanding. Moreover Kohli argues (p. 225) that India's capitalist class was minuscule and could have been tamed by Nehru. If that was the case, it is not clear how this class could help raise the level of the depressed classes.

24 After 1974 there were further nationalizations: With the take-over of Esso and Burmah Shell the entire oil sector came into the state domain, while in

1976 the large Indian firms specializing in rolling stock and structural steel, Burns Std. and Braithwate, were likewise nationalized after having gone in the red owing to dwindling business from Indian Railroads.

25 The standard treatments are Issawi, 1963; O'Brien, 1966; and Mead, 1967. Eric Davis (1983:200) argues that the precedent for the Egyptian state's handmaiden role lay in the public bailout of the private Misr Group in 1939.

26 The Marxists were initially among them, but in 1959, when they supported 'Abd al-Karim Qassim of Iraq, whom Nasser had tried to subvert, the Egyptian Communists were rounded up and put in concentration camps until 1964.

27 Hilmy 'Abderrahman, a civilian technocrat charged with drawing up the plan, resigned over the question of the target, which he found excessively optimistic. He and others have suggested it may have been Nehru and Indian planners, themselves inspired by Charles Bettelheim, who convinced Nasser it could be done.

28 On the reasons why one should expect such alternance of redistribution and retrenchment, see Albert Hirschman (1979).

3. BALD COMPARISONS

1 For general accounts of Turkish economic performance, see Hershlag, 1968, 1988; Krueger, 1974; Wålstedt, 1980; Hale, 1981; Boratav, 1982, 1988; Celâsun, 1983; Kepenek, 1983; Kopitz, 5/87; Celâsun and Rodrik, 11/87; Nas and Odekon, 1988.

2 For general treatments of India's economy, see Bhagwati and Chakravarty, 1969; Mellor, 1976; Frankel, 1978; L. K. Jha, 1980; P. S. Jha, 1980; Toye, 1981; Ahluwalia, 1985; Marathe, 1986; Weiner, 7/86; L. and S. Rudolph, 1987; Nayar, 1989.

3 For general treatments of the Mexican economy, see Clark Reynolds, 1970; Hansen, 1974; Solís, 6/71; Brun, 1980; Looney, 1985; Zedillo, 1986; Casar and Peres, 1988; Fondo de Cultura Económica, 1988.

4 For general treatments of Egypt's economy, see Issawi, 1963; O'Brien, 1966; Mead, 1967; Hansen and Nashashibi, 1975; Mabro and Radwan, 1976; Ikram, 1980; Waterbury, 1983, 10/85; Central Bank of Egypt, 1987a.

5 The debate is summarized in Varshney, 9/1/84; see also L. K. Jha, 1980; Bardhan, 1984; Acharya, 1985; Isher Ahluwalia, 1985; Marathe, 1986; Weiner, 1986.

6 After the Gulf War of 1991, the United States forgave half of the debt owed it by Egypt, and the Paris Club followed by a phased forgiveness, conditioned on implementation of a structural adjustment program. About half of Egypt's total external debt was thus actually or potentially forgiven.

7 The timing of this assistance was as follows: 1978, $1.6 billion; 1979, $2.4 billion; 1980, $4.9 billion; 1981, $3.1 billion. There are those (e.g., Birand, 1986; Aricanli, 1990) who argue that the Turkish rescue operation came about because of the fall of the Shah in Iran and after the fall of the left-of-center Ecevit government in Turkey. It is implied that the Carter administration welcomed the 1980 coup, and saved the economic payoff of $4.9 billion to reward the generals. The evidence for U.S. complicity in the coup presented in Birand's book is not entirely convincing. On the issue of financial assistance, the evidence is even less clear. Nearly $2 billion in rescheduled payments and fresh funds were already in the pipeline before Ecevit left power.

The Guadeloupe economic summit, which led to the major bailout effort, took place in January 1979, before the Shah left Iran (Okyar, 1983).

8 Leopoldo Solís (1976:9) notes that between 1964 and 1970 new import categories subject to tariff were created at the rate of 1,000 per year, reaching a total of 13,000 in 1970 and covering two-thirds of all importable items. He did not question the logic of this degree of protection but, rather, called for more efficient administration of the regime.

9 Alt and Chrystal (1983:237) argue that much of the literature dealing with state expansion is founded on an illusion brought about by sustained public expenditures during the oil shocks of the 1970s coupled with declines in real GNP. It was the latter that yielded an image of increasing state economic activity. However, evidence from the 1980s would seem to indicate that the levels attained in the 1970s have been sustained subsequently.

10 It will be recalled from Chapter 1 that the generation of a financial surplus for the treasury is the principal criterion by which SOE performance is assessed in this book. Wade (1990) advances evidence that Taiwanese SOEs, which have consistently generated financial surpluses, constitute a major exception to my generalization.

11 Short defines overall deficit as the difference between current plus capital expenditure and revenue plus receipts of current transfers and of nongovernment capital transfers (1984:144).

12 The primary as opposed to the financial deficit is net of interest payments. With rising rates of inflation in EIMT during the 1980s, especially in Mexico and Turkey, the interest burden on domestic and foreign debt became increasingly heavy. In Turkey that burden represented 5% of GNP in 1988, and in India it reached 4.9% of GNP in 1988–89 or 20% of total governmental outlays. Domestic and foreign interest payments reached 6% of GDP in Mexico in 1986 but fell to 4.5% in 1988. See Garrido Noguera and Quintana López (1987:120, Table 3); World Bank (1989:45).

13 Full inventories of SOEs can be found for Egypt in USAID/Egypt, *Public Enterprise and Performance in Egypt* (typescript, 1989); for India, in Bureau of Public Enterprises (1990, annual report); for Mexico, in Rey Romay (1987) and Casar and Peres (1988); for Turkey, in YDK, *Kamu Iktisadi Teşebbüsleri Genel Raporu, 1988* (annual report).

14 Some of the public economic institutions are TEK (Turkish Electricity Corporation), TCDD (Turkish Railways), THY (Turkish Airlines), Tekel (the alcohol and tobacco *régie*, transferred to the SEE sector in 1984), Posts and Telegraph, and so on.

15 The Turkish SOE sector in 1987 was the sole producer of coal, natural gas, copper ore, bauxite, zinc, wolfram, boron salts, sulphur, and phosphates; of alcoholic beverages, cigarettes, and other tobacco products; of petrochemicals, cellophane, morphine, aluminum hydrate, calcium carbide, nitric acid, ammonium nitrate; and of railroad cars and wagons. It is the sole operator of railroads and pipelines, and is the sole provider of radio and TV services. In addition the SOEs produce 89% of all tea, 73% of sugar, 22% of fodder, 26% of chemical fertilizers, 58% of steel, and 14% of tractors.

16 The extent to which the SOE mania can propagate itself is exemplified in the Compañía Operadora de Teatros, which ran 98 cinema houses in Mexico City with a daily audience of about 100,000. It created its own SOE, Dulcerías Oro S.A., to supply its theaters with sweets at prices well below those of private suppliers.

17 Some of the principal defense SOEs are Hindustan Aeronautics, Bharat Electronics (not to be confused with Bharat Heavy Electrical Corporation or BHEL); Bharat Earth Movers; Mazagon Dock Ltd.; Garden Reach Shipbuilders; Goa Shipyard; Praga Tools; Mishra Data Nigam (specialized alloys); Bharat Dynamics. These firms in 1983 had production valued at about $800 million. In addition, the units under the supervision of the Ordinance Factories Board had production worth about $500 million (CMIE, 1983).

4. PRINCIPALS AND AGENTS

1 Inter alia, see Tawfik, Majeed, and Obeid (1977:84); Casar and Peres (1988:106).

2 The single best treatment of these issues is Aharoni (1986), esp. pp. 222–54; also Leroy Jones, ed. (1982: pt. 2, pp. 67–102).

3 In India's Lok Sabha there is a special parliamentary committee for SOE oversight, and managers consider it quite invasive. In all four countries, public auditing agencies present SOE accounts to the legislatures or to specialized committees within them. The first attacks on Egypt's SOEs emerged from Egypt's Budget and Planning Committee in 1973 (Waterbury, 1983:139).

4 Kornai wrote his article at a time when he still hoped that such systems could be reformed and made more efficient. He has subsequently abandoned that position (see Kornai, 1989).

5 More recent estimates are that cumulative unsecured debt for 278 Egyptian SOES had reached £E 45 billion in 1991 (Thabit, 7/29/91:19). By contrast, recourse to the National Investment Bank was far more complex. As one Egyptian CEO recounted, "It's like the joke about the Egyptian Chicken Factory. The government opens a new, top-of-the-line chicken factory and invites a journalist to try it out. So he enters this gleaming building at the ground floor, and an employee in a starched white uniform says, "What can I do for you?" "I would like a chicken," says the journalist. "Do you want an imported or an Egyptian chicken?" "Egyptian," the journalist replies. "Then you'll have to go to the second floor." Off he goes and finds another neatly dressed employee. Here the question is whether he wants his chicken plucked or not. "Plucked," he says. "Then you will have to go to the third floor." Same scene. "Do you want a fryer or a broiler?" "I want an Egyptian, plucked broiler," he replies in some exasperation. Fourth floor. "Do you want it cleaned or not?" "Cleaned!" he shouts. Fifth floor. "I want a cleaned, plucked, Egyptian fryer!!" Reply, "I'm sorry, sir, we have no chickens... but how do you like our system?"

6 In the spring of 1991, Egypt reached agreement with the IMF to undertake a series of structural reforms including the gradual increase in interest rates to market-clearing levels. The implications for SOE debt are momentous.

7 In the late 1980s in India, seventeen loss-making state electricity boards had debts outstanding of about $800 million in rupees to the two power SOEs, the National Thermal Power Corporation and the National Hydro-Power Corporation.

8 Coal India, the SOE that was formed from nationalized coal mines, over the period 1985–89 ran up 2.7 billion rupees in losses, was badly in arrears on interest payments, and paid no dividends. Yet it received over the same period 6.4 billion rupees in budgetary support (World Bank, 3/90:40).

9 Pursell (1990) found that the Indian government forbade the introduction of

float-glass techniques into India in order to protect an existing set of glass manufacturers, which would have been rendered obsolete by the new process.

10 Jones (1985) shows why this is a false debate.

11 SOE losses in 1991 came to almost $6 billion as the government refused any price increases in the run-up to legislative elections that the ruling Motherland Party lost anyway. The unannounced price freeze was put into effect when inflation was at an annual rate of 70% (*Turkish Daily News*, 3/23/92:5).

12 The World Bank (10/88) found that in the mid-1980s, SOE outlays on social welfare and infrastructure averaged 1.3% of production costs, but 34% of gross profits or losses.

13 Wålstedt (1980:130–86) makes systematic comparisons of productivity in Turkish SOEs with similar units in other economies.

14 It should be noted that Shapiro and Willig premise their argument on the relative advantages of public and private ownership when privatization of SOEs is being contemplated and when the state will want to regulate the activities of the firm in whichever sector it is legally included.

15 For the mid-1970s, Hernández Laos (1985:177) concluded that the most efficient industries in Mexico, whether public or private, were those with foreign partners and capital.

16 Mertoğlu (1987:47) argues that if exchange rate subsidies, preferential borrowing rates, and an accounting practice that includes interest payments as part of investments are taken into account, most Turkish SOEs are still operating at a loss.

17 In 1988 the Ministry of Industry broke down the gross transfers to the treasury in 1986–87 as follows: customs duties, £E 521 million; excise tax, £E 153 million; price differentials in favor of the treasury, £E 648 million; bond purchases, £E 15 million; deductions for workers' service, £E 21 million; state share in profits, £E 87 million; deduction for supervision and administration, £E 17 million; share of Nasr Social Bank, £E 8 million; domestic interest payments, £E 302 million; other, £E 30. Total = £E 1.935 billion (Ministry of Industry, 3/88:42). For an earlier detailed analysis of net flows, see Ahmed (1984:67–70); also INP (5/88:130, 134).

18 Egypt's Kima Fertilizer Company, established in the late 1950s when the old Aswan Dam was electrified, was brought into existence by Taha Zaki, a consummate public sector manager and politician. He inculcated a corporate managerial culture through the firm's own management institute. Kima's managers, like those of BHEL and Sümerbank, were recruited to top positions throughout the public sector.

19 There are other cases worth examination, such as P. C. Sen's turnaround of the Calcutta-based, nationalized Burns Std. Ltd. or M. M. Suri's efforts to develop an Indian-designed tractor, the Swaraj (on the latter, see V. V. Bhatt, 1982:129–40). I regret that I cannot reproduce here the rich career details provided me in interviews with V. Krishnamurthy, P. C. Sen, K. L. Puri, and Sam Patil.

20 A more typical story of entrepreneurship is that of Diesel Nacional (DINA), a Mexican SOE overhauled after 1962 by Victor Villaseñor through new product lines in collaboration with Renault, International Harvester, and Cummings Engines. By the 1970s, Villaseñor had built DINA into a successful SOE but one dependent on high tariff protection. By 1983, the firm was in deep trouble because it generated no exports, produced obsolete vehicle models, and was losing market to domestic competitors. In 1987 it was

declared bankrupt and privatized (Castrejon, 1989b). On Villaseñor's career as a protégé of Alemán, see Camp (1980:139–41).

21 Strictly speaking, Egypt's Helwan Iron and Steel Company was located not in a backward area but rather close to Cairo. It was the Nag Hammadi aluminum complex that was sited to benefit a backward area of Upper Egypt, proximate to its energy source at the High Dam at Aswan. Four of India's major complexes are all located in the east: Orissa, Bihar, and West Bengal. Durgapur Steel, for example, was a "green grass" project in West Bengal. The plant site and township were carved out of the jungle in a tribal area. In the late 1980s the plant employed 32,000, while the township housed 500,000 and scores of downstream private and public firms. One third of SAIL's entire work force consists in township employees. Karabük steel, Turkey's first large-scale mill, was built inland for strategic and developmental reasons. It was intended to create a growth pole with Zonguldak on the Black Sea coast, where significant coal deposits are located. Ciudad Sahagún in Mexico became the site for CONCARRIL and DINA, while Las Truchas was selected for the site for SICARTSA. Both were backward areas. It should be noted that some private firms have also undertaken township development without harming their economic performance. Tata Iron and Steel built the town of Jamshedpur, which is a model of its kind (Nayar, 1991:138–39).

22 Excellent case studies of steel sectors in two other LDCs are Schneider (1991) on Brazil, and Kenz (1987) on Algeria.

23 I am grateful to Joydeep Mukherji, who gathered much of this information, and to one of his interlocutors, Pranab Sen (interview, 2/10/88). See also the excellent review of Nath (1982).

24 The company's equity was distributed as follows: federal government, 51%; NAFINSA, 25%; AHMSA, 12%; private sector, 12% (Schüking, 1982:162).

25 A similar tale of long gestation and obsolescence at birth can be told for India's Visakhapatnam Steel complex, begun in 1971 and completed in 1990. See *Economic Times*, 5/5/90.

26 Deepak Lal (1/87) does argue that deregulation and financial liberalization should be seen in many LDCs as an attempt to extend the fiscal reach of the state to new or hitherto hidden sources of income and profits.

5. REFORM AND DIVESTITURE

1 The stock exchanges of Bombay, Istanbul, and Mexico City are booming (although with very different values for the volumes traded), but they do not yet involve small investors.

2 In sharp contrast to Mexico over the same period, Turkey was able to deliver real growth during the 1980s. That in turn was in substantial measure contingent on large flows of external financing from the G-7 and the World Bank (Celâsun and Rodrik, 11/87). Mexico did not have access to similar levels of external financing for reform.

3 On the period from 1956 to 1980, see Issawi (1963); O'Brien (1966); Hansen and Nashashibi (1975); Ikram (1980); Waterbury (1983). Leroy Jones (1981) provides a review of the SOE sector with sensible reform proposals premised on the conviction that they are worth doing.

4 Joint ventures were established under Law 43 of 1974 and its successor Law 32 of 1977. Both stipulated that any joint venture with a public sector partner would automatically be considered part of the private sector regardless of

the distribution of equity between the partners. Labor would not necessarily share in profits or have representation on the board, as was the case in the public sector. The joint ventures set up in the late 1970s are the closest Egypt has so far come to privatization.

5 Years later, commenting on the new business law (#203) of 1991, Minister of Industry Abd al-Wahhab made the following uncharacteristically frank avowal: "The minister is the president of the board of the companies, and he appoints the members of the board. The Authorities [which supervise each sector] have no budget independent from the state as owner; they have no right to dispose of the profits of the companies under their jurisdiction; the profits and any returns to sales of shares go directly to the state treasury; *likewise, the budgets of the Authorities and of the dependent companies are derived ultimately from the state budget* [emphasis added]." Quoted in Thabit (7/29/91:18).

6 Ibrahim al-ʿIssawi of the INP more recently wrote an unrepentant defense of SOEs in terms unchanged from those of the 1960s (1989:85–89, 112–14).

7 The $372 million standby with the IMF is briefly described in *IMF Survey*, 5/27/91:174. The agreement with the Paris Club, in *AI*, 6/10/91:14.

8 Unlike Egypt, India had not resorted to holding companies for SOEs, with a few notable exceptions such as SAIL and the National Textile Corporation.

9 India's capital market is of sufficient depth to play a meaningful role in privatization if the idea ever becomes acceptable. The capitalization of the Bombay exchange in 1989 was more than $27 billion, while the asset value of the central level SOEs in the same year was $62.5 billion.

10 For the Indian government view of the memoranda and the texts of some, see Bureau of Public Enterprises (1990). The World Bank (10/88:102–8) provides a thorough critique; also Nigam (1989:77). Nellis (10/88) and Shirley (3/89) evaluate *contrats plans* and memoranda of understanding as they have been applied in several countries.

11 The BPE has constituted a high-level committee to draw up individual memoranda and to monitor performance annually. Its members are: the cabinet secretary, the finance secretary, the expenditure secretary, the Planning Commission secretary, the chairman of the Bureau of Industrial Costs and Prices, the chairman of the Public Enterprise Selection Board, and the additional secretary of the BPE. In a different context, one SOE manager referred to such officials as "the high priests of the bureaucracy" (Luthar, 1989).

12 Professor Mustafa Aysan is hereby gratefully acknowledged for sharing with me his unique knowledge of the workings of Turkish SOEs.

13 In a similar vein, the Treasury and Foreign Trade Secretariat established a computer network for all SOEs that allowed them to follow the financial and investment status of each firm on a daily basis (*Cumhuriyet*, 2/24/90).

14 Some real bargains could be had. In 1987 Sümerbank's book value was put at Tl 3 trillion, and the value of the shares transferred to the MHPPF at Tl 200 billion (*Dünya*, 10/4/87).

15 I have explored his strategy in some detail in Waterbury (1992). The Turkish electoral law allows a party winning about a third of the national vote to capture more than half the seats in the Grand National Assembly. The electoral law adopted in Mexico in 1989 similarly provides that any party winning a third of the national vote will receive 51% of the seats in the Chamber of Deputies.

16 This is also how I have interpreted President Sadat's "open door" policies in

Egypt (Waterbury, 1983, 1985), and I would extend it to Rajiv Gandhi's policies between 1984 and 1989. Özal, by contrast, started out as a system breaker.

17 During most of 1988, the crawling peg was replaced by a fixed peso–dollar exchange rate. When Carlos Salinas acceded to the presidency, the peso was returned to a crawling peg.

18 In December 1990, 20.4% of TELMEX was bought by a consortium headed by Grupo Carso (headed by Carlos Slim), Southwestern Bell, and France Telecom. The consortium in fact pledged itself to invest a modest $2 million per annum until 1996 (*Latin American Monitor*, 1–2/91:860).

6. MANAGERIAL CAREERS AND INTERESTS

1 In an interview, Sam Patil elaborated in detail to the author the rule bending and breaking he was obliged to undertake in order to keep Hindustan Machine Tools a thriving company.

2 Throughout the fall of 1985 I attended a seminar of Egyptian public and private sector managers who debated the issue of motivation and performance. One of their repeated recommendations was to replace the self-generated concern for excellence that only a handful of managers exhibited with the discipline of the private shareholder concerned with returns to investment. See ʿAbd al-Raziq, 1985.

3 Miguel Centeno has explored these categories in depth in his analysis of Mexican bureaucratic elites. He invented the term *tecnocrata* to describe a technically competent manager with good political skills (1990:143, 194). I am grateful to him for his extensive comments on this chapter.

4 Presumably most changes in CEOs are performance related. Yet in only two instances did I come across removals explicitly attributed to poor performance. This was the fate of two company presidents in Egypt, one who ran a spinning plant and the other a rubber plant. Both were removed because of cumulative losses in their companies. Both were appointed to new jobs, one as president of another spinning and weaving plant, and the other as counsellor in the General Organization for Chemical Industries (*AI*, 11/19/85, 11/20/85).

5 This is plausible in that ʿAziz Sidqi, the man who built the industrial public sector under Nasser, was appointed prime minister by Sadat, who then dismissed him in March 1973 as Sadat became his own prime minister in anticipation of war. After the war (October 1973), Sidqi was no longer in a position to protect his clients among the managers. I am grateful to Robert Bianchi for pointing out to me the relevant section of Hussein's study.

6 In 1984, the CAOA had carried out a survey of 367 company heads (as reported in *AI*, 3/12/84:34). I was given access only to the portion dealing with superannuation. Despite months of trying, the rest was denied me.

7 I am grateful to Heather Behn for carrying out extensive analysis of these 819 individuals, and to Devesh Kapur for expert situating of India's complex system of advanced degrees.

8 The figure was not disaggregated, but inasmuch as successful completion of the secondary school exam (*al-thanawia al-ʿamma*) guaranteed admission to a university, one can assume that the overwhelming majority of the high school graduates went on to university.

9 Good studies that try to capture the role of engineers in state-led development are Farid (1/70); Moore (1980); Kenz (1987); Schneider (1991).

10 Centeno (1990:230) emphasizes the transformation of the entire bureaucracy under Echeverría, bringing it under technocratic dominance, and subordinating the PRI, a judgment with which del Carmen Pardo (1991:35) concurs.

11 It is said that President Sadat set the retirement age at sixty in order to force out of government all the senior officials appointed by Nasser.

12 In a 1983 survey of the civil service in Egypt, it was found that there were 360,000 female civil servants, including 68 directors general and 13 deputy ministers. There has generally been one woman in the cabinet. Reports on this survey suggested that through the seniority system women would gradually take over the summit of the civil service.

13 I am grateful to Engineer al-Fiqqi for sharing with me in 1985 his insights derived from long experience as a technician and a manager.

14 R. P. Billimoria, to whom I owe thanks for the time he spent with me in 1986 explaining the intricacies of PESB operations, was himself a product of Tata Iron and Steel, deputed in 1969 to Hindustan Steel.

15 Centeno (1990:171) found that for a sample of 1,278 members of the Mexican bureaucratic elite, 436 had fathers in business, 484 professional fathers, and 188 fathers who had served in government.

16 Partial exceptions are Narain (1973) on Hyderabad State SOE managers; Leila, Yassin, and Palmer (1985), and Palmer et al. (1988), who surveyed managers at the Nag Hammadi Aluminum complex in Egypt; CAPMAS (10/74) with a certain number of attitudinal questions put to its survey group of 34,208.

17 No evidence is presented, and no claims made, that the state class is collectively conscious of how it stands in relation to the mode of agricultural production that nominally sustains it.

18 They were also less kindly known as the *malinchismos,* after the Aztec mistress of Cortés, Malinche, regarded as a traitor to her people. The *científicos* were seen as the intermediaries between North American capital and the regime of Porfirio Díaz.

19 In Egypt, the ideological defense of the public sector has been most pronounced in the Institute of National Planning, where a core of economists and planners, often with Soviet or Eastern European training, have defended their intellectual turf. See INP (5/88) and 'Issawi (1989) for examples. The outlook of the managers is reflected in the National Specialized Councils 1982 report.

20 I am very grateful to Ahmad Seif al-Din Khorshid for supplying me with the published reports, and to Abdesslam Maghraoui for careful analysis and summary of their content.

21 I am grateful to Hakan Yilmaz for interviewing on my behalf Professor Toker Dereli of Istanbul University, who has been following the development of the employers' unions.

22 Although his details differ from mine, Springborg (1989:110–11) covers the case. See also Posusney (10/91).

23 This distinction between control over or relation to means of production, on the one hand, and replication of a standard of living and life-style, on the other, is drawn from that made by Gerth and Mills (1958:193) between classes and "status groups." See also Giddens (1981).

24 We can express the likelihood of defense of the public sector in terms of the

tripartite principal–agent scheme advanced by Shapiro and Willig (1990). It consists in a "framer" who sets general rules, a "minister" who directly supervises or audits agents, and "managers" who are the agents. I suggest that the framer and the managers may advocate, or at least not oppose, reduction of SOE activity, whereas the minister will oppose or obstruct it.

7. COALITIONS AND STATE-OWNED ENTERPRISES

1 Marathe may have the better part of this argument; during the mid- and late 1980s industrial growth rates increased rapidly. The coalitional basis of the government had not changed, but the industrial regulatory regime had been significantly relaxed.

2 I am grateful to Dr. Hilmy ʿAbderrahman for his trenchant dissection of Egypt's social contract, especially in an interview, 12/26/83.

3 In his "Document of National Work" of 1987, President Mubarak asserted that between 1982 and 1987, 892,000 *new* public sector jobs had been created, and that this commitment was leading to the collapse of the national economy (*AI*, supplement, 10/19/87:12).

4 In 1988 the average civil service salary was £E 1,723 per year (3.2 million employees); the average salary in the public authorities, £E 2,245 per year (450,000 employees); and the average salary in the SOEs, £E 2,775 per year (1.3 million employees). The total government wage bill (exclusive of military, police, and schoolteachers) was about 15% of GDP.

5 In 1977 the U.S. government was involved in 27,000 off-budget operations with $61 billion in nonguaranteed debt. If one adds to this similar operations at the state level, the total amount of nonguaranteed debt greatly exceeded that of voter-approved debt (Bennett and DiLorenzo, 1984:22). The politician's thirst for discretionary resources is not a function of levels of development.

6 So too had unearmarked budgetary appropriations, known as *erogaciones adicionales*, first introduced in 1947 and running at nearly a quarter of all budgetary outlays in the mid-1960s (Wilkie, 1967).

7 Necmettin Erbakan of the religious National Salvation Party was a minority partner with the Justice Party in the mid-1970s, and in control of the Ministry of Industry. There was a spate of factory openings, culminating in Süleyman Demirel's inauguration of the Isdemir steel complex at Iskenderun in 1977, before a new round of elections. Demirel was also the moving force behind the Southeast Anatolian Project (GAP) for the development of hydropower and irrigated agriculture in Turkey's most backward, and Kurdish, region.

8 The principal speakers were Prem Jha, Nitin Desai, and Raja Chelliah, at the India International Centre, 4/20/90.

9 Mexico and Turkey, both of which have pursued adjustment with the most vigor, have also witnessed a consistent turning of the domestic terms of trade against agriculture, a result at variance with neoclassical assumptions.

10 It has frequently been reported from Eastern Europe that the average citizen prefers the current situation in which there are goods in the shops, even though he or she may not be able to buy them, to the older situation in which limited goods were allocated by queuing or entitlement.

11 The primary direct tax burden has fallen on the public sector salariat. By contrast in 1988 only 673,000 businesses and self-employed persons filed income and profits tax returns. One expert estimated the amount of tax

evasion in that year at about $5 billion in Turkish lira equivalent (Çakman, 1990).

12 Significantly, some of the proceeds of privatizations have been paid into the fund with considerable fanfare, so that welfare compensation is associated in the popular mind with privatization.

8. THE PUBLIC–PRIVATE SYMBIOSIS

1 I do not know how Alpander would have classified Adnan Menderes and Celal Bayar, two prominent elected public officials at the head of the Demokrat governments in the 1950s, one a landowner and the other a public official with good private connections. In the 1980s the legitimacy of the private sector has increased greatly, and Vehbi Koç, among other businessmen, has achieved national stature.

2 The contacts between Echeverría and Garza Sada, coming in the aftermath of the student riots and killings of 1968, led some to discern a kind of perverse alliance of a radical president with reactionary business groups, summed up by the expression "from Tlatelolco [the site of police firings on students] to Monterrey."

3 Since the Salinas campaign of 1988, some Mexican businessmen have been major contributors to the PRI, doing publicly, through the party's Commission for Financing, what they had long done in obscurity (Rodríguez Reyna, 1/92).

4 Nabil Sebbagh, in the pages of *al-Ahram al-Iqtisadi,* made the cause of these shareholders his own, and for years urged the government to expand the capital base of the fifty SOEs by share offerings to the original investors, coupled with the renaissance of the Cairo stock exchange. He was totally ignored until, after his death, the government in the summer of 1991 announced it would follow roughly the course he recommended.

5 The Federation of Indian Chambers of Commerce and Industry (FICCI) commented on this role, through its president, D. N. Patodia (*Economic Times,* 5/22/86). FICCI is generally supportive of the government and obliquely questioned the realism of the plan projections. Patodia suggested that the private sector be allowed to raise additional resources by tapping rural savings and by the abolition of the capital gains and dividends taxes.

6 This material is taken from an analysis carried out by Lazard Frères and Citicorp in anticipation of the privatization of Petlaş.

7 The İş Bank, founded by Atatürk, is officially listed as private. But, as noted in Chapter 4, its major shareholders are public entities, such as the employees pension fund. I suspect that in operational terms it should be included in the public sector.

8 The creation of the National Bank for Investment in the late 1970s offered an alternative source of borrowing for Egyptian SOEs (see Chapter 5), and its lending is not included in Moore's figures, which cover the four major public sector banks and banks chartered under Law 43.

9 The four financial institutions are the Unit Trust of India, the Industrial Credit and Investment Corporation, the Life Insurance Corporation of India, and the Industrial Development Bank.

10 When Rajiv Gandhi was still prime minister, the Life Insurance Corporation sold 390,000 shares of the private firm Larson and Toubro to Dhirubhai Ambani of Reliance Textiles, through a subsidiary of the Bank of Baroda.

Ambani was put on the board of Larson and Toubro. After Congress lost the 1990 elections, the Life Insurance Corporation reacquired the shares, forced Ambani off the board, and fired the head of the Bank of Baroda (*Times of India*, 4/20/90, 5/8/90).

11 At the time of the issuance of the Business Sector Law of 1991, the minister of industry valued the fixed assets of 268 companies affected by the law at £E 77 billion, or about $22 billion at the prevailing exchange rate. There will not be much incentive for private Egyptians to buy into these assets when treasury bills with fixed, tax-exempt interest rates are available.

9. ORGANIZED LABOR AND THE PUBLIC ENTERPRISE SECTOR

1 Posusney is probably closer to the real figure for ETUF with 1.4 million members in 1973 and 2.7 million in 1983 (10/91:chap. 3).

2 In 1985, ETUF set forth another series of recommendations reflecting the tangible benefits that leadership must try to supply the rank and file. These included indexation of wages to inflation, special food allowances, raising the statutory limits on workers' shares in "profits," establishment of more workers' housing cooperatives, raising employers' contributions to social security, and increasing benefits for early retirement (*AI*, 9/26/85).

3 In an interview with the personnel manager at Durgapur Steel in 1986, I was told that the plant, with 32,000 workers, had nine unions claiming some part of the work force. The local Bengali communist union had always been dominant but was contested by INTUC, which in this instance adopted radical stances. In 1988 the Bokaro Steel plant had sixty-five registered unions in a work force of 55,000. Legislation was proposed in that year to stipulate that any legally registered union must have the declared adherence of at least 10% of the work force in the firm (*India Today*, 6/30/88:48–49).

4 One of the more colorful institutions is the *gherao*, whereby workers besiege managers in their offices, denying them exit to latrines, or food, or drink, and subjecting them to a constant stream of verbal abuse and invective. A good manager could not face his grandchildren if upon retirement he had not, at least once, been "gheraoed." Vivid accounts of this institution are to be found in Chopra (1982?).

5 The lament of public and private employers has changed little over the years. See the complaints of S. K. Birla, then president of FICCI, in *India Today*, 9/30/90:76; P. C. Neogy, the Heavy Engineering Corporation's eighteenth CMD in thirty years, attributed HEC's chronic losses to union obstructionism (*India Today*, 11/30/91:58).

6 K. Keshav (4/29/90) makes the important point that Samant had done well when he led strikes against prospering private firms in electronics and consumer durables, but he miscalculated in promoting strike activity in the thoroughly "sick" textile sector.

7 Because Fidel Velázquez gave only perfunctory support to the candidacy of de la Madrid, it is said that the latter gave quiet encouragement to the CROC at the beginning of his *sexenio*.

8 Whether or not a role model, it is said that Luis Morones, who headed the CROM in the 1920s, claimed that the diamond rings he wore were part of a reserve fund for his workers (Hansen, 1974:197).

9 Bianchi (1986, 1989) stresses the same phenomenon in Egypt.

285

10 Basic studies of Turkish labor and labor legislation are Koç (1982, 1986) and Işikli (1987).

11 Koç (1986:82–87) goes through the problems of accurate counting of unionized labor. The combination of legal reclassification of workers and the fact that unions claimed the same workers led to official estimates of unionized labor by the Labor Ministry of 2.3 million in 1971 and 5.7 million in 1980. A figure of around 2 million for the earlier date appears reasonable.

12 Sunar (1987) put DISK's membership at 400,000 on the eve of its dissolution by the military authorities in 1980.

Bibliography

AI – al-Ahram al-Iqtisadi
APSR – American Political Science Review
EPW – Economic and Political Weekly
METU/ODTÜ – Middle East Technical University
MEJ – Middle East Journal
NYT – New York Times

Abd al-Fadil, Mahmoud. 1980. *The Political Economy of Nasserism*. Cambridge: Cambridge University Press.
Abd al-Fadil, Mahmoud. 1989. "Problems in the Substitution of Private Ownership for Public Ownership in the Egyptian and Comparative Framework." In Imany Qandil, ed., *The Private Sector and Public Policies in Egypt*. Cairo: Matbá Atlas for the Center for Political Research and Studies, Cairo University, 65–84.
ʿAbd al-Raziq, ʿAdil. 1985. *Talk of the Egyptian Manager – His Challenges, Concerns, Problems*. Paper presented at the NIMD seminar "The Successful Manager," December 14, Cairo (in Arabic).
Abdel-Khalek, Gouda, and Robert Tignor, eds. 1982. *The Political Economy of Income Distribution in Egypt*. New York: Holmes & Meier.
Acharya, Shankar. 1985. "Towards Reform of Industrial Policy." In Adiseshiah, ed., *Seventh Plan Perspectives*, 141–53.
Adelman, Irma, and Erik Thorbecke, eds. 1989. "The Role of Institutions in Economic Development." *World Development*, vol. 17, no. 9, entire issue.
Adiseshiah, Malcolm, ed. 1985a. *Seventh Plan Perspectives*. New Delhi: Lancer International.
Adiseshiah, Malcolm, ed. 1985b. *The Why, the What and the Whither of the Public Sector Enterprise*. New Delhi: Lancer International.
Aguilar, Alonso. 1988. *La Burguesía, la Oligarquía y el Estado*. Mexico D.F.: Ediciones Nuestro Tiempo.
Ahali, al-. 7/13/88. "Whither the Public Sector?"
Aharoni, Yair. 1986. *The Evolution and Management of State-Owned Enterprises*. Cambridge, Mass.: Ballinger.
Ahluwalia, Isher Judge. 1985. *Industrial Growth in India: Stagnation Since the Mid-Sixties*. Bombay: Oxford University Press.

287

Bibliography

Ahluwalia, Montek. 1986. "Balance-of-Payments Adjustment in India, 1970–71 to 1983–84." *World Development*, vol. 14, no. 8, 937–62.

Ahmad, Feroz. 1977. *The Turkish Experiment in Democracy, 1950–1975*. Royal Institute of International Affairs. London: Hurst.

Ahmad, Feroz. 1980. "Vanguard of a Nascent Bourgeoisie: The Social and Economic Policy of the Young Turks, 1908–1918." In Osman Okyar and Halil Inalcik, eds., *Social and Economic History of Turkey*. Ankara, 329–50.

Ahmad, Feroz. 1981. "The Political Economy of Kemalism." In Ali Kazancigil and Ergun Özbudun, eds., *Atatürk: Founder of a Modern State*. Hamden, Conn.: Archon Books.

Ahmed, Sadiq. 1984. *Public Finance in Egypt: Its Structure and Trends*. World Bank Staff Working Papers, no. 639. Washington, D.C.

Ahmed, Sadiq, et al. 1985. "Macroeconomic Effects of Efficiency Pricing in the Public Sector in Egypt." World Bank Staff Working Papers, no. 726. Washington, D.C.

Aitken, Hugh, ed. 1959. *The State and Economic Growth*. Social Science Research Council, New York.

Akder, Halis. 1987. "Turkey's Export Expansion in the Middle East, 1980–1985." *Middle East Journal*, vol. 41, no. 4, 553–73.

Akgüç, Oztin. 1979. "The Development of the Public Sector in Turkey's Mixed Economy." In Mukerrem Hiç, ed., *Turkey's and Other Countries' Experience with the Mixed Economy*. Istanbul, 433–57.

Aksoy, Ataman. 1980. "Wages, Relative Shares and Unionization in Turkish Manufacturing." In Özbudun and Ulusan, eds., 409–54.

Akyüz, Yilmaz. 1990. "Financial System and Policies in Turkey in the 1980s." In Aricanli and Rodrik, eds., *Political Economy of Turkey*, 98–131.

Albanán de Alba, Gerardo, and José Martinez. 1/12/89. "Con MMH se Inició el fin del Imperio La Quina." *El Financiero*, 54–55.

'Ali, 'Izza. 3/2/87. "The Wafd and the Policy of Taming the Public Sector." *AI*, 24–26 (in Arabic).

Almanac: Turkey 1989. Turkish Daily News, Ankara.

Alonso, Jorge. 1976. *La dialéctica clases – élites en México*. Mexico D.F.: Ediciones de la Casa Chata.

Alpander, Güvenç. 1968. "Entrepreneurs and Private Enterprises in Turkey." In Jerry Hopper and Richard Levin, eds., *The Turkish Administration, A Cultural Survey*. USAID, Public Administration Division. Ankara, 235–50.

Alt, James, and Kenneth Chrystal. 1983. *Political Economics*. Berkeley: University of California Press.

Amin, Galal. 1987. "Adjustment and Development: The Case of Egypt." In Said El-Naggar, ed., *Adjustment Policies and Development Strategies in the Arab World*. Washington, D.C.: IMF, 92–116.

Amin, Samir. 1976. *La nation arabe: nationalisme et luttes de classe*. Paris: Editions de Minuit, Paris.

Amsden, Alice. 1991. "The Diffusion of Development: The Late Industrializing Model and Greater East Asia." *American Economic Review*, vol. 81, no. 2, 282–86.

Anand, Ritu, and Sweder van Wijnbergen. 1989. "Inflation and the Financing of Government Expenditure: An Introductory Analysis with an Application to Turkey." *World Bank Economic Review*, vol. 3, no. 1, 17–38.

Anand, Ritu, Ajay Chhibba, and Sweder van Wijnbergen. 1990. "External Bal-

Bibliography

ance and Sustainable Growth in Turkey: Can They Be Reconciled?" In Aricanli and Rodrik, *Political Economy of Turkey*, 157–82.

Anderson, Charles. 1968. "Bankers as Revolutionaries." In W. P. Glade and C. W. Anderson, eds., *The Political Economy of Mexico*. Madison, Wis.: University of Wisconsin Press, 104–85.

Ansari, Hamied. 1986. *Egypt: The Stalled Society*. Albany: State University of New York Press.

A.R.E. 4/30/78. *Telecommunications Sector Study*. Vol. 2, *The Present Organization, Management and Financial Condition of ARETTO*. Telephone Holdings Corp., Cairo.

A.R.E. Ministry of Economy. 2/12/79. *Policy Study on Issuing Shares of Public Sector Companies*. Mimeo, Economic Studies Unit. Cairo.

Arat, Yeşim. 4/87. "Social Change and the 1983 Political Elite in Turkey." Boğaziçi University, Istanbul.

Arat, Yeşim. 1991. "Politics and Big Business in Turkey: Janus Faced Link to the State." In Metin Heper, ed., *Strong State and Economic Interest Groups: The Post-1980 Turkish Experience*. New York: Walter de Gruyter, 135–47.

Aricanli, Tosun. 1990. "The Political Economy of Turkey's External Debt." In Aricanli and Rodrik, *Political Economy of Turkey*, 230–55.

Aricanli, Tosun, and Dani Rodrik. 1990. "An Overview of Turkey's Experience with Economic Liberalization and Structural Adjustment." *World Development*, vol. 18, no. 10, 1343–50.

Aricanli, Tosun, and Dani Rodrik, eds. 1990. *The Political Economy of Turkey: Debt, Adjustment and Sustainability*. New York: St. Martin's Press.

Arya, Prakash. 1980. "A Study of Militancy Among Workers." *Indian Journal of Industrial Relations*, vol. 15, no. 4, 537–61.

Aspe Armella, Pedro. 1/92. "La Privatización del Sector Privado" (interview conducted by Federico Reyes Heroles and René Delgado). *Este País*, no. 10, 13–23.

Assaad, Ragui. 1989. *The Employment Crisis in Egypt: Trends and Issues*. Unpublished, American University in Cairo.

Association of Graduates of the National Institute for Higher Administration and Development. 1964–85. *Recommendation of Annual Conferences*. (One pamphlet for each year, in Arabic.)

ʿAtaruzy, Mahmud Fahmy al-. 1969. *Administrative Relations in General Authorities and [Public] Companies*. ʿAlam al-Kutab, Cairo (in Arabic).

Aybuk, Ural and Boduroğlu, Emre. 1/89. "Turkish Interest Groups Facing the European Community." *Yapi Kredi Economic Review*, vol. 3, no. 2, 125–58.

Aydemir, Şevket. 1968. *Inkilap ve Kadro*. Ankara: Bilgi Yayinevi.

Ayres, Ron. 1983. "Arms Production as a Form of Import Substituting Industrialization." *World Development*, vol. 11, no. 9, 813–23.

Aysan, Mustafa. 1982. "Atatürk's Economic Views." In Turhan Feyzioğlu, ed., *Atatürk's Way*. Istanbul: Gün Matbaasi, 77–118.

Aysan, Mustafa, and Selahattin Özmen. 1981. *Public Enterprise: In Turkey and in the World*. Istanbul: Kardeşler Basimevi (in Turkish).

Ayub, Mahmood Ali, and Sven Hegstad. 1986. *Public Industrial Enterprises: Determinants of Performance*. World Bank, Industry and Finance Series, vol. 17. Washington, D.C.

Ayub, Mahmood Ali, and Sven Hegsted. 1/87. "Management of Public Industrial Enterprises." *World Bank Research Observer*, vol. 2, no. 1, 79–101.

Bibliography

Ayubi, Nazih. 1980. *Bureaucracy and Politics in Contemporary Egypt*. London: Ithaca Press.

Ayubi, Nazih. 1981. "The Administrative Apparatus and Its Leadership." In Saad al-Din Ibrahim, ed., *Egypt in the Quarter Century, 1952–1977*. Beirut, 86–119 (in Arabic).

Ayubi, Nazih. 1982. "Organization for Development: The Politicoadministrative Framework of Economic Activity in Egypt Under Sadat." *Public Administration and Development*, vol. 2, 279–94.

Ayubi, Nazih. 1989a. "Bureaucracy and Development in Egypt Today." *Journal of Asian and African Studies*, vol. 24, no. 1–2, 62–78.

Ayubi, Nazih. 1989b. *The Centralized State in Egypt*. Center for Arab Unity Studies, Beirut (in Arabic).

Babai, Don. 1988. "The World Bank and the IMF: Rolling Back the State or Backing Its Role?" In Raymond Vernon, ed., *The Promise of Privatization*. New York: Council on Foreign Relations, 254–85.

"Babu Power: How Bureaucrats Rule India." 4/29–5/5/90. *Sunday*, 22–31.

Badawy, ʿAbd al-Salam. 1973. *The Administration of the Public Sector in Egypt*. Anglo-Egyptian Bookshop, Cairo (in Arabic).

Baer, Werner, Richard Newfarmer, and Thomas Trebat. 1976. "On State Capitalism in Brazil: Some New Issues and Questions." *InterAmerican Economic Affairs*, vol. 30, 69–96.

Baklanoff, Eric. 1986. "The State and Economy in Portugal: Perspectives on Corporatism, Revolution and Incipient Privatization." In William P. Glade, ed., *State Shrinking: A Comparative Inquiry into Privatization*. Institute of Latin American Studies, University of Texas at Austin, 257–81.

Balassa, Bela. 1983. "Outward Orientation and Exchange Rate Policy in Developing Countries: The Turkish Experience." *MEJ*, vol. 37, no. 3, 429–47.

Banerjee, Sanjoy. 1984. *Dominant Classes and the State in Development Theory and the Case of India*. Boulder, Colo.: Westview Press.

Bardhan, Pranab. 1984. *The Political Economy of Development in India*. Oxford: Basil Blackwell.

Bardhan, Pranab. 1989. "The New Institutional Economics and Development Theory: A Brief Critical Assessment." *World Development*, vol. 17, no. 9, 1389–95.

Bardhan, Pranab. 1/21/89. "The Third Dominant Class." *EPW*, 155–56.

Barkey, Henri. 1989. "State Autonomy and the Crisis of Import Substitution." *Comparative Political Studies*, vol. 22, no. 3, 291–314.

Basáñez, Miguel. 1983. *La Lucha por la Hegemonía en México, 1968–1980*. Mexico D.F.: Siglo Veintiuno.

Basáñez, Miguel. 1990. *El Pulso de los Sexenios: 20 Años de Crisis en México*. Mexico D.F.: Siglo Veintiuno.

Bates, Robert. 1981. *Markets and States in Tropical Africa*. Berkeley: University of California Press.

Bayart, Jean-François, and Vaner, Samih. 1981. "L'Aremée turque et le théâtre d'ombre kemaliste (1960–1973)." In Alain Rouquié, ed., *La Politique de Mars*. Paris: le Sycamore.

Baysan, Tercan, and Charles Blitzer. 1990. "Turkey's Trade Liberalization in the 1980s and Prospects for Sustainability." In Aricanli and Rodrik, *Political Economy of Turkey*, 9–36.

Bazdresch, Carlos. 5/88. "El cambio que viene." *Nexos*, vol. 11, 37–42.

290

Bibliography

Bazdresch, Carlos, and Victor Urquidi, eds. 1990. *Privatización: Alcance y Implicaciones.* CIDE y Centro Tepoztlán.

Becker, David. 1983. *The New Bourgeoisie and the Limits of Dependency: Mining Class and Power in "Revolutionary" Peru.* Princeton, N.J.: Princeton University Press.

Beinin, Joel. 1989. "Labor, Capital, and the State in Nasserist Egypt, 1952–1961." *International Journal of Middle East Studies,* vol. 21, no. 1, 71–90.

Bennett, Douglas, and Kenneth Sharpe. 1/80. "The State as Banker and Entrepreneur." *Comparative Politics,* vol. 12, no. 2, 165–89.

Bennett, James, and Thomas DiLorenzo. 1984. "Political Entrepreneurship and Reform of the Rent-Seeking Society." In Colander, ed., 217–28.

Berger, Morroe. 1957. *Bureaucracy and Society in Modern Egypt.* Princeton, N.J.: Princeton University Press.

Bernard, Jean-Alphonse. 1985. *L'Inde: Le pouvoir et la puissance.* Paris: Fayard.

Bhagwati, Jagdish. 1982. "Directly Unproductive, Profit-Seeking (DUP) Activities." *Journal of Political Economy,* vol. 90, no. 5, 988–1002.

Bhagwati, Jagdish. 1985. In Gene Grossman, ed., *Essays in Development Economics.* Vol. 1, *Wealth and Poverty.* Cambridge, Mass.: MIT Press.

Bhagwati, Jagdish. 1989. "Is Free Trade Passé After All?" *Weltwirschaftliches Archiv,* Band 125, Heft 1, 17–44.

Bhagwati, Jagdish, and Sukhamoy Chakravarty. 1969. "Contributions to Indian Economic Analysis: A Survey." *American Economic Review,* vol. 59, no. 4, 2–73.

Bhagwati, Jagdish, Richard Brecher, and T. N. Srinivasan. 1984. "DUP Activities and Economic Theory." In Colander, ed., 17–32.

Bhatia, V. G. 1986. "Pricing Policy for Public Sector." In S. B. Jain, ed., *Management and Role of Public Enterprises: Indo-French Experiences.* Vol. 1, 159–88.

Bhatt, V. V. 5/27/78. "Decision Making in the Public Sector: A Case Study of Swaraj Tractor." *EPW,* vol. 13, no. 21, 30–45.

Bhatt, V. V. 1982. "Decision Structure, Technological Self-Reliance, and Public Enterprise Performance." In Leroy P. Jones, ed., 129–40.

Bhatt, V. V. 1984. "Institutional Framework and Public Enterprise Performance." *World Development,* vol. 12, no. 7, 713–21.

Bhatt, V. V. 5/27/89. "On Competitive Impulses and Public Enterprise Performance." *EPW,* 50–54.

Bhattacharya, B. B., and Srabani Guha. 4/14/90. "Internal Public Debt of the Government of India." *EPW,* vol. 25, no. 15, 780–88.

Bhaya, Hiten. 1983. *Methods and Techniques of Training Public Enterprise Managers.* International Center for Public Enterprises in Developing Countries, Monograph Series, no. 6. Ljubljana.

Bhaya, Hiten. 5/83. "Public Sector: Colossus with Feet of Clay?" *EPW,* vol. 18, no. 22, 50–65.

Bianchi, Robert. 1984. *Interest Groups and Political Development in Turkey.* Princeton, N.J.: Princeton University Press.

Bianchi, Robert. 11/85. "Businessmen's Associations in Egypt and Turkey." *Annals,* no. 482, 147–59.

Bianchi, Robert. 1986. "The Corporatization of the Egyptian Labor Movement." *Middle East Journal,* vol. 40, no. 3, 429–44.

Bianchi, Robert. 1989. *Unruly Corporatism: Associational Life in Twentieth Century Egypt.* New York: Oxford University Press.

291

Bibliography

Bienen, Henry, and John Waterbury. 1989. "The Political Economy of Privatization in Developing Countries." *World Development*, vol. 17, no. 5, 617–32.

Bilgiç, Mehmet. 1987. "Privatization: the Case of Turkey." In S. H. Hanke, ed., *Privatization and Development*, 195–203.

Billimoria, R. P. 1985. "Role of the Public Enterprises Selection Board in the Recruitment of Top Public Sector Personnel." In S. Ravishankar and R. K. Mishra, eds., *Management of Human Resources in Public Enterprises*. New Delhi: Vision Books, 67–82.

Birand, Mehmet Ali. 1986. *12 Eylül SAAT 04.00*. Istanbul?: Karacan Yayinlari.

Birtek, Faruk. n.d. "The Economic and Political Changes in Turkey in the Years 1947–1950: The Demise of Etatism." Manuscript, METU Public Administration Reading Room.

Blair, Calvin. 1964. "Entrepreneurship in a Mixed Economy." In Raymond Vernon, ed., *Public Policy and Private Enterprise in Mexico*. Cambridge, Mass.: Harvard University Press, 191–240.

BM. 8/8/87. "Privatization Indian Style." *EPW*, 1324–27.

Boillot, Jean-Joseph. 1989. "Liberalisation sous contraintes: dette publique et dette extérieure." *Revue Tiers Monde*, T. 30, no. 119, 513–44.

Bonifaz, Francisco Javier. 1/12/89. "PEMEX, Macroempresa Estatal Pilar de la Economia del Pais." *El Financiero*, 38–39.

Boratav, Korkut. 1981. "Kemalist economic policies and étatism." In Kazancigil and Özbudun, eds., 165–90.

Boratav, Korkut. 1982. *Türkiye'de Devletçilik*. 2d ed. Ankara: Gerçek Yayinevi.

Boratav, Korkut. 1986. "Import Substitution and Income Distribution Under a Populist Regime: The Case of Turkey." *Development Policy Review*, vol. 4, 117–39.

Boratav, Korkut. 1988. *Türkiye Iktisat Tarihi: 1918–1985*. Istanbul: Gerçek Yayinlari.

Boratav, Korkut. 1989. "The Turkish Bourgeosie and the State During a Major Reorientation of Economic Policies." Prepared for the Conference on Dynamics of States and Societies in the Middle East, Center for Political Research and Studies, June 17–19, Cairo.

Boratav, Korkut. 1990a. "Contradictions of 'Structural Adjustment': Capital and the State in Post-1980 Turkey." Conference on Socioeconomic Transformation, State and Political Regimes: Egypt and Turkey, July 26–28, Istanbul.

Boratav, Korkut. 1990b. "Inter-class and Intra-class Relations of Distribution Under 'Structural Adjustment': Turkey During the 1980s." In Aricanli and Rodrik, *Political Economy of Turkey*, 199–229.

Boratav, Korkut, and Galip Yalman. 10/89. "A Study of the Political Economy of Structural Adjustment: Workers and Peasants During a Major Reorientation of Economic Policies, Turkey, 1980–1987." International Development Research Centre, Ottawa.

Bravo Ahuja, Victor. 1982. *La Empresa Publica Industrial en México*. Instituto Nacional de Administración Pública (INAP): Mexico D.F.

Bravo Mena, Luis. 1987. "Coparmex and Mexican Politics." In Maxfield and Anzaldua Montoya, eds., 89–104.

Brimmer, Andrew. 1955. "The Setting of Entrepreneurship in India." *Quarterly Journal of Economics*, vol. 69, no. 4, 553–76.

Brothers, Dwight. 12/88. "Contemporary Problem Areas and Policy Issues in the

Bibliography

Financial Sector of the Mexican Economy." Draft, Secretariat de Hacienda y de Credito Publico, Mexico City.

Brothers, Dwight. 1990. "Financial Sector Planning and Mexico's New Development Strategy." In Brothers and Wick, eds., 271–301.

Brothers, Dwight, and Adele Wick, eds. 1990. *Mexico's Search for a New Development Strategy.* Boulder, Colo.: Westview Press.

Brun, Ricardo Ramírez. 1980. *Estado y Acumulación de Capital en México: 1929–1979.* Mexico D.F.: UNAM.

Brus, Wlodzimierz. 1989. "Evolution of the Communist Economic System: Scope and Limits." In Nee and Stark, eds., 255–77.

Brus, Wlodzimierz, and Kazimierz Laski. 1989. *From Marx to the Market: Socialism in Search of an Economic System.* Oxford: Clarendon Press.

Buchanan, James. 1985. *Liberty, Market and State: Political Economy in the 1980s.* New York: New York University Press.

Buğra, Ayşe. 1989. "Political Sources of Uncertainty in Business Life in Turkey." Prepared for the Conference on Dynamics of States and Societies in the Middle East Center for Political Research and Studies, June 17–19, Cairo.

Buğra, Ayşe. 1990a. "Political Context of Entrepreneurship in Turkey." Conference on Socioeconomic Transformation, State and Political Regimes: Egypt and Turkey, July 26–28, Istanbul.

Buğra, Ayşe. 1990b. "The Turkish Holding Company as a Social Institution." *Journal of Economic and Administrative Studies,* vol. 4, no. 1, 35–51, Istanbul.

Bureau of Public Enterprises (BPE). 1984. *Top Management Personnel of Central Public Enterprises.* Ministry of Finance, New Delhi.

Bureau of Public Enterprises (BPE). 1985. *Government Policy for the Management of Public Enterprises.* 2 vols., 3d ed., New Delhi.

Bureau of Public Enterprises (BPE). 1989. *Memorandum of Understanding Between Public Sector Undertakings and Government of India, 1989–90.* Ministry of Industry, New Delhi.

Bureau of Public Enterprises (BPE). 1990. *Public Enterprises Survey, 1988–89.* Ministry of Industry, New Delhi.

Business India. 4/7–20/86. "Bombay's Textile Strike 1982–83: How the Workers Coped."

Business India. 8/10–23/87. "SAIL: Will it Succeed?" 42–52.

Çakman, M. Kemal. 1990. "The Public Finance Problem in Turkey." *The Turkish Studies Association Bulletin,* vol. 14, no. 1, 1–12.

Calder, Kent. 1989. *Crisis and Compensation: Public Policy and Political Stability in Japan, 1949–1986.* Princeton, N.J.: Princeton University Press.

Cameron, David. 1978. "The Expansion of the Public Economy: A Comparative Analysis." *American Political Science Review,* vol. 72, 1243–61.

Cameron, David. 1988. "Distributional Coalitions and Other Sources of Economic Stagnation: On Olson's Rise and Decline of Nations." *International Organization,* vol. 42, no. 4, 561–604.

Camp, Roderic Ai. 7/72. "The Middle-level Technocrat in Mexico." *Journal of Developing Areas,* vol. 6, 571–82.

Camp, Roderic Ai. 1980. *Mexico's Leaders: Their Education and Recruitment.* Tuscon: University of Arizona Press.

Camp, Roderic Ai. 1987. "Images of the Mexican Entrepreneur." In Maxfield and Anzaldua Montoya, eds., 127–44.

293

Bibliography

Camp, Roderic Ai. 7/16/90. "El poder en México, cuestión de camarillas y Salinas tiene la suya." *Proceso*, no. 715, 12–16.

CAPMAS. 10/74. *Results of Estimation and Investigation of Employment in the Administration of Public Sector Economic Activity in the A.R.E.*. Ref. 74/001. Cairo (in Arabic).

CAPMAS. 1/84. *Financial Statistics and Indicators for Public Sector Companies (Not Including Banks and Insurance Companies) 1980/81*. Doc. no. 71–12715/84. Cairo (in Arabic).

Cardoso, Eliana and Santiago Levy. 1986. "Mexico." In Rudiger Dornbusch and F. Leslie Helmers, eds., *The Open Economy: Tools for Policymakers in Developing Countries*, Vol. 2. Economic Development Institute, World Bank, Washington, D.C., 470–97.

Cardoso, Fernando Henrique, and Enzo Faletto. 1979. *Dependency and Development in Latin America*. Berkeley: University of California Press.

Carr, Barry. 1983. "The Mexican Debacle and the Labor Movement." In D. L. Wyman, ed., *Mexico's Economic Crisis: Challenges and Opportunities*. San Diego: University of California, 91–116.

Carrera Cortes, Emilio. 1989. "Aeronaves de México, S.A." Unpublished, INAP.

Carrère d'Encausse, Hélène. 1975. *La Politique Soviétique au Moyen-Orient, 1955–1975*. Paris: Presses de la FNSP.

Carrillo Arronte, Ricardo. 1987. "The Role of the State and the Entrepreneurial Sector in Mexican Development." In Maxfield and Anzaldua Montoya, eds., 45–63.

Carrillo Castro, Alejandro, and Sergio Garcia Ramirez. 1983. *Las Empresas Publicas en México*. Mexico D.F.: Miguel Angel Porria.

Casanova, Pablo Gonzalez, and Hector Aguilar Camín. 1986. *México ante la Crisis*. 2d ed. Mexico D.F.: Siglo Veintiuno.

Casar, Maria A., and Wilson Peres. 1988. *El Estado Empresario en México: Agotamiento o Renovacíon?* Mexico D.F.: Siglo Veintiuno.

Castañeda, Jorge. 1987. *México: el Futuro en Juego*. Mexico D.F.: Joaquín Mortiz Planeta.

Castrejon, Felix Aguilar. 1989a. "Macro-administrativo-Institucional de la Empresa Publica en México." Unpublished, INAP.

Castrejon, Felix Aguilar. 1989b. "Diesel Nacionál: 1951–88." Unpublished, INAP.

Celâsun, Merih. 1983. *Sources of Industrial Growth and Structural Change: The Case of Turkey*. World Bank Staff Working Papers, no. 641. Washington, D.C.

Celâsun, Merih. 1986. "Income Distribution and Domestic Terms of Trade in Turkey." *METU Studies in Development*. Special issue on the Turkish economy, 1977–84, vol. 13, nos. 1 and 2, 193–216.

Celâsun, Merih, and Dani Rodrik. 11/87. *Debt, Adjustment and Growth: Turkey*. Draft, NBER Project on Developing Country Debt.

Centeno Gutiérrez, Miguel. 1990. *The New Cientificos: Techonocratic Politics in Mexico, 1970–1990*. Ph.D. dissertation, Yale University.

Center for Monitoring the Indian Economy (CMIE). 1983. *Public Sector in the Indian Economy*. Bombay.

Center for Monitoring the Indian Economy (CMIE). 1985. *A Statistical Review of Central Government Enterprises: 1983–84*. Bombay.

Central Agency for Organization and Administration (CAOA). 6/84. *Results of*

Bibliography

Surveying Occupants of High Level Positions in Public Sector Units Expecting to Retire During the Period 1983–87. Statistical Profile Series, no. 101. Cairo (in Arabic).

Central Bank of Egypt. 1987a. "Structural Changes in the Egyptian Economy During the 1973–1986/87 Period." *Economic Review,* vol. 27, no. 1, 1–31.

Central Bank of Egypt. 1987b. "Main Features of the Second Quinquennial Plan for Economic and Social Development: 1987/88–1991/92." *Economic Review,* vol. 27, no. 2, 166–79.

Central Bank of Turkey. 1989. *1988 Annual Report.* Ankara.

Centro de Análisis e Investigación Económica (CAIE). 11/88. "Reforming the PRI: An Immodest Proposal." *The Mexican Economy: A Monthly Report,* vol. 6, no. 9, 13–19.

Cevizoğlu, M. Hulki. 1989. *Türkiye'nin Gündemindeki Özelleştirme.* Istanbul: Ilgi Yayincilik.

Chambers, Richard. 1964. "The Civil Bureaucracy: Turkey." In R. E. Ward and D. Rustow, eds., *Political Modernization in Japan and Turkey.* Princeton, N.J.: Princeton University Press, 301–27.

Chand, Gyan. 1965. *Socialist Transformation of the Indian Economy.* Bombay: Allied Publishers.

Chattopadhyay, Somnath, and K. G. Agrawal. 1977. "The Dying Ulysses: Middle-Aged Middle Managers in the Indian Public Sector." *Vikalpa,* vol. 2, no. 2, 135–50.

Chávez, Marcos. 2/4/92. "La Nueva Banca Mexicana." *El Financiero,* 8.

Chenery, Hollis, and Lance Taylor. 11/68. "Development Patterns: Among Countries and Over Time." *Review of Economics and Statistics,* 391–416.

Choksi, Armeane. 1979. *State Intervention in the Industrialization of Developing Countries: Selected Issues.* World Bank Staff Working Papers. no. 341, Washington, D.C.

Chopra, R. N. 1982? *Public Sector in India.* New Delhi: Intellectual Publishing House.

Cockcroft, James. 1983. *Mexico: Class Formation, Capital Accumulation and the State.* New York: Monthly Review Press.

Cohen, Youssef. 3/82. " 'The Benevolent Leviathan': Political Consciousness Among Urban Workers Under State Corporatism." *APSR,* vol. 76, no. 1, 46–59.

Colander, David, ed. 1984. *Neoclassical Political Economy: The Analysis of Rent-Seeking and DUP Activities.* Cambridge, Mass.: Ballinger.

Colander, David, and Mancur Olson. 1984. "Coalitions and Macroeconomics." In Colander, ed., 115–29.

Colegio de Licenciados. 1986. "Debate sobre Entidades Paraestatales." *Politico y Administración Publica,* September–December, no. 1, entire issue.

Collier, Ruth. 1982. "Popular Sector Incorporation and Political Supremacy: Regime Evolution in Brazil and Mexico." In Sylvia Hewlett and Richard Weinert, eds., *Brazil and Mexico: Patterns in Late Development.* Philadelphia: Institute for the Study of Human Issues.

Comisso, Ellen. 1990. "Crisis in Socialism or Crisis of Socialism?" *World Politics,* vol. 42, no. 4, 563–606.

Cordero, Salvador y Santín Rafael, "Los grupos industriales: una nueva organización económica en Mexico." *Revista del Centro de Estudios Sociológico.* Colegio de Mexico, no. 23.

Bibliography

Cornelius, Wayne. 1973. "Nation-Building, Participation and Distribution: The Politics of Social Reform Under Cárdenas." In Gabriel Almond et al., eds., *Crisis, Choice and Change.* Boston: Little, Brown, 392–498.

Cornelius, Wayne. 5/90. "El PRI en la encrucijada." *Nexos,* 73–79.

Coşan, F. M., and Hasan Ersel. 1987. "Turkish Financial System: Its Evolution and Performance, 1980–1986." In *Inflation and Capital Markets.* Ankara: Capital Market Board Publications, no. 7, 27–88.

Cuadernos de Renovación Nacional. 1988. *Restructuración del Sector Paraestatal.* Mexico D.F.

Cuddihy, William. 1980. "Agricultural Price Management in Egypt." World Bank Staff Working Papers, no. 388. Washington, D.C.

Cunha, Antonio-Gabriel. 1987–88. "Economic Performance and Macroeconomic Adjustment in Egypt." *American–Arab Affairs,* no. 23, Winter, 83–97.

Danielson, Michael N., and Ruşen Keleş. 1980. "Urbanization and Income Distribution in Turkey." In Özbudun and Ulusan, eds., 269–310.

Datta-Chaudhuri, Mrinal. 1985. "Le plafonnement de l'économie: une interpretation." *Esprit,* no. 107, 140–55.

Datta-Chaudhuri, Mrinal. 12/9–10/85. "The New Industrial Policy." Parts I and II, *Amrita Bazar Patrika.*

Davis, Eric. 1983. *Challenging Colonialism: Bank Misr and Egyptian Industrialization, 1920–1944.* Princeton, N.J.: Princeton University Press.

De la Madrid, Miguel. 11/86. *Criterios Generales de la Política Económica para la Iniciativa de Ley de Ingresos y el Proyecto de Presupuesto de Egresos de la Federación, correspondientes en 1987.* Presidencia de la República.

De Rossi, Flavia. 1971. *The Mexican Entrepreneur.* Paris: OECD.

de Soto, Hernando. 1989. *The Other Path: The Invisible Revolution in the Third World.* New York: Harper & Row.

"Decretos de Desincorporación de Privatizacion Entidades Paraestatales, 1982–1988." 1989. *Revista de Administración Pública,* no. 73, January–April, 105–16.

del Carmen Pardo, Maria. 1986. "La Ley Federal de Entidades Paraestatales: un Nuevo Intento para Regular el Sector Paraestatal." *Foro Internacional,* vol. 27, no. 2, 234–46.

del Carmen Pardo, Maria. 1991. *La Modernización Administrativa en México.* Mexico D.F.: Instituto Nacional de Administración Pública, Colegio de México.

Delarbre, Raúl. 1986. "The Mexican Labor Movement: 1917–1975." In Hamilton and Harding, eds., 177–203.

Delarbre, Raúl. 4/87. "La parálisis obrera." *Nexos,* 57–64.

Derin, Haldun. 1940. *Türkiye'de Devletçilik,* Istanbul.

Derviş, Kemal, and Sherman Robinson. 11/78. "The Foreign Exchange Gap, Growth and Industrial Strategy in Turkey." World Bank Staff Working Papers, no. 306, Washington, D.C.

Dethier, Jean-Jacques. 1989. *Trade, Exchange Rate, and Agricultural Pricing Policies in Egypt.* Vol. 1, *The Country Study.* Washington, D.C.: World Bank.

Díaz-Cayeros, Alberto. 1989. "INFONAVIT." (Translated chapter of a forthcoming book on housing policy.)

Dicle, Atilla. 1978. "Kamu Iktisadi Teşebbüslerinde Örgüt Geliştirme." *ODTÜ Gelişme Dergisi,* vol. 5, 1–20.

Bibliography

Dirección General de Comunicación Social de la Presidencia de la Républic. 1982. *Quien es Quien en la Administración Pública de México*. Mexico D.F.

Dixit, M. R. 1982. "Corporate Planning at HMT." In noncirculating file, Indian Institute of Management, Ahmedabad.

Djilas, Milovan. 1957. *The New Class*. London: Thames & Hudson.

DPT (State Planning Organization). *Beşinci Beş Yillik Kalkinma Plani. 1985– 1989. 1988 Yili Progami*. Ankara.

Dresser, Denise. 1991. "Neopopulist Solutions to Neoliberal Problems: Mexico's National Solidarity Program (Pronasol)." Current Issue Brief No. 3, Center for U.S.–Mexican Studies, University of California, San Diego.

Dunleavy, Patrick. 1991. *Democracy, Bureaucracy and Public Choice*. Englewood Cliffs, N.J.: Prentice-Hall.

Duvall, R. D., and J. Freeman. 1983. "The Techno-Bureaucratic Elite and the Entrepreneurial State in Dependent Industrialization." *American Political Science Review*, vol. 77, no. 3, 559–87.

Echeverri-Gent, John. 1990. "Economic Reform in India: A Long and Winding Road." In Feinberg, Echeverri-Gent, Müller et al., 103–33.

Economic and Social Studies Conference Board. 1969. *State Economic Enterprises*. Istanbul.

Ekzen, Aykut. 1981. "Approaches to the Reorganization of the State Economic Enterprises and the Policies of the Fourth Plan." In *METU Studies in Development*, special issue, "Two Decades of Planned Development in Turkey," 227–59, Ankara (in Turkish).

Eralp, Atila. 1990. "The Politics of Turkish Development Strategies." In Andrew Finkel and Nükhet Sirman, eds., *Turkish State, Turkish Society*. London: Routledge, 219–58.

Erdman, Howard. 1967. *The Swatantra Party and Indian Conservatism*. Cambridge: Cambridge University Press.

Erdman, Howard. 1978. *Politics and Economic Development in India: The Gujarat State Fertilizers Company as a Joint Sector Enterprise*. Delhi: D.K.

Erdman, Howard. 1987. "The Government–Management Interface of the Public Sector." Unpublished, with Appendix I, "The Joint Sector." Dartmouth College.

Erdman, Howard. 1988? "Politics and Industrial Management in India: The IAS in Joint Sector Fertilizer Companies." Unpublished, Dartmouth College.

Erguder, Üstün, and Richard Hofferbert. 1987. "Restoration of Democracy in Turkey? Political Reforms and the Elections of 1983." In Linda Layne, ed., *Elections in the Middle East*. Boulder, Colo.: Westview Press, 19–46.

Ersel, Hasan, and Güven Sak. 1987. "Ownership Structure of Public Corporations in Turkey." *Yapikredi Economic Review*, vol. 1, no. 2, 11–22.

Ertan, Ismail. 1969. "The Problem of the Reorganization of State Economic Enterprises." In Economic and Social Studies Conference Board, *State Economic Enterprises*. Istanbul, 133–69.

Escobar, Janet. 1982. "Comparing State Enterprises Across International Boundaries: The Corporación Venezolana de Guyana and the Companhía Vale de Rio Doce." In Leroy Jones, ed., 103–27.

Escobar Toledo, Saúl. 1987. "Rifts in the Mexican Power Elite, 1976–1986." In Maxfield and Anzaldua Montoya, eds., 65–88.

Esteva, Gustavo. 1989. "Conasupo 1988." Unpublished, INAP.

ETUF (Egyptian Trade Union Federation). 1981. *Conference on Production Growth in Peace Time Conditions*. Cairo: Dar Usama lil Taba' wal Nashr.

Bibliography

Euromoney. 12/86. Special Supplement on Turkish Banking.

Evans, Peter. 1989. "Predatory, Developmental and Other Apparatuses: A Comparative Analysis of the Third World State." *Sociological Forum,* Fall, vol. 4, no. 4, 561–87.

Evans, Peter. 1992. "The State as Problem and Solution: Predation, Embedded Autonomy, and Structural Change." In Stephan Haggard and Robert Kaufman, eds., *The Politics of Economic Adjustment.* Princeton, N.J.: Princeton University Press, 139–81.

Evans, Peter, Dietrich Rueschemeyer, and Theda Skocpol, eds. 1985. *Bringing the State Back In.* New York: Cambridge University Press.

Expansión. 9/27/89. "Las Exportadoras y importadoras más importantes de México," 37–41.

Far Eastern Economic Review. 1/14/88. "Why India's Public Sector Does Not Work," 56–61.

Farid, Saleh. 1/70. *Top Management in Egypt: Its Structure, Quality, and Problems.* Rand Corporation, Santa Monica, Calif.

Feinberg, Richard, John Echeverri-Gent, Friedemann Müller, et al. 1990. *Economic Reform in Three Giants: U.S. Foreign Policy and the USSR, China, and India.* New Brunswick, N.J.: Transaction Books for the Overseas Development Council.

Feyzioğlu, Turhan, ed. 1982. *Atatürk's Way.* Istanbul: Gün Matbaasi for Otomarsan.

Finefrock, Michael. 7/81. "Laissez-faire, the 1923 Izmir Economic Congress and Early Turkish Developmental Policy in Political Perspective." *Middle Eastern Studies,* vol. 17, no. 3, 375–92.

Fishlow, Albert. 1990. "The Latin American State." *Journal of Economic Perspectives,* vol. 4, no. 3, 61–74.

Fitzgerald, E. V. K. 1977. "On State Accumulation in Latin America." In E. V. K. Fitzgerald et al., eds., *The State and Economic Development in Latin America.* Cambridge: Cambridge University Press, 65–90.

Fitzgerald, E. V. K. 1978. "The State and Capital Accumulation in Mexico." *Journal of Latin American Studies,* vol. 10, no. 2, 263–82.

Fitzgerald, E. V. K. 1979. *The Political Economy of Peru: 1956–78.* Cambridge: Cambridge University Press.

Flores, Heriberto. 9/83. "De José Lopez Portillo à Miguel de la Madrid: la relève politique Méxicaine dans la crise économique." *Problèmes d'Amérique Latine,* no. 69, 7–28.

Floyd, Robert, et al. 1984. *Public Enterprise in Mixed Economies: Some Macroeconomic Aspects.* Washington, D.C.: IMF.

Fondo de Cultura Económica. 1988. *México: 75 Años de Revolucíon: Desarrollo Económico.* 2 vols. Mexico D.F.: Fondo de Cultura Económica.

Fortune India. 3/86. "Public Sector Enterprises: Leave 'em alone." 10–18.

Frankel, Francine. 1978. *India's Political Economy, 1947–1977.* Princeton, N.J.: Princeton University Press.

Freeman, John. 1982. "State Entrepreneurship and Dependent Development." *American Journal of Political Science,* vol. 26, no. 1, 90–112.

Freeman, John R. 1989. *Democracy and Markets: The Politics of Mixed Economies.* Ithaca, N.Y.: Cornell University Press.

Frieden, Jeff. 1981. "Third World Indebted Industrialization: International Finance and State Capitalism in Mexico, Brazil, Algeria, and South Korea." *International Organization,* vol. 35, no. 3, 407–31.

298

Bibliography

Friedman, W. 1974. *Public and Private Enterprise in Mixed Economies.* New York: Columbia University Press.

Fuentes, Carlos. 3/13/88. "History out of Chaos." *New York Times Book Review,* 12–13.

Garrido Noguera, Celso, and Enrique Quintana López. 1987. "Financial Relations and Economic Power in Mexico." In Maxfield and Anzaldua Montoya, eds., 105–25.

Gauvin, Antoine. 1984. "Choix et Contrôle des investissements dans le secteur public." *Bulletin du CEDEJ,* vol. 13, no. 16, Cairo, 49–54.

G'awini, Ahmad al- . 10/19/87. "The True Situation in the Public Sector." *AI,* no. 979, 28–29 (in Arabic).

Genel García, Julio Alfredo. 1990. "AeroMéxico: Metamorfosis Creativa." In Bazdresch and Urquidi, eds., 225–325.

General Organization for Information. 1989. *The National Encyclopedia of Prominent Egyptian Personalities,* Cairo.

Gereffi, Gary, and Donald Wyman, eds. 1990. *Manufacturing Miracles: Patterns of Development in Latin America and East Asia.* Princeton, N.J.: Princeton University Press.

Gerth, H. H., and C. Wright Mills, eds. 1958. *From Max Weber: Essays in Sociology,* New York: Oxford University Press.

Ghosh, Arun. 10/21/89. "State of Union Message from RBI." *EPW,* 2349.

Ghosh, Arun. 11/18/89. "Mystery of a Declining Capital-Output Ratio." *EPW,* 2527–30.

Ghosh, D. N. 5/25/91. "Incoherent Privatization, Indian Style." *EPW,* 1313–16.

Ghun'aim, 'Adil. 1968. "Concerning the Case of the New Class in Egypt." *al-Tali'a,* no. 4, 82–93 (in Arabic).

Giddens, Anthony. 1981. *The Class Structure of the Advanced Societies.* 2d ed. London: Hutchinson.

Glade, William. 1968a. "State Shrinking: Problems and Prospects." In William P. Glade, ed., *State Shrinking: A Comparative Inquiry into Privatization.* Institute of Latin American Studies, University of Texas at Austin, 308–21.

Glade, William. 1968b. "Revolution and Economic Development." In Glade and Anderson, 3–101.

Glade, William, and Charles Anderson. 1968. *The Political Economy of Mexico.* Madison: University of Wisconsin Press.

Goldberg, Ellis. 1986. *Tinker, Tailor, and Textile Worker: Class and Politics in Egypt, 1930–1962.* Berkeley: University of California Press.

Goldberg, Ellis. 1992. "The Foundations of State–Labor Relations in Contemporary Egypt." *Comparative Politics,* vol. 24, no. 2, 147–61.

Göle, Nilüfer. 1986. "Modernité et société civile en Turquie: l'action et l'idéologie des ingénieurs." In Altan Gökalp (Dir.), *La Turquie en Transition.* Paris: Maisonneuve et Larose, 199–218.

Gómez, Leopoldo, and John Bailey. 1990. "La Transición Politica y los Dilemas del PRI." *Foro Internacional,* vol. 31, no. 1, 57–87.

Gorkay, Omer. 1987. "Privatization of Public Enterprises: The Case of Turkey." In *Public Enterprises: Performance and the Privatization Debate.* African Association for Public Administration and Management. Delhi: Vikas, 462–71.

Government of Mexico, Poder Ejecutivo Federal. 1989. *Plan Nacional de Desarrollo 1989–1994.* Secretariat of Budget and Program, Mexico D.F.

Bibliography

Göymen, Korel. 1976. "Stages of Etatist Development in Turkey." *METU Studies in Development*, vol. 4, 89–114.

Grindle, Merilee. 1977. *Bureaucrats, Politicians and Peasants in Mexico*. Berkeley: University of California Press.

Grindle, Merilee. 12/89. "The New Political Economy: Positive Economics and Negative Politics." Working Papers, PPR. World Bank, Washington, D.C.

Grindle, Merilee, and John Thomas. 1991. *Public Choices and Policy Change: The Political Economy of Reform in Developing Countries*. Baltimore: Johns Hopkins University Press.

Gülalp, Haldun. 1985. "Patterns of Capital Accumulation and State–Society Relations in Turkey." *Journal of Contemporary Asia*, vol. 15, no. 3, 329–48.

Gupta, Anand. 1988. "Financing Public Enterprise Investments in India." *EPW*, vol. 23, no. 51, 2697–2702.

Gupta, L. N. 1977. *A Study into the Profitability of Government Companies*. Oxford: IBH.

Gupta, Meena. 1989. *Relative Performance of the Public and Private Sectors*. New Delhi: Uppal.

Gupta, S. 1973. "The Role of the Public Sector in Reducing Regional Income Disparity in Indian Plans." *Journal of Development Studies*, vol. 9, no. 2, 243–60.

Gutierrez, Carlos Sales, and Ismael Gomez Gordillo. 1989. "Aeroméxico." Unpublished, INAP.

Haggard, Stephan. 1990. *Pathways from the Periphery*. Ithaca, N.Y.: Cornell University Press.

Haggard, Stephan, and Robert Kaufman. 1992. "Institutions and Economic Adjustment." In Stephan Haggard and Robert Kaufman, eds., *The Politics of Economic Adjustment*. Princeton, N.J.: Princeton University Press, 3–40.

Hale, William. 1981. *The Political and Economic Development of Modern Turkey*. London: Croom Helm.

Halpern, Manfred. 1963. *The Politics of Social Change in the Middle East and North Africa*. Princeton, N.J.: Princeton University Press.

Hamilton, Nora. 1982. *The Limits of State Autonomy: Post-Revolutionary Mexico*. Princeton, N.J.: Princeton University Press.

Hamilton, Nora, and Timothy Harding, eds. 1986. *Modern Mexico: State, Economy, and Social Conflict*. Beverly Hills, Calif.: Sage.

Handoussa, Heba. 1980a. "The Impact of Economic Liberalization on the Performance of Egypt's Public Sector Industry." Boston University, 2d BAPEG Conference, April 2–5.

Handoussa, Heba. 1980b. *Public Sector Employment and Production in the Egyptian Economy*. International Labor Organization, publication no. 7. Geneva.

Handoussa, Heba. 11/86. "Speculations on the Industrial Public Sector in the Years of the Five Year Plan, 1987/88–1991–92." Paper presented at the 11th Annual Conference of Egyptian Economists, Cairo (in Arabic).

Handoussa, Heba. 9/88. "The Burden of Public Service Employment and Remuneration: A Case Study of Egypt." Commissioned by International Labor Organization.

Handoussa, Heba, M. Nishimizu, and J. Page. 1986. "Productivity Change in Egyptian Public Sector Industries After the 'Opening,' 1973–1979." *Journal of Development Economics*, vol. 20, 53–73.

Bibliography

Hanke, S. H., ed. 1987. *Privatization and Development.* San Francisco: ICS Press for the International Center for Economic Growth.

Hansen, Bent. 1972. "Economic Development in Egypt." In Charles Cooper and Sidney Alexander, eds., *Economic Development and Population Growth in the Middle East.* New York: Elsevier, 22–91.

Hansen, Bent, and Karim Nashashibi. 1975. *Foreign Trade and Economic Development: Egypt.* New York: Columbia University Press for the National Bureau of Economic Research.

Hansen, Bent, and Samir Radwan. 1971. *Employment Opportunities and Equity in a Changing Economy: Egypt in the 1980s.* International Labour Office, Geneva.

Hansen, Roger. 1974. *The Politics of Mexican Development.* Baltimore: Johns Hopkins University Press.

Hanson, A. H. 1959. *Public Enterprise and Economic Development.* London: Routledge & Kegan Paul.

Harbison, Frederick, and Ibrahim Ibrahim. 1958. *Human Resources for Egyptian Enterprise.* New York: McGraw-Hill.

Hardgrave, Robert. 1980. *India: Governmental Politics in a Developing Nation.* 3d ed. New York: Harcourt Brace Jovanovich.

Hassan, Ibrahim Ali. 1984. "Le Contrat d'Investissement Public et le Role de la Banque nationale d'Investissement." *Bulletin du CEDEJ,* vol. 13, no. 16, 56–62, Cairo.

Hazama, Yasushi. 1990. "Politics of Implementation: Privatization in Turkey." Unpublished, Department of Economics, METU, Ankara.

Heller, P., and A. Tait. 3/84. *Government Employment and Pay: Some International Comparisons.* IMF Occasional Paper, no. 24. Washington, D.C.

Helm, Dieter. 1986. "The Economic Borders of the State." *Oxford Review of Economic Policy,* vol. 2, no. 2, 1–26.

Henley, J. S., and Mohammed Ereisha. 1987. "State Control and the Labor Productivity Crisis: The Egyptian Textile Industry at Work." *Economic Development and Cultural Change,* vol. 35, no. 3, 491–521.

Heper, Metin. 1977. *Türk Kamu Bürokrasinde: Gelenekçilik ve Modernleşme.* Istanbul: Bosphorus University Press.

Heper, Metin. 1985. *The State Tradition in Turkey.* North Humberside, U.K.: Eothen Press.

Heper, Metin, and Ümit Berkman. 1978. "Public Administration and Development Administration in Turkey: Conceptual Theory and Methodology." *Turkish Public Administration Annual,* vol. 5, 3–30.

Herbst, Jeffrey. 1989. "Political Impediments to Economic Rationality: Explaining Zimbabwe's Failure to Reform Its Public Sector." *Journal of Modern African Studies,* vol. 27, no. 1, 67–84.

Herbst, Jeffrey. 1990. *The African State and the Politics of Reform.* Draft, Princeton University.

Herdeck, Margaret, and Gita Piramal. 1985. *"India's Industrialists."* Vol. 1. Washington, D.C.: Three Continents Press.

Hernández Laos, Enrique. 1985. *La Productividad y el Desarrollo Industrial en México.* Mexico D.F.: Fondo de Cultura Económica.

Hernández, Rogelio. 1986. "La Política y los Empresarios después de la Nacionalízación Bancaria." *Foro Internacional,* vol. 27, no. 2, 247–65.

Hershlag, Z. Y. 1968. *Turkey: The Challenge of Growth.* Leiden: E. J. Brill.

301

Bibliography

Hershlag, Z. Y. 1988. *The Contemporary Turkish Economy.* London: Routledge.

Heuzé, Gérard. 1989. "Monde Ouvrier Contemporain et Mouvements Sociaux." *Revue Tiers-Monde,* T. XXX, no. 119, 613–34.

Hill, Raymond. 1984. "State Enterprise and Income Distribution in Mexico." In Pedro Aspe and Paul Sigmund, eds., *The Political Economy of Income Distribution in Mexico.* New York: Holmes & Meier, 357–96.

Hirschman, Albert. 1965. *Journeys Toward Progress: Studies of Economic Policy Making in Latin America.* Garden City, N. Y.: Anchor Books.

Hirschman, Albert. 1967. *Development Projects Observed.* Washington, D.C: Brookings Institution, 13.

Hirschman, Albert. 1968. "The Political Economy of Import-Substituting Industrialization in Latin America." *Quarterly Journal of Economics,* vol. 82, 1–32.

Hirschman, Albert. 1977. *The Passions and the Interests.* Princeton, N.J.: Princeton University Press.

Hirschman, Albert. 1979. "The Turn to Authoritarianism in Latin America and the Search for Its Economic Determinants." In David Collier, ed., *The New Authoritarianism in Latin America.* Princeton, N.J.: Princeton University Press, 61–98.

Hirschman, Albert. 1982. "The Rise and Decline of Development Economics." In Mark Gersovitz et al., eds., *The Theory and Experience of Economic Development: Essays in Honor of Sir W. Arthur Lewis.* London: George Allen & Unwin, 372–90.

Hirschman, Albert. 1987. "The Political Economy of Latin American Development." *Latin American Research Review,* vol. 22, no. 3, 7–36.

Hirschman, Albert O. 1970. "The Search for Paradigms as a Hindrance to Understanding." *World Politics,* vol. 22, no. 3, 329–43.

Hopper, Jerry, and Richard Levin, eds. 1968. *The Turkish Administration, A Cultural Survey.* USAID, Public Administration Division. Ankara.

Hough, Jerry. 1989. "The Politics of Successful Economic Reform." *Soviet Economy,* vol. 5, no. 1, 3–46.

Huntington, Samuel. 1968. *Political Order in Changing Societies.* New Haven, Conn.: Yale University Press.

Hurtig, Christiane. 1986. "Capitalisme d'Etat et influence Soviétique en Inde." *Revue française de Science Politique,* vol. 36, no. 6, 810–26.

Hussein, ʿAdil. 1982. *The Egyptian Economy from Independence to Dependency, 1974–1979.* 2 vols. Cairo: Dar al- Mustaqbal al-ʿArabi (in Arabic).

Hussein, Mahmoud. 1971. *La lutte de classes en Egypte, 1945–70.* Paris: Maspéro.

Huvespian, Nubar, Feroz Ahmad, et al. 1985. *Turkey: Between the Bureaucratic Elite and Military Rule.* Beirut, Institute of Arab Studies (in Arabic).

Ibn Khaldun. 1981. *The Muqaddimah: An Introduction to History.* Translated by Franz Rosenthal, edited by N. J. Dawood. Princeton, N.J.: Princeton University Press.

Ibrahim, Saad Eddin. 1982. "Social Mobility and Income Distribution in Egypt, 1952–77." In Abdel-Khalek and Tignor, 375–434.

IBRD. 6/86. *Turkey: Adjusting Public Investment.* 5 vols. EMENA Projects Department, Washington, D.C.

Ikram, Khalid. 1980. *Egypt: Economic Management in a Period of Transition.* Baltimore: Johns Hopkins University Press for the World Bank.

302

Bibliography

India Today. 2/29/88. "After the Binge, the Bill," 52–56.

India Today. 4/30/91. "The Government: Wanton Ways," 52–59.

Indian Institute of Management. 7/12–28/82. *International Seminar on Management of Public Sector Manufacturing Enterprises.* Vol. 2. Technical Papers and Cases. Ahmedabad.

Insel, Ahmet. 1984–85. "L'Anatomie de l'Etatisme et des Entreprises d'Etat." *Cahiers du GETC,* no. 1, 58–72.

Institute of National Planning (INP). 5/88. *The Future of the Public Sector in Egypt,* edited by Ibrahim al-'Issawi. Cairo (in Arabic).

Iren, Cihet. 1976. "The Growth of the Private Sector in Turkey." In *International Seminar in the Turkish and Other Countries' Experience with a Mixed Economy,* Hacettepe University, Turkey.

Işikli, Alpaslan. 1987. "Wage Labor and Unionization." In I. C. Schick and E. A. Tonak, eds., *Turkey in Transition.* Oxford: Oxford University Press, 309–32.

Israfil, Cengiz. 5/87. "The Privatization Program in Turkey." World Economic Forum, Istanbul.

Israfil, Cengiz. 5/1/89. *The Privatization Program in Turkey.* Istanbul.

'Issa, Hossam. 1970. *Capitalisme et sociétés anonymes en Egypte: essai sur le rapport entre structure sociale et droit.* Paris: Librairie Générale de Droit et Jurisprudence.

Issawi, Charles. 1963. *Egypt in Revolution: An Economic Analysis.* London: Oxford University Press.

'Issawi, Ibrahim al- . 1989. *The Economic Path in Egypt and Reform Policies: Critical Studies in the Economic Crisis.* Arab Research Center, Cairo (in Arabic).

Istanbul Chamber of Commerce (ICOC). 1989. *Banking in Turkey.* Publication no. 1989-18. Istanbul.

Istanbul Chamber of Commerce (ICOC). 1990. *Economic Report.* Publication no. 1990-34. Istanbul.

Istanbul University. 1981. *Kamu Iktisadi Teşebbüsleri; Gelişmi, Sorunlari ve Çözüm Yollari.* Economics Faculty. Istanbul: Mezunlari Cemiyeti Yayinlari.

'Iz al-Din, Raga. 10/30/89. "An Energy Crisis Threatens Egypt." *AI,* 70–74 (in Arabic).

Jacobs, Eduardo. 1981. "La Evolucion Reciente de los Grupos de Capital Privado Nacional." *Economía Mexicana,* no. 3, 23–43.

Jacome, Gilberto Ramirez, and Emilio Salim Cabrera. 1987. *La Clase Politica Mexicana.* Mexico City: EDAMEX.

Jain, Girilal. 3/1/86. "Politics of Rajiv Ghandi." *Mainstream,* 11–14.

Jain, S. B., ed. 1986. *Management and Role of Public Enterprises: Indo-French Experiences.* 2 vols. New Delhi: BPE/SCOPE.

Jha, L. K. 1980. *Economic Strategy for the 80s.* New Delhi: Allied Publishers.

Jha, L. K. 4/6/86. "In Search of a New Economic Order." *The Illustrated Weekly,* 20–23.

Jha, Prem Shankar. 1980. *India: A Political Economy of Stagnation.* Bombay: Oxford University Press.

Johnson, Chalmers. 1982. *MITI and the Japanese Miracle.* Stanford, Calif.: Stanford University Press.

303

Bibliography

Jones, E. L. 1988. *Growth Recurring: Economic Change in World History.* Oxford: Clarendon Press.

Jones, L. P., and E. S. Mason. 1982. "Why Public Enterprise?" In Leroy Jones, ed., 17–66.

Jones, Leroy P. 9/81. *Improving the Operational Efficiency of Public Industrial Enterprises in Egypt.* Boston University Project on "Industrialization Strategy for Egypt." Prepared for USAID. Boston.

Jones, Leroy P., ed. 1982. *Public Enterprise in Less-Developed Countries.* Cambridge: Cambridge University Press.

Jones, Leroy P. 1985. "Public Enterprise for Whom? Perverse Distributional Consequences of Public Operational Decisions." *Economic Development and Cultural Change,* vol. 33, no. 2, 331–47.

Kabra, K. N., and N. S. Jagannathan. 1985. *Black Money.* IIC Monograph Series, no. 8. New Delhi.

Kahler, Miles. 1990. "Orthodoxy and Its Alternatives: Explaining Approaches to Stabilization and Adjustment." In Joan Nelson, ed., *Economic Crisis and Policy Choice: The Politics of Adjustment in the Third World.* Princeton, N.J.: Princeton University Press, 33–62.

Kalecki, Michal. 1976. "Observations on Social and Economic Aspects of Intermediate Regimes." In *Essays in Developing Economies.* Atlantic Highlands, N.J.: Humanities Press, 30–37.

Kandil, Amany. 1989. "Labour and Business Interest Representation in Egypt." Paper presented at the Conference on Dynamics of States and Societies in the Middle East, Center for Political Research and Studies, June 17–19, Cairo.

Kannapar, Subbiah. 1959. "The Tata Steel Strike: Some Dilemmas of Industrial Relations in a Developing Economy." *Journal of Political Economy,* vol. 67, no. 5, 489–507.

Karal, Enver Ziya. 1981. "The Principles of Kemalism." In Ali Kazancigil and Ergun Özbudun, eds., *Atatürk: Founder of a Modern State.* Hamden, Conn: Archon Books, 11–36.

Karaspan, Ömer. 1986. "Turkey's Super Rich." *MERIP Report,* September–October, 3–34.

Karaspan, Ömer. 1987. "Turkey's Armaments Industries." *MERIP Report,* January–February, 27–31.

Karataş, Cevat. 1986. "Public Economic Enterprises in Turkey: Reform Proposals, Pricing and Investment Policies." *METU Studies in Development,* vol. 13, no. 1–2, 135–69.

Karataş, Cevat. 1989. "Privatisation in the U.K. and Turkey." Unpublished, University of Bradford.

Karpat, Kemal. 1959. *Turkey's Politics.* Princeton, N.J.: Princeton University Press.

Kaufman, Robert. 1989. "Economic Orthodoxy and Political Change in Mexico: The Stabilization and Adjustment Policies of the de la Madrid Administration." In Barbara Stallings and Robert Kaufman, eds., *Debt and Democracy in Latin America.* Boulder, Colo.: Westview Press, 59–74.

Kaufman, Robert. 1990. "How Societies Change Developmental Models or Keep Them: Reflections on the Latin American Experience in the 30's and the Postwar World." In Gary Gereffi and Donald Wyman, eds., *Manufacturing Miracles: Patterns of Development in Latin America and East Asia.* Princeton, N.J.: Princeton University Press, 110–38.

Bibliography

Kaufman, Robert, Carlos Bazdresch, and Blanca Heredia. 1992. "The Politics of the Economic Solidarity Pact in Mexico: December 1987 – December 1988." Draft.

Kautsky, John. 1969. "Revolutionary and Managerial Elites in Modernizing Regimes." *Comparative Politics*, vol. 1, no. 4, 441–67.

Kazancigil, Ali, and Ergun Özbudun, eds. 1981. *Atatürk: Founder of a Modern State*. London: C. Hurst.

Keegan, Victor. 12/31/89. "Sold Down the River." *Manchester Guardian Weekly*.

Kenz, Ali el-. 1987. *Le complèxe sidérurgique d'El-Hadjar*. Paris: Ed. CNRS.

Kepenek, Yakup. 1983. *Türkiye Ekonomisi*. ODTÜ, Ankara.

Kepenek, Yakup. 1990. *Türkiye'de Kamu Iktisadi Teşebbüsleri: 100 Soruda*. Istanbul: Gerçek Yayinevi.

Kerwin, Robert. 1951. "Private Enterprise in Turkish Industrial Development." *MEJ*, vol. 5, Winter, 21–38.

Kerwin, Robert. 1959. "Etatism in Turkey, 1933–50." In Hugh Aitken, ed., *The State and Economic Growth*. New York: Social Science Research Council.

Keshav, K. 4/29/90. "A Milder Shade of Red." *Spectrum*.

Keyder, Çağlar. 1979. "The Political Economy of Turkish Democracy." *New Left Review*, no. 115, May–June, 3–45.

Keyder, Çağlar. 1987. *State and Class in Turkey: A Study in Capitalist Development*. New York: Verso.

Khandwala, Pradip. 1982. "Performance Determinants of Public Enterprises." Case study files, Indian Institute of Management, Ahmedabad.

Khera, S. S. 1964. *Management and Control in Public Enterprise*. Bombay: Asia Publishing House.

Kidwai, Waris, and Baldeo Sahai, eds. 1989. *Dynamics of Management of Public Enterprises*. New Delhi: SCOPE.

Killick, Tony. 1989. *A Reaction Too Far: Economic Theory and the Role of the State in Developing Countries*. London: Overseas Development Institute.

Kirim, Arman. 1990. "Technology and Exports: The Case of the Turkish Manufacturing Industries." *World Development*, vol. 18, no. 10, 1351–62.

Koç, Yildirim. 1982. "Türkiye'de Çalişma Yaşanina Ilişkin Veriler, veri Kaynaklas ve Özellikleri." *ODTÜ Gelişme Dergisi*, vol. 9, no. 2, 213–78.

Koç, Yildirim. 1986. *Türk-Iş Neden Böyle? Nasil Değişecek?* Istanbul: Alam Yayincilik.

Kochanek, Stanley. 1971. "The Federation of Indian Chambers of Commerce and Industry and Indian Politics." *Asian Survey*, vol. 11, no. 9, 866–85.

Kochanek, Stanley. 1974. *Business and Politics in India*. Berkeley: University of California Press.

Kohl, Jürgen. 1983. "The Functional Structure of Public Expenditures." In Charles Taylor, ed., *Why Governments Grow: Measuring Public Sector Size*. Beverly Hills: Sage, 201–16.

Kohli, Atul. 1987. *The State and Poverty in India: The Politics of Reform*. New York: Cambridge University Press.

Kohli, Atul. 1989. "Politics of Economic Liberalization in India." *World Development*, vol. 17, no. 3, 305–28.

Kohli, Atul. 1990. *Democracy and Discontent: India's Growing Crisis of Governability*. New York: Cambridge University Press.

Kopits, George. 5/87. "Structural Reform, Stabilization and Growth in Turkey." IMF Occasional Paper, no. 52. Washington, D.C.

Bibliography

Kornai, János. 1981. "Some Properties of the Eastern European Growth Pattern." *World Development*, vol. 9, no. 9/10, 965–70.

Kornai, János. 1989. "The Hungarian Reform Process: Visions, Hopes, and Reality." In Victor Nee and David Stark, eds., *Remaking the Economic Institutions of Socialism*, 32–94.

Kothari, Rajni. 1970. *Politics in India*. Boston: Little, Brown.

Kothari, Rajni. 1986. "Masses, Classes, and the State." *Alternatives*, vol. 11, 167–83.

Krishnamurthy, V. 1985. "The Work Ethos in Maruti Udyog." *Productivity*, vol. 26, no. 2, 131–38.

Krueger, Anne. 1974. *Foreign Trade Regimes and Economic Development: Turkey*. New York: Columbia University Press.

Krueger, Anne. 6/74. "The Political Economy of the Rent-Seeking Society." *American Economic Review*, vol. 64, no. 3, 291–303.

Kurt Salmon Associates. 3/23/84. *Ready Made Garment/Feeder Industries*. USAID, RFP N. Egypt 83-004.

Kuruç, Bilsay. 1987. *The Economy in the Period of Mustafa Kemal*. Ankara: Bilgi Yayinevi (in Turkish).

Kuznets, Simon. 1966. *Modern Economic Growth: Rate, Structure and Spread*. New Haven, Conn.: Yale University Press.

La Palombara, J., and M. Weiner. 1966. *Political Parties and Political Development*. Princeton, N.J.: Princeton University Press.

Lal, Deepak. 1/87. "The Political Economy of Economic Liberalization." *World Bank Economic Review*, vol. 1, no. 2, 273–300.

Lal, Deepak. 1988. *The Hindu Equilibrium*. Vol. 1, *Cultural Stability and Economic Stagnation: India, 1500 B.C. – A.D. 1980*. Oxford: Clarendon Press.

Land, James. 1971. "The Role of Public Enterprise in Turkish Economic Development." In Gustav Ranis, ed., *Government and Economic Development*. New Haven, Conn.: Yale University Press, 53–87.

Leal, Juan Felipe. 1972. *La Burguesía y el Estado Mexicano*. Mexico D.F.: Ed. Caballito.

Leal, Juan Felipe. 1986. "The Mexican State, 1915–1973." In Nora Hamilton and Timothy Harding, eds., 21–42.

Leeds, Roger. 1988. "Turkey: Rhetoric and Reality." In Raymond Vernon, ed., *Promise of Privatization*. New York: Council on Foreign Relations, 149–78.

Leff, Nathaniel. 1978. "Industrial Organization and Entrepreneurship in the Developing Countries: The Economic Groups." *Economic Development and Cultural Change*, vol. 26, no. 4, 661–75.

Leff, Nathaniel. 1979. "Monopoly Capitalism and Public Policy in Developing Countries." *Kyklos*, vol. 32, fasc. 4, 718–38.

Leff, Nathaniel. 3/79. "Entrepreneurship in Economic Development." *Journal of Economic Literature*, vol. 18, 47–64.

Leibenstein, Harvey. 1968. "Entrepreneurship and Development." *American Economic Review*, vol. 58, no. 2, 72–83.

Leibenstein, Harvey. 1989. "Organizational Economics and Institutions as Missing Elements in Economic Development Analysis." *World Development*, vol. 17, no. 9, 1361–73.

Leila, Ali, El Sayed Yassin, and Monte Palmer. 1985. "Apathy, Values, Incentives and Development: The Case of the Egyptian Bureaucracy." *MEJ*, vol. 39, no. 3, 341–61.

Bibliography

Levi, Margaret. 1988. *Of Rule and Revenue*. Berkeley: University of California Press.

Levi, Margaret, and Douglass North. 1982. "Toward a Property-Rights Theory of Exploitation." *Politics and Society*, vol. 11, no. 3, 315–20.

Levine, Daniel. 1988. "Paradigm Lost: Dependence to Democracy." *World Politics*, vol. 40, no. 3, 377–94.

Levy, Brian. 1988. "The State-Owned Enterprise as an Entrepreneurial Substitute in Developing Countries: The Case of Nitrogen Fertilizer." *World Development*, vol. 16, no. 10, 1199–1211.

Lewis, Bernard. 1961. *The Emergence of Modern Turkey*. Oxford: Oxford University Press.

Lewis, John P. 1962. *Quiet Crisis in India: Economic Development and American Policy*. Washington, D.C.: Brookings Institution.

Lewis, John P. 1989. "Government and National Economic Development." *Daedalus*, vol. 118, no. 1, 69–88.

Lewis, John P. 1990. *Governance and Reform: Essays in Indian Political Economy*. Draft, Woodrow Wilson School, Princeton University.

Lewis, John P. 1991. "Some Consequences of Gigantism: The Case of India." *World Politics*, vol. 43, no. 3, 367–89.

Linz, Juan. 1975. "Totalitarian and Authoritarian Regimes." In Fred Greenstein and Nelson Polsby, eds., *Handbook of Political Science*. Vol. 3, *Macropolitical Theory*. Reading, Mass.: Addison-Wesley, 266–69.

Lipton, Michael. 1977. *Why Poor People Stay Poor: Urban Bias in World Development*. Cambridge, Mass.: Harvard University Press.

Little, Arthur D. 1/78. *An Assessment of Egypt's Industrial Sector*. Report to Interagency Task Force Reviewing Assistance to Egypt. Boston.

Loaeza, Soledad. 4/89. "Empresarios: al fin solos." *Nexos*, 7–8.

Lochan, Rajiv. 5/25/91. "How Competitive is BHEL?" *Economic and Political Weekly*, M47–M50.

Looney, Robert. 1985. *Economic Policy Making in Mexico*. Chapel Hill, N.C.: Duke University Press.

Looney, Robert E., and P. C. Frederiksen. 1987. "Fiscal Policy in Mexico: The Fitzerald Thesis Reexamined." *World Development*, vol. 15, no. 3, 399–404.

Luna, M., R. Tirado, and F. Valdés. 1987. "Businessmen and Politics in Mexico, 1982–86." In Maxfield and Anzaldua Montoya, eds., 13–43.

Luna, Matilde. 1987. "¿Hacia un corporativismo liberal? Los empresarios y el corporativismo." *Estudios Sociológicos*, vol. 5, 455–76.

Lustig, Nora. 1990. "Economic Crisis, Adjustment and Living Standards in Mexico, 1982–85." *World Development*, vol. 18, no. 10, 1325–42.

Luthar, P. C. 1989. "Interface Relationship of Public Enterprises with the Government and the Parliament." In Kidwai and Sahai, eds., 222–56.

Mabro, Robert, and Samir Radwan. 1976. *The Industrialization of Egypt, 1939–1973: Policy and Performance*. Oxford: Clarendon Press.

Machado, Jorge, Wilson Peres, and Orlando Delgado. 1986. "La Estructura de la Industria Estatal, 1970–1985." *Economía Mexicana*, no. 7, 123–35.

Madhur, Srinivasa, and Prannoy Roy. 1986. "Price Setting in Indian Industry." *Journal of Development Economics*, vol. 20, no. 2, 205–24.

Maghraoui, Abdeslam. 1990. Summary of the Reports and Recommendations of the Association of the National Institute of Higher Administration Graduates, 1964–1985. Typescript, Princeton University.

307

Mahalanobis, P. C. 7/69. "The Asian Drama: An Indian View." *EPW*, vol. 4, nos. 28–30, 1119–32.

Mahfouz, Afaf. 1972. *Socialisme et Pouvoir en Egypte.* Paris: Librairie Générale de Droit.

Mainstream. 1/6/90. "State of Economy and Action Plan," vol. 38, no. 11, 11–35.

Malenbaum, Wilfred. 1971. "Politics and Indian Business: The Economic Setting." *Asian Survey*, vol. 11, no. 9, 841–49.

Mallon, R. D. 1982. "Public Enterprise vs Other Methods of State Intervention as Instruments of Redistribution Policy: The Malaysian Experience." In Leroy Jones, ed., 313–25.

Malyanov, O. V. 1983. *The Role of the State in the Socio-Economic Structure of India.* New Delhi: Vikas.

Mañón, Jose Merino. 1989. "Tamaño y Composición de la Administración Pública Mexicána." *Revista de Administración Pública*, vol. 73, January–April, 17–32.

Marathe, Sharad. 1986. *Regulation and Development: India's Policy Experience of Controls over Industry.* New Delhi: Sage.

March, James, and Johan Olsen. 1989a. "The New Institutionalism: Organizational Factors in Political Life." *American Political Science Review*, vol. 78, no. 3, 734–49.

March, James, and Johan Olsen. 1989b. *Rediscovering Institutions: The Organizational Basis of Politics.* New York: Free Press.

Mardin, Şerif. 1969. "Power, Civil Society, and Culture in the Ottoman Empire." *Contemporary Studies in Society and History*, vol. 7, no. 3, 258–81.

Mardin, Şerif. 1980. "Turkey: The Transformation of an Economic Code." In Özbudun and Ulusan, eds., 23–54.

Mardin, Şerif. 1983. "Religion and Politics in Modern Turkey." In James Piscatori, ed., *Islam in the Political Process.* Cambridge: Cambridge University Press, 138–59.

Margulies, R., and E. Yildizoğlu. 2/84. "Trade Unions and Turkey's Working Class." *MERIP Reports*, 15–20.

Markovits, Claude. 1985. *Indian Business and Nationalist Politics, 1931–39.* Cambridge: Cambridge University Press.

Marván, Ignacio. 1977. "El Frente Popular en México durante el Cárdenismo." *Revista Méxicana de Ciencias Políticas y Sociales*, vol. 23, July–September, 9–24.

Mateo, Fernando de. 1988. "La Política Comercial de México y el GATT." *El Trimestre Económico*, vol. 55, no. 217, 175–215.

Maxfield, Sylvia. 1988? "The Mexican Bank Nationalization: Bankers versus 'National Populists.' " Unpublished, Yale University.

Maxfield, Sylvia. 1990. *Governing Capital.* Ithaca, N.Y.: Cornell University Press.

Maxfield, Sylvia, and Ricardo Anzaldua Montoya, eds. 1987. *Government and Private Sector in Contemporary Mexico.* Center for U.S.–Mexican Studies, Monograph Series, no. 20. San Diego.

Maxfield, Sylvia, and James Nolt. 1990. "Protectionism and the Internationalization of Capital: U.S. Sponsorship of Import Substitution Industrialization in the Philippines, Turkey, and Argentina." *International Studies Quarterly*, vol. 34, no. 1, 49–81.

Maza, Enrique. 2/10/86. "Para Salvarla, el Gobierno Deberá Cargar con la Deuda de la Siderurgia." *Proceso*, 6–9.

Bibliography

Mead, Donald. 1967. *Growth and Structural Change in the Egyptian Economy.* Homewood, Ill.: Richard D. Irwin.

Medhora, Phiroze B. 1973. "Managerial Reforms in India's Public Sector." *South Asian Review,* vol. 7, no. 1, 17–28.

Mellor, John. 1976. *The New Economics of Growth: A Strategy for India and the Developing World.* Ithaca, N.Y.: Cornell University Press.

Mertoğlu, Hüseyin. 1987. "Increasing Indebtedness and Decreasing Investment in SEE Balances Expected." *Yapi Kredi Economic Review,* vol. 1, no. 2, 43–97.

Migdal, Joel. 1987. "Strong States, Weak States: Power and Accommodation." In M. Weiner and S. P. Huntington, eds., *Understanding Political Development.* Boston: Little, Brown, 391–436.

Mihçioğlu, Cemal. 1968. "The General Character of the Turkish Civil Service." In Hopper and Levin eds., 59–96.

Millward, R., and D. Parker. 1983. "Public and Private Enterprise: Comparative Behavior and Relative Efficiency." In R. M. Millward et al., eds., *Public Sector Economics.* London: Longman, 199–274.

Ministry of Finance. 1990. *Economic Survey, 1989/90.* New Delhi.

Ministry of Industry. 3/88. *Report on Performance Evaluation and Final Budget Accounts for the Industrial Sector, Fiscal Year 1986/87.* Vol.2, *Financial Analysis of Ministry of Industry Companies.* Cairo (in Arabic).

Ministry of Industry. 4/90. *Industrial Public Sector Overview of Reform Program and Performance over 1983/84 to 1988/89 Period.* Minister's Office, Cairo.

Ministry of Information. 1989. *National Encyclopedia of Outstanding Egyptian Personalities.* General Organization for Information, Cairo (in Arabic).

Mishra, R. K., and S. Ravishankar. 1985. "Training Needs of Public Enterprises in India." *Indian Journal of Public Administration,* vol. 30, no. 1, 136–49.

Misr Engineering and Energy Consultants. 6/84. *Study of Compensation Practices in the Public Sector: Summary of the Final Report.* Project no. 263-F.T.-82-005, submitted to USAID. Cairo.

Moheno, Roberto Blanco. 1980. *La Corrupción en Mexico.* Mexico D.F.: Bruguera Mexicana de Ediciones.

Mohie El-Din, Amr. 11/82. *Income Distribution and Basic Needs in Urban Egypt.* Cairo Papers in Social Science, vol. 5, monograph 3.

"Money Muscle." 9/30/89. *India Today,* 66–69.

Montemayor Seguy, Rogelio. 1988. "Reflexiones sobre la Planeación en México." *Mexico: 75 Años de Revolución: Desarrollo Económico I.* Mexico D.F.: Fondo de Cultura Económica, 77–146.

Moore, Barrington. 1967. *Social Origins of Dictatorship and Democracy.* London: Allen Lane, Penguin Press.

Moore, Clement H. 1980. *Images of Development: Egyptian Engineers in Search of Industry.* Cambridge, Mass.: MIT Press.

Moore, Clement H. 1986. "Money and Power: The Dilemma of the Egyptian Infitah." *MEJ,* vol. 40, no. 4, 634–50.

Moore, Clement H. 1990. "Islamic Banks and Competitive Politics in the Arab World and Turkey." *MEJ,* vol. 44, no. 2, 234–55.

Moore, Clement H., and A. Hochschild. 1968. "Student Unions in North African Politics." *Daedalus,* vol. 97, no. 1, 21–50.

Mubarak, Husni. 10/19/87. "Charter for National Action in the Second Presidency." *AI* (in Arabic).

Muhy al-Din, A., and S. Ibrahim. 1981. "State Socialism and Economic Growth."

Bibliography

In Sa'ad al-Din Ibrahim, ed., *Egypt in the Quarter Century, 1952–1977*. Beirut, 302–34 (in Arabic).

Mulji, Sudhir. 7/88. *Public Sector Management: A Case Study of India*. Unpublished, Nuffield College, Oxford.

Mumcuoğlu, Maksut. 1980. "Political Activities of Trade Unions and Income Distribution." In Özbudun and Ulusan, eds., 379–408.

Munir, Metin. 11/9/79. "Army Keeps the Iron Flowing." *Financial Times*.

Mu'nis, Hussein. 1984. *Pashas and Super Pashas*. Cairo: al-Zahra lil'Alam al-'Araby (in Arabic).

Mursi, Fu'ad. 1976. *This Is the Economic Open-Door Policy*. Cairo: Dar al-Thiqafa (in Arabic).

Murthy, K. R. S. 10/81. "Control Environment of Public Enterprises in India." Report of the World Bank.

Murthy, K. R. S. 1982. "Strategic Management of Public Enterprise: A Framework for Analysis." Unpublished case study, Indian Institute of Management. Ahmedabad.

Nafadi, Mohammed Sadiq. 1988. *Idle Capacity in the Industrial Public Sector (with an Applied Study of the Spinning and Weaving Industry in Egypt, 1974–1984)*. Master's Thesis, Cairo University (in Arabic).

Nagaraj, R. 12/14/91. "Public Sector Performance in the Eighties: Some Tentative Findings." *EPW*, 2877–83.

Narain, Laxmi. 1973. *Managerial Compensation and Motivation in Public Enterprises*. Oxford: IBH.

Narain, Laxmi. 1981. *Organization Structure in Large Public Enterprises: Case Studies of Five Major Public Enterprises*. Delhi: Ajanta Publications.

Narain, Laxmi. 1989. *Workers' Participation in Public Enterprises*. Bombay: Himalaya.

Nas, Tevfik, and Mehmet Odekon, eds. 1988. *Liberalization and the Turkish Economy*. New York: Greenwood Press.

Nath, N. C. B. 1982. "Theory and Practice of Price Regulation in Mixed Economies – the Case of the Indian Steel Industry." Case study files, Indian Institute of Management. Ahmedabad.

Nath, N. C. B. 1986. "Public Enterprise as an Intervention Mechanism." *Public Enterprise*, vol. 6, no. 2, 95–106.

National Specialized Councils. 1980. *The Public Sector: Its Obstacles and Evolution*. Cairo (in Arabic).

National Specialized Councils. 1982. *Strategic Supports of Industry: Egypt to the Year 2000*. No. 17, parts I and II, Cairo (in Arabic).

Nayar, Baldev Raj. 1972. *The Modernization Imperative and Indian Planning*. London: Vikas.

Nayar, Baldev Raj. 1988. "State Entrepreneurship in the Nehru Era: Ideology vs. Necessity." Reprinted from *Congress in Indian Politics: A Centenary Perspective*. Bombay: Popular Prakashan, 204–44.

Nayar, Baldev Raj. 1989. *India's Mixed Economy: The Role of Ideology and Interest in its Development*. Bombay: Popular Prakashan.

Nayar, Baldev Raj. 1991. "Property Rights Theory and Government Efficiency: The Evidence from India's Public Sector." *Development Policy Review*, vol. 9, 131–50.

Nee, Victor, and David Stark. 1989a. "Toward an Institutional Analysis of State Socialism." In Nee and Stark, eds., *Remaking the Economic Institutions of Socialism*, 1–31.

Bibliography

Nee, Victor, and David Stark, eds. 1989b. *Remaking the Economic Institutions of Socialism: China and Eastern Europe.* Stanford, Calif.: Stanford University Press.

Nellis, John. 10/88. *Contract Plans and Public Enterprise Performance.* Policy Planning and Research Working Papers, no. 118. Washington, D.C.

Nellis, John, and Sunita Kikeri. 1989. "Public Enterprise Reform: Privatization and the World Bank." *World Development,* vol. 17, no. 5, 659–76.

Nelson, Joan, et al. 1989. *Fragile Coalitions: The Politics of Adjustment.* New Brunswick, N.J.: Transaction Books for the Overseas Development Council.

Neri, Alvaro Cepeda. 1/17/89. "Los intocables: de Al Capone a La Quina." *La Jornada.*

Nigam, Raj K., ed. 1981. *Eighties for the Public Sector.* Documentation Centre for Corporate and Business Policy Research, New Delhi.

Nigam, Raj K., ed. 1984. *The Management Philosophy of Prakash Tandon.* Documentation Centre for Corporate and Business Policy Research, New Delhi.

Nigam, Raj K. 1989. "Indian Public Sector at the Crossroads." In Kidwai and Sahai, eds., 64–86.

Nigam, Raj K., ed. 1990. *The Parameters of Industrial Relations in the Public Sector in India.* Document Centre for Corporate and Business Policy Research, New Delhi.

Niskanen, William. 1975. "Bureaucrats and Politicians." *Journal of Law and Economics,* vol. 18, no. 3, 617–43.

Nordlinger, Eric. 1982. *On the Autonomy of the Democratic State.* Cambridge, Mass.: Harvard University Press.

North, Douglass C. 1984. "The Approaches to the Study of Institutions." In Colander, ed., 33–40.

North, Douglass C. 1989. "Institutions and Economic Growth: An Historical Introduction." *World Development,* vol. 17, no. 9, 1319–32.

North, Douglass C. 1990. *Institutions, Institutional Change and Economic Performance.* New York: Cambridge University Press.

North, Douglass C., and Robert Thomas. 1980. *The Rise of the Western World: A New Economic History.* New York: Cambridge University Press.

Nove, Alec. 1969. *An Economic History of the U.S.S.R.* New York: Penguin.

Nove, Alec. 1977. *The Soviet Economic System.* London: George Allen & Unwin.

O'Brien, Patrick. 1966. *The Revolution in Egypt's Economic System.* Oxford: Oxford University Press.

Ocampo Arenal, Emilio. 7/88. Simposio Modernización y Empresa Publica, Colegio Nacional de Economistas, Querétaro.

O'Donnell, Guillermo. 1973. *Modernization and Bureaucratic Authoritarianism.* Studies in South American Politics, Institute of International Studies. Berkeley, California.

O'Donnell, Guillermo, Philippe Schmitter, and Lawrence Whitehead. 1986. *Transitions from Authoritarian Rule: Prospects of Democracy.* Baltimore: Johns Hopkins University Press.

OECD. 1989. *Turkey: Economic Survey 1987/88.* Paris: OECD.

OECD. 1990. *OECD Economic Surveys: Turkey, 1989–1990.* Paris: OECD.

Offe, Claus. 1975. "Theory of the Capitalist State and the Problem of Policy Formation." In L. Lindberg, ed., *Stress and Contradiction in Modern Capitalism.* Lexington, Mass.: Lexington Books, 125–44.

Okyar, Osman. 1976. "The Mixed Economy in Turkey (1930–1975)." In Osman

Bibliography

Okyar, ed., *International Seminar on the Turkish and Other Countries' Experience with a Mixed Economy*. Hacettepe University, Ankara.

Okyar, Osman. 1983. "Turkey and the IMF: A Review of Relations, 1978–82." In John Williamson, ed., *IMF Conditionality*. Institute for International Economy, Cambridge, Mass.: MIT Press, 534–61.

Olson, Mancur. 1982. *The Rise and Decline of Nations*. New Haven, Conn.: Yale University Press.

Olson, Mancur. 4/86. "A Theory of the Incentives Facing Political Organizations." *International Political Science Review*, vol. 7, no. 2, 165–89.

Öncü, Ayşe. 1980. "Chambers of Industry in Turkey: An Inquiry into State–Industry Relations as a Distributive Domain." In Özbudun and Ulusan, eds., 455–63.

Öncü, Ayşe, and Deniz Gökçe. 1990. "Banking Sector: Macro-Politics of Banks in the 1980s." Boğaziçi University, Istanbul.

Öniş, Z., and S. Özmucur. 1988a. *The Role of the Financial System in the Creation and Resolution of Macroeconomic Crises in Turkey*. Boğaziçi University, Istanbul.

Öniş, Z., and S. Özmucur. 1988b. *Supply Side Origins of Macroeconomic Crises in Turkey*. Boğaziçi University, Istanbul.

Öniş, Ziya. 1989. *Türkiye'de Diş Ticaret Politiklari ve Diş Borç Sorunu 1980–1988*. Istanbul Chamber of Commerce, Publication no. 1989–33.

Öniş, Ziya. 10/89. "Organization of Export-Oriented Industrialization: The Turkish Foreign Trade Companies in a Comparative Perspective." Draft, Center of International Studies, Princeton University.

Öniş, Ziya. 11/89. "The Political Economy of Turkey in the 1980s: The Anatomy of Unorthodox Liberalism." MESA, Toronto.

Öniş, Ziya. 1991a. "The Evolution of Privatization in Turkey: The Institutional Context of Public Enterprise Reform." *International Journal of Middle East Studies*, vol. 23, no. 2, 163–76.

Öniş, Ziya. 1991b. "The Logic of the Developmental State." *Comparative Politics*, vol. 24, no. 1, 109–26.

Öniş, Ziya, and James Riedel. 1990. *Economic Crises and Long-term Growth in Turkey*. Unpublished manuscript.

Onlooker. 4/16/86. "Fratricidal War in Public Sector," 36–39.

Oyan, Oğuz. 1987. "An Overall Evaluation of the Causes of the Use of Special Funds in Turkey and Their Place in the Economy." *Yapi Kredi Economic Review*, vol. 1, no. 4, 83–116.

Oyan, Oğuz. 1/88. "Funds, the Stabilization Program, and Privatization." *Mülkiyeliler Birliği Dergisi*. no. 91, 20–26 (in Turkish).

Oyan, Oğuz. 2/92. "SOE and Privatization Policies in Turkey in the Early 90s." *Mülkiyeliler Birliği Dergisi*, 10–14 (in Turkish).

Özbudun, Ergun. 1970. "Established Revolution versus Unfinished Revolution: Contrasting Patterns of Democratization in Mexico and Turkey." In S. Huntington and C. H. Moore, eds., *Authoritarian Politics in Modern Society*. New York: Basic Books, 380–405.

Özbudun, Ergun. 1976. *Social Change and Political Participation in Turkey*. Princeton, N.J.: Princeton University Press.

Özbudun, Ergun. 1980. "Income Distribution as an Issue in Turkish Politics." In Özbudun and Ulusan, eds., 55–82.

Özbudun, Ergun. 1981. "The Nature of the Kemalist Political Regime." In Kazancigil and Özbudun, eds., 79–102.

Bibliography

Özbudun, Ergun. 1987. "Turkey." In Myron Weiner and Ergun Özbudun, eds., *Competitive Elections in Developing Countries*. Chapel Hill, N.C.: Duke University Press, 328–65.

Özbudun, Ergun, and Aydin Ulusan, eds. 1980. *The Political Economy of Income Distribution in Turkey*. New York: Holmes & Meier.

Özmucur, Süleyman. 1989. "Social Aspects of Turkish Liberalization, 1980–88." Unpublished, Boğaziçi University, Istanbul.

Özmucur, Süleyman, and Cevat Karataş. 1990. "Total Factor Productivity in Turkish Manufacturing, 1973–1988." *Journal of Economics and Administrative Studies*, vol. 4, no. 2, 289–322.

Pai, T. A. 1981. "Public Sector: New Ethos for the Eighties." In Nigam, ed., *Eighties for the Public Sector*, 37–46.

Palmer, Monte, Ali Leila, and El-Sayed Yassin. 1988. *The Egyptian Bureaucracy*. Syracuse, N.Y.: Syracuse University Press.

Pamuk, Şevket. 1/81. "Political Economy of Industrialization in Turkey." *MERIP*, no. 93, 26–30.

Parla, Taha. 1986. *Türkiye'nin Siyasal Rejimi*. Istanbul: Onur Yayinlari.

Patil, S. M. 1981. "Experience of a Public Sector Top Executive." In Nigam, *Eighties for the Public Sector*, 1.93–1.113.

Patil, S. M. 1989. "A Challenge for Professional Managers of Public Enterprises in India." In Kidwai and Sahai, eds., 269–89.

Payaslioğlu, Arif. 1976. "Kamu iktisadi Teşebbüslerinde Yönetim-Politika Ilişkileri." *ODTÜ Gelişme Dergisi*, Winter, 115–35.

Pazos, Felipe. 1987. "Import Substitution Policies, Tariffs, and Competition." In James Dietz and James Street, eds., *Latin America's Economic Development*. Boulder, Colo.: Lynne Rienner Publishers, 147–55.

Petras, James. 1977. "State Capitalism and the Third World." *Development and Change*, vol. 8, no. 1, 1–20.

Pichardo Pagaza, Ignacio. 7/88. *El Proceso de Desincorporación de Entidades Paraestatales: el Caso de México*. Simposio Modernización y Empresa Publica, Colegio Nacional de Economistas, Querétaro.

Picot, Arnold, and Thomas Kaulmann. 1989. "Comparative Performance of Government-owned and Privately-owned Industrial Corporations – Empirical Results from Six Countries." *Journal of Institutional and Theoretical Economics*, no. 145, 298–316.

Pitzer, John. 1983. "The USSR and Eastern Europe." In Charles Lewis Taylor, ed., 97–116.

Plan Nacional de Desarrollo, 1989–1994. 1989. Poder Ejecutivo Federal, Secretaria de Programación y Presupuesto, Mexico D.F.

Pollock, Friedrich. 1982. "State Capitalism: Its Possibilities and Limitations." In Andrew Arato and Eike Gerhardt, eds., *The Essential Frankfurt School Reader*. New York: Continuum, 71–94.

Posusney, Marsha. 10/91. *Workers against the State: Issues and Outcomes in Egyptian Labor–State Relations, 1952–87*. Ph.D. dissertation, University of Pennsylvania.

Prakash, Om. 1962. *The Theory and Working of State Corporations*. London: George Allen & Unwin.

Premchand, A. 1982. "Government and Public Enterprises: Budgetary Relationships." Case study files, Indian Institute of Management, Ahmedabad.

Presidencia de la República. 1987. *Diccionario Biográfico del Gobinerno Méxicano*. Mexico D.F.: Fondo de Cultura Económica.

Bibliography

Presidency (Egypt). 8/22/83. "Law No. 97, 1983 Pertaining to Public Sector Authorities and Companies." *AI*, no. 762, 56–63 (in Arabic).

Presidency (Egypt). 4/22/85. "Implementing Legislation Presidential Decree #90 for the Law of Public Sector Authorities and Companies." *AI*, no. 849, 60–67 (in Arabic).

Prevot-Schapira, Marie-France. 9/83. "L'évolution de l'organisation syndicale Mexicaine." *Problèmes d' Amerique Latine*, no. 69, 79–121.

Pryor, Frederic. 1984. "Rent-Seeking and the Growth and Fluctuations of Nations." In Colander, ed., 155–75.

Przeworski, Adam. 1991. *Democracy and the Market: Political and Economic Reforms in Eastern Europe and Latin America*. Cambridge: Cambridge University Press.

Purcell, Susan K. 10/73. "Decision-making in an Authoritarian Regime: Theoretical Implications from a Mexican Case Study." *World Politics*, vol. 26, no. 4, 28–54.

Purcell, Susan K. 1/81. "Business–Government Relations in Mexico." *Comparative Politics*, vol. 13, 211–33.

Pursell, Garry. 1990. "Industrial Sickness, Primary and Secondary: The Effects of Exit Constraints on Industrial Performance." *World Bank Economic Review*, vol. 4, no. 1, 103–14.

Qadi, Mohammad Kemal al- . 8/3/87. "The Financial Situation of the Economic Authorities in the 1987/88 Budget." *AI*, no. 968, 36–38 (in Arabic).

Qandil, Imany. 1985. *Public Policy Making in Egypt: An Applied Study of Economic Policy 1974–1981*. Ph.D. dissertation, Cairo University (in Arabic).

Qandil, Imany. 4/29/85. "Interest Groups and the Influence in Economic Policy." *AI*, no. 850, 16–17 (in Arabic).

Qandil, Imany, ed. 1989. *The Private Sector and Public Policies in Egypt*. Matbá Atlas for Center for Political Research and Studies, Cairo University (in Arabic).

Qassem, Sami. 1967. *The New Managerial Elite in Egypt*. Dissertation, University Microfilms. Ann Arbor, Michigan.

Quien es Quien en la Empresa Mexicana. 1985. Mexico D.F.: Quien es Quien S.A.

Ragab, Muhammad (president, Alexandria Businessman's Association). 8/21/89. *AI*, interview, 14–17.

Raj, K. N. 7/7/73. "Politics and Economics of Intermediate Regimes." *EPW*, vol. 8, no. 27, 1189–98.

Ramamurti, Ravi. 1987. "Performance Evaluation of State-Owned Enterprises in Theory and Practice." *Management Science*, vol. 33, no. 7, 876–93.

Ramanadham, V. V. 1963. *The Finances of Public Enterprises*. Bombay: Asia Publishing House.

Ramanadham, V. V. 1964. *The Control of Public Enterprises in India*. New York: Asia Publishing House.

Ramanadham, V. V., ed. 1984. *Public Enterprises and the Developing World*. London: Croom Helm.

Ramírez, Carlos. 1/9/89. "Frágil Alianza Estado Sindicatos, por la Política Económica." *El-Financiero*, 68.

Ramirez, Miguel D. 1986. *Development Banking in Mexico: The Case of the Nacional Financiera S.A.* New York: Praeger.

Rangachari, K. 4/30/90. "Industrial Policy: No Clear Framework Yet." *The Statesman*.

314

Bibliography

Ranis, Gustav. 1989. "The Role of Institutions in Transition Growth: The East Asian Newly Industrializing Countries." *World Development*, vol. 17, no. 9, 1443–53.

Rao, V. K. R. V. 1982. *Indian Socialism*. New Delhi: Concept.

Republic of Turkey. 1962. *Türkiye Kamu Iktisadi Teşebbüsleri Hakkinda Birleştirilmiş Rapor*. Finance Ministry, Güzel Istanbul Matbaasi, Ankara (in Turkish).

Reserve Bank of India. 1989. *Report on Currency and Finance 1988/89*. Vol. I, Economic Review, New Delhi.

Revista de Administración Pública. 1989a. "Decretos de Desincorporación de Privatization Entidades Paraestatales, 1982–1988." January–April, no. 73, 105–16.

Revista de Administración Pública. 1989b. "Tamaño de la Administración Pública." January–April, no. 73, INAP, Mexico D.F.

Reyes Esparza, Ramiro. 1973. "La Burguesía y el Estado." In Reyes Esparza et al., 9–57.

Reyes Esparza, Ramiro, et al. 1973. *La Burguesía Méxicana: Cuatro Ensayos*. Mexico D.F.: Nuestro Tiempo.

Rey Romay, Benito. 1987. *La Ofensiva Empresarial contra la Intervención del Estado*. Mexico D.F.: Siglo Veintiuno.

Reynolds, Clark. 1970. *The Mexican Economy: Twentieth Century Structure and Growth*. New Haven, Conn.: Yale University Press.

Reynolds, Lloyd. 1971. "Public Sector Saving and Capital Formation." In Gustav Ranis, ed., *Government and Economic Development*. New Haven, Conn.: Yale University Press, 516–56.

Reynolds, Lloyd. 1985. *Economic Growth in the Third World, 1850–1980*. New Haven, Conn.: Yale University Press.

Riad, Hassan. 1964. *L'Egypte Nassérienne*. Paris: Editions de Minuit.

Richards, Alan. 1991. "The Political Economy of Dilatory Reform: Egypt in the 1980s." *World Development*, vol. 19, no. 12, 1721–30.

Richards, Alan, and John Waterbury. 1990. *A Political Economy of the Middle East*. Boulder, Colo.: Westview Press.

Riding, Alan. 12/16/89. "Sidermex: Mexico Builds a New Steel Business." *NYT*.

Rifaʿat, ʿIsam. 7/30/90. "Mubarak and 412 National Projects for Egypt: 93 Billion Pounds – Where Did They Go?" *AI*, 8–9 (in Arabic).

Rivera Ríos, Miguel Angel. 1987. *Crisis y Reorganización del Capitalismo Mexicano, 1960–1985*. Mexico D.F.: Ediciones Era.

Rivier, François. 1981. "Politiques industrielles en Egypte." *Maghreb-Machrek*. April–June, no. 92, 42–63.

Rivlin, Paul. 1985. *The Dynamics of Economic Policy Making in Egypt*. New York: Praeger.

Rodrik, Dani. 1990. "Some Policy Dilemmas in Turkish Macroeconomic Management." In Aricanli and Rodrik, eds., *Political Economy of Turkey*, 183–98.

Rodrik, Dani. 1991. "Premature Liberalization, Incomplete Stabilization: The Özal Decade in Turkey." In Michael Bruno et al., eds., *Lessons of Economic Stabilization and Its Aftermath*, chap. 9, 323–53.

Rodríguez, Rogelio Hernández. 1987. "Les Hombres del Presidente de la Madrid." *Foro Internacional*, vol. 28, 5–38.

Rodríguez Reyna, José. 1/92. "Nuevo Empresariao: La Política como Inversión." *Este País*, no. 10, 2–8.

Bibliography

Rogowski, Ronald. 1989. *Commerce and Coalitions: How Trade Affects Domestic Political Alignments.* Princeton, N.J.: Princeton University Press.

Roldán, Otto Granados. 1988. "Estado y Rectoría del Desarollo en México: Una Perspectiva Política." *México: 75 Años de Revolución,* Desarrollo Económico, vol. 1, 1–76.

Roos, Leslie, and Noralou Roos. 1971. *Managers of Modernization: Organizations and Elites in Turkey, 1950–1969.* Cambridge, Mass.: Harvard University Press.

Roy, Delwin. 1974. "The Zonguldak Strike: A Case Study of Industrial Conflict in a Developing Society." *Middle Eastern Studies,* vol. 10, no. 2, 142–85.

Roy, Delwin. 1980. "An Examination of Legal Instrumentalism in Public Enterprise Development in the Middle East." *Georgia Journal of International and Comparative Law,* vol. 10, no. 7, 271–300.

Roy, Emilio Sacristan. 1989a. "Transporte Aereo Federal." Unpublished, INAP.

Roy, Emilio Sacristan. 1989b. "Fundidora de Monterrey." Unpublished, INAP.

RoyChowdhury, Supriya. 4/92. *State and Business in India: The Political Economy of Liberalization: 1984–89.* Ph.D. dissertation, Princeton University.

Rubin, Barnett. 1986. "Financing Gross Capital Formation in Indian Public Sector: A Quantitative Model." *EPW,* vol. 21, nos. 44–45, 1943–50.

Rubio, Luis. 1988. "The Changing Role of the Private Sector." In Susan K. Purcell, ed., *Mexico in Transition.* New York: Council on Foreign Relations, 31–43.

Rudolph, Lloyd, and Susanne Rudolph. 1987. *In Pursuit of Lakshmi: The Political Economy of the Indian State.* Chicago: University of Chicago Press.

Rudra, Ashok. 1/21/89. "Emergence of the Intelligentsia as a Ruling Class in India." *EPW,* 142–50.

Rueschemeyer, Dietrich, and Peter Evans. 1985. "The State and Economic Transformation: Toward an Analysis of the Conditions Underlying Effective Intervention." In Evans et al., eds., 46–77.

Rustow, Dankwart. 1964. "The Military: Turkey." In Robert E. Ward and Dankwart Rustow, eds., *Political Modernization in Japan and Turkey.* Princeton, N.J.: Princeton University Press, 352–88.

Sabbagh, Nabil. 10/1/79. "The Evolution of the Public Sector Has Begun." *AI,* no. 579 (in Arabic).

Sabbagh, Nabil. 6/22/87. "Principal Highlights in the Coming Budget." *AI,* no. 962 (in Arabic).

Sabbagh, Nabil. 4/26/88. "Liquidation of the Public Sector Is an Unacceptable Proposition: Participation in It Is What Is at Stake." *AI,* no. 1006 (in Arabic).

Sabbagh, Nabil. 7/11/88. "Aspects of the Public Budget of the State." *AI,* no. 1017, 78–81 (in Arabic).

Sabry 'Abdallah, Isma'il. 1969. *The Organization of the Public Sector.* Cairo: Dar al-Ma'rif (in Arabic).

Sachs, Jeffrey. 1985. "External Debt and Macroeconomic Performance in Latin America and East Asia." *Brookings Papers on Economic Activity,* 2. Washington, D.C.: Brookings Institution, 523–74.

Sağlam, Dündar. 10/2–7/81. "Türkiye'de Kit Reform Çalişmalarinin Değerlendirilmesi." Türkiye Iktisat Kongresi Kalkinma Politikasi Komisyonu, Izmir.

Sa'id, Samia. 1986. *Who Owns Egypt? An Analytic Study of the Social Origins of the Economic Open-Door Elite in Egyptian Society, 1974–1980.* Cairo: Cairo Dar al-Mustaqbal al-Arabi (in Arabic).

Bibliography

SAIL. 1/86. *SAIL-Priorities for Action*. New Delhi.

Salih, Ahmad. 11/16/87. "The Truth of the Situation in the Public Sector." *AI*, no. 983, 72–74 (in Arabic).

Salmy, Aly al- . 1979. *The Egyptian Administration: A New Vision*. Cairo: General Book Organization (in Arabic).

Saman, Ahmad Hamdullah al- . 1985. "Those Who Gained and Those Who Lost from Infitah." *AI*, no. 871, 34–35 (in Arabic).

Samuels, Warren, and Nicholas Mercuro. 1984. "A Critique of Rent-Seeking Theory." In David Colander, ed., 55–70.

Sanderson, Steven. 4/83. "Presidential Succession and Political Rationality in Mexico." *World Politics*, vol. 35, 315–34.

Sanderson, Susan. 1984. *Land Reform in Mexico: 1910–1980*. New York: Academic Press.

Sankar, T. L., et al. 2/25/89. "State Level Public Enterprises in India: An Overview." *EPW*, 33–40.

Sankar, T. L., R. K. Mishra, and R. Nandgopal. 5/25/91. "Working of State-level Manufacturing Public Enterprises." *Economic and Political Weekly*, M42–M46.

Sankar, T. L., and J. S. Sarma. 1986. "An Analysis of the State-Level Public Enterprise Performance and Perspectives." In S. B. Jain, ed., vol. 2, 95–119.

Sanver, Üstün. 3/92. "Üstün Sanver Explains the New Pattern of the Public Participation Administration." *Kapital* (interview), 12–18 (in Turkish).

Sappington, David, and Joseph Stiglitz. 3/87. "Privatization, Information and Incentives." National Bureau of Economic Research, Working Paper, No. 2196. Cambridge, Mass.

Saribay, Ali Yaşar. 1985. *Türkiye'de Modernleşme Din ve Parti Politikasi: MSP Ornek Olayi*. Istanbul: Alan Yayincilik.

Sarma, N. A. 4/90. "Central Government's Budget for 1990–1991." *Business Standard*, 6–15.

Savas, E. S. 1987. *Privatization: The Key to Better Government*. Chatham, N.J.: Chatham House.

Saybaşili, Kemali. 1976. "Economic Policy and Private Enterprise in Turkey." *ODTÜ Gelişme Dergisi*, vol. 4, 83–97.

Şaylan, Gencay. 1981. "Planlama ve Bürokrasi." In "Two Decades of Planned Development in Turkey," *METU Studies in Development* (special issue), 183–205.

Schlesinger, Arthur. 1957. *The Crisis of the Old Order, 1919–1933*. Boston: Houghton Mifflin.

Schmitter, P. C. 1974. "Still the Century of Corporatism?" *The Review of Politics*, vol. 36, 85–132.

Schmitter, Philippe. 1989. "Corporatism Is Dead! Long Live Corporatism." *Government and Opposition*, vol. 24, no. 7, 54–74.

Schneider, Ben Ross. 5/89. "The Career Connection: Bureaucrats and State Strength in Comparative Perspective."

Schneider, Ben Ross. 1990. "The Politics of Privatization in Brazil and Mexico: Variations on a Statist Theme." In Suleiman and Waterbury, eds., 319–45.

Schneider, Ben Ross. 1991. *Politics Within the State: Elite Bureaucrats and Industrial Policy in Authoritarian Brazil*. Pittsburgh: University of Pittsburgh Press.

Bibliography

Schücking, Rainer Godan. 1982. *Estado y Acero: Historia Política de las Truchas.* Mexico D.F.: el Colegio de México.

SCOPE. 1978. *Performance of Indian Public Enterprises* (Macro Report). New Delhi.

SCOPE. 1985. *Government Policy for the Management of Public Enterprises.* Vol. 1, *General Management and Financial Management*; vol. 2, *Construction Management and Production Materials Management.* New Delhi.

SCOPE. 10/85. *Tenure of Chief Executives in Public Enterprises in India.* New Delhi.

SCOPE. 1987. *Top Management Personnel of Public Enterprises.* New Delhi.

SCOPE. 12/89. *Approach Paper to the White Paper on Public Enterprises.* New Delhi.

Scott, James C. 1985. *Weapons of the Weak: Everyday Forms of Peasant Resistance.* New Haven, Conn.: Yale University Press.

Secretaría de Programacíon y Presupuesto. 1986. *Antología de la Planeacíon en México, 1917–1985.* Plan Nacional de Desarrollo, Informe de Ejecucíon.

Seidman, Harold. 1983. "Public Enterprise Autonomy: Need for a New Theory." *International Review of Administrative Sciences,* vol. 49, no. 1, 65–72.

Selley, Orlando Delgado. 1989a. Estadisticas de Apoya a la Conferencia "La Participación de las Empresas Paraestatales en la Economía." Unpublished, INAP.

Selley, Orlando Delgado. 1989b. "Caso Concarril." Unpublished, INAP.

Sen, Anupam. 1982. *The State, Industrialization, and Class Formations in India: A Neo-Marxist Perspective on Colonialism, Underdevelopment and Development.* London: Routledge & Kegan Paul.

Sencer, Muzaffer. 1974. *Türkiye'de Sinifsal Yapi ve Siyasal Davranişlar.* Istanbul: May Yayinlar.

Shamim, Ahmet. 1985. "The Collapse of the Turkish Left." *New Left Review,* March–April, 1981. Reprinted in Huvespian and Ahmad et al., 153–93.

Shapiro, Carl, and Robert Willig. 1990. "Economic Rationales for the Scope of Privatization." In Suleiman and Waterbury, eds., 55–87.

Sharaf El-Din, H. A. F. 1982. *Labour Productivity in Egyptian Industry, 1965–75.* Centre for Development Studies, Monograph XVI. University College of Swansea, Wales.

Sharif, Khaled. 11/24/87. "The Experience of Developing Countries in Liquidating Loss-making Public Sector Companies." *AI,* 29 (in Arabic).

Sharif, Khaled. 1989. *Public Enterprise Development and Performance in Egypt.* Unpublished report, USAID, Cairo.

Sharif, Khaled. 9/11/89. "Public Sector Reform Reaches the Top of the Government's Agenda Again!" *AI,* 96–97 (in Arabic).

Sharif, Khaled. 1990a. "The Liberalization Experiment in Egypt and the Performance of Public Sector Companies." *AI,* Cairo (in Arabic).

Sharif, Khaled. 1990b. "The Problems Which Commercial Public Sector Companies Face and Suggested Means of Reform." American University in Cairo.

Sharif, Khaled. 7/30/90. "Reform of Public Sector Companies." *AI,* 10 (in Arabic).

Sharif, Khaled. 10/15/90. "Public Sector Companies in the Balance." *AI,* 19 (in Arabic).

Sharma, Arvind. 1985. "Corporate Dualism in the Public Sector: Its Nature and Implications." *Indian Journal of Public Administration,* vol. 31, no. 1, 117–35.

Bibliography

Sheahan, John. 1987. *Patterns of Development in Latin America.* Princeton, N.J.: Princeton University Press.

Sheahan, John B. 1976. "Public Enterprise in Developing Countries." In William Shepherd, ed., *Public Enterprise: Economic Analysis of Theory and Practice.* Lexington, Mass.: Lexington Books, 205–33.

Shelton, David. 1964. "The Banking System." In Raymond Vernon, ed., 113–89.

Shirley, Mary. 1983. *Managing State-Owned Enterprises.* World Bank Staff Working Papers, no. 577. Washington, D.C.

Shirley, Mary. 1989. "The Reform of State-owned Enterprises: Lessons from World Bank Lending." World Bank, Policy and Research Series, no. 4. Washington, D.C.

Shirley, Mary. 3/89. *Evaluating the Performance of Public Enterprises in Pakistan.* World Bank, Policy, Planning and Research Working Papers, no. 160. Washington, D.C.

Short, R. P. 1984. "The Role of Public Enterprises, an International Statistical Comparison." In Robert Floyd et al., *Public Enterprise in Mixed Economies: Some Macroeconomic Aspects.* Washington, D.C.: IMF, 110–95.

Singh, A. K. 1985. *Personnel Management in Public Enterprises.* Delhi: Mittal Publications.

Sklar, Richard. 1979. "The Nature of Class Domination in Africa." *Journal of Modern Africa Studies,* vol. 17, 531–52.

Smith, Adam. 1937. *An Inquiry into the Nature and Causes of the Wealth of Nations.* New York: Random House, Modern Library.

Smith, Peter. 1979. *Labyrinths of Power: Political Recruitment in Twentieth-Century Mexico.* Princeton, N.J.: Princeton University Press.

Sobhan, Rehman, and Muzaffer Ahmad. 1980. *Public Enterprise in an Intermediate Regime: A Study in the Political Economy of Bangladesh.* Dacca: Bangladesh Institute of Development Studies.

Solís, Leopoldo. 6/71. "Mexican Economic Policy in the Post-War Period: The Views of Mexican Economists." *American Economic Review* (supplement), Part 2, vol. 61, no. 3, 1–67.

Solís, Leopoldo. 1976. "A Monetary Will-o'-the Wisp: Pursuit of Equity Through Deficit Spending." Research Program in Development Studies, Discussion Paper No. 77. Princeton University.

Solís, Leopoldo. 1988. "Comportamiento de la Economía Mexicana a partir de 1910: Fases y Características." *México: Setenta y Cinco Años de Revolución.* Mexico D. F.: Fondo de Cultura Económica, 867–86.

Sönmez, Mustafa. 1988. *Kirk Haramiler: Türkiye'de Holdingler.* Istanbul: Gözlem Yayincilik.

Sorj, Bernardo. 1983. "Public Enterprises and the Question of the State Bourgeoisie, 1968–76." In David Booth and Bernardo Sorj, eds., *Military Reformism and Social Classes: The Peruvian Experience.* New York: St. Martin's, 72–93.

Springborg, Robert. 1989. *Mubarak's Egypt: Fragmentation of the Political Order.* Boulder, Colo.: Westview Press.

Srinivasan, T. N. 1985. "Neoclassical Political Economy, the State and Economic Development." *Asian Development Review,* vol. 3, no. 2, 38–58.

Srinivasan, T. N. 1990. "Comments." In Brothers and Wick, eds., 89–92.

State Planning Organization (Turkey)/The Morgan Bank. 1986. *Privatization Master Plan.* New York City.

319

Bibliography

Stepan, Alfred. 1978. *The State and Society: Peru in Comparative Perspective.* Princeton, N.J.: Princeton University Press.

Stiglitz, Joseph, et al. 1989. *The Economic Role of the State.* Oxford: Basil Blackwell.

Stork, Joe. 1987. "Arms Industries of the Middle East." *Middle East Report,* vol. 12, January–February, 12–16.

Sugar, Peter. 1964. "Economic and Political Modernization: Turkey." In R. Ward and D. Rustow, eds., *Political Modernization in Japan and Turkey.* Princeton, N.J.: Princeton University Press, 146–75.

Suleiman, Ezra, and John Waterbury, eds. 1990. *The Political Economy of Public Sector Reform and Privatization.* Boulder, Colo.: Westview Press.

Sümerbank: The School of Industry. 1986. Ankara.

Sunar, Ilkay. 1987. "Redemocratization and Organized Interests in Turkey." Unpublished. Boğaziçi University, Istanbul.

Sunar, Ilkay, and Sabri Sayari. 1986. "Democracy in Turkey: Problems and Prospects." In Guillermo O'Donnell et al., eds., *Transitions from Authoritarian Rule.* Baltimore: Johns Hopkins University Press, 165–86.

Sunar, Ilkay, and Binaz Toprak. 1983. "Islam in Politics: The Case of Turkey." *Government and Opposition,* vol. 18, no. 4, 421–41.

Sunday. 4/29–5/5/90. "Babu Power: How Bureaucrats Rule India." 22–31.

Szyliowicz, Joseph. 1971. "Elite Recruitment in Turkey: The Role of the Mülkiye." *World Politics,* vol. 33, 378–95.

Szyliowicz, Joseph. 1990. "Technology Transfer and Development": The Case of the Turkish Iron and Steel Industry." In Reeva Simon, ed., *The Middle East and North Africa: Essays in Honor of J. C. Hurewitz.* Middle East Institute. New York: Columbia University Press, 262–75.

T. C. Başbakanlik, Hazine ve Diş Ticaret Müsteşarliği. 1986. *Kamu Iktisadi Teşebbüsleri 1980–1986 Yilliği.* Ankara.

T. C. Maliye ve Gümrük Bakanliği. 1988. *1988 Mali Yili Bütçe Gerekçesi.* Ankara.

Tamayo, Jorge. 1988. "Las Entidades Paraestatales en México." *México: 75 Años de Revolución,* Desarrollo Económico II, 634–760.

Tamayo, Jorge. 1989. "La Racionalización del Sector de Empresas Públicas." *Revista de Administración Pública,* vol. 73, January–April, 49–68.

Tandon, Prakash. 1980. *Return to Punjab, 1961–1975.* New Delhi: Vikas.

Tanju, Sadun. 1978. *Tepedeki Dört Adam.* Istanbul: Gelişim Yayinlari.

Taub, Richard. 1969. *Bureaucrats under Stress: Administrators and Administration in an Indian State.* Berkeley: University of California Press.

Tawfik, Hassan, Ali Abdul Majeed, and Atef Obeid. 1977. "Egypt." In *Public Enterprises and Development in the Arab Countries: Legal and Managerial Aspects.* Typescript, International Center for Law and Development. New York, 63–123.

Taylor, Charles Lewis, ed. 1983. *Why Governments Grow: Measuring Public Sector Size.* Beverly Hills, Calif.: Sage.

Taylor, Lance. 1988. *Varieties of Stabilization Experience.* Oxford: Clarendon Press.

Tekeli, I., et al. 1980. *Concentration in Turkish Manufacturing Industry.* Economic and Social Research Institute, Middle East Technical University, Working Paper, no. 18. Ankara.

Tello, Carlos. 1987. *La Nacionalización de la Banca en México.* 3d ed. Mexico D.F.: Siglo Veintiuno.

Bibliography

Tello, Carlos. 8/88. "El Estado y la Economía Mixta." *Nexos*, 25–30.

Thabit, Hussein. 7/29/91. "The Business Sector Law." *AI*, 18–19 (in Arabic).

Thornburg, Max. 1949. *Turkey: An Economic Appraisal*. Twentieth Century Fund. Baltimore: Lord Baltimore Press.

Tignor, Robert L. 1984. *State, Private Enterprise and Economic Change in Egypt, 1918–1952*. Princeton, N.J.: Princeton University Press.

Tignor, Robert L. 1987. "Foreign Capital, Foreign Communities and the Egyptian Revolution of 1952: The Importance of Events." Paper presented at the conference "Egypt from Monarchy to Republic," Dayan Center, Tel Aviv University, June 8–10.

Tignor, Robert L. 1989. *Egyptian Textiles and British Capital: 1930–1956*. Cairo: AUC Press.

Tilly, Charles. 1985. "War Making and State Making as Organized Crime." In Evans et al., eds. 169–90.

Todorov, Nikolai. 1971. "The First Factories in the Balkan Provinces of the Ottoman Empire." *METU Studies in Development*, vol. 1, no. 2, 315–58, 169–91.

Toprak, Zafer. 1982. *Türkiye'de "Milli Iktisat." 1908–1918*. 2d ed. Ankara: Yurt Yayinlari.

Toye, John. 1981. *Public Expenditure and Indian Development Policy, 1960–1970*. New York: Cambridge University Press.

Trebat, Thomas. 1988. *Brazil's State-Owned Enterprises: A Case Study of the State as Entrepreneur*. Cambridge: Cambridge University Press.

Trimberger, Ellen Kay. 1978. *Revolution from Above: Military Bureaucrats and Development in Japan, Turkey, Egypt, and Peru*. New Brunswick, N.J.: Transaction Books.

Trivedi, Prajapati. 5/30/87. "Sen Gupta Report on Public Enterprises: Eloquent Fuzziness at Its Best." *EPW*, vol. 22, no. 22, 55–66.

Tuncer, Baran. 1976. "The Regulatory Role of the Government in the Turkish Economy." *International Seminar on the Turkish and Other Countries' Experience with a Mixed Economy*. Haceteppe University, Turkey.

Turkish Republic, High Auditing Board. 1987. *Kamu Iktisadi Teşebbüsleri, Yili Genel Raporu*. Ankara, 150.

Turun, Osman Nuri, et al. 1981. *Kamu Iktisadi Teşebbüsleri: Gelişmi, Sorunlari ve Çözum Yollari*. Istanbul University. Istanbul: Iktisat Fakültesi Yayinlari.

TÜSIAD. 1987. *Report on Privatization*. Istanbul.

TÜSIAD. 12/7/87. *The Socio-economic Situation and Outlook of the Turkish Household*. Istanbul (in Turkish).

TÜSIAD. 1988a. *1980 Sonrasi Ekonomide Kamu-Özel Sectör Dengisi*. Istanbul.

TÜSIAD. 1988b. *The Turkish Economy '88*. Istanbul.

TÜSIAD. 5/88. *Güncel Ekonomik Konularda Tüsiad Kamuoyu Araştirmasi*. Istanbul.

TÜSIAD. 1989. *The Turkish Economy '89*. Istanbul.

TÜSIAD. 1/90. *1990 yilina Girerken Türk Ekonomisi*. Istanbul.

Ugalde, Francisco Valdés. 1987. "¿Hacia un Nuevo Liderazgo Sociopolítico? Ensayo sobre la Convocatoria Social de los Empresarios." *Estudios Sociológicos*, vol. 15, 433–54.

Ulagay, Osman. 3/16/90. "Kamu Kesimi Açiği Faiz Yükü ve Enflasyon." *Cumhuriyet*, 13.

Ulman, A. H., and F. Tachau. 1965. "Turkish Politics: The Attempt to Reconcile Rapid Modernization with Democracy." *MEJ*, vol. 19, 153–68.

Bibliography

Urzúa, Carlos. 5/90. "El Déficit del Sector Público y la Política Fiscal en México, 1980–89." Unpublished, Centro de Estudios Económicos el Colegio de México.

USAID/Egypt. 6/76. *Egypt: Mehallah Textile Plant.* AD DLC/P-2181, Cairo.

USAID/Egypt. 1984. *Study of Compensation Practices in the Public Sector.* Project no. 263-F.T.-82-005. Cairo.

USAID/Egypt. 1989? *Public Enterprise Development and Performance in Egypt.* Typescript, Cairo.

USAID/Egypt. 1990. *An Annotated Description of the Engineering Industries Subsector: Main Text.* Integrated Development Consultants, Cairo.

Valdés, Francisco. 1988. "Los Empresarios, la Política y el Estado." *Cuadernos Políticos,* January–April, 47–70.

Van Arkadie, Brian. 1989. "The Role of Institutions in Development." *Proceedings of the World Bank Annual Conference on Development Economics.* Supplement to the *World Bank Economic Review* (1989), 153–92.

Varshney, Ashutosh. 9/1/84. "Political Economy of Slow Industrial Growth in India." *EPW*, 1511–17.

Vermeulen, Bruce, and Ravi Sethi. 1982. "Labor–Management Conflict Resolution in State-Owned Enterprises: A Comparison of Public and Private Sector Practices in India." In Leroy Jones, ed., 141–65.

Vernon, Raymond, ed. 1964. *Public Policy and Private Enterprise in Mexico.* Cambridge, Mass.: Harvard University Press.

Villareal, René. 1988a. "El Desarrollo Industrial de México: Una Perspectiva Historica." *México: 75 Años de Revolución: Desarrollo Económico I.* Mexico D.F.: Fondo de Cultura Económica, 257–340.

Villareal, René. 1988b. *Mitos y Realidades de la Empresa Pública: Racionalización o Privatización?* Mexico City: Editorial Diana.

Villareal, Rocio de, and René Villareal. 1980. "Public Enterprises in Mexican Development Under the Oil Perspective in the 1980s." Second Boston Area Public Enterprise Group Conference, Boston.

Vitalis, Robert. 1991. "Imagining Capitalists: Ideologies of Class and Client in Egyptian Political Economy." Prepared for the Conference on Middle Classes and Entrepreneurial Elites in the Middle East, University of California, Berkeley, May 9–12.

Wade, Robert. 1990. *Governing the Market: Economic Theory and the Role of Government in Taiwan's Industrialization.* Princeton, N.J.: Princeton University Press.

Walder, Andrew. 1990. "Political Upheavals in the Communist Party States." *States and Social Structures Newsletter.* Social Science Research Council, no. 12, 7–9. New York.

Wålstedt, Bertil. 1980. *State Manufacturing Enterprise in a Mixed Economy: The Turkish Case.* Baltimore: Johns Hopkins Press for the World Bank.

Waterbury, John. 1982. "Patterns of Urban Growth and Income Distribution in Egypt." In Abdel-Khalek and Tignor, eds., 307–50.

Waterbury, John. 1983. *The Egypt of Nasser and Sadat: The Political Economy of Two Regimes.* Princeton, N.J.: Princeton University Press.

Waterbury, John. 10/85. "The 'Soft State' and the Open Door: Egypt's Experience with Economic Liberalization, 1974–1984." *Comparative Politics*, vol. 18, no. 1, 65–84.

Waterbury, John. 1989. "The Political Management of Economic Adjustment

Bibliography

and Reform." In Joan Nelson et al., 39–57.

Waterbury, John. 1991. "Twilight of the State Bourgeoisie?" *International Journal of Middle East Studies*, vol. 23, no. 1, 1–17.

Waterbury, John. 1992. "Export-led Growth and the Center-Right Coalition in Turkey." *Comparative Politics*, vol. 24, no. 2, 127–46.

Weiner, Myron. 10/83. "The Political Consequences of Preferential Policies." *Comparative Politics*, 35–52.

Weiner, Myron. 7/86. "The Political Economy of Industrial Growth in India." *World Politics*, vol. 37, no. 4, 596–610.

Weiner, Myron. 1989. *The Indian Paradox*. New Delhi: Sage.

Weiss, Dieter. 7/30/90. "Ibn Khaldoun on Economic Policy." *AI*, 94–97 (in Arabic).

Wellisz, Stanislaw, and Ronald Findlay. 1984. "Protection and Rent-Seeking in Developing Countries." In David Colander, ed., 141–54.

Whitehead, Lawrence. 10/81. "On 'Governability in Mexico.' " *Bulletin of Latin American Research*, vol. 1, no. 1, 27–47.

Wilkie, James. 1967. *The Mexican Revolution: Federal Expenditure and Social Change Since 1910*. Berkeley: University of California Press.

Wilkie, James. 1990. "The Reconquest of Presidential Budgetary Power in Latin America: Liquidating Parastate Enterprises in the Mexican Case Since 1982." Unpublished.

Williams, M. L. 1975. "The Extent and Significance of the Nationalization of Foreign-Owned Assets in Developing Countries, 1956–1972." *Oxford Economic Papers*, 260–73.

Williamson, Oliver. 1988. "The Logic of Economic Organization." *Journal of Law, Economics and Organization*, vol. 4, no. 1, 65–93.

Wilson, Ernest. 1986? "Comparative Politics and Public Enterprise in Africa." Unpublished, University of Michigan.

Wionczek, Miguel. 1964. "Electric Power: The Uneasy Partnership." In Raymond Vernon, ed., 19–110.

Womack, John. 1969. "The Mexican Revolution, 1910–1940: Genesis of a Modern State." In Frederick Pike, ed., *Latin American History: Select Problems*. New York: Harcourt Brace, 298–339.

World Bank. 7/14/81. *Turkey: Public Sector Investment Review*. Vol. 3, Statistical Annex, Report no. 3472-TU. Washington, D.C.

World Bank. 1982. *Turkey: Industrialization and Trade Strategy*. World Bank Country Study. Washington, D.C.

World Bank. 1/83. *Arab Republic of Egypt: Issues of Trade Strategy and Investment Planning*. Washington, D.C.

World Bank. 10/5/83. *Arab Republic of Egypt: Current Economic Situation and Growth Prospects*. EMENA, Report no. 4498-EGT. Washington, D.C.

World Bank. 3/85. *Turkey: Agricultural Sector Adjustment Loans, Loan Implementation Volume, Part IV: Review of Sector Economic and Financing Policies*. Report no. 5576-TU. Washington, D.C.

World Bank. 1986. *Mexico: Trade Policy Loan*. Washington, D.C.

World Bank. 5/86. *India: Economic Situation and Development Prospects*. 2 vols. Report no. 6090-IN. Washington, D.C.

World Bank. 6/86. *Turkey: Adjusting Public Investment*. 5 vols. EMENA Projects Dept. Vol. 2, Main Report and Statistical Annex; Vol. 7, Main Report. Washington, D.C.

World Bank. 7/18/86. *Egypt: Public Industrial Enterprise Efficiency Study*.

Bibliography

EMENA Region, Report no. 6305-EGT, Vol. 1, main report. Washington, D.C.

World Bank. 10/22/86. *Arab Republic of Egypt: Current Economic Situation and Economic Reform Program.* EMENA, Report no. 6195-EGT. Washington, D.C.

World Bank. 3/87. *Egypt: Review of the Finances of the Decentralized Public Sector.* EMENA Region, Report no. 6421-EGT, vol. 1, Main Report; vol. 2, Annexes. Washington, D.C.

World Bank. 1988, 1989, 1990. *World Development Report.* New York: Oxford University Press.

World Bank. 3/15/88. *Turkey: External Debt, Fiscal Policy and Sustainable Growth.* EMENA Region, vol. 1, Main Report; vol. 2, Methodological and Statistical Annex.

World Bank. 4/88. *Evaluation of Structural Adjustment Lending in Turkey: Program Performance Audit Report of the Fourth and Fifth Structural Adjustment Loans.* Report no. 7205. Washington, D.C.

World Bank. 4/13/88. *Evaluation of Structural Adjustment Lending in Turkey: Program Performance Audit Report of the Fourth and Fifth Structural Adjustment Loans (Loans 2321-TU and 2442-TU) and Overview of SALs I-V.* Report no. 7205. Washington, D.C.

World Bank. 8/88. *Turkey: Country Economic Memorandum: Towards Sustainable Growth.* Report no. 7378-TU. Washington D.C.

World Bank. 10/88. *India: Review of Public Enterprises, Propositions for Greater Efficiency in the Central Government Public Enterprises.* Industry and Finance Division, Asia Country Dept. IV, Report no. 7294-IN, vol. 2, main text; vol. 3, appendixes and annexes. Washington, D.C.

World Bank. 1989. *India: An Industrializing Economy in Transition.* World Bank Country Study. Washington, D.C.

World Bank. 5/22/89. *Report and Recommendation of the President of the IBRD to the Executive Directors on a Proposed Public Enterprise Reform Loan.* Washington, D.C.

World Bank. 6/13/89. *Egypt: Industrial Sector Memorandum.* 2 vols. EMENA Country Dept. III, Report no. 7491-EGT. Washington, D.C.

World Bank. 2/90. *Arab Republic of Egypt: Country Economic Memorandum: Economic Adjustment with Growth.* Report no. 7447-EGT, 3 vols. Vol. 2: Main Report. Washington, D.C.

World Bank. 3/90. *India: Trends, Issues and Options.* Washington, D.C.

Yalpat, Altan. 1984. "Turkey's Economy Under the Generals." *MERIP Reports.* March–April, 16–24.

Youssef, Samir. 1983. *System of Management in Egyptian Public Enterprises.* Cairo: AUC Press.

Yüksek Denetleme Kurulu (YDK). 1983, 1987, 1988, 1990. *Kamu Iktisadi Teşebbüsleri Genel Raporu.* Ankara.

Zaalouk, Malak. 1989. *Power, Class and Foreign Capital in Egypt: The Rise of the New Bourgeoisie.* London: Zed Book.

Zayida, Gamal. 1/1/90. "Participation of Workers in Ownership of the Public Sector." *AI*, no. 1094, 62–67 (in Arabic).

Zedillo de Leon, Ernesto. 1986. "Mexico's Recent Balance-of-Payments Experience and Prospects for Growth." *World Development*, vol. 14, no. 8, 963–91.

Bibliography

Zeitlin, Maurice, and Richard Ratcliff. 1988. *Landlords and Capitalists: The Dominant Class of Chile.* Princeton, N.J.: Princeton University Press.

Zermeño, Sergio. 5/87. "El fin del Populismo Mexicano." *Nexos,* no. 113, 31–35.

Zutshi, Ravi. 1985. "Operating Culture and Strategy Formulation in Public Enterprises." In R. K. Mishra and S. Ravishankar, eds., *Dynamics of Public Enterprises Management.* Delhi: Ajanta Publications, 41–64.

Index

Index

economic strategy: choices, 208; inertial force of, 148; and political control, 258
economists, 168–69; in change teams, 149–50, 156
EEC, 43, 102, 226, 255
Egyptian–American Business Council, 225
Egyptian Businessmen's Association, 225, 226
Egyptian Chemicals Company, 171
Egyptian Dairy Company, 239
Egyptian Development Organization, 139
Egyptian Petroleum Authority, 92–93
Eighth Five Year Plan (India), 90
ejidos (communal farms), 46–47, 71
"election factories" (Turkey), 22, 201
elections, 28, 163; and disbursements, 200–2; and managerial careers, 170; payoffs in, 163, 164
electoral spending cycles, 201–2
electoral system(s), 215–16; unions in (India), 245–46
Electricity Authority (Egypt), 187
elites, 6, 260; bureaucratic, 10; educational levels, 167–68; and ISI, 33; political, 192, 214; state, 12, 178–79, 191
embedded autonomy (concept), 9
Emergency of 1975–77 (India), 6, 58, 144, 244
Empaneling Committee (India), 173
Employees Pension and Mutual Aid Fund (Turkey), 104
employment: guaranteed to university graduates, 143, 195, 240, 241; public sector, 96, 97t, 236, 240
employment drive: Egypt, 240–41
employment generation: function of SOEs, 107, 126, 140
employment growth: Egypt, 240; SOE, 241
employment practices, 126–27
employment share, 91
energy subsidies, 117, 124, 140, 143, 198, 199
enforcement: of property regimes, 13, 16–20
engineering technocracy, 172
engineers, 168–69
Ente Nazionale Idrocarburi (ENI), 129
entitlements, 3, 21, 23, 66, 67, 195, 211, 264; beneficiaries, 28–29; coalitions, 203; labor, 235, 248–49, 250, 258, 259, 265; preservation of, 158; reform and, 136, 137
entrepreneurial bourgeoisie, 11, 215
entrepreneurial classes, 216, 218

entrepreneurs, 233; private, 225, 268–69; public, 127–29
entrepreneurship: penalties for, 161–62
equity, 15, 98; ownership, 224; position in firms held by government, 219–20, 231
Erbakan, Necmettin, 283n7
Erdemir Steel, 129
erogaciones adicionales, 283n6
Ertuna, Özer, 186
ESOP, 142
etatism (*devletçilik*), 261; Kemalist, 67; moderate (*mutadil devletçilik*), 38–39; Turkey, 38–39, 42, 43, 44, 206, 217
Ete, Muhlis, 42
Etibank, 40, 41, 98
ETUF, 239, 241–42
Evren, General Kenan, 66
exchange rates, 106, 117; Egypt, 143, 199
Export–Import Bank (EXIM), 124
exit, 2, 16, 110, 119, 263
exogenous shocks, 135, 266; Egypt, 64; India, 55, 57–58; in radical transformation of Egypt, 61
export drive, 78–79, 220–21, 222
export-led growth, 84–85, 159; shift to, 88; Turkey, 44, 71, 75, 150
Export Promotion Fund (Turkey), 220
export sector, 138; private, 206–7
exports, 5, 145, 268; manufactured, 85, 220–21; promotion of, 85, 88; Turkey, 85, 150
external powers: and change, 23, 24–25
extrabudgetary funds, 86, 198, 199–200
Exxon, 14
Ezz al-Din, Munir, 182–83

fahlawi (Egypt), 7
Faisal Islamic Bank, 187
family holding company, 223–25
Farid, Salah, 166
Father State (*devlet baba*), 8, 186
federal (central)-level SOEs: India, 143–48
Federal District of Mexico City, 101–2
Federation of Egyptian Industries, 225, 242
Federation of Workers of the Federal District (Mexico), 249
FERA, 217
Fernandez, George, 58
Fertilizer Corporation of India, 116, 173
FERTIMEX, 50, 101, 116, 132
FICCI, 56, 184, 226–27, 284n5
FICORCA, 200, 206, 231
fideicomisos, 103, 200, 249
financial institutions, 98, 229

Index

Index

341